Global Perspectives on People, Process, and Practice in Criminal Justice

Liam J. Leonard
Northern Arizona University, USA

A volume in the Advances in Criminology, Criminal Justice, and Penology (ACCJP) Book Series

IGI Global
PUBLISHER of TIMELY KNOWLEDGE

Published in the United States of America by
IGI Global
Information Science Reference (an imprint of IGI Global)
701 E. Chocolate Avenue
Hershey PA, USA 17033
Tel: 717-533-8845
Fax: 717-533-8661
E-mail: cust@igi-global.com
Web site: http://www.igi-global.com

Library of Congress Cataloging-in-Publication Data

Names: Leonard, Liam James, 1965- editor.
Title: Global perspectives on people, process, and practice in criminal justice / Liam James Leonard, editor.
Description: Hershey : Information Science Reference, 2020. | Includes bibliographical references and index. | Summary: "This book features an international collection of chapters on criminal justice policy and processes, with a focus on incarceration and imprisonment and reflects on the differences and alternatives to imprisonment and incarceration policy in various parts of the world"-- Provided by publisher.
Identifiers: LCCN 2020033505 (print) | LCCN 2020033506 (ebook) | ISBN 9781799866466 (hardcover) | ISBN 9781799866473 (paperback) | ISBN 9781799866480 (ebook)
Subjects: LCSH: Criminal justice, Administration--Case studies. | Imprisonment--Case studies. | Prison administration--Case studies.
Classification: LCC HV7419 .G56 2020 (print) | LCC HV7419 (ebook) | DDC 364--dc23
LC record available at https://lccn.loc.gov/2020033505
LC ebook record available at https://lccn.loc.gov/2020033506

This book is published in the IGI Global book series Advances in Criminology, Criminal Justice, and Penology (ACCJP) (ISSN: pending; eISSN: pending)

British Cataloguing in Publication Data
A Cataloguing in Publication record for this book is available from the British Library.

For electronic access to this publication, please contact: eresources@igi-global.com.

Advances in Criminology, Criminal Justice, and Penology (ACCJP) Book Series

ISSN:pending
EISSN:pending

Editor-in-Chief: Liam J. Leonard, Northern Arizona University, USA

MISSION

Criminology has never been more relevant. Violence, serial murder, crime and victimization continue to remain an unfortunate staple of society. Crime is a key issue globally, nationally, and regionally. Law enforcement personnel within the criminal justice system must keep pace with ever changing modes of crime. As officials work to predict and prevent crimes, as well as apprehend offenders, they will need to devise new tools and strategies to preserve the safety of society and ensure proper justice is served.

The **Advances in Criminology, Criminal Justice, and Penology (ACCJP)** Book Series explores emerging research behind crime control strategies, crime motivation, new methods and the utilization of technology for committing illegal acts, criminal justice and reform strategies, and the effects of crime on society and its victims. The publications contained within this series are valuable resources for government officials, law enforcement officers, corrections officers, prison management, criminologists, sociologists, psychologists, forensic scientists, security specialists, academicians, researchers, and students seeking current research on international crime.

COVERAGE

- Penal System
- Prisons
- Serial Killers
- Gang Violence
- Fraud
- Drug Trafficking
- Criminology
- Restorative Justice
- Policing
- Criminal Psychology

IGI Global is currently accepting manuscripts for publication within this series. To submit a proposal for a volume in this series, please contact our Acquisition Editors at Acquisitions@igi-global.com or visit: http://www.igi-global.com/publish/.

The Advances in Criminology, Criminal Justice, and Penology (ACCJP) Book Series (ISSN pending) is published by IGI Global, 701 E. Chocolate Avenue, Hershey, PA 17033-1240, USA, www.igi-global.com. This series is composed of titles available for purchase individually; each title is edited to be contextually exclusive from any other title within the series. For pricing and ordering information please visit http://www.igi-global.com/book-series/advances-criminology-criminal-justice-penology/212650. Postmaster: Send all address changes to above address.

Titles in this Series

For a list of additional titles in this series, please visit:
http://www.igi-global.com/book-series/advances-criminology-criminal-justice-penology/212650

Combating the Exploitation of Children in Cyberspace Emerging Research and Opportunities
Hossam Nabil Elshenraki (Dubai Police Academy, UAE)
Information Science Reference • © 2021 • 165pp • H/C (ISBN: 9781799823605) • US $160.00

Comparative Criminology Across Western and African Perspectives
Simeon Peter Sungi (United States International University-Africa, Kenya) Nabil Ouassini (Dixie State University, USA) and Joyce Muchemi (Mount Kenya University, Kenya)
Information Science Reference • © 2020 • 300pp • H/C (ISBN: 9781799828563) • US $225.00

Encyclopedia of Criminal Activities and the Deep Web
Mehdi Khosrow-Pour D.B.A. (Information Resources Management Association, USA)
Information Science Reference • © 2020 • 1162pp • H/C (ISBN: 9781522597155) • US $2,450.00

Handbook of Research on Trends and Issues in Crime Prevention, Rehabilitation, and Victim Support
Augusto Balloni (Italian Society of Victimology, Italy) and Raffaella Sette (University of Bologna, Italy)
Information Science Reference • © 2020 • 553pp • H/C (ISBN: 9781799812869) • US $245.00

Global Perspectives on Victimization Analysis and Prevention
Johnson Oluwole Ayodele (Lagos State University, Nigeria)
Information Science Reference • © 2020 • 272pp • H/C (ISBN: 9781799811121) • US $195.00

For an entire list of titles in this series, please visit:
http://www.igi-global.com/book-series/advances-criminology-criminal-justice-penology/212650

IGI Global
PUBLISHER of TIMELY KNOWLEDGE

701 East Chocolate Avenue, Hershey, PA 17033, USA
Tel: 717-533-8845 x100 • Fax: 717-533-8661
E-Mail: cust@igi-global.com • www.igi-global.com

Editorial Advisory Board

Table of Contents

Preface xv

Acknowledgment xx

Section 1
Gender and Justice: Personal Perspectives

Chapter 1
Deportation as Deterrence? Social and Legal Predictors of Remigration After Deportation 1
William Estuardo Rosales, Department of Sociology, California State University, Los Angeles, USA
Katie Dingeman, California State University, Los Angeles, USA

Chapter 2
Sanctuary? A Discussion on Latinx/a Women and Girls in a Carceral State 30
Kayla Marie Martensen, University of Illinois at Chicago, USA

Chapter 3
Prisoner Re-Entry: One Story of Coming Home 50
Rebecca Hubbard Maniglia, Northern Arizona University, USA

Chapter 4
Carceral Trauma at the Intersections of Race, Class, and Gender 72
Cassandra D. Little, California State University, Fresno, USA

Chapter 5
The Causes Behind the Cause: An Explanatory Analysis on Transgender Deviance in Dhaka, Bangladesh 86
Adiba Fannana, University of Ontario Institute of Technology (UOIT), Canada

Section 2
Global Approaches to Justice and Imprisonment

Chapter 6
Prisoner Re-Entry and Desistance 99
Luis F. Nuño, California State University, Los Angeles, USA

Chapter 7
Resisting the New Punitiveness: Penal Policy in Denmark, Finland, and Norway and Contrary Trends in Ireland 110
Kevin Warner, University College Cork, Ireland

Chapter 8
How to Reduce Recidivism: Lessons From the U.S. State of Arizona 144
Kevin A. Wright, Arizona State University, USA

Chapter 9
Prison Communities: An Examination of Work, Life, and Relationships in Prison 155
Jim Howe, Irish Prison Service (Retired), Ireland

Chapter 10
Teaching Prisoners' Rights to Prison Officers to Improve Professional Performance 168
Liam J. Leonard, Northern Arizona University, USA
Paula Kenny, Dublin City University, Ireland

Section 3
Institutions: Policy and Practice

Chapter 11
Mob Justice in Contemporary Ghana 180
Daniel Tei, Mississippi State University, USA

Chapter 12
A Holistic Approach to Transitional Justice for Afghanistan 195
Parwez Besmel, Northern Arizona University, USA

Chapter 13
Foster Children and Deviance Risks After Emancipation 214
Gianna M. Strube, Independent Researcher, USA

Chapter 14
Restorative Justice as an "Informal" Alternative to "Formal" Court Processes 226
Paula Kenny, Dublin City University, Ireland
Liam J. Leonard, Northern Arizona University, USA

Compilation of References 245

About the Contributors 276

Index 279

Detailed Table of Contents

Preface xv

Acknowledgment xx

Section 1
Gender and Justice: Personal Perspectives

Chapter 1
Deportation as Deterrence? Social and Legal Predictors of Remigration After Deportation 1
William Estuardo Rosales, Department of Sociology, California State University, Los Angeles, USA
Katie Dingeman, California State University, Los Angeles, USA

This chapter interrogates the impacts of mass deportation on people recently removed from the U.S. to Mexico. It draws from a novel survey conducted in 2018 with 128 individuals at a migrant shelter in Nogales, Mexico to assess factors impacting intentions to re-migrate the U.S. after removal. Far from deportation preventing remigration to the U.S., the authors found most individuals planned to return to the U.S. at some point. The number of deportations a person experienced did not influence their future migratory plans. Rather, individuals were motivated to attempt another migration based on the location of their subjective belonging, family ties, and nature of their interactions with the U.S. legal system prior to deportation. These findings contribute to research suggesting that migratory decisions are socially embedded, while opening up new areas for research on the impact of institutional processes on re-migration plans.

Chapter 2
Sanctuary? A Discussion on Latinx/a Women and Girls in a Carceral State 30
Kayla Marie Martensen, University of Illinois at Chicago, USA

Influenced by critical carceral studies and abolition feminism, this non-empirical work identifies a political, social and economic carceral system that is fueled by existing racist, sexist, classist, homophobic, ableist and xenophobic ideologies, which both minimize resources for Latinx/a women and girls and increases the level of state violence perpetrated against them. The consequences of dispossession, subjugation and stigmatization have impacted Latina/x women's access to livable waged jobs, healthcare, safe and healthy food and water, adequate living conditions, quality education, and acceptance in American society. This violence is justified and considered necessary by constructing Latina/x women and girls as unworthy of state protection and state resource and as threats to the economy, culture and politics of the United States. Latina/x women, like other women of color, are not afforded the protections extended to white women by the state. Many Americans do not see them as the "good victim", but often they are the "bad woman", "bad mother", "sexual deviant", exploited laborer, culturally defiant, and increasingly they are "illegal", "criminal" and "terrorist". This results in Latinx/a women and girls being more likely to be imprisoned than white women and are one of the fastest growing prison populations in the United States.

Chapter 3
Prisoner Re-Entry: One Story of Coming Home 50
Rebecca Hubbard Maniglia, Northern Arizona University, USA

This chapter is part of an ongoing research book project that examines the realities of mass incarceration in Arizona through the intimate stories of the mothers, sisters, wives, and lovers left behind by incarceration. It is designed to use a narrative approach to give the reader an intimate and personal reflection on what in criminal justice we call re-entry but what to the individuals involved is just "coming home." While it provides a general overview of the formal re-entry process, it is not designed as an academic exploration of that topic.

Chapter 4
Carceral Trauma at the Intersections of Race, Class, and Gender 72
Cassandra D. Little, California State University, Fresno, USA

This chapter will provide a firsthand analysis of one woman's journey through the prison industrial complex. The intent is to bring the readers proximate to how trauma intersects with incarceration, gender, and race. The goal is to challenge our criminal justice system's need to over-criminalize and over-incarcerate women at alarming rates. Since 1980 the number of women in United States prisons has increased by more than 700%. These rates of incarceration of women have outpaced men by more than 50%. By drawing upon lived experience interacting with the United States Criminal Justice System and empirical data, the author will provide evidence that will argue that the experience of being incarcerated is traumatic and dehumanizing for many, but even more counterproductive for women.

Chapter 5
The Causes Behind the Cause: An Explanatory Analysis on Transgender Deviance in Dhaka, Bangladesh 86
Adiba Fannana, University of Ontario Institute of Technology (UOIT), Canada

Transgenders in Bangladesh are the most vulnerable group of people. This group of people are socially excluded and considered as deviant since British colonialism. The purpose of this study is to understand why they are considered as deviant as well as the reason of their deviant behavior and what are the acts done by them. Due to the importance of a few statements, in this chapter, "transgender" and "Hijra" are used and defined well. The difference between these two terms is clarified at the end of the chapter's literature review.

Section 2
Global Approaches to Justice and Imprisonment

Chapter 6
Prisoner Re-Entry and Desistance 99
Luis F. Nuño, California State University, Los Angeles, USA

Prisoner reentry is a concept that examines the reality faced by formerly incarcerated men and women upon their release from a correction facility. A primary concern from the perspective of institutions within the criminal justice system is whether formerly incarcerated men or women return to prison. Re-incarceration is a signal that the institution has failed at rehabilitating the former convict, as well as signal of personal failure on the part of the ex-con. Prisoner reentry is much more complex than the idea of reincarceration after release from prison lets on. There is an abundance of research on the reentry experience. This chapter reviews some important findings relevant to our understanding of the prisoner reentry experience.

Chapter 7
Resisting the New Punitiveness: Penal Policy in Denmark, Finland, and Norway and Contrary Trends in Ireland 110
Kevin Warner, University College Cork, Ireland

This chapter builds on PhD research into the penal policies of Nordic countries and in particular Denmark, Finland, and Norway. Essentially, the investigation asked whether the increase in punitiveness in relation to prison systems that is presumed to occur under the 'culture of control' of late modernity can be found in these countries. The scale of imprisonment, the 'depth' of imprisonment, and the perception of the person imprisoned were all examined. The prison systems were investigated through analysis of documentation and recorded interviews with key personnel, supplemented by visits to a representative range of prisons. While there have at times been some signs of 'new punitiveness', especially in Denmark and Norway, in general it can be said that none of the Nordic countries have followed the path predicted by Garland.

Chapter 8
How to Reduce Recidivism: Lessons From the U.S. State of Arizona.............144
Kevin A. Wright, Arizona State University, USA

Nearly everyone sent to prison will one day return to the community. This means that understanding recidivism is of critical importance to members of that community. At the most basic level, recidivism can be defined as "the reversion of an individual to criminal behavior after he or she has been convicted of a prior offense, sentenced, and (presumably) corrected." Recidivism therefore requires that some sort of involvement with the criminal justice system has taken place, and that then the individual again comes into contact with the system after additional transgressions. Recidivism, in other words, is officially detected, repeat unlawful behavior.

Chapter 9
Prison Communities: An Examination of Work, Life, and Relationships in Prison.............155
Jim Howe, Irish Prison Service (Retired), Ireland

This chapter will examine the prison as a community. This enclosed community is a place for the incarceration of criminals tried in the courts. It is also a workplace for corrections officers, and a microcosm of wider society, with work related and prison related relationships developing within the institution's walls. The chapter examines these themes from the perspective of the corrections officer, a perspective not always discussed in penological literature, or understood in wider society. The focus of literature rarely involves discussion on prisons as places of work, or in terms of the individuals for which society invests the care of its incarcerated. The study of the history of imprisonment and prisons and its sociological implications is significant but outside the scope of this work.

Chapter 10
Teaching Prisoners' Rights to Prison Officers to Improve Professional Performance.............168
Liam J. Leonard, Northern Arizona University, USA
Paula Kenny, Dublin City University, Ireland

This chapter is based on the experiences of both authors as part of a multi-disciplinary team of academics who brought changes to the prison system in the Republic of Ireland by leading an academic training program for recruit corrections officers in that country's prison system. The goal was to improve the professional performance of the corrections officers and to increase their understandings of the significance of human rights and prisoner's rights as a key part of their daily work practices. The award-winning recruit prison officer training program was the first of its kind globally.

Section 3
Institutions: Policy and Practice

Chapter 11
Mob Justice in Contemporary Ghana 180
Daniel Tei, Mississippi State University, USA

Mob justice/instant justice/vigilantism in Ghana serves as an indictment on the 1992 Constitution of Ghana, creates a heightened sense of fear among citizens that they could become victims, and also undermines the legitimacy of the police and legal authorities. Several studies have shown that communities use mob justice as a tool to respond to crimes and an ineffective criminal justice system. The current study aims to describe the mob justice situation in Ghana through the lens of the procedural justice theory. Specifically, the study asks the following research question: How does the media in Ghana describe mob justice? Drawing data from two Ghanaian newspapers—the Daily Graphic and The Ghanaian Times—the study relies on the content analysis method to explore how media in Ghana describe mob justice. The study reveals that lynch mobs are more likely to subject males, especially between the ages of 20-29, to lethal punishment than their female counterparts. Men's overrepresentation and women's underrepresentation as victims are theorized to be based on gender stereotypes. Finally, the study does not find support for the procedural justice theory. Thus, the study finds that police effectiveness is not sufficient enough to elicit police legitimacy that will enhance widespread public compliance. The study recommends that the Ghana Police should embark on policing styles that respect the rights and dignity of citizens, in addition to being effective, to remedy the mob justice problem. Further research is needed to combine official homicide data from the Ghana Police and other sources of homicide to highlight the phenomenon in Ghana, given the data source of the current study.

Chapter 12
A Holistic Approach to Transitional Justice for Afghanistan 195
Parwez Besmel, Northern Arizona University, USA

This chapter will examine the transition from war to a form of peace that embraces justice for all participants in the long running civil war in Afghanistan. The chapter examines the initiatives for peace and justice established by the Afghan government and incorporates a review of the relevant literature on this approach to transitional justice. Finally, the chapter will examine the author's concept about the potential for the truth and recondition commission combined with amnesty as a pathway to a successful transitional justice framework.

Chapter 13
Foster Children and Deviance Risks After Emancipation 214
Gianna M. Strube, Independent Researcher, USA

The subject of this chapter is how foster children may become at risk of displaying deviant behavior after emancipation from care. The chapter argues that there is a special need to provide for young people's legal protection and care after emancipation. The chapter then highlights the issues surrounding of foster children being abused and neglected, aging out of the system, and the programs offered as they overcome certain measures during their adolescent years. This research advocates for foster children in this category and outlines how their deviant behavior is perceived and defined and asks if this perception is just a stereotype. The research methodologies included interviews from those involved in the foster care system, in addition to literature and research from professional foster agencies.

Chapter 14
Restorative Justice as an "Informal" Alternative to "Formal" Court Processes 226
Paula Kenny, Dublin City University, Ireland
Liam J. Leonard, Northern Arizona University, USA

This chapter will examine the manner in which restorative justice provides an informal alternative to the formal processes of the adversarial court within the criminal justice system overall. In so doing, the chapter highlights the significance of restorative justice as a facet of a 'Sustainable Justice' within the community. While members of the public may be intimidated by the formal processes of the court system, the informal nature of the restorative justice conference may provide the community with a better exchange, and thereby see true justice served more fully.

Compilation of References 245

About the Contributors 276

Index 279

Preface

In this, the first book of my term as Editor of the *Advances in Criminology, Criminal Justice and Penology* Book Series, we have an outstanding collection of international academics, researchers and practitioners who have all experienced the institutions of incarceration or other institutional centers for those deemed deviant or outside the bounds of social acceptance. Many are from the United States. The United States incarcerates a very high percentage of its population, in addition to using internment camps for refugees on its southern border, and historically interning ethnic Japanese citizens during World War Two and creating an oppressive system of reservations for Native populations who had their lands seized and stolen. This overreliance on incarceration is made worse by a long standing and systemic racism in the American criminal justice system, which has led to the rise of the Black Lives Matter movement nationally, with global support.

With this in mind, this volume is titled *Global Perspectives on People, Process, and Practice in Criminal Justice.* I included the word 'people' in the title quiet deliberately, as this is a reflection of the Sociological concept of 'giving voice' to those who aren't always heard in the debates about incarceration and justice per se. This includes some of our contributors who have been incarcerated, who have had family members incarcerated, who have researched and interviewed those who have experienced prison, and those who have worked within the walls of the prison system. This provides the book with somewhat of a unique collection of perspectives on an area of society that is rarely discussed, the world of the prison and those who have experienced it as a lived institution, a 'house of pain' that many abolitionists and criminologists now feel has served its purpose and is too cruel and unjust a form of punishment for most non-violent crimes. The book is divided into three section. The first is titled 'Gender and Justice: Personal Perspectives'.

In the book's first chapter, 'Deportation as Deterrence? Social and Legal Predictors of Remigration after Deportation', William Estuardo Rosales and Katie Dingeman of California State University Los Angeles interrogate the impacts of mass deportation on people recently removed from the U.S. to Mexico. It draws from a novel survey conducted in 2018 with 128 individuals at a migrant shelter in Nogales, Mexico to assess factors impacting intentions to re-migrate the U.S. after removal. Far from deportation preventing remigration to the U.S., the chapter finds that most individuals planned to return to the U.S. at some point. The number of deportations a person experienced did not influence their future migratory plans. Rather, individuals were motivated to attempt another migration based on the location of their subjective belonging, family ties and nature of their interactions with the U.S. legal system prior to deportation. The chapter's findings contribute to research suggesting that migratory decisions are socially embedded, while opening up new areas for research on the impact of institutional processes on remigration plans.

Kayla Martensen is the author of Chapter 2. In her study, titled 'Sanctuary? A Discussion on Latinx/a Women and Girls in a Carceral State', she argues that ideas of sanctuary can mean different things to different people at different times. This chapter associates ideas of sanctuary with spaces of refuge, networks of safety, and a life of necessity that is free from violence. The chapter focuses on elements of equity, safety and state violence- namely, criminalization, hyper-surveillance and imprisonment- which can prevent or make it challenging to access state supported sanctuary. When space is made for the testimonies (testimonios) of Latinx/a women and girls, like other women and girls of color, we witness resiliency and the creation of networks and strategies to survive, protect and create a space of sanctuary. Therefore, this chapter does not claim that Latinx/a women and girls do not have spaces or networks of sanctuary. But rather, it focuses on how structural inequities, lack of state protection and increasing state violence challenge access to sanctuary, and perhaps restrict many Latinx/a women and girls from state supported sanctuary.

Chapter 3 is a personal reflection from Rebecca Hubbard Maniglia, titled 'Coming Home'. This chapter is part of ongoing research from the author that examines the realities of mass incarceration in Arizona through the intimate stories of the mothers, sisters, wives and lovers left behind as well as through the author's own story of loving someone behind bars. It includes a discussion of rentry and parole as aspects of the criminal justice system, and examines the journey taken by prisoners and their families as a part of the reentry process once sentences have been served.

Chapter 4 continues this theme of personal reflection. In 'Carceral Trauma at the Intersections of Race, Class, and Gender', Cassandra D. Little provides a firsthand analysis of one woman's journey through the Prison Industrial Complex. The intent is demonstrate how trauma intersects with incarceration, gender and race. The chapter's goal is to challenge our Criminal Justice System's need to over criminalize and over incarcerate women at alarming rates. Since 1980 the number of women in United States prisons has increased by more than 700%. These rates of incarceration of women have outpaced men by more than 50%, according to The Sentencing Project. By drawing upon lived experience interacting with the United States Criminal Justice System and empirical data, the author provides evidence that will argue that the experience of being incarcerated is traumatic and dehumanizing for many, but even more counterproductive for women.

Chapter 5 is a study from Adiba Fannana titled 'The Causes Behind the Cause: An Exploratory Analysis on Transgenders' Deviance in Dhaka, Bangladesh'. Transgenders in Bangladesh are the most vulnerable group of people, a biological being neither male nor female or sometimes both in one body. This group of people are socially excluded and considered as deviant since the British colonialism, throughout the whole South Asia (Notches, Onni Gust, 2014). The purpose of this study is to understand why they are considered as deviant as well as the reason of their deviant behavior and what are the acts done by them, which is considered as deviant as well. Due to the importance of few statements in this chapter, "transgender" and "Hijra" are both words which are used and defined well. The difference between these two terms is clarified at the end part of the chapter's literature review.

Section 2 of the book is titled 'Global Approaches to Justice and Imprisonment'.

Chapter 6, 'Prisoner Reentry and Desistance', by Luis F. Nuño, argues that prisoner reentry is a concept that examines the reality faced by formerly incarcerated men and women upon their release from a correction facility. A primary concern from the perspective of institutions within the criminal justice system is whether formerly incarcerated men or women return to prison. Re-incarceration is a signal that the institution has failed at rehabilitating the former convict, as well as signal of personal failure on the part of the ex-con. Prisoner reentry is a much more complex than the idea of reincarceration after release from prison lets on. There is an abundance of research on the reentry experience. This chapter reviews some important findings relevant to our understanding of the prisoner reentry experience.

In our seventh chapter, 'Resisting the New Punitiveness: Penal Policy in Denmark, Finland, and Norway and Contrary Trends in Ireland', Kevin Warner's investigation asked whether the increase in punitiveness in relation to prison systems that is presumed to occur under the 'culture of control' of late modernity (Garland, 2001) can be found in these countries. The scale of imprisonment, the 'depth' of imprisonment, and the perception of the person imprisoned were all examined. The prison systems were investigated through analysis of documentation and recorded interviews with key personnel, supplemented by visits to a representative range of prisons.

Chapter 8, 'Reentry and Recidivism', by Kevin Wright states that nearly everyone sent to prison will one day return to the community. This means that understanding recidivism is of critical importance to members of that community. At the most basic level, recidivism can be defined as "the reversion of an individual to criminal behavior after he or she has been convicted of a prior offense, sentenced, and (presumably) corrected". Recidivism therefore requires that some sort of involvement with the criminal justice system has taken place, and that then the individual again comes into contact with the system after additional transgressions. Recidivism, in other words, is officially detected, repeat unlawful behavior.

Chapter 9 by Jim Howe is titled 'Prison Communities: An Examination of Work, Life, and Relationships in Prison'. Here, the author examines the prison as a community. This enclosed community is a place for the incarceration of criminals tried in the courts. It is also a workplace for corrections officers, and a microcosm of wider society, with work related and prison related relationships developing within the institution's walls. The chapter examines these themes from the perspective of the corrections officer, a perspective not always discussed in penological literature, or understood in wider society.

Chapter 10, 'Teaching Prisoners' Rights to Prison Officers to Improve Professional Performance', by Liam Leonard and Paula Kenny, is based on the experiences of both authors as part of a multi-disciplinary team of academics who brought changes to the prison system in the Republic of Ireland by leading an academic training program for recruit corrections officers in that country's prison system. Their goal was to improve the professional performance of the corrections officers and to increase their understandings of the significance of Human Rights and Prisoner's Rights as a key part of their daily work practices. The award-winning recruit prison officer training program was the first of its kind globally.

The third section of the book is titled 'Institutions: Policy and Practice'.

In Chapter 11, 'Mob Justice in Contemporary Ghana', Daniel Tei states that 'Mob justice' or 'instant justice' or 'vigilantism' in Ghana serves as an indictment on the 1992 Constitution of Ghana, creates a heightened sense of fear among citizens that they could become victims, and also undermines the legitimacy of the police and legal authorities. Several studies have shown that communities use mob justice as a tool to respond to crimes and an ineffective criminal justice system. The chapter aims to describe the mob justice situation in Ghana through the lens of the procedural justice theory. Specifically, the study asks the following research question: How does the media in Ghana describe mob justice? Drawing data from two Ghanaian newspapers—the *Daily Graphic* and *The Ghanaian Times*, the chapter relies on the content analysis method to explore how media in Ghana describe mob justice. The chapter reveals that lynch mobs are more likely to subject males, especially between the ages of 20-29, to lethal punishment than their female counterparts. Men's overrepresentation and women's underrepresentation as victims are theorized to be based on gender stereotypes. Finally, the study does not find support for the procedural justice theory.

In Chapter 12, 'A Holistic Approach to Transitional Justice for Afghanistan', Parwez Besemel examines the transition from war to a form of peace that embraces justice for all participants in the long running civil war in Afghanistan. The chapter examines the initiatives for peace and justice established by the Afghan government and incorporates a review of the relevant literature on this approach to transitional justice. Finally, the chapter will examine the author's concept about the potential for the truth and recondition commission combined with amnesty as a pathway to a successful transitional justice framework.

Gianna Strube's thirteenth chapter is titled 'Foster Children and Deviance Risks After Emancipation'. The subject of this chapter examines how foster children may become at risk of displaying deviant behavior after emancipation from care. The chapter argues that there is a special need to provide for young people's legal protection and care after emancipation. The chapter then highlights the issues surrounding of foster children being abused and neglected, aging out of the system, and the programs offered as they overcome certain measures during their adolescent years. This research advocates for foster children in this category and outlines how their deviant behavior is perceived and defined and asks if this perception is just a stereotype.

Chapter 14, 'Restorative Justice as an "Informal" Alternative to "Formal" Court Processes', by Paula Kenny and Liam Leonard, examines the manner in which restorative justice provides an informal alternative to the formal processes of the adversarial court within the criminal justice system overall. In so doing, the chapter highlights the significance of restorative justice as a facet of a 'Sustainable Justice' (Leonard & Kenny, 2010) within the community. While members of the public may be intimidated by the formal processes of the court system, the informal nature of the restorative justice conference may provide the community with a better exchange, and thereby see true justice served more fully.

REFERENCES

Leonard, L., & Kenny, P. (2010). Sustainable Justice and the Community (Advances in Ecopolitics 6). Bingley: Emerald Group Publishing.

Onni Gust. (2014). India's Section 377: India, Britain and the ongoing legacies of imperialism. *Notches*. http://www.notchesblog.com

Acknowledgment

I would like to acknowledge all who contributed to the origin of this project, which began at the 2018 at the Annual Justice Studies Association Conference at Northern Arizona University. This conference was organized by Professor Rebecca Maniglia, who brought together a remarkable collection of academics, practitioners and activists as part of a statement of intent about the need for greater justice for those experiencing incarceration from all perspectives. Professor Maniglia's conference was also reflective of the vibrant ideology of the Department of Criminology and Criminal Justice at NAU, where I had the pleasure of working before this book was completed. Here, Rebecca is joined by activist academics and researchers such as Raymond Michalowski, Luis Fernandez, Robert Schehr, Linda Robyn and Marianne Neilson, who promote justice in their teaching and output across the board. I would like to dedicate this book to them, and to Janice Harter, to my family and those who have supported me as Advances in Criminology Series Editor at IGI Global.

Section 1

Gender and Justice: Personal Perspectives

Chapter 1
Deportation as Deterrence?
Social and Legal Predictors of Remigration After Deportation

William Estuardo Rosales
Department of Sociology, California State University, Los Angeles, USA

Katie Dingeman
California State University, Los Angeles, USA

ABSTRACT

This chapter interrogates the impacts of mass deportation for people recently removed from the U.S. to Mexico. It draws from a novel survey conducted in 2018 with 128 individuals at a migrant shelter in Nogales, Mexico to assess factors impacting intentions to re-migrate the U.S. after removal. Far from deportation preventing remigration to the U.S., the authors found most individuals planned to return to the U.S. at some point. The number of deportations a person experienced did not influence their future migratory plans. Rather, individuals were motivated to attempt another migration based on the location of their subjective belonging, family ties, and nature of their interactions with the U.S. legal system prior to deportation. These findings contribute to research suggesting that migratory decisions are socially embedded, opening up new areas for research on the impact of institutional processes on re-migration plans.

DOI: 10.4018/978-1-7998-6646-6.ch001

INTRODUCTION

On January 20, 2017, Donald J. Trump was inaugurated into office as the 45th president of the United States. The billionaire celebrity entrepreneur ran on a platform of white nationalism and economic protectionism to be garnered in large part through immigration restriction. During his campaign Trump promised to build a "great wall" between the U.S. and Mexico, which Mexico would finance. He also vowed to create a "deportation force" to round up the estimated 10.5 million undocumented people residing in the country at the time. Trump defended such proposals by constructing a moral panic around Mexican migrants, portraying them "drug dealers," "rapists," "criminals," and "bad hombres" who threatened the social and economic order (Phillips 2017). He argued that eliminating the undocumented and deterring future migration mostly from Latin America and the Middle East would help restore domestic civility and return the U.S. to its rightful place atop the global economy.

While distancing neoliberal capitalism and the global elite from the production and perpetuation of economic insecurities he promised to address, Trump stoked the xenophobic fears of his base to garner political allegiance. He affirmed that outsourcing promoted deindustrialization and eliminated jobs, as epitomized by the 1993 North American Free Trade Agreement (NAFTA), while also employing misleading evidence to support claims on the purportedly negative economic impact and criminality of the undocumented. Even though conservative economists posit that the undocumented have a net positive impact on the economy (Borjas 1990), Trump claimed they mostly steal jobs and diminish wages. Research consistently finds that the foreign-born, including the undocumented, are incarcerated at lower rates than the U.S.-born (Dingeman-Cerda 2017), yet Trump reified them into criminal scapegoats for a precarious economy.

Over the course of his term, Trump instituted a consistent attack against immigration and immigrant rights. He rescinded the *Deferred Action for Childhood Arrivals* (DACA) program offering protection against deportation for immigrants who entered the US as children. He instituted a campaign of child separation from their parents at the border, expanded the incarceration of asylum seekers, attempted to eliminate *Temporary Protected Status* (TPS), instituted a ban on refugees from Muslim-majority countries, expanded the "public charge" clause that makes poor migrants largely inadmissible, and removed key asylum protections for domestic abuse survivors and other vulnerable groups. Trump also cut humanitarian aid to Central America, forced asylum seekers to wait in Mexico while attempting to access the US humanitarian system, and established Guatemala as a "safe third country" for asylum despite Guatemala being a key sending state of asylum seekers. In 2018, Trump rolled back enforcement priorities established under Obama toward a zero-tolerance policy that criminalizes unlawful border entry. Though unable to coerce Mexico to fund a wall, at the time of this writing, U.S. taxpayers funded approximately 650 miles of border barriers ostensibly to prevent new arrivals from entering unlawfully (CBP 2020).

Trump's rhetoric and barrage of anti-immigrant measures sent shockwaves through the U.S. largely because it broke from a longstanding notion of the U.S. as a nation of immigrants. Scholarship, media, and human rights reports suddenly attended to the lesser acknowledged but deeply pervasive history of immigrant exclusion, containment, and banishment from the U.S. (Kanstroom 2007). They found that deportation practices long existed in the U.S. along racial, gendered, and class lines, while targeting other groups on the basis of political ideology, health status, sexual activity, and criminal history (Ibid.). When today's mass deportation erupted in the mid-1990s, the U.S. has continued to target black and brown men without legal status who labor in agriculture, service, construction, and the informal sector (Golash-Boza and Hondagneu-Sotelo 2013; Vásquez 2015). An increasingly large population of long-term noncitizens with legal status have also been made deportable (Kerwin, Alulema, and Nicholson 2018). This has been especially been the case as enforcement expands from the border to the interior, the criminal justice system and immigration system have grown entwined, and immigration violations have become routinely criminalized (García Hernández 2013).

Since 1996, over *6 million people* have been formally removed from the U.S.[1]; with 632,651 removed in Trump's first two years in office (USDHS 2019). Deterrence logics underpinning this mass deportation assume that once noncitizens are removed, society is effectively cleansed of unwanted or threatening migrants, the cycle of migration slows, and potential migrants will consider other options. Yet, research consistently shows that immigration enforcement historically has done little to stem undocumented migration (Cornelius and Salehyan 2007). After every major enforcement initiative--the Mexican Repatriation of the 1930s, Operation Wetback in the 1950s, the tightening of border and employer sanctions by the Immigrant Responsibility and Control Act (IRCA) of 1986, and expansive border militarization and legal restrictions of the mid-1990s--undocumented migration from Mexico continued to grow (Balderrama and Rodríguez 2006; Massey, Durand, and Malone 2002; Nevins 2002). Anti-immigration measures continued to prevail to the present, yet most evidence indicates that these measures did not deterred undocumented migration (Hagan, Eschbach, and Rodriguez 2008; Slack, Martinez, and Whiteford 2018; Wong 2018).

This article contributes to our understanding of restrictionist immigration initiatives by examining the effect of the Trump Administration's rhetoric, threats, and measures *at the individual level*, drawing from the perspectives of recently deported people. Specifically, we examine the factors that contribute to *intentions to return to the U.S.* after deportation to Mexico. Our analysis draws from a novel survey administered in early 2018 at a migrant shelter in Nogales, Mexico with 128 people of Mexican origin deported within the last 6 months (see also Kerwin et al. 2018). We examined whether migrants at the shelter planned to return to the U.S. or remain in Mexico through a series of logistic regressions that examine the relative impact of various demographic, migratory, socioeconomic, and legal factors.

We find that, contrary to the notion that deportation inherently dissuades remigration, most surveyed people planned to come back to the U.S. at some point. Their plans to stay in Mexico or return to the U.S. were unaffected by the number of times they were deported. Instead, intentions to remigrate were mostly predicated on factors associated with *social membership and family ties* to the U.S. Further, we examine legal factors, such as being advised of legal rights and or receiving legal assistance before deportation, in predicting post-deportation intentions to return. In doing so, we build on Abrego's (2011) *stratified legal consciousness* and how it affects intentions to return alongside socioeconomic and identificational factors. Our study finds that securing legal assistance increases the likelihood of intending to remigrate to the U.S. While more research is needed to understand the mechanisms that support this positive association between securing legal assistance and intending to return to the U.S., our findings contribute to the literature on legal consciousness and it's differential impact on migration intentions among deported persons.

MEXICAN DEPORTABILITY AND DEPORTATION TO MEXICO

According to Drotbohm and Hasselberg (2015: 551), "Deportation the forced removal of foreign nationals from a given national territory, is not a singular event. It is a process that begins long before, and carries on long after, the removal from one country to another takes place." Deportation to Mexico is one such historically rooted process, deeply entwined with U.S. empire (González and Fernández 2003), transnational capital and labor dynamics (Calavita 1999; Sánchez 1993), displacement and migration (Massey et al. 2002), the production of undocumented and deportable statues (De Genova 2002; Ngai 2004), and the creation and intensification of border and interior immigration enforcement (Kanstrom 2007; Lytle Hernández 2010; García Hernández 2013). The U.S.-Mexico border, as both a socio-legal formation and site at which deportation as an event occurs, has likewise come into being and been given new meanings at distinct historical moments.

The process of U.S. border formation with Mexico has unfolded since the Treaty of Guadalupe Hidalgo (1848) when the U.S. annexed the northern territories of Mexico following the Mexican-American War (1946-1948). Migration from Mexico appeared almost immediately thereafter as tens-of-thousands were converted into U.S. citizens and some 20,000 Mexican moved to the U.S. in search of gold (Sánchez 1993). Migration continued to intensify at the turn of the 20th century as US railroads and labor recruiters penetrated Mexico, displacing local communities and setting migrants on a journey to the US in search of economic opportunities in mining, railroads, agriculture, construction, and service (González and Fernández 2003). The border was porous, permitting the flow of people back and forth, often seasonally and without constraint.

Observers note that Mexico has "long been considered an ideal 'back-door' source of cheap labor for U.S. employers,'' with the U.S. encouraging a "revolving door" of Mexican labor migration (Calavita 1999). Mexican migration to the U.S. remained unregulated until 1924, when the National Origins Quota Act essentially "created the illegal alien" by mandating no migrant could enter without a visa issued from abroad (Ngai 2004). That same year the Border Patrol was instituted to enforce constricting immigration laws, but remained too small to play a significant role (Lytle Hernández 2010). Seasonal and permanent migration patterns thus continued relatively unabated until the Great Depression. At that time, "Americans, reeling from the economic disorientation of the depression, sought a convenient scapegoat. They found it in the Mexican community" (Balderrama and Rodríguez 2006). In an unprecedented move the Border Patrol rounded up around one million people of Mexican descent—60 percent of whom were U.S. citizens—and expelled them to Mexico.

After World War II, the U.S. began to recruit Mexican laborers through the Bracero Program. From 1948 to 1964, approximately 200,000 braceros per year worked under temporary, 2-year contracts. Though thousands of undocumented people were given status through the program braceros lived under the threat of deportation as there was no pathway to citizenship (González 2006). By the mid-1950s, Mexicans were once again blamed for a struggling economy. Between 1954 and 1959, the INS deported nearly 1.5 million through Operation Wetback. A racist program to its core, INS officers regularly stopped individuals who appeared to be of Mexican-origin to verify if they were authorized, and many of those deported were U.S. citizens (González 2006).

A year after the termination of the Bracero Program in 1964, the U.S. passed the 1965 Immigration Act, which replaced restrictive national origins quotas with family and employer preferences, but also placed quotas on the Western Hemisphere. The effect of this law over the next several decades was not only a dramatic increase in lawful migration from a diversity of countries around the globe, but a proliferation in the size of the undocumented population, especially from Mexico. In effect a Mexican migrant illegalization campaign, by the mid-1980s, the undocumented population had reached the millions. The U.S. aimed to rectify this problem in 1986 with the Immigration Responsibility and Control Act (IRCA), which provided an amnesty that legalized over 2 million. However, it was also responsible for laying the foundation for today's mass deportation. IRCA instituted immigration controls like militarizing the southern border and instituting employer sanctions first time, moves that coincided with the Wars on Drugs and Crimes, the growth of the prison industrial complex, and broader racialized neoliberal efforts to privatize, deregulate, and divest from social safety nets.

In the 1990s, the Clinton Administration passed the free trade agreement, NAFTA. As capital, raw materials, and consumer goods began to move across borders with greater ease, border controls increasingly aimed to deter and deport displaced people (Andreas 2000; Massey et al. 2002). As racialized xenophobia ran rampant, border technology advanced and the U.S. militarized the border at key entry points through Operations Gatekeeper and Hold the Line (Nevins 2002). During this time, like IRIIRA and AEDPA in 1996, that criminalized undocumented migration, expanded crimes eligible for deportation, stipped immigration judges of discretionary power, and made difficult to re-open cases after removal (Kanstroom 2007). Border enforcement moved toward the interior, first into jails and prisons to identify noncitizen people, and later through collaborative agreements with local law enforcement (García Hernández 2013). The result has been the hyper-criminalization and removal of noncitizens, most of whom are convicted of minor and immigration-related offenses.

These trends have only accelerated to the present. This has been especially the case since 9/11 and after the formation of the Department of Homeland Security in 2003 (Kanstroom 2007). Yet, despite the removal of over 6 million people in two decades (USDHS 2019), the size of the total undocumented population held steady (Passel and Cohn 2019). As of 2017, about 10.5 million lived in the U.S., largely from Mexico and Central America. Most are long-term residents, with 66% of residing here for 10 years or more (Ibid.). Such statistics corroborate the notion that, far from serving as a deterrent, restrictionism also confines deportable people *within* the U.S., creating an underclass of legally and thus socially and economically vulnerable migrants (Coutin 2010; De Genova 2002). The undocumented population and their supporters have pushed back against illegalization campaigns, garnering important victories, like Deferred Action for Childhood Arrivals (DACA) in 2012. Meanwhile, ongoing processes of border externalization to Mexico and internalization inside the U.S. have made journeys and departures more costly, dangerous, and risky than ever before (Slack et al. 2018).

Trump's policies have not so much changed this process as diversified and expanded it. Trump entered into a humanitarian migration crisis largely of Central Americans in flight, many of whom were seeking political asylum on account of social, economic, and political insecurities in Honduras, Guatemala, and El Salvador. Migration from Mexico had already been on the decline since the Great Recession and as economic conditions in Mexico improved in the 2000s (Schultheis and Ruiz Soto 2017). Statistically speaking, the result has been a slight *reduction* in removals under Trump compared to Obama, but a remarkably high 410,253 people of Mexican origin were nonetheless deported between 2017 and 2018 (USDHS 2019). This study examines the impacts of this expulsion on intents to remigrate back to the U.S. In doing so, it interrogates both the effectiveness and humaneness of mass deportation, ultimately concluding that the system polices migration for mostly political and economic ends.

INTENTIONS TO REMIGRATE POST-EXPULSION

The extant literature on migration is diverse in advancing various factors that explain peoples' migratory decisions. While studies have examined the factors motivating the initial migratory trip and subsequent trips as well as circular movement between countries of origin and destination, less is known about the complex set of factors influencing remigration after expulsion. Though observed migration *behaviors* are commonly used in migration studies, studying *intentions to return* after being recently deported provides unique insight into the effects of restrictionist policies on individuals as they navigate their decision to remain or return. Scholars agree that not all expelled immigrants will reintegrate and or settle in the country where they are returned, but rather many will seek to remigrate (Hagan et al. 2008; Schuster and Majidi 2014). Studying intentions is a critical first step to grasping which returnees are more likely to stay or leave, while providing a foundation for understanding whether, how, and why individuals might later change their minds or prolong their plans.

Deterrence Policies and Remigration

Though the United States has engaged in enacting policies of expulsion affecting not only migrants themselves, but spouses, children, and communities (Hagan et al. 2008; Hernández-Leon and Zuniga 2016), various academic studies have demonstrated the ineffectiveness of these policies. Specifically, Massey and Espinosa (1997) find that repressive restrictionist policies, such as increased border enforcement and employer sanctions, do not fulfill intended policy goals of deterring unauthorized migratory trips. Although the authors find that, "raising apprehension probabilities and implementing employer sanctions have modest effects in lowering the odds of taking additional illegal trips, these are counterbalanced by positive effects of first trips to yield a net effect close to zero" (Massey and Espinosa 1997: 990). Further, Cornelius and Salehyan (2007) find that migrants who, "report being well-informed about current Border Patrol efforts are *more likely* to cross" (147). When limiting the sample to focus on migrants who have previous migration experience, the authors find evidence of a small deterrent effect of border enforcement, but, "the result barely reaches statistical significance at the 0.1 level," and the effect is, "substantively small compared to other factors" (Cornelius and Salehyan 2007: 149). Similarly, in the more recent Migrant Border Crossing Study (MBCS), involving a survey of over 1,600 migrants in Mexico, Slack, Martinez, and Whiteford (2018) found that, "most deportees are highly connected to the U.S., and despite increased enforcement, they still largely intend to cross again." This landmark study demonstrates that, though border enforcement has accelerated to unprecedented levels, the effects of deterrence initiatives on migration reduction continue to be suspect.

Neoclassical vs. New Economics of Migration

Regardless of whether it's the first trip or return trip to the destination country, frameworks such as neoclassical economics highlight the role *economic factors* likely play in migration decision-making. Neoclassical economics argue that migrants are "rational" individuals that engage in a cost-benefit analysis based on prior knowledge of risks and opportunities when deciding to migrate (Massey and Espinoza 1997). Migrants will move to wherever is most economically favorable given their unique financial circumstances and needs. Economic factors such as the utility of increased wages in destination countries (Harris and Todaro 1970), public social transfers in countries of origin (Stecklov et al. 2005), and labor demands in destination countries (Krissman 2005) among others are central in predicting decisions to migrate.

Though economic factors certainly play a role in migration decisions, scholars such as Massey and Espinosa (1997) build a new economics of migration approach by pointing additionally to *social and human capital* in migration decision-making, especially at the household level. They find that the odds of additional trips (return migration) to the U.S. after departure are predicted by migration-specific social capital as measured by whether a migrant's wife and children have begun migrating to the U.S. and whether any children have been born there (1997: 940-45). Palloni and colleagues further support the importance of social capital in migration decision-making finding that, "having an older sibling who has been to the United States triples the likelihood of migrating to the United States and that this differential in the odds of movement persists when controls for human capital, common conditions, and unobserved heterogeneity are introduced" (Palloni et al., 2001: 1295).

Intentions of return might very well depend on a migrant's stock of social capital available to them and where they are located--country of origin or country of destination. Social capital affects the decision-making process at various stages of the migration process and through the different relationships within a migrant's social network. As Stecklov et al. (2005) note, relationships in migration networks are convertible to affect migration decision-making by *directly* providing direct forms of support such as housing and cash and or *indirectly* through the acquisition of information such as employment information in the country of destination.

Though a significant segment of the migration literature discusses the factors of motivating migration and subsequent trips to the country of destination in terms of *economics* and *capital*, and as consequence, these theoretical and empirical analyses are inevitably subsumed under theories of *rationality* and rational choice framework. Other scholars, however, view this process of decision-making as far more complex and involve non-economic and coercive factors that move beyond rational choice theory of behavior. They claim that divorcing an understanding of *relationships* from capitalistic and neoliberal economic framing (Golash-Boza 2015), factors such social membership and social ties broaden and capture the lived realities of migrants and have important ramifications for remigration prospects after deportation.

National Identity, Social Membership, & Belonging

Research further highlights the importance of *social belonging and membership in the U.S.* in predicting post-deportation experiences and plans. The undocumented population, particularly those of Mexican origin, have spent an increasing amount of time in the U.S. (Passel and Cohn 2019) largely due to immigration restrictions that inhibit them from lawfully re-entering the U.S. if they leave voluntarily (Coutin 2010). This population, many of whom were children when they first entered, have established lives in the U.S., including being educated (Gonzales 2015), establishing families (Abrego 2014), laboring in essential industries and as entrepreneurs (González 2006), and becoming involved in civic (Rosales 2017; Terriquez 2011) and political life (Terriquez 2015). While many have retained transnational ties to Mexico (Smith 2005), others have come to view the U.S. as their principal site of social belonging and membership (Coutin 2013; Gonzales 2015). A similar trend follows for the growing portion of non-citizens deported *with* legal status as a result of the criminalization of immigration (García Hernández 2013). Research on the post-deportation experience indicates that individuals who feel stronger identification with the U.S. than their country-of-origin are likely to experience heightened longing to return (Brotherton and Barrios 2011; Dingeman-Cerda 2017).

Removal is often experienced as *expulsion*, not only from the nation of one's subjective belonging, but from family and kinship ties, particularly for those who entered the U.S. as children or otherwise had lengthy stays (Baker and Marchevsky 2019; Dreby 2015). Involuntarily family separation in turn becomes a key driver of intentions to go back (HRW 2009). Hagan and colleagues (2008), found that 38% of their sample intended to return to the U.S., with another 25% leaving the option open[2]. For those intending to return, family separation was the greatest predictor of plans to try again (Amuedo-Dorantes, Pozo, and Puttitanun 2015; Cardoso et al. 2018). In another study, Zayas (2015) found children separated from their parents sometimes are pushed into the foster care system or move to Mexico to reunify with their parents. Most live with the remaining parent in a single-mother arrangement without a key breadwinner (Baker and Marchevsky 2019; Dreby 2012). The emotional trauma and financial burdens deportation abruptly thrusts on families pushed into such a transnational relationship becomes a highly powerful motivator to return and rebuild shattered lives in the U.S., the site of their familial belonging.

Post-Deportation Embeddedness & Mobilization of Support

The degree which deported persons come to be successfully reintegrated after deportation also appears to impact plans to remigrate. Deportation literature has dedicated substantial attention to social reintegration after return, especially whether migrants feel socially accepted in their families and communities. Shame, guilt, stigmatization and "spoiled" identities are a set of outcomes commonly experienced by migrants post-expulsion that might motivate them to remigrate to the U.S. Schuster and Majidi (2015) find in their interviews of Afghans deported from Iran that, "many of those who had been deported advanced feelings of shame as reasons for remigration" (14). Similar findings around stigma have been corroborated in other deportee receiving countries around the globe (Hagan and Wassink 2020). In certain contexts, like El Salvador and the Dominican Republic, deported men who grew up in the U.S., claim heightened stigma due to local stereotypes around gang members in those countries (Brotherton and Barrios 2011; Dingeman-Cerda 2017; Golash-Boza 2015). Such individuals are also among those more likely to feel a sense of belonging in the U.S. themselves, claiming intense longings to return.

While Schuster and Majidi (2015) examine stigmatized identity in the country of origin for returning migrants as a factor, others argue that factors, "ranging from joblessness and social maladjustment to boredom and frustration," could serve as barriers to "reintegrating" in the country of origin (Arowolo 2000). Because of inhospitable economic conditions after removal, some migrants might be coerced into re-migrating to the U.S.; effectively a non-choice (Dingeman-Cerda 2017; Golash-Boza 2015; Heidbrink 2019). In studying the migration decision of indigenous youth Heidbrink recounts the stories of deported youth who not only feel great shame in being forcefully removed from the United States, but are *compelled* to remigration to the United States: "Coerced by financial debt and structural poverty, [Rodrigo] reflected: 'I go, or we all suffer and die, maybe not tomorrow but the next month or next year. *This is not a choice*' (author emphasis)" (Heidbrink 2019: 267).

Just as these experiences of negative social and economic embeddedness after removal might encourage or coerce remigration, positive post-deportation experiences might very well encourage migrants to settle. Examining a sample of deported persons and voluntary returnees in Mexico, Hagan et al. (2018) find that, "deported migrants are an adaptable and resilient population whose divergent mobility pathways can be largely explain by human agency and the skills and resources acquired abroad and mobilized upon return" (2). By studying these groups of migrants over time, Hagan et al. (2018) are able to observe labor mobility and find evidence of upward labor mobility for both deportees and volunteer returnees. Similarly, in a comparative analysis of reintegration across Guatemala, the Dominican Republic, and Brazil, Golash-Boza (2015) found that deported persons facing more favorable social and economic conditions are more likely to successfully reintegrate. From this it may be conjectured that relatively receptive national and local contexts of return may have a mitigating effect on the likelihood to remigrate after removal.

Legal Experience--or Lack Thereof--of Deported Persons

Another area of interest in understanding intentions of remigration of deported persons is how experiences with the legal system, or lack thereof, during detention and deportation affects their legal consciousness. We adopt Merry's conceptualization of legal consciousness as, "commonsense understanding of the law" (1990). Further, we build on Abrego's research finding that the legal consciousness of the undocumented population is not monotholic, but is in fact stratified depending on the experiences with other institutions, such as education (2011). While legal consciousness might be associated with factors such socioeconomic status as measured by income and education and reflect class interests, Ewick and Sibley (1992) argue that everyday understanding of the law is, "neither fixed, stable, unitary, nor consistent...[but rather]..."something local, contextual, pluralistic, filled with conflict and contradiction" (742).

Just as lawyers and judges construct legal narratives that they advance in legal briefs and decisions (Lakhani 2013), so too do migrants "construct" the contours and understanding of legal institutions as they are exposed, experience, and interact with various legal and non-legal actors. Experience with the *law* and legal institutions might endow migrants with a "new" set of understanding of their subjective self in relation to the nation state. As Peutz (2007) finds in her field research of deported persons that it was, "during such run-ins with 'the law' that they deportees started to regard themselves as rights-bearing subjects" (184). Further, Abrego (2011) finds that undocumented young adults in the U.S. vis-a-vis socialization in educational and social institutions, "inform [their] legal consciousness," in different ways from undocumented older adults; thereby "shaping how they make claims and incorporate into U.S. society" (345). For migrants who are removed or voluntarily return to their country of origin, the legal consciousness acquired in the country of destination is potentially *remitted* to the country of origin (Kubal 2015). As argued by Kubal (2015), "legal consciousness of migrants...is remitted in both directions through the practices and imaginations of migrants and their families" (84).

Other than being more informed about the law and where they are situated within any particular legal context, legal consciousness of deported persons can exert itself in, "quotidian activities seemingly removed from where the law most directly exerts its effect, in a way that goes beyond simple knowledge of the law" (Menjívar, 2011). The extant research on legal consciousness among migrants demonstrates that it is not only stratified, but that this stratification affects various outcomes, such as claims-making (Abrego 2011). It remains unclear, however, how stratified legal consciousness affects the intentions of deported persons to remigrate to the U.S. Given the previous research, one can conjecture that increased knowledge and experience with legal entities and actors through the detention and deportation process will affect future decision-making to remigrate to the U.S.

ANALYTICAL STRATEGY

This study investigates the degree to which the observed difference in intentions to remigrate to the U.S. are accounted for by number of deportations, legal experience, national identity, and mobilization of support in Mexico. Using the CRISIS Survey, we first provide a descriptive analysis of this unique sample of deported persons (Tables 1-3). We then use logistic regression to examine the relative likelihood of expressing intentions to remigrate to the U.S. for deported persons. We then test whether the differences in intentions to remigrate are due to the number of deportation, legal experience, national identity, and mobilization of support in Mexico (Table 4). Given the sample size, we estimate a parsimonious model testing only six independent variables and control for seven variables; a reasonable number of total variables given the sample size of 128.

Given the above review of the extant literature, we advance the following hypotheses:

Hypothesis 1: Net of migration-specific factors and demographic controls, we expect that restrictionist policies as measured by the number of deportations is unlikely to deter migrants from intending to remigrate to the U.S.

Hypothesis 2: Given the limited research on the effects of legal experience, as measured by legal right and legal assistance, on intentions to remigrate to the U.S., we do not hypothesize any specific association.

Hypothesis 3: Given the extant literature of social embeddedness in the country of origin, we expect that national identity, expected remittances in Mexico, and community support in Mexico are negatively associated with intentions to remigrate to the U.S., net of migration-specific factors and demographic controls.

METHODS AND DATA

The data for this study comes from the CRISIS (Catholic Removal Impact Survey in Society) survey, produced through a collaboration between the authors, the Kino Border Initiative (KBI), the Center for Migration Studies (CMS), and the Office of Justice and Ecology (OJE) of the Jesuit Conference of Canada and the United States (Kerwin et al. 2018). In 2017, the CMS and KBI reached out to Drs. Katie Dingeman and Rebecca Galemba to develop a survey and two interview instruments to collect data from deported people and their family members for a report on the impact of deportation in both the US and Mexico under the Trump Administration. The survey included eighty-five closed-ended questions on demographics, migration and deportation histories, social support networks, financial and emotional resources, and future plans. Originally in English, the survey was translated to Spanish by a team of bilingual research assistants at Cal State LA, and then verified and revised for translation errors by bilingual service providers at KBI who work directly with the population.

Over the first five months of 2018, the Kino Border Initiative administered the CRISIS survey to 133 recently deported people at its Aid Center for Migrants (CAM in Spanish) in Nogales, Sonora, Mexico at the US border with Arizona. Survey participants were identified by staff through convenience and snowball strategies. To be selected, participants had to have been deported within two years, or since approximately January 2016. All interviews were conducted in Spanish by bilingual staff of KBI; specifically Sister Maria Engracia Robles, ME and Sister Maribel Lara Hernández, ME, assisted by KBI interns Samantha Kunin and Lucy McAuliffe. These research team members engaged in an informed consent process with potential participants, affording them the right to not be identified in the data and any resulting reports. Upon completion of the surveys, KBI staff input raw, de-identified survey data into an Excel spreadsheet, which was shared with us in a collaborative agreement.

DEPENDENT VARIABLE

In this study, we operationalize a dichotomous dependent variable that captures whether respondents intend to return to the U.S. The CRISIS survey specifically asked respondents, "Do you plan to return to the U.S.?" One respondent failed to indicate whether they intended to return to the U.S. and was deleted from the analytical sample used in this study.

INDEPENDENT VARIABLES

To test the effect of restrictionist migrant deterrence initiatives advanced under the Trump Administration, we utilize the number of deportations. Deportation is experienced at the *individual* level and is a direct result of policies of expulsion. Specifically, respondents were asked, "How many times have you been deported by the U.S. government?" This measure ranges from 1 to 11, with the average number of deportation being 1.97. Two respondents failed to answer this question and they were deleted from the sampe.

The CRISIS Survey asked respondents several questions regarding their legal experience during their deportation process. The questions dealt with notice of legal right to counsel ("Were you given notice of your right to access legal advice or an attorney?"), legal contact ("Did you or your family try to contact an attorney?"), and legal assistance ("Did you secure legal assistance?"). All three questions were transformed into dichotomous variables and examined using tetrachoric correlation estimation procedure to assess correlations between the variables. Our analysis found legal assistance and legal contact were highly correlated (approximately 0.85.) Given the ambiguity contained in the legal contact question ("Did *you* or *your family* contact an attorney?) and the fact that legal contact is highly correlated with legal assistance, we dropped legal contact from our statistical estimation (See Table 4).

The literature provides evidence about the role of non-economic factors in affecting the intentions to remigration to the U.S.. For this study, we operationalized and tested three independent variables that potentially influence the decision-making process of respondents after being deported: national identity, remittances expected support in Mexico, and community support in Mexico. With regard to national identity, the CRISIS Survey asked respondents, "Do you identify with your country of birth?" Respondents were given the options of "strongly," "somewhat," "weakly," and "not at all," Given the distribution of responses, we transformed this measure into a dichotomous variable, collapsing and coding "strongly," and "somewhat" as a "1" (identifies with country of origin) and collapsing and coding "weakly" and "not at all" as "0" (does not identify with country of origin).

In capturing support in the way of remittances, the CRISIS Survey asked respondents, "Do you have people able to send you money from the U.S.?" This variable was transformed into a dummy variable with "1" representing an affirmative answer to this question and "0" representing a negative answer to this question. Finally, respondents were asked, "Do you have people in your community of origin willing/ able to support you?" This question captures community support in the country of origin and was operationalized as a dichotomous variable with "1" indicating that respondents have community support in their country of origin and "0" indicating no community support.

MIGRATION-SPECIFIC AND DEMOGRAPHIC CONTROLS

For this study, we control for several migration-specific and demographic variables. With regard to migration-specific variables, we control for whether respondents experienced any abuse during their migration journey, legal status, and years in the U.S. For demographic variables, we control for age, education, and whether the respondent's spouse and at least one child is in the U.S. For abuse, the CRISIS survey specifically asked respondents the following: "Did you suffer any abuses or extortion along the journey to the United States?" We created a dichotomous variable for this abuse variable with "1" indicating they experience abuse or extortion and "0" indicating no abuse experienced during the migration journey. To capture legal status, the CRISIS Survey asked, "What was your most recent immigration status prior to the most recent deportation from the U.S.?" We operationalized three legal statuses given the responses from respondents: permanent residency (green card); temporary visa or protective status such as DACA; and undocumented. Respondents were asked the numbers of years they had been in the years in the U.S., which ranged from 2 years to 44 years. Age is a straight-forward measure of respondent's age at the time the survey was administered during the first five months of 2018. For education, respondents were asked to specify their level of education by years. Given the variation in responses, we operationalized education as a dichotomous variable where "1" indicates respondents graduated high school or graduated high school and obtained some further education beyond high school and "0" indicating less than a high school level education. For marriage and children, we used information from several questions asking respondents which country their spouse and children lived in to operationalize a dichotomous variable where "1" indicates that respondent's spouse and at least 1 child is in the U.S. and "0" indicating that spouse and child not living in the U.S.

DESCRIPTIVE RESULTS

The sample characteristics shown in Table 1 highlight that, of the 128 people interviewed, all participants were of Mexican origin and all but one participant identified as men with an average age of 39.58. Consistent with reporting that most deportable people in the U.S. have been in the country for 10 years or more (Passel and Cohn 2019), participants had spent an average of 20.01 years in the U.S. prior to removal to Mexico. The population also reported meaningful financial ties to the U.S., with 96 percent reporting employment, with a mean monthly salary of $2,743 and an average employment length of 9.8 years. Although a significant portion of the respondents indicated they were undocumented (60.16 percent), over a quarter indicated some form of status: 13 percent held permanent residency and 21 percent has another form of visa to be in the U.S.

The population also reported significant social ties and social engagement in the U.S. Over 59.38 percent of the sample indicated that their spouse was in the U.S. and had an average of three children as demonstrated in Table 2. Additionally, the respondents indicated substantial civic and religious engagement with 43.75 percent indicating some religious participation and 19.53 percent indicating some form of civic and community engagement.

With regard to the main outcome of interest---intent to remigrate to the U.S.--approximately 73 percent of respondents indicated that they plan to return at some point. Further, respondents were asked as to the kind of support that they could avail themselves in their country of origin. Approximately, 74 percent indicated they expected some support in terms of remittances, 33 percent owned property in the country of origin, and 19.5 percent indicated that they have some form of community support. Lastly, only little over half (53.12%) of respondents indicated that they identify with the country of origin and 46.88 percent identified more with the U.S..

Table 3 provides insightful descriptive analysis of the various stages of migration that some respondents experience, as follows: migration experience; detention experience; deportation experience; and legal experience. As demonstrated in Table 3, over one third of respondents experienced some form of abuse or extortion during their *migration journey* with the average age of 1st time migration at 16.82. With regard to apprehensions as demonstrated in Table 3, respondents reported various sites of apprehension: while driving (36%), at home (26%), at work (6%) or in the street or community (16%). Respondents indicated that they spent an average of 68 days in detention. Importantly, respondents indicated that most of their deportations were "formal" (80.83%), rather than voluntary, and thus included some form of ban on their reentry. Lastly, respondents on average reported 1.97 deportations, thus many were already repeat entrants to the U.S. Further, according to Kerwin et al.'s (2018) analysis of the same survey, more than half of the sample did not commit a

Table 1. Sample Characteristics of Deported Persons (n=128)

Characteristic	Number	Percent	Mean (if applicable)
Gender			
Male	127	99.2	
Female	1	0.78	
Age			
18-30	35	27.34	39.58
31-40	31	24.22	
Over 40	62	48.44	
Years in United States			
0 to 5	9	7.03	20.01
More than 5 to 10	10	7.81	
More than 10 to 20	58	45.31	
More than 20	51	39.84	
Employed Prior to Deportation			
No	4	3.12	
Yes	124	96.88	
Employment Length Prior to Deportation			9.8 years
0 to 5 years	46	35.94	
More than 5 to 10 years	30	23.44	
More than 10 to 20 years	43	33.59	
More than 20 years	9	7.03	
Spoken Language (n=124)			
English	2	1.61	
English and Spanish	100	80.65	
Spanish	22	17.74	
Education			
0 to 5	42	32.81	
6-8	14	10.94	
9-11	50	39.06	
12 years	15	11.72	
Some College/College	7	5.47	
Average Monthly Income Prior to Deportation			$2,743
Legal Status			
Permanent Residency	16	12.50	
Asylum/Refugee	2	1.56	
U Visa	2	1.56	
Deferred Action (DACA)	4	3.12	
Undocumented	77	60.16	
Other Visa	27	21.09	

Source: CRISIS Survey, 2018

crime prior to deportation. Of the 37 individuals convicted, most were convicted of immigration violations and traffic offenses (35%), followed by drug offenses (22%) and violent crimes (22%), as classified by the uniform crime codes of the FBI (See Kerwin et al. 2018). Less than 1% of the sample reported their deportations began with a Customs and Border Protection (CBP) agent. Further, Kerwin et al. (2018)

Table 2. Social Ties & Connections, National Identity, and Intentions to remigration of Deported Persons (n=128)

Social Ties and Connections	Number	Percent
Respondent's Spouse is in the U.S.	76	59.38
Average Number of Children	3.01	
Average Number of Siblings (n=127)	4.96	
Civic and Social Participation		
Civic/Community Participation	25	19.53
Religious Participation	56	43.75
Mobilization of Support in Country of Origin (MX)	**Number**	**Percent**
Respondent's Spouse is in Mexico	7	5.47
Remittances Support[1]	95	74.22
Respondent Owns Property in Country of Origin	42	32.81
Respondent has Community Support	25	19.53
Nationality Identity and Intent to Return	**Number**	**Percent**
Respondents Who Plan to Return to the U.S.	93	72.66
Respondents that Identify with Country of Origin	68	53.12

Source: CRISIS Survey, 2018

(1) Respondents answered "yes" to"[D]o you have people to able to send you money from the U.S.?"

found that over 65% began with a police arrest and another 30% with Immigration and Customs Enforcement (ICE).

The CRISIS Survey provides a unique opportunity to examine the legal experience of deported persons. As the fourth panel in Table 3 indicates, approximately 30 percent of respondents indicated that they signed legal papers that they did not understand during their deportation process, over 70 percent indicated that they were provided with information as to their right to access legal advice; meaning one third of the sample were denied that right. Half of the sampled respondents indicated that they or their family contacted an attorney, with under 30 percent (27.3%) indicating that they secured legal assistance.

Table 3. Migration and Deportation Experiences of Deported People (n=128)

Migration Experience	Number	Percent
Respondent Experienced Abuse During Migration Journey	40	31.25
Average Age of 1st Time Migration to the US	16.82	
Respondent Sent Remittances to Family Members in Country of Origin (n=117)	79	61.65
Detention Experience	**Number**	**Percent**
Location of Recent Apprehension		
Workplace	8	6.25
Home	33	25.78
Street/Community	21	16.41
While Driving	46	35.94
In Jail	5	3.91
ICE Check-In	8	6.25
Other	7	5.47
Average Days in Detention Center (Mean)	67.56	
Deportation Experience	**Number**	**Percent**
Type of Recent Deportation (n=120)		
Voluntary	23	19.17
Formal	97	80.83
Average Number of Deportations	1.97	
Legal Experience	**Number**	**Percent**
Signed Legal Papers that Respondent Did Not Understand	39	30.47
Respondent Provided with Right to Access Legal Advice/Attorney (Legal Right)	91	71.09
Respondent or Family Contacted Attorney (Legal Contact)	54	50.00
Secured Legal Assistance (Legal Assistance)	35	27.34

Source: CRISIS Survey, 2018

STATISTICAL RESULTS

The descriptive results above provide a complex and insightful examination of this unique sampled population of deported persons. Given the small nature of the sampe, however, our study manages to estimate a parsimonious model of intentions to remigrate to the U.S. The statistical results serve as preliminary findings in examining relevant and untested factors predicting intentions to remigrate to the U.S.

Table 4 presents the estimated log odds of intent to remigrate to the United States. Four models were estimated where variables are entered into the respective models piece-wise to examine how our main independent variables of interest--number of deportations, legal experience, national identity and mobilization of support--explain the likelihood of intent to remigrate to the U.S.

Table 4. Parameters from logistic regression models predicting any intent to re-migrate to the U.S. (n=128)

	Model 1	Model 2	Model 3	Model 4
Number of Deportations	-0.013	-0.001	-0.002	0.014
Legal Experience				
Legal Right		0.037	0.079	-0.048
Legal Assistance		**1.057****	**0.960****	**0.964****
National Identity and Mobilization of Support				
Identifies with Country of Origin			**-0.956****	**-1.274****
Remittances Expected Support in Mexico			0.202	0.428
Community Support in Mexico			-0.239	-1.017
Migration-Related Controls				
Experienced Any Abuse				-0.257
Legal Status (Ref. Group=Perm. Resident)				
Undocumented				-0.065
DACA/U Visa/Other Visa				0.404
Years in the US				-0.055
Demographic Controls				
Age				-0.035
HS Graduate Plus (HS Grad and HS + Some College)				**1.730****
Spouse and at least one Child in the United States				**0.919┼**
Constant	1.004**	0.509	0.973	3.109**

Source: CRISIS Survey, 2018
┼ $p < 0.10$, * $p < 0.05$, ** $p < 0.01$, *** $p < 0.001$ (two tailed)

Across models 1-4, the number of deportations is not significantly associated with intent to remigrate to the U.S. (Hypothesis 1). Specifically, the full model--Model 4--accounts for migration-specific factors and demographic controls, and the number of deportations is unrelated to the likelihood of intent to remigration; therefore we fail to reject the null hypothesis of no association between restrictionist policies as measured by the number of deportations on the intent of remigration.

With regard to the effects of legal experience, securing legal assistance is positively associated with intent to remigrate to the U.S.. Specifically, as demonstrated in Table 4, net of national identity, mobilization of support, and migration related and demographic controls, securing legal assistance versus not securing legal assistance increases the log odds of the intent to remigration to the U.S. by 0.964. This result is significant at the 0.05 significance level. According to the results in Table 4, legal right is not associated with the intent to remigrate to the U.S.

With regard to Hypothesis 3, we hypothesized that national identity, expected remittances support in Mexico, and community support in Mexico are negatively associated with the intent to remigrate. As demonstrated in Table 4, Model 4, we fail to reject the null hypothesis with regard to expected remittances support and community support in Mexico of no association with the intent to remigrate to the U.S. With regard to national identity, we reject the null hypothesis, finding a negative relationship with identifying with the country of origin and intent to remigration to the U.S. Specifically, identifying with the country of origin versus not identifying with the country of origin decreases the log odds of intent to remigrate to the U.S. by 1.274. This finding is statistically significant at the 0.05 significance level and strengthens when we control for migration-related and demographic controls.

Finally, education and having a spouse and children in the U.S. is positively associated with intent to remigrate. Specifically, having a high school degree or more versus having less than a high school degree increases the log odds of intent to remigrate to the U.S. by 1.730. This finding is statistically significant at the 0.05 significance level. Having a spouse with at least one child in the U.S. versus having no spouse and no children in the U.S. increases the log odds of intent to migrate in the U.S. by 0.919. This result is marginally significant at the 0.10 significance level.

Given that log odds ratios are not immediately intuitive, we also estimated probabilities with varying assumptions using Model 4 estimations in Table 4. For example, the estimated probability of intending to remigrate to the U.S. is 0.946 for a respondent with one deportation, who was informed of their legal right to access legal advice/counsel, secured legal assistance, and identifies with the country of origin.[3] The probability of intending to remigrate drops to 0.876 for a respondent that was not informed of their legal right to access legal advice/counsel and did not secure legal assistance. Lastly, the estimated probability of intending to remigrate to the U.S. drops to 0.557 for someone with the same characteristics, but who has less than a high school degree.

DISCUSSION OF FINDINGS AND CONCLUSION

The findings of this study correspond with existing research arguing that migratory decision-making is impacted by a host of factors that extend well beyond the immigration policies and practices of a receiving state. Specifically, we find evidence that costly and repressive measures of expulsion do not achieve their intended goals of stopping or deterring unauthorized migration. In fact, most of the individuals in our study reported a desire to return to the U.S. at some point. Moreover, when measured by the number of deportations, we find that the effects of restrictionist policies do not deter immigrants from intending to remigrate to the U.S. post-expulsion. While our study does not capture the impact of specific restrictionist policies, such as increasing border enforcement as examined by Cornelius and Salehyan (2007), it uniquely captures the direct result of these policies: increased deportations. The number of deportations someone had had no effect on their intentions to return. Thus, at the level of individual decision-making, people's intentions to remigrate after deportation remain strong, especially if they spent a long time and are socially connected to the U.S. (Cornelius and Salehyan 2007; Hagan et al. 2008; Slack et. al 2018; Wong 2018). Such findings are in line with the extant literature that consistently show that at the macro-level, the modern deportation regime has done little to reduce the total size of the unauthorized population in the U.S. (Cornelius 2018; De Genova 2002; Passel and Cohn 2019).

While this study evaluated a set of factors that speak to Hagan et al.'s (2018) mobilization of support factors and site of social belonging and identity (Coutin 2013), only migrant's sense of identity with the country of origin was found to be statistically significant and negatively associated with intent of remigration. This finding is in line with previous research that indicates that the site of social belonging and identification plays a critical role in whether to settle in their country of origin or return (Coutin 2013; Brotherton and Barrios 2011; Dingeman-Cerda 2017). A reason for not finding factors such as community support in the country of origin is that the CRISIS survey is cross-sectional whereas Hagan et al. (ibid.) examined migrants' adaptive strategies in play over a significant period of time. Given the limited sample and non-longitudinal research design, further research should examine factors relating to mobilization of support and how they affect intentions to settle or return to the U.S.

With regard to legal consciousness, it is clear from our descriptive analysis that legal access and experiences of deported persons are not the same and therefore, unequal. Specifically, only 27 percent of our sample respondents secured legal assistance, 50 percent contacted an attorney, 71 percent were advised of their right to seek legal advice, and 31 percent signed legal papers they did not understand. This study further finds that this variation in legal experience matters in that having secured legal assistance increases the probability of stating an intention to remigrate to the U.S. One possible explanation for this finding could be that deported persons that secured legal assistance are now more fully aware of the "rights" they now have as "rights-bearing subjects" (Peutz 2007: 184) and therefore, have a legal consciousness that endows them with an empowered sense of their subjective self in relation to the legal institutions in the U.S. This legal consciousness, therefore, allows them to navigate the legal system and legal actors once they re-enter the U.S.; in a manner distinguishable from their legal consciousness on their first trip to the U.S. Further research should investigate the possible mechanisms that explains this statistically significant association between securing legal contact and expressing an intent to return to the U.S.

Overall, this research suggests that regardless of immigration restrictions migrants will continue to travel north even if their entry is delayed because of social, economic and political insecurities at home, forced separations from family abroad, the demand for cheap migrant labor, and promise of more sustainable livelihoods. Yet, the U.S. continues to finance a deportation apparatus unprecedented in scope and punitive effect (Kanstroom 2007). Scholars argue that its sustained growth mostly serves economic and political interests, including maintaining a vulnerable surplus labor force (De Genova 2002) and targeting racialized and gendered bodies to maintain a lucrative immigration industrial complex involved in a host of for-profit activities from wall construction, to surveillance technologies, to upholding the largest private prison industry in the world (Ibid.). Deportation also serves a powerful symbolic function, allowing the state to give off the impression that it is "doing something" about perceived problems of migration, crime, and even terrorism, even if these problems are misrepresented sociologically and discursively crafted through the state itself (Andreas 2000; De Genova 2002). Walters (2002) refers to this process as the governmentalization of government, a practice in which the state effectively governs itself in ways that serve to reproduce its own legitimacy, its own sovereignty.

More research is needed. The sample from the CRISIS survey was small, non-representative, and administered at one point in time. Our findings nonetheless remain illustrative and can serve as a useful guide for broader analyses on reintegration and remigration of deported people. Future research should include larger, random and representative samples capable of interrogating the relationship between immigration policies, social and institutional factors affecting migrants directly, and intents to remigration. Particularly promising is the relationship we uncovered here between migrants' legal assistance prior to removal and their post-deportation plans and realities. This project also suggests more research is needed on the relationship between national identity, post-deportation re-integration, and return. Finally, future research should consider viewing migratory decision-making as a process that unfolds over time in space within socially and economically embedded, often contingent relations. Scholars would do well to capture the dynamism in this process through ethnographic and longitudinal work that maps onto the complex unfolding of the lived experiences of deported people and their families.

REFERENCES

Abrego, L. (2011). Legal Consciousness of Undocumented Latinos: Fear and Stigma as Barriers to Claims-Making for First- and 1.5-Generation Immigrants. *Law & Society Review*, *45*(2), 337–370. doi:10.1111/j.1540-5893.2011.00435.x

Abrego, L. J. (2014). *Sacrificing Families: Navigating Laws, Labor, and Love Across Borders*. Stanford University Press. doi:10.1515/9780804790574

Amuedo-Dorantes, C., Pozo, S., & Puttitanun, T. (2015). Immigration Enforcement, Parent–Child Separations, and Intent to Remigrate by Central American Deportees. *Demography*, *52*(6), 1825–1851. doi:10.100713524-015-0431-0

Andreas, P. (2000). *Border Games: Policing the U.S.-Mexico Divide*. Cornell University Press.

Arowolo, O. O. (2000). Return Migration and the Problem of Reintegration. *International Migration (Geneva, Switzerland)*, *38*(5), 59–82. doi:10.1111/1468-2435.00128

Baker, B. F., & Marchevsky, A. (2019). Gendering deportation, policy violence, and Latino/a family precarity. *Latino Studies*, *17*(2), 207–224. Advance online publication. doi:10.105741276-019-00176-0

Balderrama, F. E., & Rodriguez, R. (2006). *Decade of Betrayal: Mexican Repatriation in the 1930s*. University of New Mexico Press.

Blust, K. (2020). Migrant Aid Group Opens New Shelter in Nogales, Sonora. *Fronteras Desk*. Accessed May 12, 2020. https://fronterasdesk.org/content/1441501/migrant-aid-group-opens-new-shelter-nogales-sonora

Borjas, G. J. (1990). *Friends or Strangers: The Impact of Immigrants on the U.S. Economy*. Basic Books.

Brotherton, D. C., & Barrios, L. (2011). *Banished to the Homeland: Dominican Deportees and their Stories of Exile*. Columbia University Press.

Calavita, K. (1999). Mexican Immigration to the USA: The Contradictions of Border Control. In R. Cohen (Ed.), *The Cambridge Survey of World Migration*. Cambridge University Press.

Cardoso, J. B., Hamilton, E. R., Rodriguez, N., Eschbach, K., & Hagan, J. (2016). Deporting Fathers: Involuntary Transnational Families and Intent to Remigrate among Salvadoran Deportees. *The International Migration Review*, *50*(1), 197–230. doi:10.1111/imre.12106

Cornelius, W. (2018). Constructing Deterrence in the Age of Trump: Restricting Asylum, Separating Families, and Criminalizing Migration. *LASA Forum, 49*(4), 37-41.

Cornelius, W. A., & Salehyan, I. (2007). Does Border Enforcement Deter Unauthorized Immigration? The Case of Mexican Migration to the United States of America. *Regulation & Governance*, *1*(2), 139–153. doi:10.1111/j.1748-5991.2007.00007.x

Coutin, S. B. (2010). Confined Within: National Territories as Zones of Confinement. *Political Geography*, *29*(4), 200–208. doi:10.1016/j.polgeo.2010.03.005

Coutin, S. B. (2010). Confined Within: National Territories as Zones of Confinement. *Political Geography*, *29*(4), 200–208. doi:10.1016/j.polgeo.2010.03.005

Coutin, S. B. (2013). In the Breach: Citizenship and its Approximations. *Indiana Journal of Global Legal Studies*, *20*(1), 109–140. doi:10.2979/indjglolegstu.20.1.109

Customs and Border Patrol (CBP). (2020). *Border Wall System*. Customs and Border Patrol, Department of Homeland Security. Retrieved June 10, 2020. https://www.cbp.gov/border-security/along-us-borders/border-wall-system

DeGenova, N. (2002). Migrant "Illegality" and Deportability in Everyday Life. *Annual Review of Anthropology*, *31*(1), 419–447. doi:10.1146/annurev.anthro.31.040402.085432

Dingeman-Cerda, K. (2017). Segmented Re/integration: Divergent Post-Deportation Trajectories in El Salvador. *Social Problems*, (0), 1–19.

Dreby, J. (2015). *Everyday Illegal: When Immigration Policies Undermine Immigrant Families*. University of California Press. doi:10.1525/9780520959279

Drotbohm, H., & Hasselberg, I. (2015). Deportation, Anxiety, Justice: New Ethnographic Perspectives. *Journal of Ethnic and Migration Studies, 41*(4), 551–562. doi:10.1080/1369183X.2014.957171

Ewick, P., & Silbey, S. S. (1992). Conformity, Contestation, and Resistance: An Account of Legal Consciousness. *New England Law Review*, (26), 731–749.

Golash-Boza, T. (2015). *Deported: Immigrant Policing, Disposable Labor, and Global Capitalism*. New York University Press. doi:10.18574/nyu/9781479894666.001.0001

Golash-Boza, T., & Hondagneu-Sotelo, P. (2013). Latino immigrant men and the deportation crisis: A gendered racial removal program. *Latino Studies, 11*(3), 271–292. doi:10.1057/lst.2013.14

Gonzales, R. G. (2015). *Lives in Limbo: Undocumented and Coming of Age in America*. University of California Press. doi:10.1525/9780520962415

González, G. (2006). *Guest Workers or Colonized Labor: Mexican Labor Migration to the United States*. Paradigm Publishers.

González, G., & Fernández, R. (2003). *A Century of Chicano History: Empire, Nations and Migration*. Routledge.

Hagan, J., Eschbach, K., & Rodriguez, N. (2008). U.S. Deportation Policy, Family Separation, and Circular Migration. *The International Migration Review, 42*(1), 64–88. doi:10.1111/j.1747-7379.2007.00114.x

Hagan, J., & Wassink, J. H. (2020, July 30). Return Migration Around the World: An Integrated Agenda for Future Research. *Annual Review of Sociology, 46*(1), 533–552. Advance online publication. doi:10.1146/annurev-soc-120319-015855

Harris, J. R., & Todaro, M. P. (1970). Migration, unemployment and development: A two-sector analysis. *The American Economic Review, 60*(1), 126–142.

Heidbrink, L. (2019). The Coercive Power of Debt: Migration and Deportation of Guatemalan Indigenous Youth. *Journal of Latin American and Caribbean Anthropology, 24*(1), 263–281. doi:10.1111/jlca.12385

Hernández, G., & Cuauhtémoc, C. (2013). Creating Crimmigration. *Brigham Young University Law Review*, 1457–1516.

Hernández-Leon, R. & Zuniga, V. (2016). Introduction to the Special Issue: Contemporary Return Migration from the United States to Mexico-Focus on Children, Youth, Schools and Families. *Mexican Studies/Estudios Mexicanos, 32*(2), 171–198.

Human Rights Watch (HRW). (2015). *Forced Apart: Families Separated and Immigrants Harmed by U.S. Deportation Policies*. HRW.

Kanstroom, D. (2007). *Deportation nation: Outsiders in American history*. Harvard University Press.

Kerwin, D., Alulema, D. & Nicholson, M. (2018). *Communities in Crisis: Interior Removals and Their Human Consequences*. Kino Border Initiative (KBI), Center for Migration Studies (CMS), and Office of Justice and Ecology (OJE).

Krissman, F. (2005). Sin Coyote Ni Patron: Why the "Migrant Network" Fails to Explain International Migration. *The International Migration Review*, *39*(1), 4–44. doi:10.1111/j.1747-7379.2005.tb00254.x

Kubal, A. (2015). Legal consciousness as a form of social remittance? Studying return migrants' everyday practices of legality in Ukraine. *Migration Studies*, *3*(1), 68–88. doi:10.1093/migration/mnu032

Lakhani, S. M. (2013). Producing Immigrant Victims' 'Right' to Legal Status and the Management of Legal Uncertainty. *Law & Social Inquiry*, *38*(2), 442–473. doi:10.1111/lsi.12022

Lytle Hernandez, K. (2010). *Migra! A History of the U.S. Border Patrol*. University of California Press. doi:10.1525/9780520945715

Massey, D., Durand, J., & Malone, N. J. (2002). *Beyond Smoke and Mirrors: Mexican Immigration in an Era of Economic Integration*. Russell Sage Foundation.

Massey, D. S., & Espinosa, K. E. (1997). What's Driving Mexico-U.S. Migration? Theoretical, Empirical, and Policy Analysis. *American Journal of Sociology*, *102*(4), 939–999. doi:10.1086/231037

Menjívar, C. (2011). The Power of the Law: Central Americans' Legality and Everyday Life in Phoenix, Arizona. *Latino Studies*, *9*(4), 377–395. doi:10.1057/lst.2011.43

Merry, S. E. (1990). *Getting Justice and Getting Even: Legal Consciousness Among Working-Class Americans*. University of Chicago Press.

Nevins, J. (2002). *Operation Gatekeeper: The Rise of the "Illegal Alien" and the Remaking of the US-Mexico Boundary*. Routledge.

Ngai, M. (2004). *Impossible Subjects: Illegal Aliens and the Making of Modern America*. Princeton University Press.

Palloni, A., Massey, D. S., Ceballos, M. K., & Spittel, M. (2001). Social Capital and International Migration: A Test Using Information on Family Networks. *American Journal of Sociology*, *106*(5), 1262–1298. doi:10.1086/320817

Passel, J. S., & Cohn, D. (2019). *Mexicans Decline to Less than Half the U.S. Unauthorized Immigrant Population for the First Time*. Pew Research Center.

Peutz, N. (2007). Out-laws: Deportees, Desire, and "The Law.". *International Migration (Geneva, Switzerland)*, *45*(3), 182–191. doi:10.1111/j.1468-2435.2007.00415.x

Phillips, A. (2017). 'They're rapists.' President Trump's campaign launch speech two years later, annotated. *Washington Post*. Retrieved June 10, 2020. https://www.washingtonpost.com/news/the-fix/wp/2017/06/16/theyre-rapists-presidents-trump-campaign-launch-speech-two-years-later-annotated/

Rosales, W. E. (2017). *Effects of Neighborhood Diversity on Civic Engagement and Social Trust* (Doctoral Dissertation). Retrieved from ProQuest Dissertations & Theses Global database. (UMI ID: 0031D_16507)

Sánchez, G. J. (1993). *Becoming Mexican American: Ethnicity, Culture, and Identity in Chicano Los Angeles, 1900-1945*. Oxford University Press.

Schultheis, R., & Ruiz Soto, A. G. (2017). *A Revolving Door No More? A Statistical Profile of Mexican Adults Repatriated from the United States*. Migration Policy Institute.

Schuster, L., & Majidi, N. (2015). Deportation Stigma and Re-migration. *Journal of Ethnic and Migration Studies*, *41*(4), 635–652. doi:10.1080/1369183X.2014.957174

Slack, J., Martinez, D., & Whiteford, S. (2018). *In the Shadow of the Wall: Violence and Migration on the US-Mexico Border*. University of Arizona press. doi:10.2307/j.ctt20krzfr

Smith, R. C. (2005). *Mexican New York: Transnational Lives of New Immigrants*. University of California Press. doi:10.1525/9780520938601

Stecklov, G., Winters, P., Stamini, M., & Davis, B. (2005). Do Conditional Cash Transfers Influence Migration? A Study Using Experimental Data From the Mexican PROGRESA Program. *Demography*, *42*(4), 769–790. doi:10.1353/dem.2005.0037

Terriquez, V. (2011). Schools for Democracy: Labor Union Participation and Latino Immigrant Parents' School-Based Civic Engagement. *American Sociological Review*, *76*(4), 581–601. doi:10.1177/0003122411414815

Terriquez, V., & Kwon, H. (2015). Intergenerational Family Relations, Civic Organisations, and the Political Socialisation of Second-Generation Immigrant Youth. *Journal of Ethnic and Migration Studies*, *41*(3), 425–447. doi:10.1080/1369183X.2014.921567

USDHS. (2019). *Yearbook of Immigration Statistics*. Office of Immigration Statistics. Department of Homeland Security.

Vázquez, Y. (2015). Constructing crimmigration: Latino subordination in a "post-racial" world. *Ohio State Law Journal*, *76*(3), 599–657.

Wong, T. K. (2018). *Do Family Separation and Detention Deter Immigration?* https://www.americanprogress.org/issues/immigration/reports/2018/07/24/453660/family-separation-detention-deterimmigration/

Zayas, L. H. (2015). *Forgotten Citizens: Deportation, Children, and the Making of American Exiles and Orphans*. Oxford University Press.

ENDNOTES

1. Formal removals are defined by the Department of Homeland Security as, "the compulsory and confirmed movement of an inadmissible or deportable alien out of the United States based on an order of removal" (USDHS 2019). These are distinguished from "voluntary returns," which are state administered but do not include an order of removal and typically have no ban on lawful re-entry. Returns are said to measure activity at the Southern border and the same people are often returned more than once. Still, when returns are included, the U.S. completed over *18 million deportations* since 1996 (Ibid.).
2. Hagan et al. (2008:13) noted that Salvadorans may be less likely to return to the U.S. than Mexicans: "One reason is that Mexican migrants are the largest national category of deportees (70 percent), and they have a much easier time in migrating again because of accumulated social capital and years of experience in migrating, along with their close proximity to the United States."
3. Other assumptions made to estimate this probability include: receiving no support in the country of origin, undocumented, with a spouse and at least one child in the US, having at least a high school degree, and holding years in the US and age at the sample mean.

Chapter 2
Sanctuary?
A Discussion on Latinx/a Women and Girls in a Carceral State

Kayla Marie Martensen
University of Illinois at Chicago, USA

ABSTRACT

Influenced by critical carceral studies and abolition feminism, this non-empirical work identifies a political, social and economic carceral system that is fueled by existing racist, sexist, classist, homophobic, ableist and xenophobic ideologies, which both minimize resources for Latinx/a women and girls and increases the level of state violence perpetrated against them. The consequences of dispossession, subjugation and stigmatization have impacted Latina/x women's access to livable waged jobs, healthcare, safe and healthy food and water, adequate living conditions, quality education, and acceptance in American society. This violence is justified and considered necessary by constructing Latina/x women and girls as unworthy of state protection and state resource and as threats to the economy, culture and politics of the United States. Latina/x women, like other women of color, are not afforded the protections extended to white women by the state. Many Americans do not see them as the "good victim", but often they are the "bad woman", "bad mother", "sexual deviant", exploited laborer, culturally defiant, and increasingly they are "illegal", "criminal" and "terrorist". This results in Latinx/a women and girls being more likely to be imprisoned than white women and are one of the fastest growing prison populations in the United States.

DOI: 10.4018/978-1-7998-6646-6.ch002

INTRODUCTION

When we think of sanctuary, ideas that come to mind include safety, refuge, peace, protection. For many of us, we think of sanctuary in only positive ways. However, "sanctuary" came under fire during the 2015 presidential election campaign when U.S. cities broadly defined as "sanctuary cities" were targeted by suggested immigration policy 'reform'. The lack of legal conceptualization of what defines a sanctuary city, at the time, allowed narratives of sanctuary cities to be painted with a broad brush (McBeth and Lybecker, 2018). But for many people living in the margins, sanctuary that is offered by a state or municipality is nonexistent. This political conversation pushed some scholar activists to question, what does sanctuary mean for those living in the margins, or at and around the border, of the carceral United States? At the 2016 Justice Studies Association conference in Flagstaff Arizona, we gathered to discuss this question. One thing that was painfully clear in my work is Latinx/a women and girls are intentionally banned from state sanctuary. Exposed to a form of peaceful state violence (Trask, 2006), Latinx/a women and girls are exposed to structural inequities resulting in increased levels of poverty and interpersonal violence. The lack of safety net and state protection allotted for women of color in the United States, leaves Latinx/a women and girls in vulnerable positions. Latinx/a women and girls are targeted by aggressive forms of state-based violence through acts of domestic war. During the COVID-19 pandemic, it is ever more pressing to critique the idea of sanctuary for Latinx communities in general, and for Latinx/a women and girls in particular.

Influenced by critical carceral studies and abolition feminism, this non-empirical work identifies a political, social and economic carceral system that is fueled by existing racist, sexist, classist, homophobic, ableist and xenophobic ideologies, which both minimize resources for Latinx/a women and girls and increases the level of state violence perpetrated against them. This chapter will highlight structural inequities that result in a 'peaceful' form of state violence, such as poverty and access to education, followed by a deeper dialogue on direct state violence which has disproportionally impacted Latinx/a women and girls. This chapter will address the ways that the state paints a narrative on the bodies of Latinx/a women and girls which serves to criminalize them and identify them as threats, diminishing social support. Although immigrant and undocumented women suffer immensely from state violence, this chapter centers research on Latinx/a women and girls of all documentation status[1]. There is a lack of research and inclusion of Latinx/a women in discussions of racist state violence, racial justice and equity. Because there is substantial work that focuses specifically on immigrant and undocumented women, the intention is to be inclusive of all Latinx/a women no matter what their documentation status. Furthermore, an obscure war on immigration impacts anyone who *looks like* an immigrant, which can be the case for many Brown women in and around the borders of the United States.

A Note on Terminology

The use of Latinx as a gender-neutral pan-ethnic term is used to describe a variety of people from diverse backgrounds. The use of this term does not intend to erase the individual identity of Latinx/a women and girls, nor does this chapter assume that Latinx/a women and girls identify as Latinx. The use of this term is solely a political choice made by the author to identify a diverse group of women and girls which the state has identified as Hispanic and do so in a gender inclusive way. In an effort to be inclusive, I use the term Latinx/a women and girls to include all spectrums of gender and age. It is important to note that there is no singular Latinx/a identity. The experiences of the women that identify as Latina/x are as diverse as the countries they are from, or their mothers are from, or their grandmothers. Generationally and culturally the experiences of Latinx/a women are different. And given the extent for which race is a risk factor of state violence, it is important to note that many Latinx/a women can pass as white, while others are Mestiza or *India* (indigenous appearance), while Afro-Latinas are often identified (and self-identify) as Black. The author[2] understands the complexities of this and that some of the experiences described in this chapter vary for different people.

STRUCTURAL INEQUITIES: 'PEACEFUL VIOLENCE'

Trask (2006) identifies denial of basic needs as a form of *peaceful* [state] *violence* that is rooted in a history of colonial violence. Structural racism, sexism, ableism and heteronormativity have inherently rendered the bodies of Latinx/a women and girls as targets of peaceful state violence. The consequences of dispossession, subjugation and stigmatization have impacted people of colors' access to livable waged jobs, healthcare, safe and healthy food and water, adequate living conditions, quality education, and acceptance in American society (Trask, 2006). Latinx/a women and girls are impacted by these structural inequities within the United States, at the U.S. Mexico border, and within many countries in Latin America at the hands of the U.S. government. In the paragraphs that follow, several distinct, yet interconnected, inequities will be discussed.

On November 20th, 2019, "Latina Equal Pay Day" was declared as the symbolic day when the earnings of Hispanic and Latina women "catch up" to the earnings of white men from the previous year, as Latinas make 54 cents to every dollar made by white men (Twillie, 2019). Latinx/a women experience the largest wage gap compared to any other racial or ethnic group of women, and in an era of mass incarceration and mass deportation, single mother headed households are on the rise in Latinx families. When we think of what this means generationally and over time, we see huge disparities in wealth. White women on average "had a median wealth of $45,400, compared to $100 and $120 respectively for African American and Latina women" (Richard, 2014, p. 1). In fact, discussions around the gender wage gap pay little attention to the ways that white women are paid significantly more than women of color, and in fact, are often paid higher wages than men of color, on average (Richard, 2014).

According to Paz and Massey (2016),

Latinas are more likely to be employed in low-paying, part-time, or seasonal jobs and experience twice the rate of unemployment (7.7%) compared to White women (3.3%). Recent documented weekly income for a full-time employed Latina was $570 compared to $621 for Black women, $745 for white women, and $943 for Asian women.

There is a rich history of exploiting the labor of Latina migrant workers compared to that of even Latino migrant workers. In 1986, the Immigration Reform and Control Act granted citizenship to a mostly male group of undocumented workers that were already in the United States. This partial provision was passed because the war waged on the U.S. Mexico border prevented the needed labor from undocumented Mexican workers. This provision ensured the United States had a 'supply' of low-waged laborers. However, to entice these workers to accept U.S. citizenship, the provision allowed the spouses of these workers to migrate and receive citizenship as well. This put the Latina spouses in a vulnerable position as their labor was not valued, as compared to that of their husbands. And, as bearers of children, their presence represented permanence, something that would put a target on their backs and that of their children for decades to come (Escobar, 2016).

Wage inequities and labor exploitation contribute to high rates of poverty in Latinx families. Latinx families experience consistently high levels of poverty compared to other racial and ethnic groups (Lopez, 2011). It is likely that if incomes of undocumented families or households of mixed documentation status was considered, the poverty rates for Latinx people would be higher still. In Chicago, Latina/x young women and girls experienced the highest levels of poverty compared to other racial and ethnic groups of young women and girls, with 16% having experienced homelessness (Coalition on Urban Girls Chicago (CUG), 2018). And, one in two Latinx/a young women and girls are living in poverty and neighborhoods classified as low opportunity and under resourced (CUG, 2018). This could be considered a national issue, or even a women's rights issue, but it is not. High rates of poverty among Latinx/a women go unaddressed by any mainstream movements. Poverty comes with many other structural inequities that can impact quality of life. Namely, poverty impacts child development and well-being and is associated with greater risk of illness and barriers to quality healthcare (Chaudry and Wimer, 2016).

Navigating healthcare systems can be complex for Latinx families. Issues around cultural sensitivity, health care literacy, and a shortage of Latinx health care providers make accessibility challenging (Velasco-Mondragon, Jimenez, Palladino-Davis, 2011). According to the 2016 census, Latinx people were most likely to be uninsured than other racial and ethnic groups. Latinx/a women have higher mortality rates, compared to other racial and ethnic groups of women, from breast and cervical cancers, which is linked to disparities in access to preventative care (Paz and Massey, 2016). Black and Latinx/a women are disproportionately exposed to serious health conditions, in comparison to Asian and white women, this is especially the case for breast cancer, HIV infection, and coronary heart disease (Karliner, Marks, Mutha, 2016). Other barriers that impact Latinx women's access to healthcare are language barriers and access to healthcare education. Undocumented Latina/x women and girls must navigate additional barriers presented to them through federal and state law. Laws create restrictive circumstances for Latina/x women and girls that impact their ability to seek preventative and emergency medical services, including access to reproductive and sexual health care (Bissonnette, 2020). There is also a lack of access to mental or emotional health care to address previous traumas, or just the traumas enforced by the state, including being restricted from healthcare (Bissonnette, 2020). Lack of access to emotional and mental health services is particularly scant for Latina/x women and girls who are navigating systems of interpersonal violence.

Latina/x women and girls are systematically left outside of the protections of the state, especially in cases of intimate partner violence (Messing, Vega and Durfee, 2017; Harper, 2017). The previously mentioned inequities are risk factors of interpersonal violence for Latina/x women and girls (Gonzalez, Benuto and Casas, 2018). These same inequities, in fact, restrict Latina/x women and girls' access to state safety nets, and thus present challenges to accessing state sanctuary. Structural issues like language barriers, absence of laws which consider their needs, gender and racial inequities, and economic disadvantage may leave the criminal legal system out of reach (Vidales, 2010). It is important to specify that in terms of intimate partner violence and sexual violence, there are challenges with navigating the criminal legal system in general. Many have called for the decriminalization of these intimate types of violence to be replaced with healing forms of response that would work to repair the harm and prevent future occurrences (Goodmark, 2018). It is the case that for many survivors of color, the system is not an appropriate response because it is not structured to keep them safe, and in fact, only perpetrates violence against survivors, the person who harmed them, and the families and communities impacted (INCITE, 2000).

In addition to these intimate forms of violence, Latina/x women and girls are disproportionally exposed to violence that happens in their communities, which we often see as a repercussion of the structural inequities previously mentioned (Ayón, Messing, Gurrola and Valencia-Garcia, 2018). Latina/x young women and girls are often exposed to interpersonal violence at a young age. In Chicago, Latina/x young women and girls have the highest rates of dating violence, compared to other racial and ethnic groups of young women and girls, and also have the highest reported rates of attempting suicide (CUG, 2018). This speaks volumes to how Latina/x young women and girls access sanctuary as well as access appropriate healthcare. Some scholars highlight the role that schools have in marginalizing girls, and in essence restricting their access to state sanctuary (Flores, 2016; Lopez 2017).

Latinx students have the highest high school dropout rate compared to other racial and ethnic groups who attend public schools. Although the number of Latinx youth who are dropping out has hit a record low, 10% of Latinx high school students drop out of school (Gramlich, 2020). Latinx students are disproportionately impacted by negative school policies at every level (Castillo, 2014) even though their levels of misbehavior in school does not represent their rates of punishment (Peguero and Shekarkhar, 2011). Latinx students are disproportionately suspended and expelled from school, referred to school police and referred to the juvenile courts for things that happen in school (Castillo, 2014). Latina/x young women and girls, specifically, are more likely than their white counterparts to be impacted by these harsh punishments (Peguero and Shekarkhar, 2011). Zero-tolerance policies demand harsh punishments for students who break school rules and leaves no room for discretion. These policies were implemented after mass school shootings, in predominantly white attended rural schools. The consequences, however, were Latinx students in urban schools being pushed into the juvenile court system for minor infractions (Triplett, Allen, and Lewis, 2014). And when Latina/x young women and girls are pushed out of schools into the system, they are at constant risk of detainment because of an alliance between schools and the juvenile courts (Flores, 2016). For immigrant students whose documentation has expired, or perhaps never had documentation, they find school doors literally closed to them through surveillance tactics and state legislation (Macias, 2020). Latinx/a student's experience with discrimination in school as well as academic underachievement in under-resourced schools is believed to impact these disproportionate dropout rates (McWhirter, Garcia and Bines, 2018).This has consequences for the parents, especially mothers, of these punished Latinx youth who endure what Dunning- Lozano (2018) calls secondary discipline, a form of state discipline that impacts those around the primary person being disciplined (p. 2). This adds to the hyper-surveillance of Latinx communities more generally, and of Latinx/a mothers specifically, which tells Latinx people that they are not accepted in American society, an often-neglected element of the peaceful violence Trask (2006) describes. What does sanctuary mean for whole racial and ethnic groups of people that are not accepted by society, whose very presence is labeled criminal, illegal and/or terrorist?

The Story *They* Tell

There is a history of painting, and repainting, a narrative on the bodies of Latina/x women to fulfill the agendas of the western world. Historic and modern practices of imperialism throughout Latin America and within the United States have prescribed gendered, racialized and heteronormative scripts on the bodies of Latina/x women and girls, which present barriers to spaces of sanctuary by placing them in vulnerable situations and exposing them to state violence. These narratives are then placed in the consciousness of western society to diminish social support, minimize the harm of state violence against Latina/x women and girls, and in fact, justify and instruct private citizens to engage in the same harmful behavior, or at the very least be complacent in it. This violence is justified and considered necessary by constructing Latina/x women and girls as unworthy of state protection and state resource *and* as threats to the economy, culture and politics of the United States. In this way, the idea of state sanctuary for Latina/x women and girls is irrelevant to the state as Latina/x women and girls, as it is understood, in fact threaten white supremacy, heteropatriarchy and capitalism, or the sanctuary and safety of "law-abiding", "tax-paying" (white) Americans, as the story is told.

Being both abandoned by *and* targeted by the state is illustrated in the work of Hill (2016) who describes what it means to be "nobody" in America. People, based on their social identities, are placed in vulnerable circumstances and left with no social or state safety-net (Hill, 2016). When people with social power, people with wealth, and people who are white are facing a crisis, the state responds. In fact, state resources are often times allocated to address the emerging needs, of said people, when they are in crisis, like the recent opioid epidemic, which completely reconceptualized what it means to be addicted to drugs and what the response to drug addiction should be. The nation must stop, take a pause, re-evaluate our conceptions of behaviors, support change in legislation and the reallocation of money and resources, create task forces when white people, especially the wealthy, come into a crisis. Mass school shooting, acts of domestic terror, sexual assault of mostly white celebrities, the housing crisis, the banking crisis, and most recently the opioid crisis demand public attention and response. Yet, all of the issues mentioned in the previous section are accepted, or ignored, without doubt.

Latina/x women, like other women of color, are not afforded the protections extended to white women by the state. Many Americans do not see them as the "good victim", but often they are the "bad woman", "bad mother", "sexual deviant", exploited laborer, culturally defiant, and increasingly they are "illegal", "criminal" and "terrorist". These narratives minimizes their social value (Cacho, 2012), their humanness. It allows peaceful violence to go unquestioned, and it supports explicit violence against their bodies, families and cultures. The very identities of Latinx/a women and girls have been criminalized. And like other criminalized populations, they are not just restricted from protection, they are not just targeted by state violence, but they are in fact understood as the reason why punitive and harsh punishments exist (Cacho, 2012). And therefore, the scripts that have been written *for* them, not by them, work to diminish social support. Non-Latinx people and communities, sometimes unintentionally, support the domestic, border and global wars waged on the bodies of Latinx/a women and girls by the carceral United States. Certain groups of people, including Latinx/a women and girls, are permanently placed in a criminalized position and will never establish humanhood as their very existence is deemed criminal, illegal and threatening. Cacho (2012) argues that:

targeted populations do not need to break laws to be criminalized. Their behaviors are criminalized even if their crimes are victimless (using street drugs), even if their actual activities are not illegal at all (using health care), and even if the evidence is not actually evidence ("looking like a terrorist"). Criminalization can operate through instituting laws that cannot be followed. People subjected to laws based on their (il)legal status — "illegal aliens," "gang members," "terrorist suspects" — are unable to comply with the "rule of law" because U.S. law targets their being and their bodies, not their behavior Cacho p. 6, 2012).

Now, more than ever, we see Latinx/a women, girls and mothers being criminalized and directly targeted by the state through our punitive immigration systems, our welfare systems, the criminal legal system, at our borders, and in our communities by private citizens. This sort of harm and violence enacted on their bodies directly impairs access to sanctuary, and in fact, creates a set of circumstances where they must seek sanctuary from the state.

Criminalized and Punished: State Violence Against Latinx/a Women and Girls.

Research on the extent and impact of the criminal legal system on Latinx/a women and girls is minimal. The U.S. government classifies Latinx ('Hispanic') as an ethnicity, not a race. This results in a lack of consistent and comprehensive data related to Latinx people and their contact with the criminal legal system. Additionally, official data rarely considers both sex and race/ethnicity in its statistics. Latinx people are often classified as white, which skews our idea of how many white people are impacted by the system. This also means that Latinx people are often left out of conversations (and research) on racial inequities and racial discrimination. This is especially the case for Latinx/a women and girls. Some studies 'add and stir' by including Latinx/a women and girls in their samples, but this can lead to a comparative analysis, which often marginalizes Latinx/a women and girls. Very rarely does research center the experiences of Latinx/a women and girls, but when it does, readers can witness the nuances of those experiences and how they are incomparable to other women and girls (Lopez, 2017; Escobar, 2016). Although there are similar experiences to non-Latinx/a women and girls of color, when we consider race/ethnicity, gender, class, geographic location, age, we uncover a very unique story (Jones, 2009). The paragraphs that follow will piece together some of the ways Latinx/a women and girls are impacted and targeted by legislation and policy which renders their bodies punishable, and often times, criminal.

There is a long history of controlling Latinx/a women and girls' bodies, sexuality and reproductive freedoms. Throughout the early to mid 1900's there is documentation of forced sterilization of Chicana women (Mexican descendants) (Lira and Stern, 2014). These women were "pathologized as mentally defective and overly fecund in order to justify sterilization" and endured forced and coerced sterilization practices throughout the 1920's-1950's, although this was not done without resistance (Lira and Stern, 2014, p. 9). This violence also targeted the bodies of Puerto Rican women, both on the island and the mainland. The sterilization of Puerto Rican women was so common, that between 1930-1970, a third of sterilized women were Puerto Rican (Andrews, 2017). 'La Operación' documents a similar story of deception and coercion which generationally impacted Puerto Rican women (García, 1982). These same women were used as guinea pigs by U.S. pharmaceutical companies testing new drugs (Andrews, 2017). State violence on the reproductive systems, and bodies, of Latinx/a women and girls works in more covert ways in today's society, but nonetheless, impacts decisions to punish, police and incarcerate Latinx/a women as a form of reproductive control.

The narratives of Latinx/a mothers as sexually deviant and over-fertile are used today to control the bodies of Latinx/a women and girls by a variety of state institutions. Latinx/a young women and girls report an emphasis on pregnancy prevention in sex-ed curriculum (García, 2009). Educators make direct and indirect assumptions of Latinx culture and blame said culture on the unsafe sex practices of Latinx/a young women (García, 2009). For system-involved Latina/x young women and girls, we see this same stereotypical emphasis by court actors. Court actors express distain around working with Latinx/a young women and girls because of reasons associated with what they describe "Latino culture" (Pasko and Lopez, 2018). Decision-makers in the juvenile justice system, in fact, were cited as using their discretion to incarcerate Latinx/a girls in residential facilities to avoid teenaged pregnancy (Pasko and Lopez, 2018). This same pattern is represented in the foster care system, where disproportionately Latinx/a young women and girls are classified as having behavioral health issues by case workers with stereotypical ideas of Latinx culture, which degrade women and prioritize heteronormative relationships, including pregnancy (Restrepo, 2019). And, similarly to other systems, the foster care system targets their bodies and may refer them to the juvenile justice system for assumed engagement in sexual behavior (Restrepo, 2019). Policing and controlling the bodies of Latinx/a young women and girls funnels them directly into the criminal legal system for no actual crime. When Latinx/a women become mothers, they face narratives of being bad, criminal, and state dependent mothers, which gains social support for policies and tactics that wage war on Latinx/a women's body.

The *welfare queen* is one of the criminalizing narratives that has been ascribed on the bodies of Black women and Black mothers for decades (Cammett, 2016). Briggs (2002) argues that this narrative has been used on women from Latin American countries, especially Puerto Rican women (Briggs, 2002). Also attributed to a *cultural of poverty*, Puerto Rican and other Latinx/a women and mothers are described as being over-fertile and over-sexual, deviant and criminal (Briggs, 2002). Briggs (2002) argues that in unique ways, Puerto Rican women and were used as the basis of welfare reform laws in the mid-1990's, which is reminiscent of policy change that centered around the bodies of Black women and mothers. Although the experiences of Black mothers and Latinx/a mothers are distinct, Escobar (2016) argues we must consider the ways that the criminalization of Black mothers leaves a narrative in the minds of American society which can also be ascribed on the bodies of Latinx/a mothers. This neoliberal criminalizing narrative targets Latinx/a mothers as being both criminal and state dependent, as well as critique their ability to raise law-abiding children. This leads to strict policies around public assistance and welfare that are largely targeted towards families of color.

Harsh welfare reform laws make navigating this system difficult, especially if there are cultural or language barriers. If benefits are accessible, the demands of receiving benefits are incredibly high. Latinx/a women and mothers are disproportionately disciplined by case workers[3] who sanction them for not complying with the terms set forth by the state, which according to Schram, Soss, Fording and Houser (2009) include, "fail[ure] to complete required hours of participation in countable work activities such as job search, job-readiness classes, vocational education, training, community work, and paid employment" (p.2). Due to mass incarceration and mass deportation, Latinx families are increasingly put into situations where they need resources due to parent removal. When a parent is removed from the home, families are at an increased need of state support (Sugie, 2012). Although, parent removal has a traumatic impact on families, it is often minimized when the culprit of that removal is the Carceral State. Research indicates that at every level of the child welfare system, Latinx families are disproportionately impacted, compared to white families and are the least likely to receive social services (Davidson, Morrisey and Beck, 2019). In addition, Latinx youth that have immigration status are more likely to be placed outside of kinship care (with other family members or friends) than other youth (Scott, Faulkner, Cardoso, Berger and Burstain, 2014) making it that more challenging for Latinx/a mothers to reunite their families. Latina/x women and mothers who are removed from their homes through the immigration and prison systems face increasing surveillance and imprisonment by the Carceral State.

The pathways created by the Carceral State into the prisons systems (including detention) have severe repercussions for Latinx/a women and girls and directly attacks spaces of potential sanctuary, including social services. In fact, the expansion of carceral logic into everyday social institutions has its greatest impact on women of color. Nowhere is this more apparent than for Latinx/a young women and girls who are court-involved. The everyday social institutions they encounter are linked with the juvenile court systems. Latinx/a young women and girls adapt to this hyper-surveilled environment by not going to school, not going home and keeping a low-profile in their communities (Flores, Camacho & Santos, 2017), all of which are primary institutions that should be a space of sanctuary for young women and girls. Flores (2016) finds Latinx/a young women and girls do not see a difference between schools and secure detention. These two institutions are so inherently linked that they pose a threat to reincarcerate girls for either "academic or criminal infractions" (Flores, 2016, p. 72). Schools and detention centers ally to provide *wraparound services*- services that extend throughout youth institutions, such as youth centers, schools, police - but the consequences amount to what Flores (2016) calls "wraparound incarceration", leaving Latinx/a girls with a constant threat of incarceration.

Latinx/a women *and* girls are more likely to be imprisoned than white women and are one of the fastest growing prison populations in the United States (Sentencing Project, 2019). And since 2015, the incarcerated Latinx/a population has skyrocketed compared to all other racial and ethnic groups of women (United States Commission on Civil Rights, 2020). This is also true for Latinx/a girls who now account for 19% of girls confined, which is disproportionate to their population size (Kajsturua, 2019). The war on drugs has made a big impact on these statistics, Latinx/a women are 20 percent more likely to be criminalized for drug laws than white women, although they are no more likely to engage in drug crimes (Drug Policy Alliance, 2018). Within community, Latinx/a women are more likely to be arrested during a stop compared to white women (Prison Policy Initiative, 2019). But nowhere is state war on Latinx/a women and girls more apparent than through our immigration system. Although there is little research that highlights the impact of gender, Escobar (2016) intends that we must view immigration through a racialized, gendered lens. When we do, we see the complexities that women face in the immigration system. This is especially the case for trans-women who are often intentionally misplaced into male only detention, which leaves them exposed to increased violence at the hands of guards and detainees. Latinx/a Trans women are left out of both immigrants' rights movements and queer liberation movements, although many argue that these movements must center the experiences of trans women (Gutíerrez and Portillo, 2018). This is especially concerning as many trans women migrate to the U.S. to escape violence because of their gender identities. The violence of incarceration on top of the violence one experiences inside of detention is argued as cruel and unusual punishment (Arkles, 2009). And, for trans women, being placed in solitary confinement can result in severe repercussions for their emotional and mental well-being (Arkles, 2009). Other issues women face while in detention are language and cultural barriers, food and living conditions, labor exploitation, lack of access to phone calls to communicate with their children and loved ones, access legal assistance and contact child protective services (Rabin, 2008).

Many of the women that end up in detention have not committed any criminal offense. Despite this, immigrant women testify to being treated like criminals, handcuffed, shackled and strip searched by ICE officials (García Hernandez, 2014). One of the biggest complaints among women in federal detention is their health needs go unmet. From minor issues like headaches to major issues like cancer and diabetes, these women are met with complete disregard (Rabin, 2008). Trans women are left without their hormonal treatments, and for HIV positive women, the results of their detainment can literally mean death, as was the case with Roxanna Hernández (Gutíerrez and Portillo, 2018; Sevelius and Jenness, 2017). Women who are pregnant are restricted from receiving prenatal care and having routine doctor visits (Rabin, 2008). Women with mental health issues are often neglected. This is especially concerning when many of the women in federal detention seeking asylum have just escaped traumatic experiences, usually related to domestic and/or sexual violence (Parish, 2017). Furthermore, the journey itself is incredibly traumatic on both sides of the border (and at the border) just to be met with the harsh realities of detention, which provide no sanctuary (Goodman, Vesely, Letiecq and Cleaveland, 2017). Perhaps the most severe collateral consequence of detaining immigrant mothers is family separation. Despite having little to no risk on society, ICE uses their discretion to incarcerate mothers and strip them away from their children with complete disregard of the consequences; furthermore, many women get placed in detention centers that are states away from their children (Rabin, 2008). The violence of ICE can be traced to a history of police violence against women of color, including border patrol agents who use their militarized power to assault and harass immigrant women in the United States and at our borders (Falcon, 2001). Women who migrate to the United States are at risk of being sexually and physically assaulted by the police and civilian men alike (Pickering, 2011). Rape has long been a weapon of war, and as the U.S.-Mexico border has become increasingly militarized, this space of war is no exception (Falcon, 2006). Of great significance is that very few cases of abuse by state agents are reported back to the state, for obvious reasons (Ritchie, 2016). For immigrant women especially, fear of deportation leaves them vulnerable to abuse by state agents (Ritchie, 2016).

CONCLUDING NOTES

The conversation of state violence and sanctuary would be left incomplete without considering the resistance and survival strategies which create alternative spaces of sanctuary for women of color. The emotional labor it entails to survive active efforts of violence and create a space of safety is a testament to the resiliency of Latinx/a women under centuries of U.S. invasion, colonialism and gender-based state violence. Although this chapter does not intend to highlight movements towards liberation, it is important to acknowledge that these movements exist.

The mainstream immigrants' rights movement often times creates binaries, of the good and deserving immigrant and the bad, usually criminal, immigrant. But this binary only further perpetrates violence against Latinx communities. Some of the concluding efforts in Escobar's (2016) book push us to consider the ways that the immigrant rights movement can utilize liberation strategies from the abolition movement by acknowledging the similarities in Black and Latinx state oppressions. Technologies of punishment that target Latinx/a migrants are connected to a history of anti-Black punishment (Escobar, 2009). Escobar (2009) links the connections between the war on drugs, that targets Black communities, with the war on immigration, and argues that we must understand not just the criminalizing narratives discussed previously, but also the carceral technologies, such as surveillance by local law enforcement for federal agendas. The acceptance and normalcy of Immigrant Customs Enforcement (ICE) and immigrant detention centers are directly related to the ways the police and prison are deeply embedded in our society as agencies of control and punishment on Black bodies (Escobar, 2009).

Lastly, it is incredibly important to emphasize the impact of the COVID-19 pandemic on Latinx/a women and girls as a direct reflection of the racial and ethnic inequities that Latinx communities face as a whole. This is a clear illustration of the ways this peaceful violence has a direct impact on ending lives of Latinx/ women and girls early. What does social distancing mean to laborer's who must work?

To immigrant farmers bunking 6 people to a room? What does social distancing mean to all the people locked up in detention and prison across the nation? There are hundreds of confirmed COVID-19 cases in our detention centers and prisons each day (Rascon-Canales, 2020). And in the community, the situation is bleak. The El Milagro tortilla factory in Chicago had to shut down as the mostly Mexican employees were exposed to the virus, causing the deaths of at least two people, with much speculation to the plants efforts to keep its employees safe (Jimenez, 2020). In the same Mexican American community, "re-developers", locally called "gentrifiers", have demolished an old coal plant covering the community in dust during a global pandemic which targets the human respiratory system (Pope, 2020). Mujeres Latinas en Accion (2020), a key organization in Chicago of sanctuary for Latinx/a women and girls, surveyed predominantly Latinx neighborhoods and found that 63% of community members lost their jobs and 53% are ineligible for unemployment and stimulus checks. Beyond this, Mujeres Latinas en Accion (2020), remind us what does it mean to protect Mujeres (women) from sexual violence and intimate partner violence that happens in their homes during a stay-at-home order. In fact, what does the idea of "stay-safe" even mean during this time for women who do not have access to sanctuary to begin with?

REFERENCES

Andrews, K. (2017). *The Dark History of Forced Sterilization of Latina Women.* Retrieved on April 3rd, 2020, https://www.panoramas.pitt.edu/health-and-society/dark-history-forced-sterilization-latina-women

Arkles, G. (2008). Safety and solidarity across gender lines: Rethinking segregation of transgender people in detention. *Temp. Pol. & Civ. Rts. L. Rev., 18*, 515.

Ayón, C., Messing, J. T., Gurrola, M., & Valencia-Garcia, D. (2018). The oppression of Latina mothers: Experiences of exploitation, violence, marginalization, cultural imperialism, and powerlessness in their everyday lives. *Violence Against Women, 24*(8), 879–900. doi:10.1177/1077801217724451

Bissonnette, A. (2020). "Caged Women": Migration, Mobility and Access to Health Services in Texas and Arizona. Journal of Borderlands Studies, 1-22.

Bolivar, A. (2017). For Chicago's Trans Latina Sex Workers, A Cycle of Fear, Violence, and Brutality: From employment discrimination to incarceration to deportation, trans Latina sex workers face a triple threat of sexism, racism, and classism through policing. *NACLA Report on the Americas, 49*(3), 323–327. doi:10.1080/10714839.2017.1373959

Briggs, L. (2002). La Vida, Moynihan, and other libels: Migration, social science, and the making of the Puerto Rican welfare queen. *Centro Journal, 14*(1), 75–101.

Cacho, L. M. (2012). *Social death: Racialized rightlessness and the criminalization of the unprotected*. NYU Press.

Cammett, A. (2016). Welfare Queens Redux: Criminalizing Black Mothers in the Age of Neoliberalism. *S. Cal. Interdisc. LJ, 25*, 363.

Castillo, J. (2014). Tolerance in schools for Latino students: Dismantling the school-to-prison pipeline. *Harvard Journal of Hispanic Policy, 26*, 43–58.

Chaudry, A., & Wimer, C. (2016). Poverty is not just an indicator: The relationship between income, poverty, and child well-being. *Academic Pediatrics, 16*(3), S23–S29.

Coalition on Urban Girls Chicago (CUG). (2018) Girls in the City: A Status Report on Teen Girls Residing in Chicago. Retrieved May 8, 2020, from http://cugchicago.org/wp-content/uploads/2018/12/CUG-2018-REPORT-UPLOAD-1.pdf

Davidson, R. D., Morrissey, M. W., & Beck, C. J. (2019). The Hispanic Experience of the Child Welfare System. *Family Court Review, 57*(2), 201–216.

Drug Policy Alliance. (2018). *Women, Prison, and the Drug War*. https://www.drugpolicy.org/sites/default/files/women-and-the-drug-war_0.pdf

Dunning-Lozano, J. L. (2018). Secondary discipline: The unintended consequences of zero tolerance school discipline for low-income Black and Latina mothers. *Urban Education*. doi:10.1177/0042085918817343

Edwards, A. (2019). Hispanic Poverty Rate. *United States Census*. Retrieved May 8, 2020, from https://www.census.gov/library/stories/2019/02/hispanic-poverty-rate-hit-an-all-time-low-in-2017.html

Escobar, M. (2009). Understanding the Roots of Latina Migrants' Captivity. *Social Justice (San Francisco, Calif.), 36*(2), 7.

Escobar, M. D. (2016). *Captivity beyond prisons: Criminalization experiences of Latina (im) migrants*. University of Texas Press.

Falcon, S. (2001). Rape as a weapon of war: Advancing human rights for women at the US-Mexico border. *Social Justice, 28*(2 (84), 31-50.

Flores, J. (2016). *Caught up: Girls, surveillance, and wraparound incarceration*. Univ of California Press. doi:10.1525/california/9780520284876.001.0001

Flores, J., Camacho, A. O., & Santos, X. (2017). Gender on the run: Wanted Latinas in a southern California barrio. *Feminist Criminology, 12*(3), 248–268.

García, A. M. (1982). *La Operación* [Film]. Latin American Film Project.

García, L. (2009). "Now Why Do You Want To Know About That?": Heteronormativity, Sexism, and Racism in the Sexual (Mis)education of Latina Youth. *Gender & Society, 23*(4), 520–541. doi:10.1177/0891243209339498

García Hernández, C. C. (2014). Immigration detention as punishment. *Immigr. & Nat'lity L. Rev., 35*, 385–453.

Gonzalez, F. R., Benuto, L. T., & Casas, J. B. (2018). Prevalence of interpersonal violence among Latinas: A systematic review. *Trauma, Violence & Abuse*. doi:10.1177/1524838018806507

Goodman, R. D., Vesely, C. K., Letiecq, B., & Cleaveland, C. L. (2017). Trauma and resilience among refugee and undocumented immigrant women. *Journal of Counseling and Development, 95*(3), 309–321. doi:10.1002/jcad.12145

Goodmark, L. (2018). *Decriminalizing domestic violence: A balanced policy approach to intimate partner violence*. Univ of California Press. doi:10.1525/9780520968295

Gramlich, J. (2020). panic dropout rate hits new low, college enrollment at new high. *Pew Research Center.* Retrieved on April 3rd, 2020, from https://www.pewresearch.org/fact-tank/2017/09/29/hispanic-dropout-rate-hits-new-low-college-enrollment-at-new-high/

Gutíerrez, J., & Portillo, S. (2018). Trans (formation) of a Movement: Roxsana Hernández, an immigrant transgender woman from Honduras, died in ICE detention earlier this year. LGBTI activists refuse to let her death be in vain. *NACLA Report on the Americas, 50*(4), 392–394. doi:10.1080/10714839.2018.1550983

Harper, S. B. (2017). No way out: Severely abused Latina women, patriarchal terrorism, and self-help homicide. *Feminist Criminology, 12*(3), 224–247. doi:10.1177/1557085116680743

Hill (2016). Nobody: Casualties of America's War on the Vulnerable, from Ferguson to Flint and Beyond. Atria Publishing Group: Miami, FL.

INCITE! (2000). *Mission Statement.* Retrieved on April 3rd, 2020, from https://incite-national.org/history/

Iriondo, J. (2018). Income, Poverty and Health Insurance Coverage in the United States: 2017. *U.S. Census*. Retrieved on April 3rd, 2020, from https://www.census.gov/newsroom/press-releases/2018/income-poverty.html

Jimenez, A. (2020). El Milagro Temporarily Closes Plant. *Chicago Tribune*. Retrieved May 8, 2020, from https://www.chicagotribune.com/coronavirus/ct-coronavirus-chicago-el-milagro-closing-factories-20200427-v5onmmvgvfhs5bwl64z4j2x4eq-story.html

Jones, N. (2009). *Between good and ghetto: African American girls and inner-city violence*. Rutgers University Press. doi:10.36019/9780813548258

Kajsturua, A. (2019). Women's Mass Incarceration: The Whole Pie 2019. *Prison Policy Initiative*. Retrieved on April 3rd, 2020, from https://www.prisonpolicy.org/reports/pie2019women.html

Karliner, L., Marks, A., & Mutha, S. (2016). Reducing health care disparities for minority women in the era of the affordable care act: Opportunities within primary care. *Journal of Health Care for the Poor and Underserved, 2*(27), 392–415. doi:10.1353/hpu.2016.0098

Lira, N., & Stern, A. M. (2014). Mexican Americans and eugenic sterilization: Resisting reproductive injustice in California, 1920–1950. *Aztlán, 39*(2), 9–34.

Lopez, C., & Cohn, D. (2011). Hispanic Poverty Rate Highest In New Supplemental Census Measure. *Pew Research Center-Hispanic Trends*. Retrieved on April 3rd, 2020, from https://www.pewresearch.org/hispanic/2011/11/08/hispanic-poverty-rate-highest-in-new-supplemental-census-measure/

Lopez, V. (2017). *Complicated lives: Girls, parents, drugs, and juvenile justice*. Rutgers University Press. doi:10.36019/9780813586571

Macias, J. K. (2020). *Rompiendo Alambres: Immigrant Youth Navigating School and Life in St. Louis* (Doctoral dissertation). Washington University in St. Louis.

McBeth, M. K., & Lybecker, D. L. (2018). The narrative policy framework, agendas, and Sanctuary cities: The construction of a public problem. *Policy Studies Journal: the Journal of the Policy Studies Organization, 46*(4), 868–893. doi:10.1111/psj.12274

McWhirter, E. H., Garcia, E. A., & Bines, D. (2018). Discrimination and other education barriers, school connectedness, and thoughts of dropping out among Latina/o students. *Journal of Career Development, 45*(4), 330–344. doi:10.1177/0894845317696807

Meiners, E. R. (2015). Trouble with the Child in the Carceral State. *Social Justice (San Francisco, Calif.), 41*(3), 120–144.

Messing, J. T., Vega, S., & Durfee, A. (2017). Protection Order Use Among Latina Survivors of Intimate Partner Violence. *Feminist Criminology*, *12*(3), 199–223. doi:10.1177/1557085116678924

Mujeres Latinas en Accion. (2020). *A Letter from our President and CEO*. Sent to Listserv.

Parish. (2017). Gender-Based Violence against Women: Both Cause for Migration and Risk along the Journey. *Migration Policy Institute*. Retrieved on April 3rd, 2020, from https://www.migrationpolicy.org/article/gender-based-violence-against-women-both-cause-migration-and-risk-along-journey

Pasko, L., & Lopez, V. (2018). The Latina penalty: Juvenile correctional attitudes toward the Latina juvenile offender. *Journal of Ethnicity in Criminal Justice*, *16*(4), 272–291. doi:10.1080/15377938.2015.1015196

Paz, K., & Massey, K. (2016). Health Disparity among Latina Women: Comparison with Non-Latina Wome. *U.S. Library of Medicine National Institutes of Health*. Retrieved on April 3rd, 2020, from https://www.ncbi.nlm.nih.gov/pmc/articles/PMC4955974/

Peguero, A. A., & Shekarkhar, Z. (2011). Latino/a student misbehavior and school punishment. *Hispanic Journal of Behavioral Sciences*, *33*(1), 54–70. doi:10.1177/0739986310388021

Pickering, S. (2011). Women, borders, and violence. In *Women, Borders, and Violence* (pp. 109–119). Springer. doi:10.1007/978-1-4419-0271-9_6

Pope, B. (2020). Little Village residents rip Chicago officials during virtual town hall on botched smokestack demolition. *Chicago Sun Times*. Retrieved May 25th, 2020, from https://chicago.suntimes.com/2020/5/23/21268518/little-village-chicago-residents-hilco-smokestack-power-plant-demolitions-frydland-arwady

Prison Policy Initiative. (2019). *Policing Women: Race and gender disparities in police stops, searches, and use of force*. Retrieved on April 3rd, 2020, from https://www.prisonpolicy.org/blog/2019/05/14/policingwomen/

Rabin, N. (2008). Unseen prisoners: Women in immigration detention facilities in Arizona. *Geo. Immigr. LJ*, *23*, 695–717.

Rascon-Canales. (2020). "If they come for her child in the morning…": Detained/Incarcerated Children in the time of COVID-19, retrieved on April 3rd, 2020, https://abolitionjournal.org/if-they-come-for-her-child-in-the-morning-detained-incarcerated-children-in-the-time-of-covid-19/

Restrepo, I. C. (2019). Pathologizing Latinas: Racialized Girlhood, Behavioral Diagnosis, and California's Foster Care System. *Girlhood Studies*, *12*(3), 1–17.

Richard, K. (2014). The wealth gap for women of color. *Center for Global Policy Solutions*. Retrieved on April 3rd, 2020, from http://www.globalpolicysolutions.org/wp-content/uploads/2014/10/Wealth-and-women-of-color.pdf

Ritchie, A. J. (2017). *Invisible no more: Police violence against Black women and women of color*. Beacon Press.

Schram, S. F., Soss, J., Fording, R. C., & Houser, L. (2009). Deciding to discipline: Race, choice, and punishment at the frontlines of welfare reform. *American Sociological Review*, *74*(3), 398–422. doi:10.1177/000312240907400304

Scott, J., Faulkner, M., Cardoso, J. B., & Burstain, J. (2014). Kinship Care and Undocumented Latino Children in the Texas Foster Care System: Navigating the Child Welfare-Immigration Crossroads. *Child Welfare*, *93*(4).

Sentencing Project. (n.d.). *Incarcerated Women and Girls*. Retrieved on April 3rd, 2020, from: https://www.sentencingproject.org/publications/incarcerated-women-and-girls/https://www.sentencingproject.org/publications/incarcerated-women-and-girls/

Sevelius, J., & Jenness, V. (2017). Challenges and opportunities for gender-affirming healthcare for transgender women in prison. *International Journal of Prisoner Health*, *13*(1), 32–40. doi:10.1108/IJPH-08-2016-0046

Sugie, N. F. (2012). Punishment and welfare: Paternal incarceration and families' receipt of public assistance. *Social Forces*, *90*(4), 1403–1427. doi:10.1093fos055

Trask, H. K. (2006). The Color of Violence. In *INCITE! Women of Color Against Violence (Ed.), Color of Violence the incite! Anthology* (pp. 81–87). South End Press.

Triplett, N. P., Allen, A., & Lewis, C. W. (2014). Zero tolerance, school shootings, and the post-Brown quest for equity in discipline policy: An examination of how urban minorities are punished for white suburban violence. *The Journal of Negro Education*, *83*(3), 352–370. doi:10.7709/jnegroeducation.83.3.0352

Twillie, J. (2019). November 20, 2019, is Latina Equal Pay Day. It's not a celebration, it's a day of awareness. Retrieved on April 3rd, 2020, from: https://publicmediawomeninleadership.org/announcements/2019/11/20/november-20-2019-is-latina-equal-pay-day-its-not-a-celebration-its-a-day-of-awareness

United States Commission on Civil Rights. (2020). *Women in Prisons: Seeking Justice Behind Bars*. Retrieved on April 3rd, 2020, from: https://www.usccr.gov/pubs/2020/02-26-Women-in-Prison.pdf

Velasco-Mondragon, E., Jimenez, A., & Palladino-Davis, A. G. (n.d.). *Hispanic health in the USA: A scoping review of the literature*. Retrieved on April 3rd, 2020, from: https://www.latinaequalpay.org/about

Vidales, G. T. (2010). Arrested justice: The multifaceted plight of immigrant Latinas who faced domestic violence. *Journal of Family Violence*, *25*(6), 533–544. doi:10.100710896-010-9309-5

ENDNOTES

1 See Escobar (2016) for work that centers the experience of immigrant Latinx/a women.

2 The author identifies as a mixed-race Filipina (mestiza).

3 Noteworthy is that Black women face greater sanctions compared to Latina women.

Chapter 3
Prisoner Re-Entry:
One Story of Coming Home

Rebecca Hubbard Maniglia
Northern Arizona University, USA

ABSTRACT

This chapter is part of an ongoing research book project that examines the realities of mass incarceration in Arizona through the intimate stories of the mothers, sisters, wives, and lovers left behind by incarceration. It is designed to use a narrative approach to give the reader an intimate and personal reflection on what in criminal justice we call re-entry but what to the individuals involved is just "coming home." While it provides a general overview of the formal re-entry process, it is not designed as an academic exploration of that topic.

INTRODUCTION

At least 95% of Americans currently in prison will, at some point, be released from behind bars (BJS 2020). In criminal justice terminology, this is known as reentry. In its narrowest understanding, reentry is nothing more than "the process of leaving prison and returning to society" which "reflects the iron law of imprisonment: they all come back" (Travis 2005, p. XXI). Historically this portion of a prisoner's progression through the system has consisted of nothing more than the basic supervision provided by parole officers, hired and maintained by the state department of corrections. Parole, then, is not designed as a community-based, rehabilitative approach to enabling the successful transition from prison into society. Instead it is the state-mandated way of ensuring a prisoner successfully completes their prison sentence. As Travis (2005) explains,

DOI: 10.4018/978-1-7998-6646-6.ch003

"because a prison term for a felony conviction is owed to the state, the remainder that is not served in a state prison—the period of parole supervision—is still considered time owed to the state. Hence, parole is a state function" (p 58).

This approach has meant that the primary purpose of parole was to provide a former prisoner with a level of accountability to the state for whatever time was left on their sentence; what was still owed. Parole, in many states, then, focuses on ensuring former prisoners stay out of "trouble", are employed, and are able to meet their financial obligations to the state. If they falter, a parole officer is able to rescind freedom and force the individual to finish their sentence behind bars. This model of parole is the one primarily used in Arizona. In fact, the nature of reentry as a fundamental component of corrections is perhaps best demonstrated by the state's recent name change from the Arizona Department of Corrections to the Arizona Department of Corrections, Rehabilitation and Reentry.

In recent years, many states have begun to think more inclusively about the nature of reentry, creating specialized community-based programs which, while not supplanting the role of parole, do attempt to address the societal challenges of coming back into society after a period of incarceration. These services in Arizona are very limited, but where they do exist, they tend to address housing, employment, and drug prevention—the same structural issues about which parole holds former inmates accountable. In many cases, involvement in this programs can be mandated by parole, inadvertently creating another avenue through which a former prisoner is at risk of technical parole violations which may result in future incarceration. Thus how to effectively and humanely support the difficult transition from prison back into society remains an open question for criminal justice professionals focused on reentry.

But this chapter is not about reentry. It is about coming home.

This is a narrative of one coming home story, shared with the intent of showing how "coming home" is a parallel process to prisoner reentry. By using storytelling rather than academic exploration, it hopes to reveal the personal nature of the coming home experience. It is designed to demonstrate the invisible role families play in whether or not former prisoners successfully reenter society, and to explore the emotional and relational costs of incarceration.

"It has to be Perfect."

She struggled to catch her breath as she drove the 90 miles to meet him. She'd been waiting for this moment for almost five years, and now it was here. She'd spent the night before doing all the little things to get ready. She'd selected her outfit--nothing fancy or too sexy. She wanted to look pretty but normal to him. She'd done her hair.

She'd cleaned every inch of the house. She'd stressed over every detail, and now it was actually happening.

"It was like I just woke up, and I was in this fairy tale. My hair had to be perfect, my clothes. The room had to be perfect. The whole house had to be perfect. The kids needed to be perfect. I wanted everything to be just so perfect, and on the drive over there I was like a little kid who was going for the first time ever to a carnival or something. That's how excited I was."

She pulled up in the parking lot and got out of the car. She only had to wait for a few moments for his bus. He was the fourth or fifth person off, looking around for his family. Then their eyes met. She ran forward and jumped into his arms, surprising him and almost knocking both of them to the ground. And in that instant, the moment she had dreamed of for almost five years, she knew things were not perfect.

"Once I ran to him, and I saw the reaction, I realized this was not the same man that left me five years ago. I could tell right then that something was different about him."

She released him, and he moved to greet his sons. Handshakes and hugs, and they started the long trip home. They had planned to stop for lunch but Danny said he didn't want to go out to eat. He was still on prison time and wasn't hungry. She drove in silence, stealing side glimpses of him. The boys tried to make conversation, but they all felt Danny didn't seem present.

"He did a lot of wandering. They would be talking to him, and he'd be listening but he'd be looking out the window or spaced out, coming back and forth. He would leave reality, and then he'd come back."

They all assumed it was just the shock of freedom so, even with the disappointment creeping in, they tried to be patient and give Danny space.

"I thought ok he's been gone for a long time and maybe it's a little bit overwhelming for him. So I just rode it out. I let it go. I didn't let it rent space in my heart."

They headed home and had a quiet dinner, just the family. They laughed together and pretended everything was okay. The family put away their expectations of a perfect homecoming and let Danny adjust. But in the coming weeks, the differences in Danny didn't dissipate. They became more obvious. Sylvia's frustrations became harder to conceal as her disappointment mounted. She kept trying new approaches to make him feel loved, secure, safe, empowered but nothing seemed to work.

"Into the second week I just realized that he wasn't the same person...I knew that I wasn't happy because of the way he came out. I got a lot of rejection. I was rejected no matter what I did or said. He was negative all the time."

It started with the little things. Danny stayed on prison time for weeks. The family struggled to understand and accept but the tension was palpable. They had a routine established in the five years Danny had been away, and they didn't want to adjust it because dad was home. The family struggled as prison rules found their way into the home instead of Danny finding his way out of prison.

"He was still on a schedule when to eat and when to bathe, when to go, when to come, lights out at ten or whatever. We didn't like it. We'd talk amongst ourselves and the kids would be like, 'Dad just needs to calm down. He's not in there no more, and he doesn't have to act like that.'"

Then there was the fear. For Danny, life on the outside was not shaped by a sense of relief, but by a sense of fear. He felt a lack of control over his own life because, while on parole, and even afterwards, he knew he could be sent back for the slightest infraction.

"He was really scared about going back. Whenever the probation officer would call and say 'give me the address to your job' he was really worried about it. What if he wasn't on the wall? What if he was in the bathroom when she pulled up? He didn't want to miss her no matter what."

But it wasn't just at work Danny worried about being sent back.

"Every little thing worried him. Like we would get in the car, and if I would forget to fasten my seatbelt, he would be like 'I'm not looking to get pulled over. I don't wanna go back.' He was very much afraid of every little thing going wrong."

To try to control his lack of security about his own future, Danny limited the parameters of his life and by default those of his family.

"We're not really sociable with the outside. If we get invited somewhere, and a certain person is going, he doesn't want to go because he knows that person is gonna drink, and he doesn't want to be around any of that in case someone calls the cops. We are kind of isolated. If we are going to do something it's just me and him and the immediate family."

This was hard for a family that had pinned so many dreams to Danny's return home. They had expected Dad returning as the re-beginning of a happy, normal life, but instead the prison cage seemed to extend to the whole family. Sylvia and the kids tried to be patient, to wait it out, to respect the transition Danny was going through. But the truth was that they had been sustaining themselves for years off the vision of what life would be like when dad came home, and now here he was, and it wasn't what they thought, and the unspoken disappointment was devasting.

"Eventually I gave up the picture. It took me maybe the first year but I just gave it up. I kept blaming myself. Maybe it was something I was doing. Maybe it was something the kids were doing. When I finally realized that it wasn't us. It was him..."

This kind of intensity of expectation is not Sylvia's alone. It is true for many of us who love someone behind bars. The thousands of words sent in letters or whispered in visitation create an image of how life will be when this is over. The image of a future homecoming is all there is so it becomes its own kind of reality. It's the company you keep when you're lonely. It's what sustains you when you're overwhelmed. You catch yourself daydreaming about it while doing the dishes or riding the bus to work. How he will look, how he will feel, what he will say. You build every little detail of what the first moments, hours, days will be like and that's how you survive the years apart. Then he comes home, and for some of us the distance between the vision and the reality is unbearable, as Sylvia explains.

"I carry the disappointment every day. I think it's always gonna be with me."

In my own experience, relational disappointment is a powerful emotion because it often encompasses many related feelings. If we are disappointed by someone, it is because we had an expectation of them. We believed or desired something to be true that ultimately wasn't, and that leaves lingering questions. Were our desires of the other misplaced, unrealistic or inappropriate? Did we fail in some way? Did we not try hard enough or love completely enough? What would have made the outcome different? For families with loved ones behind bars, the questions feel familiar because they are the same ones they have been asking all the years the person was gone. They are the same ones they have asked a million times in relation to the events leading to the incarceration itself. This is what makes having to ask them again upon the loved one's return so devastating.

Yet no return happens in a vacuum. Sylvia's dream of Danny's coming home is fundamentally shaped by the totality of their lives together, by their individual and collective choices not just while he was gone but before he ever left. Yet incarceration changes people, often forever. Being left behind to manage life's challenges during an incarceration does the same. Neither party lives through the event unscathed, unaltered. Coming home to one's family then is not a singular event, a moment. It is instead the forced blending of two (or more) parallel realities that must now find one path forward all while managing stated and unstated expectations. This is the emotional truth of Danny's coming home, and it is the often unspoken reality of reentry for every American who returns to life outside the prison gates.

The Emotional Terrain of Coming Home

Every week, 10,000 women and men walk out of American prisons and back into their lives (DOJ 2019). If they are lucky, there is someone they love waiting at the prison gate ready to welcome them back to citizenship. These mothers, fathers, daughters, sons, husbands and wives have brought clothes to the prison so that their loved one can face the world looking fresh. There will be hugs and kisses and tears as families are free to touch without supervision, sometimes for the first time in years. While the desire may be to cling, most will attempt to act casual, not sure what to expect or trying to give space to adjust to freedom. They will get in the car, and head off for the first meal (something the former prisoner has been planning for weeks). Many will then go straight to the parole office as the nagging fear of being sent back has already begun. Then there may be a barbeque or a coming home party or simply a quiet evening of freedom being surrounded by family and friends.

The less lucky ones may be dropped by prison officials at a bus stop. They will re-enter their lives with all the same emotions – apprehension, relief, excitement, foreboding—but they will do it alone. They may take a long ride to another part of the state where they have relatives or friends. They may arrive unannounced, surprising people who have long since stopped checking DOC records to see where they were or what their release date was. They may be welcomed in for the night or for a few days and then asked to move along as everyone has pressures, busy lives, and after all "you're grown and need to find your own way".

Many of the newly released may hug children that have moved from toddlers to teenagers in their absence. They make love to partners who they haven't touched for years while secretly wondering who has been meeting the needs in their absence. If welcomed home, they will try to find old rhythms and fit into the family's new patterns of operating, the ones developed without them. They will feel overwhelmed by the noise or the quiet or the space or the seemingly unlimited choices, but they will likely never speak of these things. They will try to make up for what they lost, for the guilt they feel, in tangible and intangible ways. Some of these will go unnoticed, and some will cause conflict as those tasks—parenting, making money, fixing things—have long ago been assigned to others.

They will eat foods they have craved and then not tell anyone when they are made sick by the satisfaction of their own cravings. They may struggle to not get drunk or high, especially at the celebrations of their return where friends and family party the way they always have. They may hide the addiction they developed inside that makes these desires even worse. They may be so relieved to be home and yet unable to find the right words to describe escaping life inside or what the taste of liberty feels like. Yet, for some, within days, they will also quietly and secretly long for the structure and security of the yard or the walls where life at least made sense, and they knew the rules.

Coming out of prison, life makes a dramatic and immediate shift. A former prisoner goes from being told when to get up, when to eat, when to go to bed, where to stand, what to wear, when to shower—sometimes for years—to walking out of the gate and being responsible for every decision of every hour of every day. Little choices can feel overwhelming. What should I eat when everything that I have craved for years is suddenly available? Where should I go now that I can go anywhere? The stress of freedom can come as a surprise, especially as it has been the former prisoner's sole desire throughout the years of imprisonment.

By the same token the former prisoner goes from being largely responsible only for oneself to immediately being responsible for navigating the emotional needs of parents, siblings, spouses, children and friends, all of whom have expectations and needs that have been put on hold during the incarceration. The prisoner has lived emotionally and sexually closed off, trying to survive in small spaces with strangers who may pose a risk to their safety. At release they are forced to maneuver and understand the emotional needs of people who have been craving their presence for years and so demand immediate intimacy, emotional and physical. As Sylvia explains,

"Inside all he had to worry about was Danny. What was Danny gonna do to manage? Where was Danny gonna get his next meal? It was just Danny, Danny, Danny. He's still in that mentality. I tell him, 'You chose to come home to a family. You had a choice. You chose to come home to me. This is where you said you wanted to be. You said you missed your family, you wanted your family, but he doesn't show us that."

For Sylvia, one of the reasons, the unexpected changes in Danny affected her so deeply was because she thought she did know what to expect. This was not the first time Danny had been away so she had done the coming home process before. She thought she knew how it worked. Days before Danny was to return, Sylvia told me,

"I know what I'm going up against. It makes me feel more confident. I'm okay... No matter how things end up I'm going to be okay. I want things to work between me and Danny. I want us to be together. I want us to pick up from where we left off

and move forward from there. I want that more than anything, but at the same time if he comes home and tells me that he can't do it, and that he still needs time, I'm going to be okay with that. I'm not going to let it bring me back down anymore."

But Sylvia was to find that the speeches she had made to herself were a lot harder to put into practice with Danny standing in front of her after his longest sentence yet. She wanted to be loved and rewarded for all she had held together and how she had grown as a woman, and he wanted her to be the passive, traditional Latina wife he had left. Eventually they would both realize that Danny wanted her to be someone she no longer was, and that their parallel experiences during his imprisonment were never going to align into a singular future. That devasting truth was one for which she was far from prepared.

Societal Reintegration and the Realities of Reentry

Most people will never have to trod the emotional terrain of coming home. Perhaps it equates in some ways with families who must re-integrate loved ones returning from deployment, but there are key differences. Incarceration is a forced, shameful separation supposedly earned by the unlawful actions of an individual. The expectation of those untouched by the prison experience is that the former prisoner, now released, should welcome freedom by becoming a productive member of society. After all he or she was the cause of their own incarceration because they failed to follow this path initially. Therefore, the debt was justly earned and justly paid and deserves no additional accommodation. These individuals most now re-integrate without causing more trouble for the society from which they were exiled, and they must never forget what cost them their freedom in the first place. Thus the official language of reentry is fraught with labels that imply this relationship—i.e. formerly incarcerated persons, ex-convict. The idea is even inherent in the most progressive language used to describe prisoners after their release, "returning citizens". As the title implies, the former prisoner was removed from society based on their behavior, and now they are returning to prove their right to remain in the larger social system.

"Returning citizen", however, ignores the structural reasons for crime by assuming the separation from society was individually motivated and thus individually solved by individual punishment. More importantly, however, the title does not address the realities a "returning citizen" will face when trying to regain their place in society. The truth is that the ex-prisoner, while returning, is no longer a citizen in the truest sense of the word, despite having completed their sanctioned punishment. They have had removed from them many of the unalienable rights that come with United States citizenship. For instance, they may have lost the right to vote, sometimes permanently, and thus are unable to participate in democracy, a foundational element of American citizenship. They have also lost the right to access Federal financial aid for college, thus pragmatically removing them from higher education, long touted as the path to success in the American dream. Life simply does not go back to normal. You do not pick up where you left off.

But beyond the structural rights that have been taken away, the former prisoner will likely struggle to reintegrate into society in basic ways. Housing can be a challenge. Most rental properties ask on their application if a person has ever been convicted of a felony. Many apartments will deny renting privileges based on that information alone, regardless of the ability to pay. If a prisoner cannot provide parole with a viable living environment, they may be forced to go to a halfway house until they can obtain a more permanent address. Even if family members are willing to allow the former prisoner to live with them, they will be prohibited from doing so if there are other convicted felons in the home or if the family is living in subsidized housing. Having a parolee live with you also requires that you are willing to be subjected to interviews and sometimes a walk-through of your own home to ensure the appropriateness of the environment. And after release, parole officers can come to the family home unannounced to check on the former prisoner. Thus living with a parolee requires the entire family to be on parole in some sense.

Former prisoners returning to small towns or convicted of crimes that received a lot of publicity may not be able to overcome the community's preconceived judgments. They may feel shamed in public or not be welcomed back as full members of the community. If they have been convicted of a sex offense, even if only minor, they likely have to register as sex offenders resulting in their mug shot and address being published in the local paper. Thus while still trying to adjust emotionally to their freedom, the "returning citizen" is on display, prejudged by the home to which they return.

There will also be pressure both internally and externally to find meaningful employment. Arizona parole departments require that parolees work, and many inmates themselves feel shame at having relied financially on their families during their imprisonment and so feel obligated to quickly pull their own weight. Yet the simple act of finding work remains one of the most difficult tasks the former prisoner will face. Most job applications ask directly if a person has ever been convicted of a felony. While this question does not ask about incarceration, the existence of a previous felony conviction almost always disqualifies one for employment. In an attempt to eliminate this barrier, in 2019, Congress passed the Fair Chance Act building on initiatives President Obama had introduced earlier. This new legislation effectively "band the box" asking about previous felony convictions for all Federal jobs and Federal contractors. An additional 35 states have similar laws although they are have not always resulted in eliminating barriers to employment for the formerly incarcerated (Barthel 2019). Even with effort to "ban the box" a former prisoner who had legitimate work experience before incarceration, now has a hole in their work history that must be explained or may even eliminate them before an interview. Many jobs requiring a background check will also reject persons convicted of certain types of crimes regardless of the circumstances of those convictions. Even entry level positions such as those in gas stations or convenience stores are often not available to people with drug offenses or financially related crimes such as robbery or fraud.

Incarceration also means that the former prisoner has been absent from the informal social networks that help people find employment. They do not have a presence on social media or job oriented sites such as LinkedIn. They have not been able to keep up on technological advances and so may not possess job skills related to technology. They may struggle with basic data entry or to work computerized systems required at many entry level jobs such as fast food restaurants or grocery stores. Even the transition from paper applications to online applications may be a stumbling block for former prisoners who were incarcerated before the proliferation of the internet.

Former prisoners sometimes are not able to give potential employers a permanent address, especially if they are living at a shelter or a halfway house. They also may not have access to reliable transportation to and from work, or they may have travel restrictions placed on them by parole. They may not have a bank account into which their checks can be automatically deposited, and many employers will not issue paper checks. They may not possess a suitable wardrobe, having not bought clothes for many years, and may not be able to acquire one before finding employment. This has implications beyond professional jobs, affecting manual labor as well. While many prisons have certificate programs for inmates interested in specialized labor, these positions require employees to supply their own tools and work clothes. For someone just out of prison, even something as basic as steel toed boots can be beyond their grasp, putting construction jobs out of immediate reach. Manual labor jobs can be difficult for other reasons as well. Many former prisoners have health issues related to poor nutrition and health care while inside. Inmates may have long term injuries from prison fights. These can make manual labor difficult.

These structural challenges to reentry have been well documented in the literature on mass incarceration (example cites) and encompass many of the issues that new state and local reentry programs seek to address. They are seen as the stumbling blocks that must be removed if a former prisoner is to successfully complete parole. But even in this more inclusive picture of reentry, what remains absent from the literature is the emotional, relational and personal terrain of "coming home"; the backdrop to the official reentry process. In fact, it has been suggested that former prisoners with supportive family networks on the outside might benefit from being removed from official parole programs because they don't need the kind of support parole provides (Horn 2001). However, while this absence of state controlled parole might remove the former prisoner from state influence, it also requires the family to assume responsibility for solving the myriad of practical reentry issues while still navigating the emotional and relational ones.

It is my assertion, then, that coming home needs to be recognized as a separate and parallel process to reentry—one which acknowledges the damage that systems of incarceration inflict on prisoners and their loved one alike. While every former prisoner's process will be unique, and some may transition back into their families and home environments with minimal disruption, many others will not. Former prisoners may in fact slip back into old behaviors not just because of a lack of employment, housing, motivation, or counseling support, but because of the inability to overcome the relational damage that incarceration and absence has caused. They may come home to loving and supportive families who long for their presence and still not be able to effectively integrate into these environments and thus back into society. This is what happened to Sylvia and Danny, and their story—all of it—matters as it illuminates what has long remained private and personal and thus irrelevant.

Before Coming Home: The Beginning

For Sylvia the changes in Danny after his return were difficult to understand and move past. They had been married 16 years at the time of his release and had been together for 28. They had raised six children, and when Danny came out of prison this time, they had seven grandchildren. They had both invested a great deal of their lives in one another, and in the years of Danny's incarceration, they had struggled in order to make it possible to have a future together. So Sylvia expected having "the love of my life" come home to be reminiscent of the emotions she had when things all began.

"The day I knew Danny was coming home was one of the best days of my life, other than the first day that I met him...The first time that I met him, he swept me off my feet."

But looking back, the problems that would plague Danny and Sylvia after his release had always been there. They had both just handled them differently.

Sylvia met Danny when she was 23, and the prison experience was part of their lives from the very beginning. Danny, a traditional Phoenix Latino full of machismo, didn't try to hide the fact that he had been out of prison for just a few weeks after serving six months on a driving while intoxicated (DWI) charge. Sylvia, who had two children from a previous relationship, was "skeptical" but not entirely put off.

"Did I really want to put myself into something I wasn't sure of? I kind of just played it by ear. I just gave him my phone number and thought if he called he did and if he doesn't he doesn't."

But he did call, and they started spending time together. Danny *"didn't go into detail as far as his experiences being in there"*, and truthfully Sylvia was more concerned with the behavior that had led him into prison than with prison itself.

"My questions to him were not about what went on in prison but were more like what made you get in there. Are you an alcoholic? What's going on here?"

She discovered that Danny had started drinking at a young age because it was expected behavior. *"His mom and dad didn't give two cents whether he drank or not so he did."* While she was a little worried about his drinking, Sylvia was swept away. She put her fears aside and began a life with this man she had come to love. She had been raised in a very strict, traditional Latino home, where her father's power reigned unchallenged. Her mother, who Sylvia loved dearly, was a homemaker, a mother, a wife. She accepted her role to be seen and not heard, to stand behind and support, to remain quiet and submissive. This never completely settled in Sylvia, who was head strong and determined, but she knew the power of expectations.

"You have to understand my upbringing was not a very good one. We were not talked to about a lot of things. I did not want the same life I watched my mother live. It was a very sad life and very controlling. She wasn't allowed to laugh or smile. She was not allowed to be herself."

While Sylvia didn't want the limitations of her mother's life, Danny represented a way out of her struct immediate family, and Sylvia was in love. They were together for a couple of years before they had a son and then a daughter—another clear expectation that Sylvia internalized. Danny's drinking got worse, and three years after the birth of Little Danny, a year after the birth of their daughter, and only a few months after they got married, Danny went back to prison for aggravated driving/ DWI. This time he was gone for two years, but Sylvia had family support to care for the kids, and life still seemed full of possibilities.

"It was rough but I was at a young age still. Danny was still at a young age. We only had the little kids together. I wasn't devasted like I should have been. It was like, hmm, well you were fresh outta prison when I met you so I wasn't surprised."

Part of the reason it was not immediately devastating to her was because Danny's behavior had been causing a great deal of stress in their relationship.

"He was doing things that I knew were a risk. He loved to drink. He was an alcoholic. He just couldn't admit it so I knew it was eventually gonna come back and bite him, and that's exactly what it did…I was more relieved than I was angry because I was tired of all the restless nights. Is he going to get into a car accident? Is he gonna kill somebody? What if I get a phone call, and they say that he died?"

But after his arrest, Sylvia let her anger come to the surface. *"I wasn't there when they sentenced him. I didn't go. I guess I didn't care. I really didn't care."*

After Danny was sentenced, Sylvia pulled herself together and began to do what she thought a good wife was expected to do. After all this was how she was raised. Men sometime get into trouble and it the job of a good wife to keep things together in their absence. *"You step up to the plate and take care of business"* she explained. So she did just that. She went to visitation. She took the children. She wrote letters. She put money on his books. And then it all just got to be too much. She was young and overwhelmed and those old voices of wanting more for herself started to ring in her ears again.

"I did it for maybe the first year, and the last year I just gave up. I just didn't want it. I couldn't see myself doing that. It was a struggle. It was more of a struggle to get up, do the whole kid thing, pack them in the car, drive hours away or whatever. It just got to be too much. I stopped everything (phone calls too). I was just young, and I wasn't ready for that in my life. I didn't know how to deal with that. I didn't know how to cope. He wrote me. He was very hurt, couldn't understand why. Said that he would love me to the end no matter what, said that I broke his heart."

She stuck to her decision, however, and for a year they had no contact. Sylvia even began another relationship briefly and had a daughter, but Danny was never far from her thoughts. After her daughter was born, Sylvia figured she and Danny were a thing of the past. He wouldn't be able to forgive her for becoming involved with someone else even though that had not lasted long, and she had created too much distance between them to start again.

"When he came home that time I hadn't had any contact with him in a year. I had gotten a letter from him two days before his release date letting me know that he was going to be coming home on this day, and asking if would it be okay if his mom came to pick up the kids so he could see them. I said that was fine."

"When that day came, they left, and when the time came for them to come home, he was there to drop them off. When I seen him, I felt instant love for him, and he treated me like I had never left him, like I had never done nothing wrong to him. He just acted like nothing was wrong, like everything was normal. But I knew something was wrong. I felt shame because I had met somebody else. I'd gotten pregnant. I had a daughter so I just felt like it couldn't be between me and him."

But Danny only wanted his family back, and so nine months later, Sylvia and Danny were back together. They had another son and things were stable for a long time, years. Sylvia thought life was solid now. They were growing old together as a solid Latino couple, maybe a little too much like her parents for her liking, but Danny was a good man, and life was okay. Then slowly the old behaviors that had always plagued Danny started to return.

"At first he would drink but he wouldn't drive. Then he started being around my brother. They drank together, and they did it proudly. They started using cocaine so they were staying up longer. They started drinking more. When they ran out of one or the other, they would try to get a ride to go get more. Then the ride started to not be there, and so they started to drive, and it eventually it just caught up with him."

"It was a weekend, and we got into a little bit of an argument because he was drinking, and he said "I'm just gonna drive down the street and get something to eat. I'll be right back. He left, and he never came back."

In 2013, when his youngest son was 12 and almost 14 years since he was last in prison, Danny was arrested for aggravated assault resulting from an argument at the bar he had gone to when he left that night. The police found his 9mm in his truck, and as a former felon he was charged with misconduct involving weapons. In an instant, Sylvia's life was once more thrown into chaos.

Danny's movement back toward prison, even after 14 years of freedom, is not usual. According to the Bureau of Justice Statistics' study of recidivism among former state prison inmates, 43% of former offenders are arrested during their first year of release but that percentage rises to almost 80% after nine years of freedom (BJA 2018). In fact, six in ten new arrests by those formerly incarcerated didn't happen until four to nine years after their release (BJS 2018).

The dismal rates of recidivism are one of the reasons that states have attempted to refine their efforts at reentry. Reentry was seen as the pivotal moment when a former prisoner would find their way back into society or back into prison. But after 14 years, Danny's progress back toward incarceration had more to do with the demons of alcoholism and relational tension than his inability to hold a job and he had long since moved out the state's efforts to keep him on the straight and narrow.

"We Are Not Supposed to Be Here Again"

Danny's court process didn't last long. He had two prior felony convictions, and he was charged with a violent crime so things were not in his favor. Yet Sylvia hung on to her hope.

"Honestly I really didn't want to accept the fact that it was going to happen again because it had been such a long gap since he was in. I was just thinking he's not gonna go to prison. They are gonna give him probation because he's shown for so long that he's okay. But as the court dates went on, they kept talking about all these aggravating factors. Then they say 'you're looking at six years" and I was just like in disbelief. This is not supposed to be happening to us right now. We're older, and we've shared so much and done so much, and to think that's going to be taken away in the blink of an eye. It was too much. It was over-whelming."

While their relationship had been struggling prior to his arrest, the threat of prison threw them back together. *"I went back to being a good wife, to fulfilling expectations. I went to every court date."* Eventually Danny signed a plea agree which allowed the judge to sentence him to 6 to 25 years in prison. The day came for Danny's sentencing., and the reality of the choice she had to make was staring her in the face.

"I was there when they sentenced him. I asked myself, 'do you really want to wait and do the time with him or are you just gonna say this is it? This is where we park. This is where everything ends.'"

After Danny was sentenced to five years, he was given five minutes to say goodbye to his wife. He looked her in the eyes and gave her permission not to wait for him.

"He said to me, 'I love you more than anything in this world but I'm going to be a man and accept my time. And I'm gonna be gone a lot time, Sylvia. I don't want you to wait for me. I want you to move on with your life. When I get out if you're by yourself, then we will try and make things work but I'm not gonna ask you to wait."

That was the moment Sylvia decided, and she went back to all she had learned about the kind of wife she was supposed to be. She went back to the way she had been raised.

"That day I realized that I was really in love with him, and that I would wait a lifetime for him. Don't ask me how that just clicked but I felt it so strong in my heart. I just knew that I didn't care if they had given him 25 years, I would be there for him."

Sylvia left the courtroom to begin life on her own again. This was different, though. She and Danny had been raising six children and three grandchildren when he was arrested. Her mother had died and she didn't have the family support she had had before. Sylvia had never worked, as Danny was the sole breadwinner for the family. They had been living comfortably off Danny's salary for 14 years, renting a nice home in a good neighborhood. That was all about to change.

"It doesn't happen overnight, but everything happens so fast. I didn't have job. I didn't know where to begin. Once I did figure it out, it was kind of a little too late. The bills had started piling up. No matter how much I paid, it was never enough, and I found myself deeper and deeper and deeper. The water got shut off. The gas got shut off. Rent started being late, and it kept being late, and finally it just couldn't be like that anymore, and we had to move. We had to get rid of the house. There would be days when I would go without eating as long as the kids ate."

"I depended on him for everything for 14 years. He was my rock. He was everything to me, to the kids. You gotta understand that when you're in a situation like that having everything taken away from you, and not being educated, it can destroy a whole entire family. It destroys, it manipulates you. It makes you think crazy. It makes you angry. You are vulnerable to so many things."

Sylvia let the family spiral out of control for months. She tried to keep visiting Danny, sometimes getting a ride with me, but eventually the cost was just too much. The truck was reprocessed. More grandkids came because Sylvia didn't feel strong enough to handle her own children, and the weight of what she was suffering began to take a toll on her relationship with Danny.

"Danny blames himself for everything that has gone wrong since he went in. It's his fault we lost the house. It's his fault that I don't have a vehicle. It's his fault that the kids are all separated. Whenever anything goes wrong on the outside, it's all his fault. If he wouldn't be in there none of this would have happened."

"There is truth to that. If he never would have gone in, we would still be living at the house. All these grandbabies that we've had since he's been gone...I think that would have been under more control. I know that a few of my kids say he has failed them as a father because the times they needed him the most he wasn't around. There

is truth to that too. Especially when you're a Latino boy growing into a young man, and you need that father figure in your life, and he's not there."

"He is the one to blame. He did end up there, and he's paying for his actions. I just didn't know when he left that I was going to hit rock bottom this hard too. How do you know you're going to hit rock bottom? I get mad but I'm more hurt. What I've gone through emotionally since Daniel's been gone, I really can't compare to anything. The amount of hurt and anger and frustration and pity I've felt since he's been gone is unbelievable. I think I've felt every emotion that a person could feel."

"'I felt like I was doing the time too, and I was. Not just me, but my kids. My family was doing it too."

After living for months with her children on the brink of eviction with no running water and no steady income, Sylvia started to pull herself out of her own depression. While she felt like she was doing the time with Danny, she started to realize that she was on the outside and still responsible for her children and her grandchildren. She couldn't allow herself to float away into her own suicidal thoughts. Danny was gone, and she had responsibilities. This was not the ethnic picture of the self-sacrificing wife she has been raised with. This was survival.

"One morning I got up, and I was just done. I got tired of feeling sorry for myself. I got tired of crying all the time. I got tired of being nobody. I got tired of how my kids would look at me just lying there not doing nothing, not caring, not wanting to live anymore, not wanting anything. Not caring that I had grandkids. Not caring that I had kids that still needed me."

"I got on the cell phone, and I started applying to every place I could think of. Then all of a sudden I got a job, started picking myself up. A few months went by, and I would fall back behind a little bit because I would get worried about Daniel. It would weigh in the back of my mind not knowing what was going on with him and that would kind of set me back. For the first year I went through jobs like crazy because of trying to deal with him and myself and the household. I was juggling a lot."

Sylvia's experience of being thrust into the role of breadwinner is not unique. According to the Federal Bureau of Prisons, the prison population is 93% male, and in their absence, it is women who bear the brunt of the pressure for making ends meet. Even when women themselves are incarcerated, children often do not become the responsibility of the father. In most cases, grandmothers raise their grandchildren until the mother's return. Therefore the aftermath of prison falls most heavily on women. While not all men who are incarcerated have been taking care of their families financially at the time they are sentenced (only 17% of the men in state prison report living in a single parent home with their children prior to their incarceration), for women relying on their husband's paychecks, prison strikes a hard blow (Christian 2009).

For the women who survive it, it can create personal growth. But this too has a dark side. Women who become aware of their own power and abilities during their partner's incarceration, can sometimes experience relational tension upon his release. When men exit a prison environment where aggression and respect are the tools of survival, they struggle to re-integrate into relationships with women who have found their own voices in their absence. This has been enough of a consistent problem that the Federal Office of Violence Against Women has created Project Safe Return, a research and advocacy program designed to address the rates of domestic violence against African American women from men returning from incarceration (Hairston and Oliver 2005). While violence was not a part of Sylvia and Danny's story, there were strong tensions about the way Sylvia had found it in herself to save the family while Danny was away.

Eventually Sylvia started work as a custodian for a company at the airport. It required her to walk to the bus for a long ride before the sun was up, to work hours on her feet, and then repeat the process to get home at suppertime. But she did it because it had to be done.

After three months, her supervisor suffered an accident and didn't return to work. Sylvia earned herself a supervisory position. She stayed with the company for another year until she got laid off. But this time she was stronger, more aware of her gifts, more confident in her abilities. She immediately applied for a supervisor position at another cleaning company in the same location. She stayed in that position for about two years until the company lost its contract in a rebid. But this didn't stop her. Sylvia was able to transition to the new company and was put in a management position over one of their airline contracts, where she still works.

She paid the bills. Got the family a new place to live, and eventually bought herself a new car. Sylvia did what she did not believe she could do. She went from working just to pay the bills and keep the family out of ruin to being able to provide for her kids in a meaningful way. In the process she discovered herself and how angry she was inside.

"I didn't realize it then but all of that was just making me stronger, and it was changing me at the same time because all the sadness was turning into anger. I started to have all this anger in me."

But she worked through the anger as she continued to discover her own confidence. She remained faithful to Danny, visiting when she could and putting money on his books. She was developing into the strong Latina woman she had envisioned herself to be before she met Danny, but she also stayed committed to having Danny home, to being a family.

Then Danny came home, distant and emotionally unavailable, and all the anger she thought she'd worked through rose again.

"Now that he's home, the kids say to me when he's not around, 'mom, you know that we can forgive dad. We can forgive him for everything he's ever done but there's one thing that you cannot ask us to do because we refuse to do it. We will forgive that man—our dad—but we'll never forget. We cannot forget.'"

"I can forgive him too. I already have. But I can't forget what our lives were when he made the choice to leave. I can't forget that. I don't think I ever will. When I think about the things we had to go through it makes me so angry. I blame him for what me and my kids went through those five years he was gone. I blame him for everything I ever lost in that house. I blame him for everything that ended up at the pawn shop. I blame him for losing my truck. I blame him for everything."

If Danny's coming home had been the perfect story that Sylvia and the kids had been dreaming about, they all might have conquered the pain of the past. But it wasn't. Danny had no skills in managing his own guilt and regret, and this kind of counseling was unavailable to him. As Sylvia explains,

"He's not happy because he lost five years of his life. He's never gonna get those five years back. He lost five years of all his kids' lives. When he left Jose was just twelve years old. He left at the most crucial point of Jose's life. Jose needed him at that age. Jose is now 17. He doesn't go to Danny for anything. None of my kids go to him for anything because when he was gone we had to learn to live without him, to make ends meet without him. He's like 'nobody even needs me.' He sees that. None of the kids need him."

"I tell him, 'granted these kids grew up without you. There's nothing you can do or nothing you can say that is gonna make these five years better. I'm sorry. That's time lost. So forget about the time lost because there is nothing we can do to bring that back.'"

"I tell him, 'what you have to do is pick up from where you left off and try and move forward. You have to think on the level your kids are on. Your oldest son is running

work now. Your other son has his own family. Jose is getting ready to graduate from high school. You can't treat him like he's 12 years old anymore. You have to start moving forward from where they're at now. Reach out to them.'"

"He doesn't do any of that. I said to him, 'You have to reach out to them because how they grew up was with tough love. They had to suck it up. Dad's gone. That's it. Dad's gone, and Mom's only one person. She can only do so much. They had to fend for themselves so they are not going to go to you for anything.' He just stays quiet. His response is 'well I guess I have nobody to blame but myself.'"

"And he's right. I tell him 'well you were the one who chose the path that you did that night you left here. You had a choice, and you chose to walk out that door when we all begged you not to leave because we saw the condition you were in. You still chose to leave. You pushed your way out from in front of us and you left anyway.'"

But beyond Danny's need for help with his emotional adjustment to freedom and family, Sylvia's development as a woman was not part of Danny's reentry plan. In fact, there was nothing offered to Danny as part of his standard parole that discussed how he should understand and adjust to the changes in his relationships. Reentry addressed the basics--his requirement to work and the legal expectation that he was not taking drugs or engaging in criminal behavior. The emotional rehabilitation required in coming home fell to Sylvia and the family. They were considered personal in nature and so not under the purview of the state.

Yet as is obvious in their larger story, and those of most families affected by mass incarceration, the inter-personal dynamics of Sylvia and Danny's relationship had always played a role in Danny's "criminal" behavior. It would only be expected then that their inability to find a new life with one another now would be a key factor in Danny's inability to stay on the "straight and narrow" and out of prison in the future.

"He feels that I don't need him. He says, 'you're making good money. You don't need me for anything. You can hold this down.' And you know what? He's right. He was all I ever knew. He was my provider. He was everything. He was the backbone of that family. I thought I had no choice but to wait. I love my husband. But I built a life for myself and the kids, and let me tell you it was super hard. I've grown to be a very independent woman. I don't need a man to take care of me now because I know I can do that on my own. I just wanna live, and now we will just take it one day at a time."

CONCLUSION

The choices Daniel made led him into a prison cell over and over again. The drinking and the drugs took him away from his family, cost him his confidence, and ultimately destroyed his relationships with the people he loved the most. He has always accepted responsibility for those decisions even while being unable to alter their consequences. The system in which he found himself sought punishment of him and his family as the solution. It focused on the potential dangers of his actions – he could have hurt someone else-- instead of seeking to understand their source. After more than 18 months home, Danny started drinking again and experimented with drugs a little. Fear of punishment is not a strong enough tonic to heal years of pain, disappointment and isolation, and a struggling, loving family has proven to be not enough to heal years of incarceration. Danny finished reentry and parole successfully, but after almost two years of begin home, he and Sylvia have decided to divorce, and Danny may be headed down the path that lead him back to prison in the first place.

Sylvia has struggled with her own guilt at not being able to get it right. She has spent hours alone asking if her expectations were realistic, fair, appropriate? Did she love unconditionally enough? What there anything else she could have done that would have changed things? The same, old, familiar questions.

At the same time she also now recognizes that the burden of rehabilitating Danny should not have been hers alone and that assistance with the emotional side of Danny's return might have helped them to not be in this place.

"There's no education for families that lose a loved one to the system for years, and then when they come out nobody tells you what to expect. If there was more education, families would be saved."

She had been helped by having gone through it twice before and by her friendships, but it wasn't enough. Many women don't even have that. They face what comes alone, shouldering their own predictable expectations and disappointments alone. The unflinching truth is that many women and families are not able and maybe should not be expected to finish the rehabilitation process that incarceration began, and that coming home cannot remain just a silent, private process.

REFERENCES

Barthel, M. (2019). Employers are Still Avoiding Former Inmates. *Atlantic (Boston, Mass.)*.

Bureau of Justice Statistics. (2018). *2018 Update on Prisoner Recidivism: A Nine-Year Follow-Up Period*. Bureau of Justice Statistics.

Christian, S. (2009). Children of Incarcerated Parents. *National Conference of State Legislatures*.

Hairston, C. F., & Oliver, W. (2005). *Domestic Violence and Prisoner Reentry*. Vera Institute of Justice.

Horn, M. (2001). Rethinking Sentencing. *Corrections Management Quarterly*, *5*(3), 34–40.

Hughes & Wilson. (n.d.). *Reentry Trends in the United States*. Washington, DC: Bureau of Justice Statistics.

Travis, J. (2005). *But They All Come Back: Facing the Challenges of Prison Reentry*. The Urban Institute.

Chapter 4
Carceral Trauma at the Intersections of Race, Class, and Gender

Cassandra D. Little
California State University, Fresno, USA

ABSTRACT

This chapter will provide a firsthand analysis of one woman's journey through the prison industrial complex. The intent is to bring the readers proximate to how trauma intersects with incarceration, gender, and race. The goal is to challenge our criminal justice system's need to over-criminalize and over-incarcerate women at alarming rates. Since 1980 the number of women in United States prisons has increased by more than 700%. These rates of incarceration of women have outpaced men by more than 50%. By drawing upon lived experience interacting with the United States Criminal Justice System and empirical data, the author will provide evidence that will argue that the experience of being incarcerated is traumatic and dehumanizing for many, but even more counterproductive for women.

INTRODUCTION

July 13, 2013 marked the beginning of a personal transformation that will forever change the trajectory of my life. I had to wrap my mind around something so profound, intimidating, and labyrinthine, I knew I had no other recourse but to accept my fate. On that day, I began my journey to discovering other parts of myself heretofore unknown while remaining impervious to being and feeling defeated.

DOI: 10.4018/978-1-7998-6646-6.ch004

Grounded in structures of capitalism and imperialism, the Prison Industrial Complex is marred with serious pitfalls. It is well-documented that the United States has the highest rate of incarceration in the world. I was sentenced to 33 months and served 23 months incarcerated at a Federal Prison Camp in Victorville, California—giving me entry into a unique subset of American womanhood, that of women charged with a felony. My journey from growing up in the inner city of East Palo Alto, California, to graduating college, earning a Ph.D. and ultimately becoming a CEO of my own company to the details of my carceral period that charts my days under sentence to my ascent into freedom. I had become a part of the quickly growing statistic in America, I was an incarcerated woman .

As an artist, academic, intellectual, person of color, mother and a woman—I have always embodied the capacity to view my experiences in a broad context. This paper will expound on the impact of being a part of a growing epidemic of imprisoned women, and the roles that were compromised as a result. I will provide evidence that the collateral damages for incarcerating women are exponential to the individual as well as the family.

The increased incarceration of women appears to be the outcome of larger forces that have shaped U.S. crime policy (Covington & Bloom, 2003).

Mass Incarceration and the War on Drugs

As a Black queer, educated mother who was given the opportunity to experience the carceral state very early in childhood--so early that my subconscious mind stored evidence of what was paved before me--I have to admit that it took some of the most epic soul-searching and heartfelt conversations for me to find the root of my personal experience with also being label as a felon. My introduction into the Prison Industrial Complex began when I was 9 years old, in the fall of 1973. Right around the time my parents' divorce was still fresh in my mind, and the United States was in political turmoil. I was constantly trying to drown out everything that was deemed unimportant, including the headline news, concerning the president's transgressions—which seemed to follow me everywhere. They played the news about the Watergate scandal at the corner store, at our neighborhood candy store, in my grandparents' car, and at my friends' houses. Back in those days, it seemed as if I had to bury my head completely in the sand in order to not hear about an impending impeachment.

At home, which I shared with my maternal grandparents, mother and two younger sisters--my grandfather's FM radio often played in the kitchen. He'd sit at the table his legs shook, alternately. At the same time, he'd have a cup of coffee with the newspaper in front of him, while the television blasted from his and my grandmother's bedroom. This happened constantly. I recalled hearing President Nixon declare from multiple media devices, "I am not a crook!" (Kilpatrick, 1973)

Not only did my grandmother adopt the word "crook", alongside a trail of other ungodly nouns and finally, "God bless you!" repeatedly echoed from my brown skinned, big-boned grandma's mouth, thereafter. I instinctively knew to trust her wisdom—her martyrdom, her bleeding heart. I paid attention to my role models with a fiery defiance that flipped how I felt about responsibilities and relationships. My elders were living in survival mode, and as a young girl, I knew it—it was innate. During this impressionable period of my life, I began visiting any given uncle in San Quentin prison. I was young but fully aware of the consequences of breaking rules and laws. As the oldest child, I was an outgoing, very independent, strong-willed little girl, I knew that my grandmother's New Orleans tendencies volleyed between martyrdom and courage. Looking back, I see how my grandparents essentially became full time babysitters. My father became an alcoholic and remarried, and my mother began a life of abusing drugs, which included serving time in jail and prison—for multiple, non-violent, drug related offenses. In 1975 my sisters and I were being raised by both maternal and paternal grandparents because the writing was on the wall. My family dynamic was dysfunctional at a level that was too far gone for me to embrace. By 1977 my mother had two additional little girls, the youngest was born addicted to heroin and picked up from the hospital by my aunt, while my mom went to serve time in prison.

There were occasions when I witnessed my mother's criminal activities firsthand. One of those times happened towards the end of summer in 1980. My mother took my sister's and I shopping for school clothes and ended up getting arrested for using someone else's checks and identification for the purchases. Instead of allowing my grandparents to pick us up, as I had begged the officers to do, they made me drive my mother's car to the police station as she sat in the back of the police car. There was one police car driving in front of me with my mother yelling and screaming in the back seat--and another police car trailed behind me. I couldn't comprehend why she did this to me? I was equally angry at the Police Officers for insisting that my sisters and I endured such a traumatic experience, when there were other more humane and age appropriate options.

I grew up in East Palo Alto, California—a fairly safe hood, located approximately 32 miles from Oakland. During my childhood, I witnessed a slow, yet impactful evolution of the effects of living in a carceral existence. Up until 1985, my hometown had an ambiance of a broken village, but thereafter, EPA became a warzone. (De-Bug, 2015). In 1992, East Palo Alto made headline news for birthing the highest homicide rate in the country. Crack cocaine, incarceration, on-going killings and broken families peppered throughout my community. The aftermath of growing up in such trauma haunted me and my strides towards living the American Dream, for years to come.

In an article written by Douglass James Fort, a criminologist who also grew up in EPA, a heartfelt chronological journey related to the impact of growing up in a carceral state is noted, when he says, "The Crack Epidemic was capitalized upon the criminal justice system, triggering policy makers to make laws that put a lot of family and friends in prison for a long time, and in many ways are still sitting in these prisons today." His personal insight holds a level of truth that I've experienced; Growing up in an environment peppered with drug abuse, trauma and routine prison visits that may have assisted with me becoming familiar with an environment that never left my psyche, nor my direction in life. I was bound to familiarizing myself with the prison industrial complex, no matter how optimistic I was about paving the way for a life free of restrictions by conducting myself properly, which entailed being a law abiding, ambitious person--with an air of stubbornness.

After I graduated from college in December 1987 with my Bachelors' degree in Sociology with an emphasis in Criminal Justice, I started working full time at a child welfare agency called Child help USA.

Upon graduating with my Masters' in Social Work, I obtained my clinical license and worked as a Licensed Social Worker in the field of Child Welfare for 5 years. During my college years, one of my sister's fell victim to crack-cocaine addiction and gave birth to 9 crack-exposed babies from 1987-1999. After I was notified that she had given birth to her youngest child, and he was going into foster care, and very ill with a heart problem, my partner at the time and I decided that we would gain custody of my nephew. After six months of completing legal paperwork and preparing our home for a baby, we were allowed to take Aaron home from Fresno, California and moved him to Reno, Nevada, to become a part of our family. My partner at the time had to incredible sons, who were 9 years old and 10 years old when we met, and she was a Registered Nurse. So, it seemed like a perfect scenario for us all. When I initially saw Aaron, it was love at first sight. I remember holding him for the very first time, and how his little hands seemed to be touching every area of my face as we smiled at each other; It was an immediate connection, one that reflects the beauty of a mother-son relationship. It is a feeling of love I get from him that has always kept me centered and whole.

In 2000 I decided I wanted to pursue my Doctorate in Counseling Educational Psychology. This was in line with my long-term goal to eventually become a professor at a University someday. By 2002 I've acquired enough expertise, professional relationships and courage to start my own Foster Care Agency. I also decided that I have always felt a strong desire to provide a nurturing yet therapeutic environment that not only provided the basic requirements of shelter, food, clothing, access to a team of healthcare professionals, and education—but also life and relationship building skills. Because of my childhood, I felt it was necessary to guide abused children to dream outside of what they endured in the past.

After a lot of thought and planning, on March 5, 2003, Ujima Youth Services opened its doors to provide services for abused kids in the foster care system. Aside from my son, it was one of the proudest moments in my life, to align myself with the results of all the hard work it took to even consider opening up a community-based business. I borrowed the name Ujima from a Kwanzaa principle that means, "Collective work and responsibility." My goal was to provide a safe, loving, supportive, purposeful program for all youths who were considered by many in the community as being "unsalvageable". It reminded me of my childhood days of helping my grandmother and her friends at the Co-op community store in our neighborhood. And I had wonderful memories such as communities working together to help each other and listening to Angela Davis speech in East Palo Alto after she was released. I remember her standing on a podium in front of the co-op with her big beautiful afro and her fist raised signifying black power.

Many of the youth that were referred to Ujima were severely traumatized. Ujima had nearly 10 youth in the program and the need for more beds. This population was rapidly increasing, as cycles of drug abuse and incarceration continued to separate children from their parents. My "adopted" city had a growing need for providers, such as myself, and I had all the available resources to manage a successful business that would benefit the youth, alongside the community in which we all resided.

The Female Experience and the Prison Industrial Complex

At the end of 2009, Ujima had grown to 65 youths from ages five to twenty-two years old, and over 50 staff members. My goals and dreams were becoming a reality; I had my four sisters at my side, many of my family members, and close friends—who provided the love and care to the youths in Northern Nevada. Seven years passed with the promise of continued service, and on October of 2009 an IRS agent, and Medicaid Fraud Investigator entered my office asking about the whereabouts of my brother in law—who was also the chief financial officer of Ujima Youth Services. This inquiry began the unraveling of my hard-dedicated work and service and opened a criminal case that transformed me from being a mother, community leader, caring foster mother, Licensed Clinical Social Worker and professional, to a suspect in a white-collar crime (Rubino, n.d.).

In April 2010, I received a letter stating that my agency would no longer receive funding and that the 65 youths continued in my program would have to be removed by May 20, 2010. My dream had become one of my worst nightmares. For the next two years I spent most of my time in my blue lounge chair, contemplating suicide, mindlessly watching television, praying like I've never pray before for answers as to why this was happening to me, and what was going to happen next. I knew I was traumatized by the sudden investigation into my business affairs. I wasn't prepared for the most intense anxiety I could ever experience as an adult. The mystery of not knowing what was going on with my life, catapulted me into a major depressed and paranoia state. I began to feel like my house was being watched, and frequently peered through the blinds in my upstairs room. I was 100% convinced that my home was under surveillance every time I saw a police car drive down the street. I didn't speak much on the phone, because I began hearing strange noises during conversations, and I was sure someone was listening in on my calls. I'd often receive messages that investigators were speaking to friends, family, community members and some of my former foster care youths, to gather information about me and my organization. One day I received a frantic call from my nephew who was in one of my offices that I had converted to a music studio for kids in the community, that Federal Bureau Investigators (FBI) were raiding my office. I got into my car and drove to see what was going on. By this time my agency had been closed over a year. When I reached the office, I asked what was going on? The young Medicaid Fraud Unit (MFU) Investigator abruptly told me that I was not the one asking questions they were (HHS, Accessed 2018).

The investigation lasted for nearly another two years, during which time I had no frame of reference for what was happening to me. I tried with everything inside me to gain insight into what I did that was legally or even morally wrong. I began to feel personally attacked. Did the government wage war against me because of the color of my skin? Was it due to my gender, or sexual preference? In the past I had very little concern over how people judged me, but this was completely different. My freedom and livelihood were in their hands, rendering me powerless; I had no income, no business, and no job. I was so financially in the hole, I wasn't able to afford an attorney, leaving me at the mercy of the system. Like, my childhood, the carceral state was in full control of the narrative, and all I could do was sit in my blue lounge chair and wait for the unknown to reveal itself. The only thing that kept me hopeful was the time spent with my son, my grandkids and close family members.

A year later, in 2013, there was a knock at my door from the same two investigators who paid me the fateful visit earlier. They asked if they could enter my home and handed me an indictment. The United States vs. Cassandra Little was underway and all I could say to myself was, "Finally!" At least I was in the position to find out what the government wanted from me. As I read the indictment my hands began to shake. I could not get pass the heading, "The United States vs. Cassandra Little." It was the scariest document I have ever held in my hands. The next day I called the Federal Public Defender's office and arranged to meet with someone who could assist me with understanding exactly what was happening with my case, and how I could possibly fight it.

My assigned public defender was very helpful. She was about to retire and did not waste anytime telling me that everything would move quickly from this time forward. Every time I presented her with an argument for what the Government was asserting, she'd remind me that the Carceral State was not about the truth, it was about what they could and would try to prove. In other words, I was at their mercy and therefore powerless.

After many sleepless nights researching and trying to understand the process of being indoctrinated into the Prison Industrial Complex (Florida International, 2011). I succumbed to the reality that the Federal Government has a 93% conviction rate. I question the systems decision to incarcerate me instead requiring me to repay the $84,000. When you look at it, taxpayers paid for the Governments three years investigation, the court hearings, my 23 months of incarceration and my 5 months of halfway house. Let's not forget about the 64 youth who many had to be placed in higher level, high cost facilities and the many staff members who were forced to get on welfare, food stamps or unemployment.

Childless Incarcerated Mother

On our last day together before I had to leave to drive to California and self-surrender to the Bureau of Prisons, I loaded up the car with my son's things and my suitcase. While driving my son to his new, temporary home—I looked at him and told him that he had everything he needed while I was away. He quietly put his head down, started crying and said, "Yea, I have everything except my mom!" I couldn't respond, since deep down inside I knew he was rightfully saddened by our separation.

I had never been away from my son for more than a weekend. The first month away from him caused me a tremendous amount of anxiety. I learned to savor every minute we spoke on the phone, while trying to maintain composure. At night I would stare at his picture that I taped on the brick wall. I would say a silent prayer for my son and myself, and our healing. I prayed for his safety, and I prayed that he knew that even though I was absent from his life, I deeply loved him. I reminded myself that my son was just as resilient as myself, and we would get through this period of our lives.

As I made my way to my visit, I wondered how visiting me would it impact him? Would it be traumatic? How would I feel once he left and I had to go back to the unit? Fortunately, it all went well. When I walked into the visiting room and saw his chocolate face, I could not help but smile. As I sat next to him, he leaned over and put his head on my shoulder. By this time, he had grown to be a very handsome, 6-foot-tall young man. We talked about school and football and his plans for the next weekend. It was wonderful to see him face to face, to kiss and hug him. Prior to my incarceration, we had our nightly routine where I would come in and tuck him in and discuss the plans for the next day. I missed those days and promised myself once I returned home, I would never take any of our moments together for granted. At the end of the visit on the second day I prepared myself to say goodbye and I hugged him as long as he allowed, then watched as he exited the visiting area. I distinctly remember hearing mothers crying after their visits with their children. I can still hear their voices trying to reassure their children that everything was going to be okay. I considered myself a professional mother. I took that role seriously and understood clearly what my absence for nearly two years would do to my son and to our relationship. I understand the sense of vulnerability and fears a mother can have when parting from their children, and all I could do was be present—in the moment, as a witness, and move with some sort of grace. I also felt a kinship with the expecting mothers. During my incarceration there were six pregnant, nonviolent, low-level offenders.

One of the pregnant women did not know she was pregnant until she received the news from the physician assistant at the Federal Prison Camp. After her initial shock and frustration at being told that she was pregnant, she quickly started counting her good days to see if she would be released from custody prior to her baby being born. After she realized that for nine months, she would have to rely on the marginal medical care at the Prison Camp, she started crying. She explained to me that she had been fighting her indictment for nearly three years and was just relieved to get it over with. As the days and weeks and months went by, I continued to check on her diligently and she would always smile and reassure me that they were both doing okay.

The maternity care in prison was frighteningly marginal and non-existent (Altman, 2007), I would pray daily that the women would go into labor before 5pm on the weekdays, and after 5pm—on the weekends, we were basically on the Federal Camp with one guard who would spend most of his time in the office or socializing with their colleagues from the other prisons, on the facility (Law, 2015). For my own sanity, I started asking questions about what needs to happen in case one of the women went into labor during off hours. I was told that the red phone on the wall, was used for emergencies, but every one of the women on the camp knew that no one ever responds to the red phone calls.

The Bureau of Prisons has a written policy that if at all possible, incarcerated persons would not be sent more than 500 miles away from their hometown and support, so I was sent to Victorville California which was 475 miles away from my son. I was hoping to be sent to the facility in San Francisco, which was 218 miles away, and easier for my family members to bring my son to visit me. I hadn't seen my son for nearly 8 months after I self-surrendered myself to the Prison Camp (Smyth, 2012). The costs and distance made it nearly impossible to maintain a parental relationship with him during this period. The day before he was coming to visit, I could not sleep, I was questioning my decision to have him come see me imprisoned. Would the experience cause him additional trauma that would impact him and his future?

As a Nation we must create Criminal Justice reforms that address the ending of incarcerating women and girls (James, 2019).

Trauma of the Incarceration Experience

That fateful day finally came, and I found myself incarcerated in a Federal Prison Camp in Victorville California. I decided to actively participate in a process that was constructed to deconstruct my consciousness and destroy my way of being. I deemed myself as a conscious prisoner by practicing radical acceptance, which is defined as accepting life without resistance. There's no need to do anything to change outcomes, as it's fruitless. Radical acceptance is about saying yes to life, just as is (Görg, et al., 2017). I survived the worse period of my life, and somehow escaped suicide or insanity. After the closing of Ujima Youth Services, my dream and my life work were over. I visualized myself peacefully laying in a shiny casket, wearing my Sunday best outfit, as my loved ones cried and spoke about what a wonderful, loving person I was. As I walked away from a life, I had planned my entire childhood, I was heading closer to what I've been avoiding as a person of color in the United States. As I looked back and waved goodbye to my close friend, my designated person, Rebecca, I took a deep breath and pulled open the heavy door. My heart began racing as I slowly stepped into a world I've always feared. I recalled thinking that it would be great to just drop dead from a heart attack, right there in the hallway, that way I would bypass my Federal Prison Camp sentence of 33 months for healthcare fraud and money laundering.

After waiting anxiously for nearly 2 hours to be processed, I was escorted to the women's bathroom by one of the correctional officers, where she nervously instructed me to strip out of my clothing. As a middle-age woman, I've grown into being conservative about who I expose my body to, but when she asked me to bend over, tears filled my eyes, and I decided to complete my intake with as little eye contact as possible. I stuck out my tongue without regard for my privacy and coughed directly in front of me while looking through the correction officer. When asked to lift my breast for contraband, I held them towards my face without pause. I was operating outside of my body, which was fine with me, at the moment. The emotional and traumatic impact of that 3-minute interaction remains with me to this day. After it was clear that I was free of any unauthorized materials, I was handed a black mesh laundry bag that had a green smock dress, three pairs of larger men tube sock, 4 panties, travel size toiletries, a pair of oversized and used slip on tennis shoes, and a pair of black used crocs. As I searched through the bag for something to wear, the officer said, "Welcome to the BOP" (Golden, 2013).

(Orange is the New Black 2013), came to Netflix in 2013 at the same time I was being indicted. I spent many of my days attempting to research the Federal Criminal Justice System and the Federal Prison system. Most of the information that was provided was specific to the experiences and the needs of men. So, when I heard there was a book, by Piper Kerman, who was imprisoned within the Federal Prison System I was immediately drawn to it. It was the first current point of reference that was available to me at the time. After reading Piper Kerman's memoir, I had a difficult time watching the Netflix series, as it played mostly towards entertaining the masses, but I was torn, because at least there was something that spoke to the experiences of women. At that moment I decided that it was my duty to share my story and my truths, so that women like myself would have a narrative that would speak to our experiences from a space of truth not entertainment.

I was amazed as I walked pass the prison tv room, where women were lined up in green plastic chairs, sitting with commissary overpriced, clear transistor radios, that were programmed to pick up the audio signals from the televisions that were mounted on the white concrete barren walls. Often to my dismay the women would be watching shows such as "Lock up". I would always feel deeply offended when I would walk by the small, crowded room and see the women intently watching these shows. Quite often I would ask many of them how could you watch a show that provides a chronicle to those on the outside that we belonged in prisons. As an educated woman I understood how media was providing a narrative, that would desensitize the general population to the dehumanizing and traumatic aspects of the incarceration black and brown bodies. This show continues to give Americans the okay to not complain about people being locked in cages and treated as animals at a high rate (Loader & Sparks, 2014).

During my incarceration, I created a daily routine which I followed exactly the same every day until my release. That routine began with walking the dirt track outside of the recreation room every morning. I would then return to the unit, shower, dress for my so called "work detail", which for the Prison Industrial Complex, should be define as legal slavery and abolished as expressed by Angela Davis (Davis, Are prisons obsolete, 2003). After completing my work detail, I would spend the rest of the afternoon reading Angela Davis, James Baldwin, Buddhist teachings, and whatever else material that spoke to my heart. Drawing and writing kept my trauma and anxiety at a low level and tethered to my female soul (Cox, 2012) . It was essential that I remain grounded in daily faith and rituals.

There was no routine or personal strength—however—that could protect any loving, caring woman from not being impacted by the visceral behaviors, routines or rules within the Federal Prison Camp. From the daily human counts, to being berated and treated in a dehumanizing manner by correctional officers, to hiding food in your locker so you could have something to eat when the hunger pangs start to hit, and many other freedom snatching atrocities that those on the outside could never ever fully understand. These types of traumatic occurrences would often remind me of my childhood and the experiences of many of those foster youth, I care for over the years, who were taken out of their homes and mistreated in foster care. I would often think, so who in the world will hold the American Criminal Justice System accountable, for being abusive and neglectful to those they are in charge of caring for within the prison walls.

Reentry: Coming Home

On April 15, 2018 when I was released from Supervised Release and from the legal shackles of the Carceral State. The collateral consequences for being a Black, Queer, Woman and Felon at times have felt insurmountable. Since my release and return, I have lost my home, my business, my career, my Clinical License, I have been fired from a minimum wage job, I have been refused assistance by Equal Employment Opportunity Commission, I have not been able to secure employment in my field of practice after submitting over 100 applications. I wonder about the women who do not have the education, clinical experience, resources and support that I have? I have a saying that reminds me that I was born and raised to move through anything, anywhere at any given time. I have an innate ability to tap into my childhood resiliency and radical acceptance, my education to enhance and empower me. But I truly have a clear understanding of how and why recidivism occurs. Unlike many women who are reentering after enduring such a traumatic experience, I am fortunate. Which is why I will continue to share my story and my methods for not just surviving but thriving through one of the most horrendous and traumatic periods in my life.

Dr. Angela Davis has made apparent in her compositions, that the Prison Industrial Complex is doing exactly what its structured to do, and that is why it must be abolished (Davis & Shaylor, Race, Gender, and the Prison Industrial Complex California and Beyond, 2001). The Carceral State has affected generations of families—specifically Black Americans. My journey serves as an example of how our government policy concerning mass incarceration is a detriment to all Americans.

I'm free, but in a lot of ways I'm far from being free. The collateral consequences (Turanovic, Rodriguez, & Pratt, 2012) for formerly incarcerated persons are often more challenging than incarceration itself. Because of my childhood, I have always strategically placed myself in position to be financially secure and gainfully self-employed. After returning home from prison, the first thing I was told by my probation officer was that to remain in compliance with my probation, I must obtain a job. In the past prior to my being a felon, I never worried about employment or creating a job for myself. Now I was faced with seeking employment with a list of restrictions and a felony. My employment restrictions barred me from working in Child Welfare, being self-employed, working for a friend, working for family, or working in the Healthcare field. The structural barriers within the criminal justice system and collateral consequences for being labelled a felon, made it very difficult for me to obtain gainful employment upon my release (McNair-Williams, 2019). After applying for over 50 jobs, I finally got hired at Patagonia Clothing for $12.65 an hour. I had not made that small amount of money since college, but I was so happy to be employed and once again being a productive citizen in my community. After three months I was summoned into an office where there were the Area Manager, Human Resource Manager and my Supervisor. The Area Manager informed me I was being fired because they were notified by someone on Facebook of my indictment. I will never ever forget his words to me when he stated, "We never would have hired you if we knew you had a record". I was appalled and heartbroken, not because I was losing the $12.65 an hour job, but mainly because this young man felt privileged to speak to me in such a dehumanizing and disgusting manner. I quickly gathered myself emotionally and regally told him that he was missing out because I am an incredible, wonderful woman and it was his company's loss. As I was escorted out of the Patagonia Clothing building, I kept telling myself don't cry. I kept my head up his and just left peacefully. As I walked to my car, I took three deep breaths and I thought about all that I had been through and survived. I got into my car, cried and returned home to my son.

I have memories that are still marred with questions, and a host of emotions associated with my incarceration. For the life of me, I can't understand the lack of humanity within our Criminal Justice System. I guess that will have to remain a question, one which has forever changed my life.

It is very difficult to explain to others the impact of Carceral Trauma has on me and many other women I know. It is not normal for a loving human, woman and mother to endure the insolence, pain and dehumanizing system without having some residual pain. When I speak about my journey it is not just about my time spent in prison. Most of my trauma was endured prior to being incarcerated, during my incarceration and within my re-entry. The realization that as a woman in America who did not have millions of dollars, I had little no value. I will never forget that for a period of time in America, I was not Dr. Cassandra Little, a community worker, mother, foster mother, sister, aunt, friend, academic or woman, I was just inmate 47078-048.

My time spent in prison allowed me to assess and reevaluate how to utilize my inherent strength, redirect my life passions and goals, and to stand up against the wrongful mass incarceration of women. elements that we, as persons in the United States, can begin to digest in efforts to induce necessary changes, to bring about healing for self and for our future generations. The impact of Mass Incarceration on women has a lasting imprint on their mental health, physical health, family relationships, employment outcomes and mental health (Cox, The Impact of Mass Incarceration on the Lives of African American Women, 2012). It is proven fact that when you incarcerate a woman you incarcerate the entire family.

REFERENCES

Altman, R. J. (2007). *The health of incarcerated women: An analysis of existing conditions and recommendations for future programs*. Retrieved from http://d-scholarship.pitt.edu/10135

Baldwin, J. (1963). *The Fire Next Time*. Dial Press.

Covington, S. S., & Bloom, B. E. (2003). *Gendered Justice: Women in the Criminal Justice System*. Carolina Academic Press.

Cox, R. (2012). The Impact of Mass Incarceration on the Lives of African American Women. *The Review of Black Political Economy*, *39*(2), 203–212. doi:10.100712114-011-9114-2

Davis, A. (2003). *Are prisons obsolete*. Seven Stories Press.

Davis, A., & Shaylor, C. (2001). Race, Gender, and the Prison Industrial Complex California and Beyond. *Meridians (Middletown, Conn.)*, *2*(1), 1–25. doi:10.1215/15366936-2.1.1

De-Bug, S. V. (2015). *East Palo ALto and Crack Epidemic That Tried to Kill the Black Family*.

Florida International. (2011, June 10). *Slavery and the Prison Industrial Complex-Angela Davis*. Retrieved from Youtube: https://www.youtube.com/watch?v=yQ2cC7LHMxA

Golden, D. (2013). The Federal Bureau of Prisons: Willfully Ignorant or Maliciously Unlawful? *Michigan Journal of Race & Law*, *18*(2), 275–294.

Goodwin, M. (2015). Invisible Women: Mass Incarceration's Forgotten Casualties. *Texas Law Review*, *94*(2), 353.

Görg, N., Priebe, K., Böhnke, J. R., Steil, R., Dyer, A., & Kleindienst, N. (2017). *Trauma-related emotions and radical acceptance in dialectical behavior therapy for posttraumatic stress disorder after childhood sexual abuse*. Retrieved from https://ncbi.nlm.nih.gov/pmc/articles/pmc5508787

HHS. (2018). *Medicaid Fraud Control Units*. HHS.

James, A. (2019). *Ending the Incarceration of Women and Girls*. The Yale Law Journal Review.

Kilpatrick, C. (1973). *Nixon Tells Editors, 'I'm Not a Crook'*. Washington, DC: The Washington Post.

Law, V. (2015). Pregnant and behind bars:How the US Prison System Abuses Mothers-to-be. *The Guardian*, 15.

Loader, I., & Sparks, R. (2014). Beyond mass incarceration. *The Good Society - PEGS, 23*(1), 114–120. doi:10.5325/goodsociety.23.1.0114

Lorde, A. (1984). *Sister Outsider:Essays and Speeches*. Crossing Press.

Love, M. C., & Shay, G. (2012). *Incarceration in the United States: Issues in America's Jails and Prisons: Gender & Sexuality in the ABA Standards on the Treatment of Prisoners*. Retrieved from https://papers.ssrn.com/sol3/papers.cfm?abstract_id=2063916

MacDonald, M. (2013). Women prisoners, mental health, violence and abuse. *International Journal of Law and Psychiatry, 36*(3), 293–303. doi:10.1016/j.ijlp.2013.04.014

McNair-Williams, S. S. (2019). *The Impact of a Felon's Overall Well-Being on Education, Employment, and Recidivism*. Retrieved from https://digitalcommons.liberty.edu/doctoral/2197

Rubino, E. P. (n.d.). *White Collar Crime - An Overview*. Retrieved 5 3, 2020, from https://www.frankrubino.com/CM/FSDP/PracticeCenter/Criminal-Law/White-Collar-Crime.asp?focus=overview

Sherman, R. (2019). *Understanding Mass Incarceration of African American Women*. Retrieved from https://wisc.pb.unizin.org/english100coursereader/chapter/understanding-mass-incarceration-of-african-american-women

Smyth, J. (2012). *Dual Punishment: Incarcerated Mothers and Their Children*. Retrieved from https://cswr.columbia.edu/article/dual-punishment-incarcerated-mothers-and-their-children

Turanovic, J. J., Rodriguez, N., & Pratt, T. C. (2012). The collateral consequences of incarceration revisited: A qualitative analysis of the effects on caregivers of children of incarcerated parents. *Criminology, 50*(4), 913–959. doi:10.1111/j.1745-9125.2012.00283.x

Chapter 5
The Causes Behind the Cause:
An Explanatory Analysis on Transgender Deviance in Dhaka, Bangladesh

Adiba Fannana
University of Ontario Institute of Technology (UOIT), Canada

ABSTRACT

Transgenders in Bangladesh are the most vulnerable group of people. This group of people are socially excluded and considered as deviant since British colonialism. The purpose of this study is to understand why they are considered as deviant as well as the reason of their deviant behavior and what are the acts done by them. Due to the importance of a few statements, in this chapter, "transgender" and "Hijra" are used and defined well. The difference between these two terms is clarified at the end of the chapter's literature review.

INTRODUCTION AND SIGNIFICANCE:

Transgenders in Bangladesh are the most vulnerable group of people, a biological being neither male nor female or sometimes both in one body. This group of people are socially excluded and do not enjoy any basic human rights comparing with the cis genders all around in this country. Prior researches show that the rate of sex trade, drug trafficking and extortion is getting high day by day among transgender people in Bangladesh. It means transgenders are involving in deviance at an alarming rate. The purpose of this study is to highlight the reasons behind this deviant behavior of transgenders all over in Bangladesh. This paper will answer the question of how social exclusion affects any transgender's life and creates a pathway towards deviance. The

DOI: 10.4018/978-1-7998-6646-6.ch005

study finds out that social exclusion comes from lack of proper knowledge regarding Transgenderity among Cis gender people in Bangladeshi society. In terms of being socially excluded, transgender community suffers from illiteracy and unemployment which indirectly force them to involve in illegal sex trade, extortion and drug trafficking as well. The sociological importance of this paper is to develop a precise idea through which people will be able to know why transgenders in Bangladesh involve in deviance. Research shows that, in Bangladesh gender diversity is not accepted warmly and this diverse group of people is continuously being a subject of humiliation, abuse, harassments and most often transgenders are being labeled as deviant. This labeling tendency makes them stigmatized and also narrow down their opportunities to choose healthy occupation for themselves. Most transgenders often claim that there are no other options left for them rather than involving in deviant activity to earn their daily bread. Independent variables here in this chapter are social exclusion, and labeling and the dependent variable is deviance. This paper concludes that understanding the reason of deviance will help to control deviance rate among transgenders in Bangladesh.

The unit of analysis in this research is the Bangladeshi transgender and cis genders individual, which is a micro level unit of analysis. The major concepts in this chapter are Transgender, Social Exclusion, labeling, Stigma, and deviance. Transgenders claim themselves neither male nor female; sometimes combine both in one body. They historically exist in Indian sub-continent and do not conform the traditional and social notion of gender identity. Normally they are known as Hijra in India, Bangladesh and Pakistan but they do have so many other names through which they are being addressed socially. Such as *Bakla* in Philippines, *Xaniths* in Oman, *Serrers* among Pokot people in Kenya and many more. Whatever the name they have but the meaning of their existence is, their biological orientation is different from their psychological gender belief. In India they are known as impotent man or barren woman, who has incomplete genital organ and cannot participate in reproduction. In Bangladesh, the concept is same. The use of the concept social exclusion in this paper focuses upon the rejection of a person or a group of people from participating in all social activity. As soon as the transgender identity disclose in their family they got abandoned. They become the victim of exclusion from their family first. All peers deny their blood relationship and so does the whole society. They cannot go to school and receive education; they don't have access to join social celebrations like Marriage. They do not enjoy even a single human right to lead a decent life. This exclusion causes high rate of illiteracy and unemployment among the transgenders in Bangladesh. According to Criminological explanation, deviance is any kind of act which is considered as a violation of norms including a formally enacted rule. In transgender group, there are many forms of deviances that they are involved with but among all those activities, showing threat on public to ask money is the most common one. Research shows that in some extreme level of public harassment, transgenders expose their genital or private body parts to those persons who refuse to give money. Most often, this trick of collecting money actually succeed. Moreover, illegal sex business, drug trafficking and different forms of extortion keep continuing in their whole life cycle. This paper finds out that transgenders in Bangladesh violet social norms and legal rules just to earn their livelihood. Comparing to any cisgender individual, most transgenders commit crime just to meet up their basic human needs. Here Cisgender can be defined as group of people who's biological and psychological gender identity is same. A definite male or a definite female is considered as Cisgender, according to Gender and sexuality education. Transgenders believe that outer world and the Cisgender community do not understand their culture and the natural logic of their existence. Most layman hates and scared of any Transgedner existence around him, just because of their deviant activity.

Literature Review

The socio–cultural notion regarding transgender is almost same in Indian Subcontinent including India, Bangladesh and Pakistan. Historically, these three countries were used to be known as same before 1947. Through the rule of the British for almost 200 years in that sub continent actually created some typical socio –cultural point of view among the residents and these notions are still the same. Negative outlook towards transgender mostly known as Hijra, is one of those notions that is still deep rooted in our society and which is really hard to discuss and describe in its true manner. The aim of this literature review is to find out some historical explanation of being Hijra. This part of the paper analyses that how historically the Hijra community is being neglected, why they are still the most marginalized group of people in Bangladesh, why they commit crime or involve in deviance and what are those particular type of crime that they usually commit historically.

Although my area of study is Dhaka, Bangladesh but for the sake of good historical explanation, this part will cover articles from India, Bangladesh and Pakistan context because without bringing these three countries explanations together, it is hard to understand where did we get the notion of Hijra from. Most of the people in Bangladesh neglect Hijra saying that they are the curse of the nature (*Common Gender,*2012). This is why this paper does the investigation regarding this statement to throw light on this age old socio –traditional notion. Literature review always helps to understand an issue from its historical context. The purpose of this review is to discover and realize the Hindu mythological explanation of Hijrahood so that this paper can encourage the reader to understand the Hijra origin and do further research on their deviance behavior and its reason in Bangladesh.

The history of transgenders in Indian Sub–Continent is same. In India, Bangladesh and Pakistan, transgenders are known as Hijra. No matter which country they are coming from and which religion they belong to, their deep rooted historical evolution is same. I found a clear explanation regarding transgenderity in Hindu mythology. S. Nanda (1986) explores that the hijra are commonly believed by the larger society to be intersexed, impotent man who undergo emasculation in which all or part of the genitals are removed. They adopt female dress and some other aspects of female behavior. The most common definition of Hijra in English publications is "eunuchs" or "hermaphrodites"(Chakrapani 2010; Hahm 2010). In both terms, impotence is the key concept to clarify the biological structure of Hijra. Either they remove their genital in latter life in terms of joining the Hijra group or they were born with incomplete genitals, one has to be impotent to consider as hijra, first (Nanda, 1984). The Master's thesis paper by Tahmima Habib says that Hijra are usually live or prefer to live the opposite gender of their biological sex. "Transgender" is often used as umbrella terms to signify individuals who denied binary gender construction and present a blurry of culturally prevalent stereotypical cultural role (Chakrapani 2010). In Bangladesh, the consideration of Hijra is quite critical. According to Chakrapani 2010, Hijra are biologically male but refuse their masculine identity in due course of time to identify as women or "not men". As they are preferring themselves as women and having sex with men, they are perceived by the society as homosexuals (Chakrapani 2010). Homosexuality in this part of explanation opens up a new door of information which is directly pointing out one of the deviant activity among Hijra. In Oman Hijra are known as *Xenith* but the core difference between hijra and xenith is, xenith is considered to marry and they are also at least potent but hijra are considered as impotent and not eligible for marriage (Nanda, 1984). In Oman having sex with xenith is "sinful but not deviant", but in India, Bangladesh and Pakistan, homosexual activities are considered as deviant and are a term to legally punished for (Nanda, 1984).

Discussion of Methods and Samples:

Secondary source is used to get conceptual, theoretical and historical information. Literature review worldwide, seemed the best option for this chapter because of the scarcity of enough research work based particularly on Bangladesh, under this research title. The study will be conducted through Questionnaire survey around several places in Dhaka, where transgenders mostly live. 5 in depth interviews, and three case study analysis is intended to be taken. WVS database will be using to code survey results. Cis gender samples are selected in a random sampling method and the samples are the residents of Dhaka city, Bangladesh. And in case of transgender sampling, Snow ball sampling will be using with the help of two non government organizations (NGO) placed in Bangladesh, "Shustho Jibon" and "Bondhu". The reason behind this snow ball sampling is, it is hard to get network of transgenders without having pre connection with any NGOs. These NGO will be helping to trace out the leaders of several transgender communities, who will convince the samples to take survey, give interview or to share their stories for case study as well.

The sampling frame of this study will be in two parts. One part is for cis gender samples, and it will be the areas of Uttara (Higher middle class society resides here), Gulshan area (Higher class society resides here), University of Dhaka campus (Highly educated community) and Kamalapur Slum area (lower class society resides here). From this four selected frames, samples would be selected randomly to avoid biasness and to get a good sample size for this study. Second part of sampling frame will be two NGO, placed in Dhaka city. A full list of transgender members in these two organizations will be selected to do snow ball sampling in order to get the actual transgender sample size as well.

Face to face interview will be the first delivery method in terms of conducting the research. As there are few questions like "have you ever committed any crime in your life", in terms of avoiding validity measurement error, telephone (mobile) interview may be a way of delivery method, depending upon the circumstance as well. I cannot use email in terms of surveying and interviewing Bangladeshi transgenders because most of them do not have access to internet over there.

Hypotheisis:

Hypothesis 1: Social exclusion causes high involvement in crime.
Hypothesis 2: Less institutional (family, school, religious places etc.) attachment creates the pathway to involve in crime.
Hypothesis 3: Lack of gender based education is increasing gender discrimination rate among transgenders in Bangladesh.

Findings:

1. **One shot case study:** One shot case study has been proposed to do the experiment. The diagram would be;

   X O
   Transgender subjects Cis Gender sbject (Compare group)

This experiment directly address hypothesis 2, "Less institutional (family, school, religious places etc.) attachment creates the pathway to involve in crime." Participants will first be providing the information of experiment, but not clarifying them about the hypothesis. Twenty transgender and twenty cis gender will be separated in two groups and will be asked to write down their life story. These stories then will be reviewed by the research team by careful reading and observing each and every statement in each case. It is assumed that, in their life history, they will mention about social exclusion, throwing out from family, being neglected by the society, victim of school bullying etc. Then two groups' case studies will be compared to determine the role of institution like family, school, religious institutions and many more.

Limitation: The main limitation of this experiment could be measuring the crime as the participants' occupation. In their case study they may be biased in terms of their occupation which will create low external and internal validity. To address this limitation, factorial survey would be conducted.

2. Vignette:

To test the first hypothesis, and to see the validity and reliability for experiment 01, developing *Vignette* is proposed to use because social judgment concepts like social exclusion and deviance can be fruitfully measured by vignettes (Willoughby et al, 2005). A passage indicating multiple dimensions will be given to participants and their response will be measured.

The same groups of respondents will be asking to participate in this experiment three days after the first experiment. This time span will help to see if there is any biased information in the case studies, received from the first experiment. A printed copy of vignette is proposed to provide every 40 participants on the 2nd experiment day. They will be asked to response on every factors depending upon the vignette dimensions. This may take hardly 25-30 minutes and after that the first and second experiment responses will be observed.

The vignette is as follows;

Rana is a 12 years teenager lives in Dhaka with his family, with two more siblings, a brother and a sister. He is the eldest son and so far doing very good in education and dance. He loves dancing and specially wearing make ups and jewelries like women. Because of his girlish attitude he often faces bully in school and feels like he cannot take it anymore. He is also a good student and love studying but he scares of being thrown out of his school anytime if everybody comes to know about his secret desire. He likes wearing his mom's saree and most often when he stays alone in house, he uses his sisters dupatta and make up kits to look more pretty. Yes, he doesn't want to see himself a "macho man" but a "pretty lady" in his young age. He does like to say his prayer but mostly with his mom, not going to mosque with his father. One day he wrote in his diary that, he feels like there is a female soul caged in his male body, and someday coming out from that closet, is his ultimate dream.

The vignette assessment question will ask the participants to make three judgments,, “disagree”, “agree”, “strongly agree” on 1-5 point scale where 1= disagree and 5=strongly agree. The higher the score will be, the higher the concern it will prove. The high score will be more likely to represent those participants’ attitude and concern towards their transgender friends or family member, they will socially exclude them or not and also the reaction of institutions regarding this transgenders’ social engagements like going to school and Mosque.

3. **Factorial analysis:** Factorial analysis in this stage of experiment is proposed to get clear outcome about social exclusion and rejection of transgenders from the society. After vignette assessment the same participants will be asked to fill up a factorial questionnaire containing 15 factorial questions which is related with the vignette mentioned above and those will be measured through scoring scale. Questions including factors are;

    a. Sexual relationship with Ratan disgust me.
    b. Sex change operations for Ratan are morally wrong.
    c. Ratan should change his behavior as soon as possible and do the study as his parents want him to do.
    d. If a friend like Ratan wants to go through emasculation process I would support him openly.
    e. Ratan who dresses as a woman is a sinful person.
    f. Ratans parents should exclude him from family if he does not change himself.
    g. Ratan also has sexual need like any male or female but he should change his behavior before to get married and have a healthy conjugal life.
    h. Ratan can be harmful for cis gender children in schools, mosques and madrasas.
    i. Ratan has to be either male or female to be able to complete his study.
    j. Ratan has to be either male or female to be able to claim for property right.
    k. Ratan has to be either male or female to be able to apply for decent jobs in Bangladesh.
    l. Ratan does not deserve to get a partner in his life unless he becomes either male or female.

Experiment 2 will bring the high external and internal validity in this research. These factors will describe the attitude towards a transgender in contemporary Bangladeshi society. Social exclusion can makes a transgenders life more complicated than we could have thought before and these factors will indicate those complexity by the higher scoring of each factors depending upon the vignette. It will help us to see in what extent transgenders are excluded from family and society and how less opportunities they have to earn money in decent way.

A pretest and post test experiment is suggested.This experiment will be conducted to see if gender education can decrease the rate of gender discrimination in Bangladesh. The same group of people will be the participants but this experiment will be done on the cis gender group only, to see any particular educational session can change their mind regarding transgender or not. Among 20 cis gender participants, 10 respondents will be selected randomly and they will be provided a short course for two months, on transgender issues like what is transgender, what are the medical conditions of transgenders, what religions say about them, their historical social status and how their became labeled during British colonials. Different types of presentations, seminars and symposiums will be arranged throughout this two months time span and the experiment will be given books, articles to read and assignments to done on those readings. After two months of short course, the same factors with same vignette will be analyzed with all 20 cis gender participants. It is proposed to observe the result of before experiment factorial survey and after experiment factorial survey, which will help to understand if there is any importance of gender education in terms of fighting against gender discrimination for transgenders in Bangladesh.

R O x O (10 cis gender in experiment)

R O O (10 cis gender out of experiment)

Fig: Diagram for experiment 03

DISCUSSION AND CONCLUSION:

We always try to see the gender identity around us only in two forms, male and female. Transgenders are such a group of people whose existence we really cannot deny or avoid. But they have been facing discrimination on the basis of their duel gender identity which is considered "confusing" to the cis gender people. From the introduction to experiment part of this proposal, I have been trying to focus only on one issue, that is even if transgenders are being considered as deviant in our society, but somehow the social structure, educational system and stereotypical mentality among cisgenders are responsible to force them to involve in deviance. Case studies will help to know the stories of each respondent by their own words. Cis gender group of respondents will also get opportunity to write down their privileges what they have enjoyed in their life so far just for having a definite gender identity. There is huge potentiality of their biased responses but to address this limitation three types of experiments are also proposed, so that the outcome we get, could be a set of solution to resolve transgender issues in Bangladesh. If we could bring fruit full outcome through this research project, potentiality for bringing sufficient policy changes in terms of transgender human rights establishment as well.

Throughout the study, transgender vulnerability has been observed. They are the group of people who is becoming the continuous victim and also involving in crime to earn their daily bread. They do not have any family accountability and social institutional involvement but they are being cursed for their biological existence. It has been observed that transgenders used to have good social status and get reputation but that scenario had been changed right after the British regulatory act. Since then the inhuman life for transgenders begins.

Transgender people are not like a gay or lesbian that we see around us. A gay has a definite male body but his psychological gender belief is different than his physical appearance. A lesbian has a definite female body but her psychological gender belief is just the opposite of her physical gender. Though gay, lesbian, cross dressers etc. all include in the list of transgender community members, but the transgenders are literally more vulnerable than any other gender disorder people. They go through mental trauma and physical confusion all the way of their lives and die with the deep desire to be a part of the community.

These three findings will show in what extent they are being socially excluded. This will also help us to see the connections between social boundlessness and illiteracy and unemployment which could be a reason for transgender deviance in Bangladesh. The result of this survey is to get high external and internal validity in this research. All social status respondents are being included to get the survey done. On the other hand case study, survey report and three types of experiments will help to get high internal validity. The questions in the questionnaire are valid. There are questions like the respondents have ever been thrown out from their family or not, how often they go to social institutions like Church, Mosques, Schools and many more, how many friends they have or how often they meet with their peers etc. is helpful to understand their family bonding, involvement in institutions or social liability to be good citizen. What type of occupation they are involved in is another criterion which will focus their deviant involvement as an occupation as well. There is no invalid questions that should not match with the hypothesis or that cannot go with the research topic or is unethical to ask.

As suggested by Kvale and Brinkmann (2009), validity is an essential concept regarding social research which encompasses the entire stages from the thematizing to producing a scientific report. Following this, the validity has been concerned during the whole process of this study. In line with that for this study, the subject and the interview project have been designed. Transgender population in Bangladesh is living under the poverty line and also less educated than any other transgender around the world. There is a huge question of validity in terms of dealing with such population of interest because to take interview I may have to pay them money for their time and information. To deal with such risk, Convergent Validity Assessment is intended to be done to accomplish research objective.

To deal with reliability, Test –Retest method will be using to measure reliability. In order to testing reliability, surveys will be done in two parts at both of the NGOs in Dhaka. After first survey, two weeks gap is planned to take prior to the second survey on same questionnaire with the same respondents as well.

Kvale and Brinkmann (2009) describes that an analytical generalizability can be applied on the basis of analysis of similarities and differences of situation. The respondents will be only from Dhaka city and the situation of Bangladeshi Trangenders are different from many other countries. So, the result which is going to be achieved through this research could not be generalized worldwide, in fact it would be generalized depending upon the challenging transgender situation and also the recommendations that might be taken after the research as well.

Ethical Consideration:

According to Kvale and Brinkmann (2009), informed consent, confidentiality, consequences and the role of the researcher are addressed as ethical guidelines. In line with this the ethical principles for social research have been considered in the report. Confidentiality and privacy had been ensured throughout the pre test, to all the respondents irrespective of transgender and cis gender respondents. Again this confidentiality and security concerns for transgenders in Dhaka will be assured through proper way.

REFERENCES

Aslam, M. (2009). *Education Gender Gaps in Pakistan: Is the Labor Market to Blame?* The University of Chicago Press.

Ferdaush, Jannantul, & Rahman. (2011). *Gender Inequality in Bangladesh, Unnayan Onneshan-The Innovators*. Christian Aid Trust.

Hossain, A. (2010). Bangladesh. In C. Stewart (Ed.), *The Greenwood encyclopedia of LGBT Issues Worldwide* (Vol. 1, pp. 333–346). Greenwood press.

Hossain, A. (2012). *Beyond Emasculation:Pleasure, Power and masculinity in the making of Hijrahood in Bangladesh* (PhD Thesis). University of Hull.

Khan, Hussain, M. I., Parveen, S., Bhuiyan, M. I., Gourab, G., Sarker, G. F., Arafat, S. M., & Sikder, J. (2009). Living on the Extreme Margin: Social Exclusion of the Transgender Population *(hijra)* in Bangladesh. *Health. Population and Nutrition*, *27*(4), 441–451. doi:10.3329/jhpn.v27i4.3388

Khan, S. I., Hudson-Rodd, N., Saggers, S., & Bhuiya, A. (2005). Men who have sex with men's sexual relations with women in Bangladesh. *Culture, Health & Sexuality*, *7*(2), 159–169. doi:10.1080/13691050412331321258

Khan, S. I., Hussain, M. I., Parveen, S., Bhuiyan, M. I., Gourab, G., Sarker, G. F., Arafat, S. M., & Sikder, J. (2009). Living on the extreme margin: Social exclusion of the transgender population (hijra) in Bangladesh. *Journal of Health, Population and Nutrition*, *27*(4), 441–451. doi:10.3329/jhpn.v27i4.3388

Nanda, S. (1984). The Hijras of India: Preliminary Report. *Medicine and Law*, *3*, 59–65.

Nanda, S. (1986). The Hijras of India. *Journal of Homosexuality*, *11*(3-4), 3–4, 35–54. doi:10.1300/J082v11n03_03

APPENDIX

TG: Transgender
BD: Bangladesh
UKS: Unnayan Kormo Shangsthan
F1: Findings 01
F2: Findings 02
F3: Findings 03
STD: Sexually Transmitted Disease
HIV: Human Immunodeficiency Virus
SKTN: Social Knowledge and Technology Network
DV: Dependent variable
IV: Independent Variable

Section 2

Global Approaches to Justice and Imprisonment

Chapter 6
Prisoner Re-Entry and Desistance

Luis F. Nuño
California State University, Los Angeles, USA

ABSTRACT

Prisoner reentry is a concept that examines the reality faced by formerly incarcerated men and women upon their release from a correction facility. A primary concern from the perspective of institutions within the criminal justice system is whether formerly incarcerated men or women return to prison. Re-incarceration is a signal that the institution has failed at rehabilitating the former convict, as well as signal of personal failure on the part of the ex-con. Prisoner reentry is much more complex than the idea of reincarceration after release from prison lets on. There is an abundance of research on the reentry experience. This chapter reviews some important findings relevant to our understanding of the prisoner reentry experience.

"PRISONER REENTRY AND DESISTANCE"

Prisoner reentry is a concept that examines the reality faced by formerly incarcerated men and women upon their release from a correction facility. A primary concern from the perspective of institutions within the criminal justice system is whether formerly incarcerated men or women return to prison. Re-incarceration is a signal that the institution has failed at rehabilitating the former convict, as well as signal of personal failure on the part of the ex-con. Prisoner reentry is a much more complex than the idea of reincarceration after release from prison lets on. There is an abundance of research on the reentry experience. Here I review some important findings relevant to our understanding of the prisoner reentry experience.

DOI: 10.4018/978-1-7998-6646-6.ch006

The structure of prison life is gone the moment a formerly incarcerated man or woman walks out through the prison gates to reenter free society. For many first-time convicts, entering prison is a daunting experience. All individuals sentenced to segregation inside correctional facilities must adjust to confinement in total institutions. The behavioral and attitudinal adaptations to prison life that Clemmer described as "prisonization" must be shed in the process of reentry to free society, otherwise further criminality is likely to occur (1950). Prisonization occurs as a result of the "pains of imprisonment," which is defined by a set of deprivations: loss of liberty, autonomy, goods-and-services, and heterosexual relationships (Sykes 1971). The shock to daily life defined by the conditions of confinement in a total control institution leads to behavioral and psychological adaptations to the social structure of prison life. There exist interesting debates in prisoner reentry literature about whether prisonization is imported from the code of the streets or exported to the streets from prison (Mears and Cochran 2014; Lopez-Aguado 2018.). The criminal lifestyle is understood as a disdain for conventional values. The attitudes and value system of the criminal lifestyle revolve around three central ideas: beating the system, living on the edge, and pursuit of fast money (Crank and Brezina 2013: 786-7). The attitudes and behavioral adaptations to prison life may impact the pathways for readjusting to free society. The process of reentry is shaped by real life trajectories present in an individual's life before, during, and after incarceration (Harding and Morenoff 2014; Harding, Morenoff, and Herbert 2013; Schnittker 2014). Here I review research literature on the impact of family, education, and employment on the pathways toward desistance.

Every year there are nearly one million formerly incarcerated men and women return to society after incarceration. It is important to understand how we assess prisoner reentry for policy and social justice purposes. If formerly incarcerated individuals are reentering free society for short periods, re-engaging in criminal activity that results in arrest, conviction, and return to prison, then we must reexamine the purpose of programming inside our correctional facilities. If, on the other hand, some individuals reenter society never to return to prison after serving a prison sentence, it is important to understand what went well in the reentry experience for those who desist from offending. Why do some ex-convicts return to prison and others reintegrate to free society? We do not know for certain why some formerly incarcerated men and women succeed at adapting in the transition from prison to freedom. There is a lot of research on the experiences of those that return to prison. In order to better assess this question, we must examine the different ways that researchers and policy officials approach the topic of recidivism.

Reentry and Recidivism

Key areas of research on the topic of prison reentry examine factors related to recidivism, which generally refers to the likelihood of a formerly incarcerated person returning to prison. However, conceptually, the topic of recidivism leaves many questions unanswered. Do we measure recidivism by type of offense committed? How long do we track ex-cons since their release from prison, one year, three years, five years? Do we measure only re-arrest for a similar offense or do we include re-arrests for different offenses? Does it matter if we include parole or probation violations in our measure of recidivism? Do misdemeanors count? One recent study on recidivism, for example, defined recidivism "measured as first felony conviction for a new offense within three years after prison release" (Mears, Cochran, Bales, and Bhati 2016: 98) The agencies that study recidivism have not reached a consensus about which definition of recidivism works best (Armstrong 2012: 4-5).

The Pew Center on States definition of recidivism includes committing a new crime that results in reconviction within three years since following release from prison, as well as violation of parole that results in a return to prison. Using this measure of recidivism, Pew reported on a comprehensive study on prisoner reentry across 23 states in August 2018 that recidivism rate decreased to 37% in 2012 from a high of 48% in 2005 (Gelb and Velázquez 2018). The Pew Center's perspective on recidivism leads us to conclude that approximately one out of three formerly incarcerated men and women returned to prison in 2012, which represents an improvement from 2005 when about one out of two ex-cons returned to prison within three years from release.

The Bureau of Justice Statistics measures recidivism as "criminal acts that result in the rearrest, reconviction, or return to prison with or without a new sentence during a three-year period following the prisoner's release" (Alper, Durose, and Markman 2018: 3). A 2018 study on recidivism published by the Bureau of Justice Statistics reports that the recidivism rate across 30 states between 2005-2013 is as high as 83% by looking solely at rearrest. Using this measure of recidivism would lead one to believe that prisons fail at rehabilitating offenders since more than eight out of ten ex-cons reengage in criminal offending resulting in arrest within three years from their release from prison. This definition overlooks the fact that some arrests do not result in conviction, much less resenting to prison.

The United States Sentencing Commission measures recidivism with a primary and secondary definition. The primary definition includes any one of these three events happening within two years of release from prison: reconviction for new offense; re-arrest with no conviction; violation of parole that results in return to prison. Their secondary definition limits recidivism to re-conviction only (U.S. Sentencing Commission 2004). The rationale for the varied definition of recidivism is to allow future researchers to use different aspects of the definition to suit their individual particular study, since access to data varies by region and state. In April 2020, the U.S. Sentencing Commission released a report that studied the impact of length of incarceration on recidivism, measured as return to prison. The report found that sentences of longer than 60 months had a deterrent effect on formerly incarcerated individuals. The likelihood of returning to prison is less likely for individuals that served sentences longer than 120 months. What is missing from this perspective is analysis of whether length of sentence is the variable that had a direct effect on desistance, as opposed maturity of the individual released from prison. A truism in criminology is that patterns of offending decrease as individuals age. There are many possible reasons for this: poor physical health resulting from years of alcohol and drug abuse; network of peers moved away, married, or became employed; cognitive development that comes with aging and maturity.

The National Institute of Justice defines recidivism in a more general, all-encompassing format. Recidivism includes behaviors that result in citations not leading to return to prison. (National Institute of Justice 2008). The National Institute of Justice includes behaviors that result in state interventions, such as drug treatment or counseling, in addition to state sanctions, such as "fines, community supervision and imprisonment" (Armstrong 2012: 4). From this perspective, then, recidivism would include measuring behaviors of formerly incarcerated individuals that never return to reside in a correctional facility. In light of other measures of recidivism, this definition seemingly includes its counting individuals that others would count as having desisted from offending.

In sum, there is agreement that it is an important policy decision to track formerly incarcerated individuals for some time period ranging from one year to five years since their release from prison. From a theoretical and policy perspective, researchers need to assess whether formerly incarcerated individuals are engaging in behavior that results in rearrest, reconviction, or resentencing to prison. Depending on how we measure recidivism, formerly incarcerated men and women return to prison at alarmingly high rates that suggest rehabilitative programs in prison fail or reincarceration rates for first-time offenders are low, which suggests that prison programs work. Recidivism is shorthand for returning to prison as a result of criminal reoffending. For some analysts the recidivism rate, or rate of return of ex-offenders back to state prison as high as seventy percent; prisons are carceral institutions that recycle the poor in spaces of confinement, first in the hyper-ghettoes of the modern metropolis, then in prisons spread across rural landscape (Wacquant 2010: 611). For others, the subject to recidivism is more problematic since there is little agreement about what we mean, as well as poor measuring instruments for distinguishing between different categories of the reentry population. Tonry shows, for example, that recidivism rate for first time prisoners is extraordinarily low: as many as two-thirds of people sent to prison for a first offense never return to serve a second sentence (2004: 186-187). A recent study of formerly incarcerated men and women in Boston shows the re-incarceration rate within one year from release is as low as eighteen percent (Western 2018: 122). Further, those who reoffend, are rearrested, reconvicted, and resentenced to a state prison, the likelihood of returning for a third or fourth stint in prison rises as high a slightly above seventy percent, the reverse of the recidivism rate for first time convicts (Tonry 2004: 187). Trapped in the logic of corrections, particularly the likelihood of rearrest, reconviction or return to prison sidesteps the important issue of desistance. Why do some ex-convicts desist from criminal activity?

Reentry and Desistance

A measure of the successful transition from prison to society is desistance. Desistance appears comparatively straightforward in relation to the concept of recidivism. When measuring desistance, researchers refer to the act of desisting from offending within a time period of typically five years from the time that one was released from prison. An interesting puzzle that researchers weigh when speaking about the topic of desistance is: What motivates formerly incarcerated men and women to desist from offending? What happens in the lives of some men and women that leads them to engage in patterns of behaviors that keep them from returning to prison? The search for insights on pathways toward desistance examines the interaction between structure and agency. To simplify the vast literature, I examine three main areas of research on desistance: family, education and employment. In the narrative below, I highlight relevant research findings in criminological and sociological literature that weigh in on the factors that motivate formerly incarcerated persons to desist from offending.

Here I review one hypothesis that is common in the research literature on desistance is the role of ties to institutions of informal social control: family, school, and work. First, I review some research on family bonds to explain the pathways toward desistance. Then I consider the research that test the function of ties to educational institutions in the pathways to desistance, particularly the pursuit of higher education for ex-convicts. I conclude with a summary of the research that highlights the role that ties to meaningful work in the transition to reentry for desistance.

Family

Most men in prison are fathers, brothers, and uncles. While in prison, some men feel the pains of imprisonment through social isolation and removal from the family home. Western notes that a common feature across the lives of men as they reenter society after incarceration is the presence of a mother, wife, daughter in their transition (2018). Crank and Brezina's survey research on anticipatory stigma management among incarcerated men in a Colorado correctional facility found that marital status at time of confinement had a "significant and positive impact on the perceived severity" of the prison sentence (793). For married men, the pains of imprisonment were more harshly felt than non-married incarcerated men. The findings suggest that individuals who perceive incarceration as painful are more likely to prepare for successful reentry and desist from of future offending. Married men and fathers are more likely to perceive segregation in a correctional facility as wasted time away from membership in a community of meaningful intimacy.

Education

For some incarcerated individuals, education can be transformative. The pursuit of higher education can transform mind and soul. Many prison education programs operate on the premise that transforming mind and soul during incarceration can improve the prospects for that individual to have a successful reentry to society. Men and women in prison are likely to have poor educational skills in quantitative and literary reasoning (Ellison, Szifris, Horan, and Fox 2017: 110). Educational opportunities allow incarcerated men and women to gain insight into their individual agency, as well as structural limitations impacting that agency. It is difficult to measure the impact of education as "a catalyst for change or enabler for change" (Ellison et al. 2017: 124). Nonetheless, much evidence suggests that prison education programs allow individuals to gain some control and self-efficacy in their pathways toward desistance (Ellison et al 2017; Runell 2017; Newbold, Ross, Jones, Stephens, and Lenza 2014).

Employment

It is widely recognized that ties to our occupational roles form our most meaningful identity as we adjust to the adult world of work. Central to California's rehabilitative efforts are programs inside correctional facilities designed to prepare men and women for a successful reentry by learning how to write a resume, search for work, and prepare for job interviews (Transition Program Curriculum, "Another Chance A Better Choice"). For young men incarcerated for offenses tied to financial struggles, obtaining meaningful work can be as transformative as becoming a father or graduating from college. Nevertheless, it remains true that employers hesitate to hire ex-felons (Pager 2007). Survey data on employers has shown, for example, that most employers would rather not hire formerly incarcerated men and women (Visher, Debus-Sherril, and Yahner 2011: 701). A felony conviction is a stigma marking a deviant behavior, which implies that the individual has made the choice to engage in that stigmatizing behavior. Winnick and Bodkin (2008) study how male prisoner anticipate handling the stigma of a felon label. They found that a successful reentry requires a combination of individual agency with structural opportunities. The larger society interprets the mark of a criminal record as the stigma of offending behavior, which is different from the stigma of physical disability. A deviant condition is something over which the individual has little to no control over, whereas deviant behavior is something resulting from choices an individual makes. A pervasive challenge for the ex-convict reentering society is finding meaningful employment. What does the research show about the role of work in encouraging desistance?

Western's study of formerly incarcerated men and women in Boston suggests that the role of employment in desistance is complicated (2018). Visher, Debus-Sherril, and Yahner found that "most men could not be characterized as having found a steady job with sufficient income to support themselves and any dependent family members" eight months after release from prison (2017: 209). It does not take long for ex-convicts reentering society to confront the very real discrimination against their ex-felon status. The complex realities of money-making opportunities after incarceration make it difficult to assess the significance of work in motivating desistance. Many parolees are paired with temp agencies in their transition to free society. While these employment agencies possess the intent to assist an ex-convict to develop structure and routine necessary to find success in free society and the adult world of work, the harsh reality is that the jobs offered by temp agencies pay poorly, come with limited benefits, and require a lot of patience for one to see fruitful gains that come only after moving on to more permanent employment with higher pay.

In Western's Boston Reentry Study, those formerly incarcerated men and women with the highest success in desistance were the few who gained meaningful employment in a skilled trade. The role of programming inside correctional facilities did not have much of a factor in the transitions to desistance. Those who found meaningful work did so through family contacts. Meaningful work was obtained through union jobs. The reentry population that found greatest success in their transition to desistance were primarily white men over age forty, working union jobs where they earned more than $28,000 a year. Black and Latino men earned $5,000 less that white men in the reentry study. Most nonwhites were relegated to "minimum wage work and thus remained dependent on family support or public assistance" (Western 2018: 98-99). Visher et al's study on employment after prison found similar results (2017: 711).

Successful Desistance Signaling

Strategies for reentering society after incarceration may be about more than family, education, and work. Individual agency plays a role. Circumstances under which individuals can exercise agency are limited by harsh conditions of physical disability, mental illness, or addiction to drugs or alcohol. "Research estimates that approximately two thirds of ex-prisoners remain unemployed for up to 3 years after their release from prison" (Maruna 2012: 750). Desistance may be about more than simply finding one factor causing success. For Maruna, desistance is a strategy. A successful desistance strategy requires work, not necessarily family support, educational attainment, or employment alone. The successful desister identifies as an agent of change and performs the role of the desister. In psychology, one might refer the successful desistance strategy as self-efficacy. Self-efficacy is the confidence to overcome challenges by exercising agency to identify pathways for success. The ability to exercise agency in some respects also means performing a hustle to make things work. The successful desister signals to others that one has embraced a new role as a change agent, beginning with the initiation of change within oneself.

While agency is important on the pathways toward desistance, it is equally important to recognize the impact of structure confronting agency. Prisons in the age of mass incarceration serve a dual purpose as places of confinement for individuals convicted of a criminal offense and places of treatment for individuals lacking educational credentials, or access to mental health and addiction services. Race plays an important role in shaping the reentry experiences of men and women exiting America's prisons. Black and Latino men and women leaving prison face challenges tied to their structural disadvantages rooted in decades of segregation (Lopez-Aguado 2018; Western 2018; Rios, Carney, and Kelekay 2017: 502-3). Whites, on the other hand, face challenges tied to "the deficits of support for the health problems of mental illness and drug addiction" (Western 2018: 169). To understand the pathways toward desistance for prisoner reentry, our focus should remain on interactions between agency, history, and structure. Meaningful belonging in a community requires the desire to participate on the part of the desister and the willful embrace on the part of the community.

REFERENCES

Alper, M., Durose, M. R., & Markman, J. (2018). *2018 Update on Prisoner Recidivism: A 9-Year Follow-Up Period (2005-2014)*. Available at https://www.bjs.gov/index.cfm?ty=pbdetail&iid=6266

Armstrong, B. (2012). Notes on Recidivism. *Alaska Justice Forum, 28*(4), 4-5.

California Department of Corrections and Rehabilitation. (2015). *Transition Program Curriculum, "Another Chance A Better Choice" Part 1: Participant Guide*. Division of Rehabilitative Programs, Office of Offender Services.

Clemmer, D. (1950). Observations on Imprisonment as a Source of Criminality. *The Journal of Criminal Law and Criminology*, *41*(3), 311–319. doi:10.2307/1138066

Crank, B. R., & Brezina, T. (2013). 'Prison Will Either Make Ya or Break Ya': Punishment, Deterrence,and the Criminal Lifestyle. *Deviant Behavior*, *34*(10), 782–802. doi:10.1080/01639625.2013.781439

Dilts, A. (2014). *Punishment and Inclusion: Race, Membership, and the Limits of American Liberalism*. Fordham University Press.

Ellison, M., Szifris, K., Horan, R., & Fox, C. (2017). A Rapid Evidence Assessment of the effectiveness of prison education in reducing recidivism and increasing employment. *Probation Journal*, *64*(2), 108–128. doi:10.1177/0264550517699290

Gelb, A., & Velázquez, T. (2018). *The Changing State of Recidivism: Few People Going Back to Prison.* Available at https://www.pewtrusts.org/en/research-and-analysis/articles/2018/08/01/the-changing-state-of-recidivism-fewer-people-going-back-to-prison

Harding, D. J., Morenoff, J. D., & Herbert, C. W. (2013). Home Is Hard to Find: Neighborhoods, Institutions, and the Residential Trajectories of Returning Prisoners. *The Annals of the American Academy of Political and Social Science*, *647*(1), 214–236. doi:10.1177/0002716213477070

Hay, C., & Meldrum, R. (2016). *Self-Control and Crime Over the Life Course*. Sage Publications. doi:10.4135/9781483397726

Lopez-Aguado, P. (2018). *Stick Together and Come Back Home: Racial Sorting and the Spillover of Carceral Identity*. University of California Press. doi:10.1525/california/9780520288584.001.0001

Maruna, S. (2012). Elements of Successful Desistance Signaling. *Criminology & Public Policy*, *11*(1), 73–86. doi:10.1111/j.1745-9133.2012.00789.x

Mears, D., & Cochran, J. C. (2016). *Prisoner Reentry in the Era of Mass Incarceration*. Sage Publications.

Mears, D. P., Cochran, J. C., Bales, W. D., & Bhati, A. S. (2016). Recidivism and Times Served in Prison. *Criminology*, *106*(1), 81–122.

Morenoff, J. D., & Harding, D. J. (2014). Incarceration, Prisoner Reentry, and Communities. *Annual Review of Sociology*, *40*(1), 411–429. doi:10.1146/annurev-soc-071811-145511

National Institute of Justice. (2008). *Measuring Recidivism*. Available at https://nij.ojp.gov/topics/articles/measuring-recidivism

Newbold, G., Ross, J. I., Jones, R. S., Richards, S. C., & Lenza, M. (2014). Prison Research From the Inside: The Role of Convict Autoethnography. *Qualitative Inquiry*, *20*(4), 439–448. doi:10.1177/1077800413516269

Pager, D. (2007). *Marked: Race, Crime, and Finding work in an Era of Mass Incarceration*. The University of Chicago Press. doi:10.7208/chicago/9780226644851.001.0001

Rios, V. M., Carney, N., & Kelekay, J. (2017). Ethnographies of Race, Crime, and Justice: Toward a Sociological Double-Consciousness. *Annual Review of Sociology*, *43*(1), 492–513. doi:10.1146/annurev-soc-081715-074404

Runell, L. L. (2017). Identifying Desistance Pathways in a Higher Education Program for Formerly Incarcerated Individuals. *International Journal of Offender Therapy and Comparative Criminology*, *61*(8), 894–918. doi:10.1177/0306624X15608374

Schnittker, J. (2014). The Psychological Dimension and Social Consequences of Incarceration. *The Annals of the American Academy of Political and Social Science*, *651*(1), 112–138. doi:10.1177/0002716213502922

Sykes, G. (1971). *The Society of Captives: A Study of a Maximum Security Prison*. Princeton University Press. (Original work published 1958)

Tonry, M. (2004). *Thinking About Crime: Sense and Sensibility in American Penal Culture*. Oxford University Press.

United States Sentencing Commission. (2004). *Measuring Recidivism: The Criminal History Computation of the Federal Sentencing Guidelines*. Available at https://www.ussc.gov/sites/default/files/pdf/research-and-publications/research-publications/2004/200405_Recidivism_Criminal_History.pdf

United States Sentencing Commission. (2020). *Length of Incarceration and Recidivism*. Available at https://www.ussc.gov/sites/default/files/pdf/research-and-publications/research-publications/2020/20200429_Recidivism-SentLength.pdf

Visher, C. A., Debus-Sherrill, S. A., & Yahner, J. (2011). Employment After Prison: A Longitudinal Study of Former Prisoners. *Justice Quarterly*, *28*(5), 698–718. doi:10.1080/07418825.2010.535553

Wacquant, L. (2010). Prison reentry as myth and ceremony. *Dialectical Anthropology*, *34*(4), 605–620. doi:10.100710624-010-9215-5

Western, B. (2018). *Homeward: Life in the Year After Prison*. Russell Sage Foundation. doi:10.7758/9781610448710

Winnick, T. A., & Bodkin, M. (2008). Anticipated Stigma and Stigma Management Among Those to be Labeled 'Ex-Con'. *Deviant Behavior*, *29*(4), 295–333. doi:10.1080/01639620701588081

Chapter 7
Resisting the New Punitiveness:
Penal Policy in Denmark, Finland, and Norway and Contrary Trends in Ireland

Kevin Warner
University College Cork, Ireland

ABSTRACT

This chapter builds on PhD research into the penal policies of Nordic countries and in particular Denmark, Finland, and Norway. Essentially, the investigation asked whether the increase in punitiveness in relation to prison systems that is presumed to occur under the 'culture of control' of late modernity can be found in these countries. The scale of imprisonment, the 'depth' of imprisonment, and the perception of the person imprisoned were all examined. The prison systems were investigated through analysis of documentation and recorded interviews with key personnel, supplemented by visits to a representative range of prisons. While there have at times been some signs of 'new punitiveness', especially in Denmark and Norway, in general it can be said that none of the Nordic countries have followed the path predicted by Garland.

INTRODUCTION

The first part of this chapter probes what Garland's analysis implies for prisons, and suggests that penal developments under the 'culture of control' can be identified via three key criteria. Each of these criteria is then studied in the three Nordic countries

DOI: 10.4018/978-1-7998-6646-6.ch007

that are focused on, with occasional reference also to Iceland or Sweden: the scale of imprisonment, the depth (or quality or content) of imprisonment, and the representation or perception of people held in prison. A concluding section contrasts these Nordic patterns with what has happened in penal policy and practice in Ireland over the past quarter of a century. Ireland's penal system had much in common with Nordic countries until the mid-1990s, especially its penal 'philosophy' and a similar level of incarceration, although its prison conditions have generally lagged well behind. However, Ireland has recently diverged considerably from Nordic norms, exhibiting many of the features Garland describes.

Garland's 'Culture of Control'

Three Summary Criteria of Punitiveness

In *The Culture of Control* (2001), Garland sets out 12 'indices' of the change he sees in the overall crime control field. Most of these relate to imprisonment, in particular a switch in aims from rehabilitation to retribution and protection, penal populism, a steep rise in incarceration, greater emphasis on control and less on offering assistance, and negative characterisation of people involved in crime - "stereotypical depictions of unruly youth, dangerous predators and incorrigible career criminals" (Garland, 2001, p.10). Pratt *et al's* (2005) term 'the new punitiveness' encapsulates well these purported new trends.

The Garland indices relevant to imprisonment can be consolidated into the three criteria of punitiveness already mentioned: the scale and depth of imprisonment, and the representation of the prisoner. Thus, for example, *the scale* is affected by the change to retributive and protection functions, as well as by the assertion that 'prison works'. *The depth* is shaped by the vengeful attitudes incorporated in Garland's second index, "punitive sanctions and expressive justice" (2001, p.8), as well as by the change in criminological thinking from a welfare-focused to a controlling perspective. Almost all indices impact on *the way the person held in prison is seen:* whether as part of society, as implied by an inclusive concept of rehabilitation, or as in the negative stereotypes often painted in politics or the media; whether one-dimensionally as an 'offender', as suggested by much of the new managerialism, or more broadly as "the whole person bearing in mind his or her social, economic and cultural context" (Council of Europe, 1990, p.8).

Penal Welfarism

It is important to note what it was this 'new punitiveness' (Pratt *et al*, 2005) or 'culture of control' was presumed to have replaced. Garland refers to the earlier outlook as 'penal welfarism', a broad paradigm that held sway for most of the twentieth century. Key attitudes in this paradigm included seeing prison as a last resort, wanting to minimise security and 'normalise' life within prison, and regarding people in prison as members of society. The "basic axiom" of penal welfarism was "that penal measures ought, where possible, to be rehabilitative interventions, rather than negative retributive punishments" (Garland, 2001, p.34). Garland sees penal welfarist features as "part of the wider scheme of things… integral elements of the post-war welfare state and its social democratic politics" (p.28). Penal welfarism assumed that "*the state was to be an agent of reform as well as repression, of care as well as control, of welfare as well as punishment*" (p.38, emphasis in original) and "claimed to bring all individuals into full social citizenship with equal rights and equal opportunities" (p.46).

Garland stresses that, in the new crime control field, "new practices and mentalities co-exist with the residues and continuations of older arrangements" (p.167). However, the 'penal mode' of penal welfarism has become "more prominent… more punitive, more expressive, more security-minded…The welfare mode, as well as becoming more muted, has become more conditional, more offence-centred, more risk conscious" (p.175). Those who commit offences are "less likely to be represented in official discourse as socially deprived citizens in need of support. They are depicted instead as culpable, undeserving and somewhat dangerous." (p.175)[1] Clearly, then, the punitive developments Garland speaks of are relative rather than absolute and refer to significant *changes in emphasis* in penal policy.

Measuring Severity

This chapter will explore the three criteria of punitiveness in the Nordic countries thematically. The scale of imprisonment and aspects of the 'depth' are amenable to quantitative examination. The rate of incarceration (the prison population per 100,000 of a country's population) is widely accepted as a broad-brush-stroke measurement of penal severity. However, the depth of imprisonment is more difficult to assess, having both quantitative and qualitative aspects.

Tangible features which indicate the depth of a prison system are, for example:

- the physical arrangements in cells, and whether these are shared or not;
- the amount of time spent out of cells;
- the extent of structured activity (work, education, therapy, sport, etc.);
- the extent of prison leave;
- the proportion in open prisons.

In assessing such features in Denmark, Finland and Norway, information came variously from documentation, as a result of specific enquiries, or during prison visits or interviews. The more qualitative aspects of the content of imprisonment, crucial to how people might experience imprisonment, were explored particularly in interviews and assessed on visits to prisons.

The third criterion, whether people in prison are seen inclusively or exclusively in relation to society, is the most difficult to assess. Inferences of inclusion or otherwise were drawn from what interviewees said, from criminological or other literature, from policy or political statements and from particular practices. For example, one can take as indicative of an inclusive attitude the presence of strong policy in relation to resettlement, while indications in another direction can be gleaned from the use of demonising or other negative language.

The Scale of Imprisonment

Garland built his analysis of the emergence of a culture of control, and, within that broader context, greater severity in penal matters, on developments in the USA and Britain in the late twentieth century. His presumption was that new patterns in crime control in America and Britain would sooner or later apply "elsewhere in the developed world" (Garland, 2001, p.viii). A core question for this research, then, was whether such trends could be found in Nordic countries.

While the USA's rate of incarceration of 655 is notorious, much lower rates of 140 for England and Wales and 149 for Scotland still stand out as among the highest in Western Europe.[2] Levels of imprisonment have risen enormously in the US since 1973, and in Britain since1993. By comparison with Britain, or even with Ireland, the Nordic countries incarcerate far fewer people. Recent rates of incarceration (per 100,000 of the country's population) and prison populations are:

Denmark **63** 3,635
Finland **53** 2,910
Norway **60** 3,190
Sweden **61** 6,210
Ireland **85** 4,209

It may be noted that, while Ireland has a lower general population than all the above countries, its prison population exceeds the numbers held in prisons in each of Denmark, Finland and Norway by considerable amounts.

Denmark

While prison numbers in Denmark have risen occasionally, its rate of incarceration has generally remained in the low 60s per 100,000 for the past 25 years. Punitive impulses have come from the political field at times, leading to some increased sentences, a clampdown on drugs and restrictions on prison leave, but these have tended to be offset by alternatives to custody, supportive drug treatment and a policy which enables many to be released ahead of the conventional two-thirds point of sentence. Such balancing features derived mainly from a coherent 'philosophy' among those running the prison system, an outlook that is very much penal-welfarist in the manner described earlier in the chapter.

Lappi-Seppala explains how sometimes Nordic countries pronounce punitive policies, but then more quietly soften these by introducing alternatives to custody, and his description is particularly relevant to Denmark:

A functional differentiation seems to prevail between sanctions policies and criminalization policies. Reforms in specific offences tended to lead in a more severe direction, whereas the changes made in the system of sanctions mostly had the opposite effect. In many cases, changes and innovations in the system of sanctions functioned as a safety valve, easing the pressure created by politically motivated reforms in the realm of criminalization. (Lappi-Seppala, 2007, p.219)

Finland

In Finland too, there have been some longer sentences for certain sex, drugs and violent offences, but these greater punishments were limited in scope and more than offset by the drive to find alternatives to custody, such as the development of community service and the virtual abolition of prison for non-payment of fines. Finland's prison population has fallen almost continually from a high level just after World War Two – except for an upward swing from 1999 to 2005, which then turned decisively downwards again. Esa Vesterbacka, the Director General, spoke in interview in 2007 of additional alternatives being introduced, such as conditional early release and electronic monitoring. These have clearly been effective, with the rate falling from 67 in 2007 to 59 in 2011, and to 53 in early 2020. Reducing prison numbers is a government objective.

Nils Christie says: "Finland's penal history illustrates that prison figures are not created by crime, but by cultural/political decisions… laws were changed, fines used more often, prisons less" (2000, pp.53-54). He credits much of the responsibility for this to "the intellectual-administrative elite" with responsibility for crime policy. In relation to the uncharacteristic rise in prison numbers for a period in the early years of the century, Esa Vesterbacka noted that a refusal by the Ministry of Finance to a request for more prison spaces at that time was a positive thing. The Finance Ministry's view was that it was better to reduce the prison population. Acknowledging that there is a tendency for any given prison capacity to be soon filled up, Esa Vesterbacka compared this to a lack of cupboard space in one's kitchen at home – when new cupboards are acquired they are quickly filled up also!

Norway

Prison populations rose in Norway at certain times this century to a rate of incarceration in the low 70s, but dropped again to a rate of 60 in 2019. One may find traces of Garland's indices of punitiveness in Norway in some longer sentences and a stress on protecting the public. However, the latter idea leads not to more imprisonment as Garland describes, but to a commitment to offer help towards change and resettlement. This is evident in the government's White Paper on punishment (Norwegian Ministry of Justice and the Police, 2008), which is notable for its strong focus on a socially-inclusive concept of rehabilitation and its recognition that this is best achieved outside prison or in open prisons. The political and administrative leadership declared a commitment to reduce prison numbers via alternatives to custody and early releases, a strategy that has clearly been put into effect over the past decade.

The Depth of Imprisonment

The physical conditions of imprisonment and the way people in prisons are treated are also indicators of penal severity. Evans and Morgan say:

Countries with the lowest incarceration rates tend also to have the shallowest systems, that is a high proportion of prisoners in small, relatively open institutions with liberal regimes. Rising incarceration rates tend to be accompanied by the growth of more restrictive prison regimes. This... reflects a political will to get 'tough on crime'. (1998, p.325)

Former British Home Secretary, Michael Howard's, promulgation in 1993 of twin punitive concepts ('prison works' and 'austere prisons') is an illustration of how the scale and depth of imprisonment tend to move together. This section will examine a number of factors which appear to contribute to the 'shallow' character of Nordic prisons, including the high usage of open prisons, the tendency to have small prisons and other important regime features. The discussion will be illustrated by reference to particular prisons.

Open Prisons

An important indicator of the depth of imprisonment is the extent to which sentences are served in open prisons. There is a widely held view in Nordic countries that open prisons have fewer detrimental effects and better facilitate reintegration. The operation of an open prison relies substantially on relationships and on the prisoner's sense of responsibility, rather than on physical restraints. Denmark holds 30 per cent of its total prison population in open centres, Finland also 30 per cent, and Norway 34 per cent (Kristoffersen, 2019). This contrasts sharply with Ireland, where the rate is less than 6 per cent.[3] Thus, each of these Nordic countries has *at least five times* the proportion in open institutions as Ireland. These figures include remand prisoners, but when one looks only at *sentenced* prisoners in Denmark, it transpires that a large majority are in open rather than closed institutions – 55 per cent in the latest available figures (Kristoffersen, 2019). As well as being seen to have fewer detrimental effects, Nordic officials report that the cost of holding someone in an open prison is about half that of a closed prison.

Small Prisons

Nordic prisons tend to be small relative to most other Western countries, with no prison in any Nordic country holding more than 400.[4] The average population in a prison is approximately 77 in Denmark, 120 in Finland, 89 in Norway and 79 in Sweden – in contrast to Ireland, where the average prison size is 350.[5] The general assumption is that such smaller institutions will have less institutionalisation, restriction and bullying. Having more small prisons rather than fewer large ones also means more of those in prison can be held near their homes and families. Such thinking is taken furthest in Iceland, where the average prison holds 26 (a population of 131 in five prisons). Iceland's former Assistant Director of the Prison Administration, Erlendur Baldursson, says that "small institutions function better" because "the problems that emerge, and there are problems in all prisons, are more visible and can therefore more easily be discussed and solved" (Baldursson, 2000, p.7). His idea of smallness is an institution with 10 to 20 places, which describes four of Iceland's five prisons. The one 'large' prison in his eyes was Litla Hraun, (which had 87 places at the time of this author's visit in 2013), and where Baldursson had seen "increasing levels of traditional problems", such as drug abuse and personal conflicts (Baldursson, 2000, p.8).[6]

Regime features

Other notable aspects of regimes for those serving sentences in Denmark, Finland and Norway are:

- single-cell accommodation for almost all men and women in prison;
- proper and private sanitation arrangements

- out-of-cell time that is generally 12 to 14 hours, with strong activity such as work, training, education and therapy;
- an increasing tendency to facilitate 'self-management' whereby those in prison carry out their own daily tasks such as cooking and cleaning;
- substantial temporary prison leave;
- sentence planning and a concomitant willingness to release people from prison early;
- substantial drug treatment;
- very few young people imprisoned.

This picture will be elaborated on below, in particular via portraits of particular prisons and details from interviews with officials.

Denmark – East Jutland prison

Despite an increased emphasis on security and a recent reduction in prison leave in Denmark, the 'depth' of prison remains very contained, best exemplified by the high proportion in open prisons. However, examining the relatively new high-security closed prison of East Jutland is just as revealing. It opened in October 2006, holds 228 and is situated amid farmland and rolling hills which can be seen from most parts of the prison. A principle in the construction of East Jutland was that there should be "scattered, low buildings toning down the institutional impression". Although it has the highest security in Denmark, there is a sense of space inside, not just in the way the perimeter wall is modulated to afford views to the countryside beyond, but within the walls also, where there is a high ratio of open space to buildings.

There are five accommodation sections spaced apart, A to D each comprising 48 places, and E, which holds 36 and has the highest security. D is dedicated to full-time drug treatment. Those held in the prison may traverse the central area between sections several times a week, walking past the football field and lake to a central building or 'culture centre', which holds a sports hall, church, library and a self-service shop where groceries and personal accessories can be purchased. Security is strong and regarded as the highest in any prison in Denmark, with a high perimeter wall and a fence beyond that, and 200 CCTV cameras.

Living spaces, which look like good-quality student accommodation, are made up of units of six single rooms grouped around a well-equipped kitchen, sitting area, laundry facilities and a balcony. Prisoners have keys to their own rooms and staff have keys to second outside locks used to close doors at 9.30pm. Rooms measure12.5 square meters, including a separate bathroom, and each has a sofa-bed, desk, chair, television, clear unbreakable glass windows and an air-vent. Each six-room unit opens on to a lobby area shared with other units, where there are recreational facilities.

As in other Danish prisons, men and women mix, although a woman may opt to be in a single-sex unit. There are usually fewer than eight women in East Jutland, the vast majority of imprisoned women in Denmark being in open prisons. At the time of this author's visit in 2008, the staff-to-prisoner ratio was 1.14 to 1.[7]

While security is relatively high, in many ways the prison day within East Jutland is similar to that in other Danish prisons, including open prisons. Out-of-cell time is 14.5 hours per day, from 7am to 9.30pm. Those in prison must be in occupation for over seven hours each day, making up the 37-hour week. From 3.30pm to 9.30pm, they are free to go about their daily tasks – shopping, washing, cooking, eating, recreating. They may spend this time outdoors if they wish. Work is similar to that offered elsewhere in Danish prisons, such as the processing of textiles, metal, wood or paper. Education consists, as elsewhere, of normal adult education courses. There are programmes such as anger management, as well as drug treatment.

The same effort to create as much normality as possible is evident in visiting facilities. There are 14 standard visiting rooms, each fairly similar to the prisoner's own room, with arm-chairs and a coffee-kettle in addition. There are also two 'visiting flats' where a family can come to stay with the person in prison for a day or two. Each of these has a double-room for adults, another room with bunk-beds for children, a kitchen/dining/sitting area, and an opening on to a small courtyard. All these visiting facilities adjoin a garden area which includes some children's play facilities.

East Jutland has managed to reconcile the imperatives of 'care' and 'custody', or what long-time Director General, William Rentzmann, called *"the soft and the hard"*, opposites that are notoriously difficult to hold in balance. A high level of security has been achieved while also doing justice to the progressive principles that govern life in Danish prisons[8] – relating activities in the prison to normal life in the community, achieving a measure of openness and enabling those in prison to take responsibility for at least some aspects of their own lives.[9]

Finland

In interview, the Finnish Director General, Esa Vesterbacka, was frank in detailing the shortcomings of his prison system. His points related mainly to structural issues: the then continuing practice of 'slopping out', which still affected close to 500 people in prison in 2007 and was slowly being phased out; the sharing of cells which affected '*a couple of hundred*'; insufficient drug treatment; the confinement of a small number of sentenced prisoners (in '*tens*' rather than '*hundreds*') to cells for up to 23 hours a day, mainly because of fear of other prisoners; and the lack of a full day's activity for many in prison. Thus, while physical conditions in Finland may not match those in Denmark, the prisons are less subject to the new restrictions experienced in the latter. So, while there are shortcomings in Finnish prisons, there appears to be steady, if slow, improvement, enhanced by a new sentence-planning process.

Resettlement is a key concept, with a stress on social supports. Housing, unemployment, drugs, alcohol and mental health are seen as the main challenges in ensuring successful reintegration. The recognition of the social dimension here corresponds to a phrase that is often cited in Finland: 'Good social policy is best criminal policy.' Clearly, the management of the prison system have an inclusive view of people in prison, regarding them as full members of society, an issue to be explored further later in the chapter.

Norway

Conditions for most people held in prison in Norway are relatively good, illustrated by an average of 13 hours out-of-cell time for those serving sentences, a strong range of activities such as work and education, and virtually none of the substandard sanitation that characterises many systems. The former Director General, Kristen Bolgen Bronebakk, spoke of a need to differentiate more between types of prisoners, suggesting "*a stricter regime*" for "*the organised crime group*", who are clearly seen as a small minority, while recognising that drug-users "*are not really a threat to society, more a threat to themselves*". The 2008 White Paper repeats this dual approach: "Some convicted persons will require stricter regimes, others more open. The Government will deploy measures along both these tracks" (Norwegian Ministry of Justice and the Police, 2008, Part 5). Overall, however, it is clear that in this policy document the government envisaged improved regimes for most prisoners, and a significant increase in the proportion in open prisons.

Despite some curtailment over a decade ago, prison leave is more substantial than elsewhere. Major cities have halfway houses from which those in prison go to education or work on the outside during the day. In addition, a person in prison normally gets home leave after serving one-third of the stated sentence. The norm then is 18 days leave per year in a closed prison and 30 days in an open, although many will transfer from a closed to an open institution at the one-third point. They pay for travel home themselves.[10] Approximately 25,000 leaves were given in 2005; less than 0.5 per cent defaulted, including late returns.

Asked to identify the strengths and weaknesses of the prison system, the Director General said the main weaknesses related to the isolation of, and lack of activity for, many pre-trial prisoners, and the confinement of a small number of high-security prisoners. She identified as the key qualities of Norwegian prisons:

The personnel. And the emphasis put on treating everybody with respect, not using more harsh methods than absolutely necessary. I think when you visit a prison in Norway, what people say to me afterwards is that they note the atmosphere and the relationship between inmates and security officers…Security officers are not locked into their own cubicle, they are out there together with inmates.[11]

The role envisaged for prison staff is centred on relating to prisoners, captured in the official slogan that reflects a decision to change the emphasis of their work: "from guard to social worker – a paradigm shift".[12] This changed role is particularly evident for the 'personal officer' (also called 'contact officer'), who has the responsibility for supporting usually no more than three people in prison in dealing with their sentences and planning their futures.

Bastoy Open Prison

The open prison on the island of Bastoy has achieved some fame within the Norwegian prison system and beyond, and is referred to in the recent White Paper as a model to be copied elsewhere. It is run on "*ecological principles*" and the idea that (as the Governor, Oyvind Alnaes, expressed it) "*people can change behaviour. We believe that if you treat each other with respect, they will treat you with respect back.*" This thinking is put into practice in many ways, including in joint seminars between staff and prisoners. The Governor explained the ecological principles:

We think that it's not one small factor that changes people. There are lots of factors. And the ecological thinking is a circle of thinking, everything is tied together… Education, working, training, and so on…We raise horses here, an old Norwegian race. And we also produce calves and when you are a prisoner and work in the agriculture department, you would get the responsibility for a cow. And that's how we train responsibility in action. This is your cow…you have to give the cow food. And when the calves come, you have to take care of the calf. You have literally to take it out... And this is teaching and training responsibility in action. This is also a way of building, or training and teaching, empathy.

Such a holistic approach is clearly a very different way of developing responsibility than Canadian-style behaviourist 'programmes' with their narrow focus on the criminogenic.

Much of the philosophy behind open prisons such as Bastoy may also be found in closed prisons in Norway, such as the new prison in Halden, which resembles East Jutland prison in Denmark in many ways and which opened in 2010 (Kriminalomsorgen, no date).

Resilient Penal Welfarism

In Norway, penal welfarism is clearly identifiable in the thinking of both the administrative and political leadership of the prison system, and this lies behind much of the restraint on punitiveness. Shortly before the Norwegian government published its White Paper in 2008, the Deputy Minister for Justice, Terje Moland Pedersen, gave an interview for this research. He was explicit at several points in distinguishing his government's approach on penal matters from what was happening elsewhere in Europe. He said:

The main issue is rehabilitation, to try to reintegrate criminals into civil society... We have also some discussion that they have in every country about security and safety, and what's security for prisoners, security for the people that work in the prison, and security for society. But I think the most important thing is what we are trying to achieve about rehabilitation.

This priority given to an inclusive form of rehabilitation over security seemed set to have major impact on the depth of imprisonment. When asked about the escalating emphasis on security in many prison systems elsewhere, Pedersen said:

I think we are going in a different way. It is very important that we have prison with high security, but not so high... I think most of the people in the prison should stay in the prison with lower security.

He made clear that what he meant by low security prisons were open prisons such as Bastoy:

We call it, for the debate, a prison with low security. We are going to have more of that kind of prison. And also we're looking at the possibility of having a prison where prisoners should take care of themselves... that they have to make their own food, maybe they could be able to have some work outside the prison area and earn some money, and control the day more than they do today. Because I think if they were able to do that it would also be easier for them to go back to the normal life afterwards. And I think that Bastoy is a really good example.... We think how to use the prisons with high security even less than we are doing today.

Garland says: "Where the older criminology demanded more in the way of welfare and assistance, the new one insists upon tightening controls and enforcing discipline" (2001, p.15). On that basis Norway is certainly following 'older criminology', given, for example, that the former Director General was of the view that "*prison should be bearable"* and also said: "*We have enough of the locks and gates and cameras… we need to have more activities."*

The Representation of the Person Held in Prison

Nordic Countries: The Larger Social Context

Turning now to the third criterion of punitiveness, the research sought to decipher how the men and women held in prison were perceived, within the prison system and within wider society. This was an attempt to assess whether they were, in Garland's terms, "represented in official discourse as socially deprived citizens in need of support", or "depicted instead as culpable, undeserving and somewhat dangerous" (2001, p.175). In all three Nordic countries focused on, human rights thinking and socially-inclusive attitudes (both related to the universal welfare state) counteract the stereotyping of people in prison typical of the 'culture of control'. Those in prison are widely seen as citizens, as members of the larger society. It is also recognised that prison has 'detrimental effects', damaging bonds with the wider community, and so should be used as 'a last resort'.

Such thinking is central to a Danish document setting out the principles for prison and probation work (Ministry of Justice, 1994), the 2006 Prisons Act in Finland and the 2008 White Paper on prisons in Norway. All broadly resonates with Council of Europe (2006) policy. A sense of the prisoner's larger social context is kept to the fore in Nordic countries. In other words, not *all* responsibility for change is put on the shoulders of the individual, as it tends to be in the USA and Britain; there is usually an awareness of contributory social factors to crime, and to reform.

This awareness is well captured in Finnish prison authority statements, such as the following:

Among the prisoners there are more and more offenders who have consciously chosen a criminal career and who are reluctant to quit it in the short term. However, the bulk of the prison population still consists of persons who have drifted into crime and who are socially maladjusted. Alcohol and other drug problems would seem to be major factors in current crime in Finland. (Ministry of Justice, 1999, p.6)

The same policy document gives as a goal for the prison system "supporting and encouraging the convicts in leading a life without crime", but also sets a goal of "influencing society as a whole in order to make work with this orientation possible" (Ministry of Justice, 1999, p.7). In this thinking, society needs to be worked with and changed, as well as people in and from prison.

Are Hoidal, the former Governor of Oslo Prison (and now Governor of the new Halden Prison referred to earlier), said of those held in his Oslo prison: "*80 per cent of them need help*". In a survey of Norwegian prisoners, Skardhamar found that their major problems related to housing, money and work. He says: "Inadequate living conditions should not necessarily be considered a cause of crime, but as a narrowed opportunity structure where other choices are limited"(Skardhamar, 2003, p.39). In similar vein, Nilsson's (2003) research on social exclusion and recidivism among prisoners in Sweden found that problems of employment, education, housing and finance (in that order) are significantly associated with recidivism. In addition, he said, "Time spent in prison serves to reduce the chances of living a conventional life – with a legitimate income – and thereby contributes to marginalisation and social exclusion" (Nillson, 2003, p.80).

Denmark: the 'Six Principles' for Prison and Probation work

A widely-accepted philosophy in the Danish penal system remains resilient, even though buffeted by different approaches coming from some politicians. This 'philosophy' is well expressed in *A Programme of Principles,* the statement of six principles adopted in 1993 (Ministry of Justice, 1994). These principles begin:

1. *Normalisation.*
   The daily activities of the Prison and Probation Service shall in general…be related to normal life in the general community…
2. *Openness.*
   Prison and probation work shall be organised so that the offender is offered good opportunities to make and maintain contact with the ongoing life of the community…
3. *Exercise of Responsibility.*
   Prison and probation work shall be so organised that the offender has the opportunity to develop a sense of responsibility, self-respect and self-confidence and become motivated to actively strive for a crime-free life…

These three principles have been referred to as the 'three cornerstones' of Danish penal policy (Rentzmann, 1992).

Such principles also underpin the Danish view that open prisons should be the norm for those serving sentences. Open prisons incorporate a greater degree of normalisation, enable those in prison to have more interaction with the outside community and take responsibility for more of their own lives. The representation of the person in prison in the *Principles* document, then, suggests a normal citizen, a member of the community, one who can be trusted to a large extent. The citizenship of people in prison is also acknowledged in Denmark, as elsewhere in Europe, via their rights to vote, appeal to the ombudsman and form representative groups.

While there has been some decline in the perception of the person in prison in Denmark, especially in the political sphere, the evidence does not suggest the kind of radical swing from penal welfarism to a culture of control that Garland describes. Employers still actively seek those released from prison for work. Inclusive concepts persist in other areas too, such as the accepting and positive view of the incarcerated person inherent in the *'principle of acknowledgement'* [13] used at Moglekaer open prison. The Head of Employment there gave striking examples of what he means by this: a paedophile can be moral in other respects; a thief can be a good parent. This approach seeks to find the positive qualities in people in prison, to acknowledge these and try to motivate them accordingly.

Finland: Prisoners as Members of Society

The representation of the person in prison in Finland can likewise be examined by probing principles, practices and attitudes to gauge whether those in prison are seen inclusively, or in stereotypical terms and as 'other'. Analysis suggests the former is the dominant approach. The 2006 Prison Act, the primary framework for penal policy in Finland, stresses that people in prison retain basic rights. The substantial focus on resettlement, and helping those in prison in relation to issues such as work, housing and addiction, reflects the view that criminal policy is part of social policy.

There is far more to the Finnish idea of rehabilitation than narrowly 'addressing offender behaviour', which indicates a one-dimensional perception of the person in prison.[14] A course at Kerava Prison, for example, seeks "the holistic rehabilitation of the client", recognising the social dimension in a way offence-focused programmes seldom do. This course addresses issues such as housing, finding meaningful activity like work or education, and help within and beyond prison with addiction and mental health. The goal "is to support the client to find new contents for life and reinforce the experience of meaningful life".[15] That wider perspective is evident too in the manual for the assessment and allocation of those held in prison and their involvement in the formation of a sentence plan (Criminal Sanctions Agency, 2004). The approach is to look for strengths as well as weaknesses, and it is expected staff must listen to and collaborated with those in prison.

The recognition that imprisonment weakens the bond with wider society is at the heart of Finnish penal thinking, and hence its decarceration policy:

The prison sentence shall be enforced so that the punishment will involve only deprivation of liberty. The harmful effects caused by the loss of liberty shall, as far as possible, be mitigated. The punishment shall be enforced so as not to unduly render difficulties, but rather facilitate, the readjustment to society. The conditions in penal institutions shall, as far as possible, be arranged to correspond to those prevailing in the society. (Ministry of Justice, 1994, 1.4)

'To Support the Self-esteem of the Prisoner'

The idea that those in their charge were mainly "*members of the community*" in need of help was pervasive among those interviewed in Finland. Such thinking is part of a deep and long tradition in Finnish penology, exemplified by K.J.Lang, an earlier and long-time Director General of the prison system. Lang translated the Finnish term for the prison service, 'Vankeinhoito', as "care of prisoners", also noting that the corresponding Swedish term 'Kriminalvard' literally means "care of criminals" (Lang, 1993, p.65). He argued that most in prison are "socially and psychologically disabled…deprived of all chances to develop and use what we can call their stronger parts" (p.66). They have, Lang said,

… very low expectations of success. They (or a majority of them) experience domestic and street violence in their childhood, often as victims. They have also been exposed to violence in their later life… they are poorly educated and unskilled and have been unemployed for long periods or all of their lives. (p.66)

Asking "what are the needs of our customers?", Lang made what might be regarded as a remarkable statement for a Prison Service Director General:

First of all prisoners/clients need to improve their self-confidence. Therefore all our efforts when organising correctional services should be analysed as to their ability to support, uphold and redress the self-esteem of the prisoner. (Lang, 1993, p.67)

He stressed the importance of work, training, education, "medico-social treatment" and "the need for shelters" - since "our customers…have been mistreated and abused both inside and outside the institutions we put them in", they should be offered in prison "shelter and protection in time, space and social environment" (Lang, 1993, p.67). It would be hard to find a more welfarist statement from the leader of any prison system. This philosophy continues to be a core part of the outlook of those running the prison system in Finland; the culture of control has made few inroads there in relation to the representation of people in prison.

Norway: Reasserting the Social Dimension

Although there is evidence of some narrowing of focus to *individual* responsibility in Norwegian penal policy around the turn of the century, the social dimension was strongly reasserted later. The idea of the person in prison as part of society, but someone in need of help, is brought out strongly in the 2008 White Paper. Just before it was issued, the Deputy Minister for Justice, Terje Moland Pedersen, spoke of the welfare state as a factor shaping the debate. He explained the Nordic welfare state model as "*about how everyone is going to carry for everyone*", and this meant "*that it is possible for us to have another kind of discussion about how we use prison and how we sentence people than I think it can be in some other countries*". For Pedersen the key issue was "*the people who really need help*". He added: "*I think it's about humanity and it's about [whether] you succeed in handling poverty.*"

This White Paper is titled, in its 'English summary' form, *Punishment that works – less crime – a safer society* (Norwegian Ministry of Justice and the Police, 2008). It suggests that fewer should be in prison, that more of those imprisoned should have lower security, that regimes should be improved and focused on rehabilitation, underpinned by the government's 'return guarantee' which assures social support in this process. The White Paper is unquestionably penal welfarist and socially inclusive in outlook, even if it speaks of strict regimes for a minority and in places cloaks discussion in the language of the culture of control.[16]

Penal welfarism is also suggested by core ideas in the White Paper:

The smaller the difference between life inside and outside prison, the easier the transition from prison to freedom. The normality principle is therefore a loadstar for penal implementation policy. It is also in accordance with the principle that deprivation of liberty is the actual penalty and that the stay in prison shall not be more onerous than security considerations demand... Strengthening the normality principle means organising a daily routine in prison that as far as possible reflects the society outside the walls. (Part 3)

The concept of the person in prison here is of a 'normal' member of society.

'A Competition Between Pictures'

Showing a tabloid headline that translated as "Blitz at Oslo emergency ward: PRISONER SHOT FREE by masked gang",[17] one governor stressed that only about 10 per cent of those in prison were dangerous in this manner. Most prisoners, he said, "*are the poor guys.*" An issue in Britain and the USA is that 'the dangerous guys' come to be seen as typical of those in prison, rather than as a small minority, and this is a basis for vengeful and punitive attitudes. Nils Christie, strongly critical of presentations of people in prison as 'monsters', said: "*The danger is now that these very physical famous criminals shall in a way cover the picture. So we think they are the prisoners. It's even competition between pictures now.*" One senses, however, that in Norway the negative stereotypes have not won this 'competition between pictures' and the entire prison system has not been moulded in response to the minority.

In its representation of people in prison, the White Paper goes strongly against the grain of the 'new punitiveness'. They are seen as members of society who "enjoy the same rights as everyone else", if not always the same access (Part 4). Social services are obliged to provide for them "in the same way as to other citizens" (Part 4). It is noted that many in prison "belong to the poorest and most alienated sectors of our society" (Part 4).The report lays great stress on the government's "return to society guarantee", which is declared to be "a public responsibility" (Part 4).

In this inclusive view of the men and women who are in prison, it is the explicit ruling out of stereotyping that is most striking. The White Paper says that "it is only a minority that constitute a threat to public or individual safety" and specifically warns against their 'demonising' (Part 2) . In similar calming vein, it states that "policy must not be based on individual incidents" (Part 1). In Norway, the perception of the person held in prison among the public, politicians and especially the prison administration, is for the most part holistic and inclusive.[18]

Conclusion: Ireland's Punitive Drift

Nordic Penal Restraint

Broadly speaking, Nordic countries have not followed the penal policy path predicted by Garland. While, in particular countries and at particular times, one can find traces of some of Garland's indices and some punitive urges, in general it can be said that Nordic countries have remained very restrained in their use of imprisonment, have adhered to high standards of humanity and human rights in the way people are treated in prison, and have largely maintained socially-inclusive approaches in responding to those who commit crime. That was the main conclusion of this author's PhD research in Denmark, Finland and Norway more than a decade ago (Warner, 2009). Around the same time, John Pratt explored penal policy and conditions in Denmark, Norway and Sweden, and his landmark study in 2008 likewise asserted that these countries are distinctive; he spoke of 'Scandinavian exceptionalism in a time of penal excess' (Pratt, 2008). Pratt's work set in motion considerable debate, both within and beyond Nordic countries, as to whether and in what ways their penal policy and practice were 'exceptional' (Ugelvik and Dullum, 2012). More widely in

Europe, other studies found considerable differences in levels of punitiveness, as well as an absence of punitiveness, in different places (Snacken and Dumortier, 2012).

At the very least, all such writing makes it clear that the Anglo-American direction of travel in penal policy is not inevitable. There can be 'resistance' to the forces that led to a 'punitive turn' in both the USA and Britain. For a country like Ireland, it is clear that alternative approaches are possible; lessons can be learned from other Western European countries, especially those of similar size with similar history, social structures and political systems – such as most of the Nordic countries.

Ireland's 'Punitive Turn'

Yet, while Ireland may not have gone as far down the punitive road described by Garland as Britain and the USA have, comparisons with Nordic (and some other) countries today indicate that it has travelled in that direction to a considerable extent. A quarter of a century ago, Ireland matched Nordic countries in its restrained inclination to imprison, having a rate of incarceration of 59 in 1994. Today, it has moved from being among those countries with the lowest rate of incarceration in Western Europe to a mid-table position in that region. Its rate of incarceration today is 85 per 100,000, much higher than that in each of the Nordic countries, and even higher than in Germany which currently has a rate of 77 per 100,000.[19]

The main driver for the surge in the numbers in prison in Ireland (which went close to 100 per 100,000 in 2011, before tapering off somewhat) came from the political field. The sense of the new punitiveness as something that crossed the Atlantic to Britain and Ireland is conveyed by finding the exact same phrases that had been used in the USA occurring in debates in Ireland and Britain. This happened most dramatically in 1997, when phrases such as 'get tough on crime', 'zero tolerance', 'prison works' and 'career criminals' were used extensively in general elections that were held in both countries that year.

In Ireland, the three centre-right parties that dominated politics at that time competed with each other in their promises to put more people in prison. So, at a time when Ireland's prison population was about 2,400, the Fine Gael Minister for Justice pledged 800 additional prison places, an increase of one-third. The Progressive Democrats, whose policy document on criminal justice was called 'Winning the War against Crime' advocated 1,500 extra places, while the then main opposition party, Fianna Fáil, committed to an additional 2,000 spaces. Fianna Fáil subsequently won the election. Fianna Fáil's policy paper on justice claimed that crime had brought "destruction, death and menace to our communities" and spoke of "hardened prisoners" and "predator criminals". A *Sunday Tribune* headline at the time of the previous Irish general election in November 1992 stated 'Crime is not an issue in this election', but the same newspaper in 1997 reported 'Crime–wave central to election battleground'.[20]

Although it did not happen as quickly as promised in that election, Irish governments did come close to doubling prison numbers over the following years – the prison population reached about 4,600 in 2011. The most extreme proposal in this escalation was the decision in 2004 to build a very large prison for 2,200 at Thornton Hall near Dublin, supplemented by another prison for 450 in Kilworth, County Cork. Approximately 3,200 were held in the Irish prison system in 2004, so building these two prisons would have represented a massive escalation in the scale of incarceration. In the economic down-turn that followed some years later, these particular construction projects were abandoned. However, considerable expansion did take place through the addition of numerous cell-blocks to existing prisons, often for several hundred at a time, and the building of a new prison for some 300 men in Cork City. Almost all of the prison expansions took place without a corresponding increase in opportunities such as education and work-training for those in prison. In both the Thornton Hall and Kilworth proposals, and in the subsequent construction that did happen, the great majority of new cells were planned to be 'doubled-up', in defiance of the European Prison Rules (2006).[21] Significantly, in planning Thornton Hall in particular, the Irish Prison Service relied heavily on consultation with an American multi-national company involved in the correctional business and the British Home Office, while ignoring suggestions that they also study the prisons being planned at East Jutland in Denmark and Halden in Norway just at that time.

Ireland's propensity to imprison is seen to be even more severe when its very high rate of committals is considered, i.e. the 'flow' into prison of many who receive short sentences. Further, most of the men and women sent to prison for short sentences are the poor, with O'Mahony stating that "while this profile of multiple disadvantage is typical of prisoners around the world… the prison population in Ireland come from the most deprived groups and lowest socio-economic classes to a far more concentrated degree than is the case in Britain" (2002, p.551). O'Mahony also finds that "the majority of convicted Irish offenders are sent to prison for relatively minor acts of property theft" and that "imprisonment rates [in Ireland] clearly point to a comparative overuse of prison, particularly in regard to the breadth of use" (2002, pp.552-3).

Reinforcing this picture, Kilcommins *et al* find that "Ireland appears relatively punitive when the prison population is expressed per 1,000 crimes. The proportionate use of custody was three times as high as England and Wales and the Netherlands, and five times as high as Finland" (2004, p.251). They also note how prison in Ireland tends to be used "as a default sanction", in the absence of sufficient options for sanctions in the community, so that there is "a strong orientation towards custody among Irish judges", a relationship which they argue is reversed in other jurisdictions (2004, p.244).

The intensification in recent decades of Ireland's inclination to imprison its marginalised groups reinforces, and is reinforced by, a clear deterioration in the representation of people held in prison, i.e. greater punitiveness in both the scale of imprisonment and in the characterization of those found to have broken the law tend to develop together. There has been a marked change in this latter aspect in Ireland since the mid-1990s. People in prison are now seen in public discourse in ways that are more demonising and socially-excluding, in marked contrast to Nordic countries, and this is reflected in their official designation – from being regarded by the Department of Justice as "valued members of society" in 1994 to a position where they are presumed to be outside such status in 2001 (see Warner, 2011).

Complacent Irish Narratives

Despite such trends in the scale of imprisonment and the representation of those held in prison, and perhaps even some starker deteriorations in the depth of imprisonment (to be discussed more fully below), there has been a degree of denial in Irish criminological discourse in relation to these developments. A certain narrative, which suggests Ireland has avoided the 'punitive turn' taken by other countries, has gained some dominance among Irish criminologists.[22] Kilcommins *et al* took the view, albeit in 2004, that in Ireland "there has been no real shift towards penal austerity, in the way that is seen elsewhere" (2004, p.259). They also stated that the Irish edition of Garland's crime complex "has emerged in a dilute and distinctive hybrid form" (2004, p.292).

While this latter statement may well be valid, as it may be for many countries, it does leave open the questions as to *how* diluted the punitive trends might be, and what components exactly make up the hybrid policies. As was noted above, Garland did, after all, argue that in the new crime control field "new practices and mentalities co-exist with the residues and continuations of older arrangements" (2001, p.167), thus recognising the hybrid nature of the new arrangements and seeing changes in thought and action in relation to crime as significant *changes in emphasis*. It is this author's argument that such changes in emphasis in a punitive direction have certainly occurred in Ireland's penal system since the mid-1990s.

Rogan's 2011 study is more assertive in making the case that Ireland has not taken a punitive turn, "that Garland's theories in *The Culture of Control* may not be applicable to contemporary Ireland" (2011, p.213). Moreover, she took the view that "penal welfarism did not become significantly apparent or embedded in Irish penal policy" (2011, p.210), somehow discounting the establishment of open prisons and other progressive institutions such as the Training Unit and the Dóchas Centre (women's prison) between the late 1960s and mid-1990s, as well as the thinking (which was very congruent with that of the Council of Europe) in Irish policy documents in the 1980s and 1990s (Brangan, 2019; Lonergan, 2010; Warner, 2011).

Brangan, in particular, "challenges the dominant narrative that Irish penal policy was stagnant or merely pragmatic" around the 1970s, and she makes the case that policy at that time is best described as 'pastoral penality', which was very much focused on "addressing the pains of imprisonment" (2019, p.1). Whatever way policy and practice in relation to prisons prior to the late 1990s is conceived, there is evidence of greater social-inclusion in the way the person in prison was seen and treated then. Moreover, despite the undoubted shortcomings in Irish prisons and penal policy in the past, it is clear that the prison system in this earlier period was at a more caring place on the 'care-custody' spectrum than is generally the case today.

A Shift Towards Penal Austerity?

However questionable was the claim by Kilcommins *et al* in 2004 that there was "no real shift towards penal austerity" (p.259) in the Irish penal system, it was certainly untenable some years later. Indeed, Ian O'Donnell, one of the authors of that earlier text, took a much more critical view of Irish penal policy nearly a decade later, noting a sharp increase in the imprisonment rate and speaking of "a punitive shift within the criminal justice system and the emergence of a less-forgiving mentality" (2013, p.321). A range of other writing has documented excessive restrictions and very poor conditions, many of which have deteriorated considerably in the past quarter of a century. John Lonergan, former Governor of Mountjoy and other Irish prisons, offered sharp insights into the Irish prison system in his autobiography, including his judgement that "the daily regime in prisons is seriously impoverished as a direct result of overcrowding, and prisons are now just warehousing" (Lonergan, 2010, p.202).

Elsewhere, John Lonergan is particularly critical of the consequences of overcrowding, including the increase in 'doubling-up' in cells, the 'one size fits all' approach to security,[23] and the fact that, with further cell-blocks and other facilities being added, existing prisons had become "dominated by concrete buildings with very little open space" so that they became bland and claustrophobic places (Carroll and Warner, 2014, pp.xvii-xix). His term 'warehousing' is a reasonable description, in particular, of the thinking inherent in the Thornton Hall and Kilworth projects and much of the additional accommodation that has been shoe-horned into the Irish prison estate. Yet, despite its intended massive scale and the sub-standard cell and other arrangements envisaged for Thornton Hall, Rogan's view was that "it cannot be said with any certainty that a punitive agenda was behind the decision to establish Thornton Hall" (2011, p.196).

Hamilton's assessment of the Irish prison system is much more critical, and challenges the narrative of other criminologists who detect little punitiveness within it. She says: "While rehabilitation certainly remains an aspiration of the Irish Prison Service… this is seriously compromised by overcrowding and… the general poverty of the daily regime" (2014, p.51). She notes that "in most institutions prisoners are locked up for 18 hours per day", in some there is a "lack of any meaningful activity… [and] violence and bullying appear endemic in Irish prisons" (2014, p.51). While also recognizing some positive aspect of the system, including a measure of humanity and reasonably good relations between staff and prisoners, she raises concern that "Irish penal policy and practice is worryingly out of line with international human rights standards in a range of areas" (2014, p.52).

Other studies point to deteriorations in regimes in recent decades, such as those by the Jesuit Centre for Faith and Justice in 2012 and 2016, the latter highlighting the very poor arrangements there are now for young men aged between18 and 24, with the closure of specific institutions for the younger part of this age group, including the open prison, Shanganagh Castle, in 2002. These young adults have, in effect, been abandoned, their particular needs and vulnerabilities not recognized by the justice system and hundreds of them are now incarcerated with full adults in large inappropriate closed prisons. Deteriorations in basic living conditions in general have also been documented, including how they fall short of those set out by a landmark government inquiry (Whitaker Report, 1985) and how standards prescribed by a recent Inspector of Prisons fall far short of those established by the Council of Europe or that pertained previously in Ireland (Warner, 2012a, 2014). Recently, the Irish Penal Reform Trust has begun to monitor annually whether the prison system meets particular targets, and, even though the targets they set often fall very far short of international best practice (and certainly short of what usually pertains in Nordic countries) – relating for example to matters such as lock-up times, cell-sharing, privacy in toilet arrangements, percentage in open prisons, access to structured activity, etc. – progress is often found to be very limited, if at all (Irish Penal Reform Trust, 2019).

Two other aspects of prison regimes in Ireland will now be explored in a little more detail. Each illuminates current thinking and practice, and the change from a relatively supportive approach to one focused more on control or punishment. Each may be seen to show the change in emphasis referred to earlier, indicative of a shift from ways of doing things that put more emphasis on care (whether that be termed penal welfarism or 'pastoral penality' or something else) to a more punitive approach. An Irish government report in 1997, generally known as the McAuley Report, stipulated that there should be a rebalancing of 'care/custody' in the direction of more care in the prison system, and as part of that a "strengthening of healthcare and of the psychological, educational and training elements" (Report of

Expert Group, 1997, p.13). This thinking resonates with that of the former Danish Director General, William Rentzmann, cited above, where he spoke of balancing "*the soft and the hard*", a balance that is clearly evident in Danish penal policy and practice. Even more so, it is in tune with thinking of the Norwegian Director General, Kristen Bolgen Bronebakk, who asserted, "*We have enough of the locks and gates and cameras... we need to have more activities.*"

However, rather than the rebalancing towards 'care' advocated by the McAuley Report, the prison system in Ireland moved sharply in the other direction, giving huge priority to 'security' in its most physically restraining sense (see Jesuit Centre for Faith and Justice, 2012).Two episodes indicating this more punitive philosophy will now be examined: one, the introduction of the so-called 'incentivised regimes' scheme in 2012; and two, the response of Irish authorities in 2011 to a critique by a Council of Europe body to the way they deal with inter-prisoner violence.

'For the few not the Many'

In noting deteriorations in Irish prison regimes or penal policy generally, or even in simply recognizing that certain poor conditions or treatment have long been present, it is important also to acknowledge that some things are done well. In all prisons and among all disciplines working within them, examples of good and professional work can be found, sometimes indeed even excellent initiatives. To criticize the overall drift of policy or practice is not to deny such positives, nor the admirable work of many genuine individuals in all spheres. Nor is it to deny that some people held in prison 'make good', sometimes even in the most unlikely of circumstances. However, neither the fact that some held in prison achieve against all the odds, nor that some working within the system manage to do extraordinary things, excuses shortcomings elsewhere or an overall drift in the prison system which leads to services and opportunities becoming more limited, tending to be available for some but not for all.

One pattern of the punitive drift that has happened in Irish prisons is that resources become 'targeted' on a minority to the detriment of the larger population. Universal rights, such as the right to education or the right to family contact, become seen as 'privileges' which are provided only to some (Warner, 2018). The fact that things may work out for certain people in prison does not excuse the reality that matters have worsened for others – indeed, at times, as we shall see, they may be somewhat worse for everyone. An example of such a pattern is the new 'incentivised regimes' system introduced into Irish prisons in 2012. A copy of the Incentives and Earned Privileges (IEP) scheme that has operated in English prisons since 1995, this departure in Ireland clearly indicates a focus on 'the few not the many' (to reverse the slogan of a British political leader).

For many decades, a man or woman held in an Irish prison received a meagre payment that was meant to cover the purchase of personal items like soap or toothpaste and whatever else they choose to buy from prison shops such as sweets, cigarettes, batteries for radio, newspapers, etc. The amount, which was €2-35 per day before 2012, was long recognized as too low to meet this purpose, so that many in prison were obliged to subsist at a poor level or pressure their families to give in money for them. However, nearly all in prison used to receive this same gratuity.

However, in 2012, Irish prison authorities cut this payment for all in prison, but cut it by more for some than others, and in the process saved about €500,000 per year in the prison budget. They created three levels of new payment: a so-called 'enhanced' rate of €2.20 per day, a standard rate of €1-70 and a 'reduced' rate of €0-95 cents. What was already a pathetically low payment was cut by 28 per cent on average. What are regarded as 'privileges' such as visiting by family members or time allowed on phone-calls – and usually meagre measures of these also – are also differentially apportioned under this scheme. The rationale for this new scheme was put by the then Director General of the Irish Prison Service: "We want to encourage prisoners to join the programmes, the education, the supports, take the drug counselling so we can create a safer society" (Warner, 2012b). Yet, the authorities have set a limit to the number of those who can be in receipt of the 'enhanced' rate; no more than one-third in prison can receive this level of payment. Further, it has been found in practice that young adults, those with disabilities or otherwise vulnerable, and those who seek protection and are thereby confined to their cells for most of the day are disproportionately on the lower rates. Moreover, one of the major and growing problems within Irish prisons is the failure of authorities to ensure that those seeking to participate in activities such as education *can actually access such services*; that is the problem rather than any need for 'incentives' to participate.

A significant aspect of this type of scheme is the neo-liberal ideology underpinning it (Crewe, 2009) and this represents a departure from previous universal principles whereby services were offered to all on the basis of a duty of care. This change is linked to a narrowing in the concept of rehabilitation, with much more emphasis now placed on the individual's 'responsibility' and choice, and much less recognition of the role of society in supporting reintegration. Previously, rehabilitation was seen in a wider social context, as in the Whitaker Report which spoke of it as efforts to help the person's "inability to cope with society" (1985, p.89), and such thinking was also evident in Department of Justice policy in the 1980s and up to the mid-1990s (see Warner, 2011). However, by the turn of the century, a shift had taken place, with the then Director General of the Irish Prison Service emphasising the centrality of a prisoner's "personal decision-making capacity" (O'Mahony, 2002, p.591). The change can also be seen in the way the role and purpose of education, still by far the largest structured activity within Irish prisons, has also been narrowed. Where once education was officially regarded within the Irish prison system as a right to which all in prison were entitled, and which was envisaged as a wide curriculum aimed at helping 'the whole person' in line with an adult education philosophy, it is now seen by prison authorities merely as one among a range of 'rehabilitation services' – but with the idea of rehabilitation now narrowly conceived as an individual choosing to 'address offending behaviour' (Warner, 2018).

'Dynamic Security and Care'

Finally, this chapter will explore an illustrative episode from around 2011. The Council of Europe inspection body, the CPT, in their report on Irish places of custody issued that year, addressed the problem of inter-prisoner violence. Among other suggestions, they gave the following advice to Irish authorities:

Addressing the phenomenon of inter-prisoner violence requires that prison staff must be alert to signs of trouble and both resolved and properly trained to intervene. The existence of positive relations between staff and prisoners, based on the notions of dynamic security and care, is a decisive factor in this context; this will depend in large measure on staff possessing appropriate interpersonal communication skills... Moreover, it is imperative that concerted action is taken to provide prisoners with purposeful activities. (Council of Europe CPT, 2011a, p.19)

It is worth exploring here two of the key strategies they recommended, 'dynamic security' and 'care'. Dynamic security is a concept that occurs often in Council of Europe documents and in the penal policies of Nordic and other countries. Dunbar (1985) defined it as encompassing three key features in the way staff deal with those in prison: relationships, activity and treating each person in prison as an individual. Coyle explains it further:

It is the opposite of the arrangement whereby staff observe prisoners at a distance, often via television monitors, and rarely come into physical contact with them. In the dynamic security model, staff mix with the prisoners. They will move among them, talk to them and listen to them; there will be the normal dynamics of human interaction. (2005, p.139)

Clearly, this is the approach advocated above by the former Norwegian Director General in speaking about the role of staff in Norwegian prisons. It should be noted also that 'interpersonal communication' between staff and prisoners, as advocated by the CPT, would clearly be much more feasible in a typical Nordic prison, where people are out of their rooms or cells for 12 to 14 hours or more in the day – East

Jutland or Bastoy, which were described earlier, being fairly typical in this regard of closed and open prisons respectively. The norm in Ireland of six hours out-of-cell time, with several hundred being locked away for much longer, obviously offers far less opportunity for such communication. Likewise, high lock-up times severely restrict the opportunities for 'purposeful activity', another of the CPT's prescriptions, while by contrast the range of activity even in a closed prison like East Jutland is considerable.

The other concept highlighted by the CPT, that of care, also has a long tradition in penology, and in many ways indicates the supportive dimension of penal welfarism. It was noted alredy that the Swedish word 'kriminalvard' and the Finnish word 'vankeinhoito', each usually translated as 'correctional services', actually literally mean 'care of criminals' and 'care of prisoners' respectively (Lang, 1993, p.65). Care clearly suggests helping rather than controlling, and complements the idea of 'dynamic security', as it does other suggestions of the CPT such as promoting communication and activity.

The unusually lengthy response by the Irish authorities to the CPT advice is striking. They set out over three pages a long list of restrictive physical measures which they had deployed or proposed to deploy, not one of which reflects the progressive concepts advocated by the CPT (Council of Europe CPT, 2011b, pp.22-24). This Irish list includes, among similar initiatives:

- solitary confinement for men deemed in danger
- tighter control and monitoring generally, including of visits
- increased random searches of cells and occupants
- greater use of cameras and probe systems
- the installation of nets over yards
- a drug detection dog service
- Operational Support Units, for searching/intelligence-gathering
- the introduction of BOSS (Body Orifice Security Scanner) chairs.

It is not easy to work out whether the Irish authorities failed to understand the concepts being proposed by the CPT or simply choose to ignore them. Either way, the chasm in thinking and practice between what the CPT proposed and what the Irish prison system considered appropriate indicates the gulf between a penology based on humane values and decency, which one finds in the Council of Europe and Nordic countries, and the punitive mind-set and unimaginative practices that now span the Irish prison system.

REFERENCES

Baldursson, E. (2000). Prisoners, Prisons and Punishment in Small Societies. *Journal of Scandinavian Studies in Criminology and Crime Prevention*, *1*(1), 6–15. doi:10.1080/14043850050116228

Brangan, L. (2019). Pastoral penality in 1970s Ireland: Addressing the pains of imprisonment. Theoretical Criminology, 1-22.

Carroll, E., & Warner, K. (Eds.). (2014). *Re-Imagining Imprisonment in Europe: Effects, Failures and the Future*. Liffey Press.

Christie, N. (2000). *Crime Control as Industry: Towards Gulags Western Style* (3rd ed.). Routledge.

Costelloe, A., & Warner, K. (2014). Prison education cross Europe: Policy, practice, politics. *London Review of Education, 12*(2).

Council of Europe. (1990). *Education in Prison*. Author.

Council of Europe. (2006). *European Prison Rules*. Author.

Council of Europe CPT. (2008). *Report to the Government of Denmark on the visit to Denmark carried out by the European Committee for the Prevention of Torture and Inhuman or Degrading Treatment or Punishment (CPT) from 11 to 20 February 2008.* Strasbourg. Download from www.cpt.coe.int

Council of Europe CPT. (2011a). *Report to the Government of Ireland on the visit to Ireland carried out by the European Committee for the Prevention of Torture and Inhuman or Degrading Treatment or Punishment (CPT) from 25 January to 5 February 2010.* Strasbourg. Download from www.cpt.coe.int

Council of Europe CPT. (2011b). *Response of the Government of Ireland to the report of the European Committee for the Prevention of Torture and Inhuman or Degrading Treatment or Punishment (CPT) on its visit to Ireland from 25 January to 5 February 2010.* Strasbourg. Download from www.cpt.coe.int

Coyle, A. (2005). *Understanding prisons: key issues in policy and practice*. Open University Press.

Crewe, B. (2009). *The Prisoner Society: Power, Adaptation, and Social Life in an English Prison*. University Press. doi:10.1093/acprof:oso/9780199577965.001.0001

Criminal Sanctions Agency. (2004). Assessment and Allocation Unit Handbook, Version 1.0. Helsinki: Author.

Dunbar, I. (1985). *A Sense of Direction*. Home Office.

Evans, M., & Morgan, R. (1998). *Preventing Torture: A Study of the European Convention for the Prevention of Torture and Inhuman or Degrading Treatment or Punishment.* Oxford: Clarendon Press.

Garland, D. (2001). *The Culture of Control: Crime and Social Order in Contemporary Society*. University Press. doi:10.7208/chicago/9780226190174.001.0001

Hamilton, C. (2014). *Reconceptualising Penality: A Comparative Perspective in Ireland, Scotland and New Zealand*. Ashgate.

Houses of the Oireachtas, Joint Committee on Justice, Defence and Equality. (2013). *Report on Penal Reform*. Author.

Irish Penal Reform Trust. (2019). *Progress in the Penal System (PIPS): a framework for penal reform*. Dublin: IPRT. Download from www.iprt.ie

Jesuit Centre for Faith and Justice. (2012). *The Irish Prison System: Vision, Values, Reality*. Dublin: JCFJ. Download from www.jcfj.ie

Jesuit Centre for Faith and Justice. (2016). *Developing Inside: Transforming Prison for Young Adults*. Dublin: JCFJ. Download from www.jcfj.ie

Kilcommins, S., O'Donnell, I., O'Sullivan, E., & Vaughan, B. (2004). *Crime, Punishment and the Search for Order in Ireland*. Institute of Public Administration.

Kriminalomsorgen (Norwegian Correctional Service). (n.d.). *Halden Prison: Punishment that Works – Change that Lasts!* Halden: Halden fengsel.

Kristoffersen, R. (Ed.). (2019). *Correctional Statistics of Denmark, Finland, Iceland, Norway and Sweden 2013-2017*. Lillestrom: University College of Norwegian Correctional Service. Download from www.krus.no

Lang, K. (1993). What kind of prisoners do we meet in the 1990s? In Report from 'Beyond the Walls', conference of European Prison Education Association, Sigtuna, Sweden.

Lappi-Seppala, T. (2007). Penal Policy in Scandinavia. In Crime, Punishment and Politics in Comparative Perspective. Crime and Justice: A Review of Research, Vol. 36. Chicago: University Press. doi:10.1086/592812

Lonergan, J. (2010). *The Governor: the life and times of the man who ran Mountjoy*. Penguin Ireland.

Ministry of Justice (Denmark). (1994). *A Programme of Principles for Prison and Probation Work in Denmark.*

Ministry of Justice (Finland). (1994). *Survey of the Enforcement of Imprisonment Sentences in Finland.*

Ministry of Justice (Finland). (1999). *Mission and Short-term Policies of the Prison Administration and the Probation Association of Finland.* University Press.

Nillson, A. (2003). Living Conditions, Social Exclusion and Recidivism Among Prison Inmates. *Journal of Scandinavian Studies in Criminology and Crime Prevention, 4*(1), 57–83. doi:10.1080/14043850310005321

Norwegian Ministry of Justice and the Police. (2008). *Punishment that works – less crime – a safer society. Report to the Storting on the Norwegian Correctional Services.* English Summary.

O'Donnell, I. (2013, Autumn). Penal Policy in Ireland: The Malign Effect of Sustained Neglect. In *Studies: An Irish. The Quarterly Review, 102*(407), 315–323.

O'Mahony, P. (Ed.). (2002). *Criminal Justice in Ireland.* Institute of Public Administration.

Pratt, J. (2008). Scandinavian Exceptionalism in a Time of Penal Excess. British Journal of Criminology, 48, 119-137, 275-292.

Pratt, J., Brown, D., Brown, M., Hallsworth, S., & Morrison, W. (Eds.). (2005). *The New Punitiveness: Trends, theories, perspectives.* Willan Publishing.

Rentzmann, W. (1992). Cornerstones in a modern treatment philosophy: normalisation, openness and responsibility. Prison Information Bulletin, 16, 19-23.

Report of Expert Group (McAuley Report). (1997). *Towards an Independent Prison Agency.* Dublin: Department of Justice.

Rogan, M. (2011). *Prison Policy in Ireland: Politics, penal-welfarism and political imprisonment.* Routledge. doi:10.4324/9780203828885

Skardhamar, T. (2003). Inmates' Social Background and Living Conditions. *Journal of Scandinavian Studies in Criminology and Crime Prevention, 4*(1), 39–56. doi:10.1080/14043850310012314

Snacken, S., & Dumortier, E. (Eds.). (2012). Resisting Punitiveness in Europe? Welfare, human rights and democracy. Abingdon: Routledge.

Stern, K. (2014). *Voices from American Prisons: Faith, education and healing*. Routledge. doi:10.4324/9780203374573

Ugelvik, T., & Dullum, J. (2012). *Penal Exceptionalism? Nordic Prison Policy and Practice*. Routledge.

Warner, K. (2009). *Resisting the New Punitiveness? Penal Policy in Denmark, Finland and Norway* (Unpublished PhD thesis). University College Dublin. Download from www.pepre.ie

Warner, K. (2011). 'Valued members of society?' Social Inclusiveness in the Characterisation of Prisoners in Ireland, Denmark, Finland and Norway. *Administration*, *59*(1), 87-109. Download from www.pepre.ie

Warner, K. (2012a). Redefining Standards Downwards: The Deterioration in Basic Living Conditions in Irish Prisons and the Failure of Policy. *Working Notes*, *70*, 3-10. Download from www.pepre.ie

Warner, K. (2012b, July 31). Negative, miserly, punitive. *Irish Examiner*. Download from www.pepre.ie

Warner, K. (2014). Regimes in Irish Prisons: 'Inhumane' and 'degrading': An analysis and the outline of a solution. *Irish Journal of Applied Social Studies*, *14*(1), 3–17.

Warner, K. (2016). What's the Difference between Ireland and Iceland? One Letter and a Decent Prison System.... *Irish Probation Journal*, *13*(October), 234–248.

Warner, K. (2018). Every possible learning opportunity: the capacity of education in prison to challenge dehumanisation and liberate 'the whole person'. *Advancing Corrections Journal*, *6*, 30-43. Download from www.icpa.org

Whitaker Report. (1985). *Report of the Committee of Inquiry into the Penal System*. Dublin: Stationery Office.

ENDNOTES

1 Examples of such stereotyping from Ireland in just a five-month period in 2009 included a front-page headline in the *Irish Daily Star* (9 February) which ran "DNA tests to nail jail scum", with the term "scum" clearly referring to people in prison in general; two (factually incorrect) references by Irish public broadcasting (RTE) journalists to Mountjoy Prison in Dublin being "full" of violent prisoners (RTE television news, 25 April, and on radio, 16 June); and the equation by the Minister for Justice of life-sentence prisoners with continuing dangerousness on an RTE radio programme ('Morning Ireland', 12 June). A former Director General of the Irish Prison Service routinely spoke of prisoners in general as "a threat to the public", including, on one occasion, the entire population of the main woman's prison.

2 The figures in this section come from www.prisonstudies.org, on 2 March 2020, other than those for Ireland, which are taken from www.ips.ie on the same date and relate to 28 February 2020.

3 This statistic is deduced from the Irish Prison Service website, www.ips.ie (visited on 2 March 2020), where it is noted that, out of a total prison population of 4,209 on 28 February 2020, just 240 were held in the two remaining open prisons in Ireland, Loughan House and Shelton Abbey.

4 Pratt says: "These countries have a large number of small prisons, often with 100 inmates or fewer… The largest prison in the region, in Sweden, holds around 350 inmates". (2008, p.120) However, Oslo Prison had 392 in November 2006, and the new Turku Prison in Finland had places for 350 in July 2008, at the time of this author's research visits.

5 Nordic figures are derived from www.prisonstudies.org on 2 March 2020. The Irish prison system held 4,209 in 12 institutions on 28 February 2020 (www.ips.ie, on 2 March 2020).

6 For further information on penal policy in Iceland, and how it contrasts with that of Ireland, see Warner (2016).

7 There were 261 full-time equivalent staff of all disciplines to the 228 prisoners at East Jutland.

8 These principles are explained further in another section.

9 In February 2008, two months after the visit to East Jutland for this research, the Council of Europe's inspection body, the CPT, visited the prison. Their description and assessment of the institution corresponds very closely with that given above. (Council of Europe CPT, 2008, pp.30-31) Additionally, the CPT examined the special units in Section E intended for "negatively strong inmates" and note that material conditions and activities there were excellent

and similar to the other units, except for "the limited amount of outdoor space available to them" (Council of Europe CPT, 2008, p.23).

10 In 2008, most people in prison in Norway were paid 51 NOK per day, the same standard rate applying whether they attend school, work, programmes or other organised activity. This amounted to about €32 per week at that time. In Ireland, the rate had been €16.45 per week for many years, but the Irish Prison Service introduced an average reduction of 28 per cent to this rate in 2012, bringing the average to €11.84 per week; it remains at this level in 2020.

11 Certainly, nothing in the three Norwegian prisons visited for the PhD research, nor in three others visited subsequently, would give rise to a questioning of that statement; the atmospheres and the relationships seemed good.

12 Similarly, in Denmark, prison officers are expected to carry out four main tasks which relate to security, welfare, occupational supervision and leisure-time guidance.

13 This is reported to be based on the thinking of the German writer, Axel Honneth.

14 Such narrow and one-dimensional views of the person in prison are challenged in Costelloe and Warner (2014) and Stern (2014).

15 Information on this course comes mainly from a brochure in English which describes it.

16 That the emphasis on protection in the 2008 White Paper leads to more 'liberal' policies rather than greater incapacitation is reflected in the statement: "Penal implementation out in the community is more effective for rehabilitation than prison and is therefore the best long-term protection" (Norwegian Ministry of Justice and the Police, 2008, Part 2).

17 The newspaper was *VG* on 7 September 2003.

18 The input of those in prison was also sought for the White Paper: "In six prisons dialogue conferences were held in which both inmates and staff participated and discussed what a good day in prison would look like for them." (Part 5)

19 The German rate is taken from World Prison Brief, www.prisonstudies.org on 2 March 2020. The rate for Ireland in 1994 is taken from the Council of Europe's *Penological Information Bulletin*, Nos. 19 and 20, December 1994-1995; the rate was 58.6 on 1 September 1994.

20 Fuller details of the 1997 general election in Ireland, including the sources for the information given above, can be found in Warner, 2009, Chapter 1.

21 In fairness to more recent Irish politicians, an all-party parliamentary report in 2013 unanimously advocated the reduction of Ireland's prison population (then, as now, just over 4,200) by one-third. They specifically pointed to Finland as a model to follow in this respect, although they might just as easily have used the recent example of Sweden. However, their progressive proposals have so

far been ignored by the Department of Justice and the Minister for Justice. (House of the Oireachtas, 2013)

22 For example, such a statement was made by Professor Ivana Bacik in her concluding keynote address to the 11th North-South Criminology Conference at University College Dublin in September 2018.

23 The approach to security in Irish prisons, designed to address the minority of very 'serious' criminals, tends to be applied to the prison population at large, so that the majority of those in prison are subject to more restrictions than is necessary. In part, this is due to the structure of the prison estate, which is mainly made up of a small number of relatively large closed prisons; in part, it is because of a particular mind-set among Irish prison authorities. The Irish approach to security contrasts sharply with the differentiated approach in Nordic countries, discussed extensively in sections 3 and 4 above.

Chapter 8
How to Reduce Recidivism:
Lessons From the U.S. State of Arizona

Kevin A. Wright
Arizona State University, USA

ABSTRACT

Nearly everyone sent to prison will one day return to the community. This means that understanding recidivism is of critical importance to members of that community. At the most basic level, recidivism can be defined as "the reversion of an individual to criminal behavior after he or she has been convicted of a prior offense, sentenced, and (presumably) corrected." Recidivism therefore requires that some sort of involvement with the criminal justice system has taken place, and that then the individual again comes into contact with the system after additional transgressions. Recidivism, in other words, is officially detected, repeat unlawful behavior.

INTRODUCTION

Multiple measures of this behavior exist, including re-arrest, reconviction and reimprisonment. Recidivism can include technical violations – acts that are otherwise not viewed as criminal, such as entering an establishment that serves alcohol – that can constitute breaches of contract for individuals on probation or parole release. Other factors can also drive the frequency of recidivism. More intensive supervision of released individuals could mean more opportunities for violations and the detection of violation. A longer time spent within the community could also mean more opportunities to recidivate. (It is often said that at least three years since release provides a good understanding of recidivism). Recidivism is complicated, featuring different definitions, the combination of unlawful behavior with technical violations,

DOI: 10.4018/978-1-7998-6646-6.ch008

varying levels of supervision and different follow-up periods. Recidivism becomes "a complex measure of criminal behavior combined with formal and informal policy and procedure mechanisms" (Wilson, 2005: 494)

These complexities of recidivism are not trivial. For example, in a national study of over 400,000 formerly incarcerated individuals released across multiple states in 2005, it was determined that 18 percent of those released had returned to prison within 6 months. In the same study, it was determined that 77 percent of those released had been rearrested within 5 years (Durose, Cooper, & Snyder, 2014). Both numbers are correct and both are valid indicators. But it is critically important to know exactly what is being measured (and what is not) to fully comprehend recidivism (Wright & Khade, 2018).

What is the extent of recidivism in the United States? The national study cited above by the U.S. Bureau of Justice Statistics (BJS) documented 404,638 formerly incarcerated individuals from 30 states for a period of five years, from 2005-2010. Within that five years, over three-quarters (77 percent) of the released individuals had been rearrested and over half (55 percent) had a parole or probation violation or a new offense that resulted in reimprisonment (Durose et al., 2014). Extended to nine years, eighty-three percent had been rearrested (Alper, Durose, & Markman, 2018).

The United States Sentencing Commission (2016) produced a report on 25,431 incarcerated individuals released from the federal prison system in 2005 with a follow-up period of eight years. Nearly half were rearrested, nearly one-third were re-convicted, and nearly one-quarter were re-imprisoned during that period.

A critical difference between this study and the BJS study is that the former also included individuals who were previously sentenced to only probation. These individuals had a re-arrest rate of 35 percent, while individuals sentenced to prison had a re-arrest rate of 53 percent. Further data are contained in a 2011 Pew Center on the States report entitled "State of Recidivism: The Revolving Door of America's Prisons." This provided aggregate recidivism rates between 2004 and 2007 for 33 states. The overall three-year recidivism rate, measured as return-to-prison, was 43 percent. This rate masked wide variation among states, with six states reporting recidivism rates above 50 percent (led by Minnesota's 61 percent) and five states reporting recidivism rates under 30 percent (led by Oregon's 23 percent).

Criminologists have long focused on identifying and targeting risk factors that might increase an individual's likelihood of recidivism. These individual-level risks are classified into two categories: static and dynamic (Bonta & Andrews, 2017).

Static risk factors are features of the person that cannot be changed, such as age, race or criminal record. Research has consistently found that younger individuals, males, minorities and those with a criminal history have a higher risk for recidivism (Benedict, Huff-Corzine, 1998; Gainey, Payne, & O'Toole, 2000; Gendreau, Little,

& Goggin, 1996; Hepburn & Albonetti, 1994; Listwan, Sundt, Holsinger, & Latessa, 2003).

Dynamic risk factors, on the other hand, are characteristics that can be changed and therefore make appropriate targets for treatment. These include antisocial values, beliefs and behaviors, which sometimes are referred to as "criminogenic needs" (Andrews et al., 1990). Consideration of static and dynamic risk factors can begin to suggest what programs are most appropriate for certain individuals in order to reduce recidivism. But to truly understand recidivism - and how to potentially reduce it - it must be learned why people recidivate.

Why Do People Recidivate?

The reasons that people continue to engage in crime are as varied as the reasons people commit crimes in the first place. A criminology textbook may include everything from biological theories of crime to psychological theories to sociological theories; from individual theories of crime to neighborhood theories to nation-state theories; and from social bond theories to social disorganization theories to social learning, to social support theories. Then there are factors such as strain, labeling, poverty, genes, masculinity, self-control, inequality, personality - the list goes on. For the general public, the reason is usually simpler and perhaps a bit obvious: Criminals choose to engage in crime.

Most criminologists tend to be wary of any explanation that whittles criminal behavior down to a simple choice - a rational, cost/benefit analysis of whether to forge that check, inject that heroin, or beat up that former associate. Part of this reluctance is that rational-choice explanations of criminal behavior by themselves can lead to punitive policy prescriptions: All we need to do, this approach says, is make the costs of crime outweigh the benefits. Thus, increasing the likelihood of going to prison and for a longer time should dissuade most people from engaging in crime.

But this line of thinking shows the limited value of the "crime as a choice" explanation. First, people who engage in crime do not always have the same set of legal, prosocial options available to them from which to choose. They often come from disadvantaged backgrounds marked by abuse and victimization, drug and alcohol addictions, and family instability. They have fewer opportunities for quality education, gainful employment or positive recreational outlets. They find themselves surrounded by crime and incarceration. Engaging in criminal behavior may be the easiest, most comfortable or only choice available to them.

The counter argument is that many people grow up in difficult situations yet refrain from criminal behavior. This is true, but leads to a second shortcoming of the "crime as choice" explanation: people who engage in crime do not always approach the decision-making process with a rational mindset. A number of different factors can impact rationality, including mental illness, past victimization, and drug and alcohol addiction. More importantly, however, what is perceived as rational may be different for people who engage in crime as compared to those who do not.

It may sound like a cliché, and perhaps a bit of a copout, but there is some truth to the idea that "crime is all they know." If you surround yourself with family and friends who engage in criminal behavior, then you are likely to develop attitudes that support that behavior and "thinking errors" that prohibit you from considering the impact of your actions on yourself and others, as well as the potential legal ramifications of those actions.

Considering these two shortcomings together helps explain why prison is not much of a deterrent to people who engage in criminal behavior, and especially those who engage in repeat criminal behavior. It does not matter how long the prison sentence is or how vile the prison conditions may be, offenders give little consideration to the punishment aspects of a criminal act. To some, incarceration is a natural part of life, and to others it may even represent a badge of honor or rite of passage.

Broadly speaking, people recidivate because 1) they have limited opportunities to obtain and sustain quality education, gainful employment, stable housing, as well as supportive professional and personal networks and relationships and, 2) they are rewarded for antisocial thinking and behavior instead of prosocial thinking and behavior, which may be influenced by prior victimization, mental illness or substance abuse.

A more direct approach to answering why people recidivate is to simply pose the question to people who are currently incarcerated. The challenge in doing this is that it may be difficult to establish the necessary rapport with incarcerated individuals that would allow for truthful responses to questions that pry at the most difficult aspects of their lives. To counter that obstacle, in the summer of 2017, researchers from Arizona State University (ASU) worked with incarcerated men to develop and implement a study that could overcome this critical obstacle. ASU faculty, graduate students and incarcerated men are part of a think tank called The Arizona Transformation Project (ATP), which evolved out of the first Inside-Out Prison Exchange Program in Arizona in spring 2016.

The ATP developed interview questions in collaboration with the Governor's Office Recidivism Reduction Project Team. Incarcerated members were trained in proper interviewing techniques and consent protocol, as required by ASU's Institutional Review Board (IRB). The five incarcerated researchers completed 409 interviews in two months at the medium-security East Unit of the Arizona State Prison Complex at Florence. The report was shared with the Governor's Office (Wright et al., 2017). It is believed to be one of the first studies in the United States in which incarcerated men served as interviewers of other incarcerated men. Both incarcerated and nonincarcerated collaborators detailed this project in academic journals (Thrasher et al., 2019; Haverkate, Meyers, Telep, & Wright, 2020).

Early in the interview, the incarcerated men were asked: Why do you think most people come back to prison? Several themes emerged. The most prominent theme that emerged (44 percent of respondents) was that a lack of resources or programming contributed to recidivism. For example, one respondent said: "*Because they are not adequately prepared for reentry into society, because they have not made successful and dedicated transformation from their old lifestyle to one that would keep them out of prison.*"

A second theme was drug and alcohol use (27 percent of respondents), captured by the respondent who said: "*A lot of felons have serious drug addiction problems. … When addicts get out, there aren't any affordable quality treatment options.*"

The third most prominent theme among respondents was an inability to change thinking and behavior, or resorting to comfort. This was best captured by the respondent who said: "*Lack of education, skills, and a desire to succeed. They stay in here for a long time, get complacent and [there isn't] any real type of job training to teach them how to be successful. So, they revert back to crime (what they know) because they're unprepared for society. … Prison isn't much of a deterrent anymore when someone isn't taught how to live.*"

Other themes that emerged included lack of a support system/mentor (16 percent), lack of education (15 percent), money issues (14 percent), stigma (14 percent), and peers, neighborhood or family environment (12 percent).

Of the 409 men interviewed, 62 percent had been to prison before (recidivists). The men who had recidivated were different in important ways from those who had not. They were older (42 years versus 39 years), had more kids (2.5 versus 1.5), more minor kids (1.4 versus 0.8), fewer months served in prison (77 versus 123), fewer years still to serve in prison (4.8 versus 7.4), and had been employed on the outside for a shorter period of time (52 months versus 72 months). They also were more likely to have less than a GED (21 percent versus 17 percent) and to have been unemployed at time of arrest (48 percent versus 35 percent).

Importantly, they were also more likely to believe that they had a substance abuse problem (52 percent versus 35 percent) and were more likely to not know where they would live upon release (31 percent versus 17 percent). But most telling are their responses to questions that were asked regarding their perceived needs upon release. Recidivists were statistically significantly more likely to report needing assistance with obtaining identification, transportation, housing, childcare, family and friend support, meals, employment, mentorship, substance abuse, healthcare and religious services.

Despite having served much longer sentences, and with much longer sentences still to serve, first-timers perceive their reentry needs to be less than that of recidivists.

There are many plausible explanations for these differences. Given their experience, recidivists' perceptions of needs may be more rooted in reality. Should this be the case, prison first timers may be woefully underprepared for the challenges that lie ahead. It is also plausible that recidivists have been particularly negatively impacted by the experience of churning in and out of prison: Bridges have been burned, stigmas have been added and failures have accumulated.

Still other reasons could include the nature of the crime and the circumstances that led to their incarceration (whereas first timers may be in for longer sentences for violence that is not tied to deficits, need or addiction), substance abuse and mental illness, or challenges associated with criminal justice supervision. Whatever the reasons, recidivists seem to differ from non-recidivists. One recidivist summed his experience this way:

"Having a negative thought pattern from prison. Frustration and lack of opportunities. Not having the tools to deal with frustration of denials and roadblocks. So, all the negative thinking from prison kicked back in. And I go back to old ways. I started with [a] positive mind-set and that quickly faded away, leading to substance abuse. Substance abuse changes people so quickly, so you must avoid those frustrations and barriers."

Re-Entry and Recidivism in Arizona

How is Arizona doing when it comes to reentry and recidivism? The challenges here are similar to the challenges elsewhere, and significant strides have been made in the last few years to reduce recidivism in the state. As of August 2020, approximately 39,000 people were incarcerated in state prisons in Arizona (Shinn, 2020). At yearend 2018, Arizona had the fifth-highest incarceration rate in the nation (559 per 100,000 adults), behind only Louisiana, Oklahoma, Mississippi, and Arkansas (Carson, 2018).

Arizona's three year return-to-prison rate is 39.1 percent. This figure puts the state below the national average for the BJS cohort study reported above, 49.7 percent within 3 years (Durose et al. 2014), and below the figure for the Pew state study reported above 43.3 percent within 3 years (Pew Center on the States, 2011). Although comparisons across states should always be done with caution, Arizona is decidedly average when it comes to recidivism – the Pew study puts Arizona between states like Minnesota (61.2 percent) and California (57.8 percent) and states like Wyoming (24.8 percent) and Oregon (22.8 percent). Importantly, however, approximately half of all of the people currently incarcerated in Arizona have served a prior term in prison (19,843) (Shinn, 2020).

The reduction of recidivism has been a primary goal for Governor Doug Ducey's administration as represented by the Recidivism Reduction Project Breakthrough Team. This project has the Arizona Department of Corrections, Rehabilitation and Reentry (ADCRR) as the lead agency and includes additional agencies such as the Department of Economic Security, the Department of Housing, and the Department of Health Services. ADCRR has made a number of changes over the last few years with recidivism reduction in mind, including modifying conditions of confinement to make prisons less restrictive, training correctional officers on motivational interviewing techniques, and supplying cognitive behavioral therapy for high-risk individuals.

ADCRR also has collaborated with some of the above agencies to introduce innovative approaches to recidivism reduction – most notably with the implementation of employment centers in three prisons. Prior to their release, eligible men and women can transfer to these units and receive assistance in employment searches from Department of Economic Security staff. Potential employers are invited to the centers for job fairs with the goal of having individuals released from prison with a job in hand.

Additional approaches to reducing recidivism include reentry centers to provide alternatives to reincarceration, a partnership with Uber to provide transportation to released individuals, enrollment of incarcerated individuals within the Arizona Health Care Cost Containment System (AHCCCS), reentry coalitions designed to mobilize support for formerly incarcerated individuals within the community, and the development of new standards for halfway house quality. Each of these approaches will require evaluation to determine how well they reduce recidivism, but they are all steps in the right direction.

CONCLUSION

How to Reduce Recidivism

Based on the above information, which is informed by scholars, currently incarcerated individuals, formerly incarcerated individuals, correctional administrators and staff, and other key stakeholders associated with recidivism reduction, the following elements could help to reduce recidivism.

Replace the Reward Structure of Incarcerated Individuals

Focus on rewarding good behavior rather than punishing bad behavior. Incentivize prosocial behavior on the inside that is expected on the outside: reward sobriety (e.g., clean UAs), and education, job, and programming performance (not only attendance or completion). Create bank accounts that allow people to save money toward their release and to visually see the savings.

Create Prosocial Opportunities for Formerly Incarcerated Individuals

Time spent in legal activities means less time to spend in illegal activities. Work to increase education, employment, housing, and productive leisure opportunities. Do not just remove barriers (e.g., "Ban the Box") – create pathways for formerly incarcerated individuals to be successful. Begin these processes while the individual is still incarcerated, and give special attention to the immediate transition period between prison and community re-entry.

Distribute Re-entry and Recidivism Efforts Across Multiple Agencies and Organizations

Recidivism is not simply a problem for the Department of Corrections (Wright, Morse, & Sutton, In Press). Employment needs, health needs, mental health needs, substance abuse needs and housing needs all point to assistance required from other agencies and organizations.

Recognize that People Recidivate for a Variety of Reasons

There never will be a magic-bullet program that works for everyone and reduces recidivism to a significant degree. Even the very best, gold standard cognitive behavioral therapy programs are difficult to scale up to reach a large population. Recidivism-reduction efforts should be multifaceted and address the many factors related to criminal behavior.

Start Re-entry on the First day of Incarceration

Re-entry programming often begins just a few months before re-entry and has to overcome the effects of years of incarceration. Instead, re-entry preparation should begin early, with individualized case plans from counselors and in-prison mentoring from those who have gone through the system.

Foster Ties to the Outside World Within Prison

Nearly all prisoners are returning to society. Re-entry into society is a shock, and the unfamiliarity of interacting with people and institutions can promote recidivism.

Opportunities for keeping prisoners connected to society, while still retaining the incapacitation effects of incarceration, include the 'Inside Out' Prison Exchange Program, parenting programs that allow family members into the institution so that skills can be practiced, work release, visitation with a focus on family reunification, mentorship programs, and job training.

Acknowledge Victimization Among People who are Incarcerated

The well-documented "victim/offender overlap" in criminology means that a significant portion of people who are incarcerated are also victims. They also often were children of incarcerated parents themselves. Women in prison in particular often have significant histories of abuse and victimization. Addressing these harms and traumas is critical toward successful re-entry.

Develop Alternatives to Re-incarceration

Prison should be reserved for violent individuals who are a continued danger to themselves or society. Prison is more costly than community alternatives. It costs approximately $24,300 to incarcerate one person per year in Arizona – $66 a day. It costs approximately $3,400 to supervise one person per year in the community in Arizona, or $9 a day. Incarcerating older people is even more costly and their likelihood of reoffending declines significantly with age. Good quality transitional housing and reentry centers or increased supervision conditions may be better responses to recidivism.

Empower and Reward Correctional Staff

Correctional staff are often underpaid and overworked and, quite simply, undervalued. They are often expected to act as change agents to alter antisocial thinking and behaviors while simultaneously ensuring safety and security. Staff should be trained and provided the best resources available to accomplish these goals, and they should be incentivized to do their job well.

Anticipate Setbacks

Resist the urge to hold up individual examples as failures of the larger program or approach. High profile negative instances can result in an otherwise successful program or policy being discarded.

The above list is certainly not exhaustive, and it generally avoids recommendations that would require significant legislative changes. It also does not explicitly address the especially pronounced impact of incarceration on the future prospects of youth, women, and racial and ethnic minorities. Arizona is making significant advancements in several of these areas, but it will take continued and additional support from community members to achieve sustained progress.

Nearly everyone in prison is coming back. It is time to acknowledge this fact and to give appropriate attention and resources to recidivism reduction in order to achieve public safety at a lower social and economic cost.

REFERENCES

Alper, M., Durose, M. R., & Markman, J. (2018). *2018 update on prisoner recidivism: A 9-year follow-up period (2005-2014)*. Bureau of Justice Statistics.

Andrews, D. A., Zinger, I., Hoge, R. D., Bonta, J., Gendreau, P., & Cullen, F. T. (1990). Does correctional treatment work? A clinically relevant and psychologically informed meta- analysis. *Criminology, 28*(3), 369–404. doi:10.1111/j.1745-9125.1990.tb01330.x

Benedict, W. R., Huff-Corzine, L., & Corzine, J. (1998). Clean up and go straight: Effects of drug treatment on recidivism among felony probationers. *American Journal of Criminal Justice, 22*(2), 169–187. doi:10.1007/BF02887256

Bonta, J., & Andrews, D. A. (2017). *The psychology of criminal conduct* (6th ed.). Routledge.

Carson, E. A. (2016). *Prisoners in 2018*. U.S. Department of Justice.

Durose, M. R., Cooper, A. D., & Snyder, H. N. (2014). *Recidivism of prisoners released in 30 states in 2005: Patterns from 2005 to 2010*. Bureau of Justice Statistics.

Gainey, R. R., Payne, B. K., & O'Toole, M. (2000). The relationships between time in jail, time on electronic monitoring, and recidivism: An event history analysis of a jail-based program. *Justice Quarterly, 17*(4), 733–752. doi:10.1080/07418820000094741

Gendreau, P., Little, T., & Goggin, C. (1996). A meta-analysis of the predictors of adult offender recidivism: What works! *Criminology, 34*(4), 575–607. doi:10.1111/j.1745-9125.1996.tb01220.x

Haverkate, D. L., Meyers, T. J., Telep, C. W., & Wright, K. A. (2020). On PAR with the yard: Participatory action research to advance knowledge in corrections. *Corrections: Policy, Practice and Research, 5*(1), 28–43. doi:10.1080/23774657.2019.1576149

Hepburn, J. R., & Albonetti, C. A. (1994). Recidivism among drug offenders: A survival analysis of the effects of offender characteristics, type of offense, and two types of intervention. *Journal of Quantitative Criminology*, *10*(2), 159–179. doi:10.1007/BF02221157

Listwan, S. J., Sundt, J. L., Holsinger, A. M., & Latessa, E. J. (2003). The effect of drug court programming on recidivism: The Cincinnati experience. *Crime and Delinquency*, *49*(3), 389–411. doi:10.1177/0011128703049003003

Maltz, M. D. (1984). *Recidivism*. Academic Press.

Pew Center on the States. (2011). *State of recidivism: The revolving door of America's prisons*. The Pew Charitable Trusts.

Shinn, D. (2020). *Corrections at a glance, August 2020*. Available at https://corrections.az.gov/reports-documents/reports/corrections-glance

Thrasher, J., Maloney, E., Mills, S., House, J., Wroe, T., & White, V. (2019). Reimagining prison research from the inside-out. *Journal of Prisoners on Prisons*, *28*, 12–28.

United States Sentencing Commission. (2016). *Recidivism among federal offenders: A comprehensive overview*. Available at https://www.ussc.gov/sites/default/files/pdf/research-and-publications/research-publications/2016/recidivism_overview.pdf

Wilson, J. A. (2005). Bad behavior or bad policy? An examination of Tennessee release cohorts, 1993-2001. *Criminology & Public Policy*, *4*(3), 485–518. doi:10.1111/j.1745-9133.2005.00304.x

Wright, K.A., Haverkate, D.L., Meyers, T.J., Matekel, C.G., Telep, C.W., Maloney, E., … Wroe, T. (2017). *Recidivism reduction in Arizona*. Report submitted to the Governor's Office Recidivism Reduction Project Team.

Wright, K. A., & Khade, N. (2018). Offender recidivism. In O. H. Griffin & V. H. Woodward (Eds.), *Routledge handbook of corrections in the United States* (pp. 494–502). Routledge.

Wright, K. A., Morse, S. J., & Sutton, M. M. (in press). The limits of recidivism reduction: Advancing a more comprehensive understanding of correctional success. In J. Gould & P. Metzger (Eds.), *Big ideas in criminal justice reform*. NYU Press.

Chapter 9
Prison Communities:
An Examination of Work, Life, and Relationships in Prison

Jim Howe
Irish Prison Service (Retired), Ireland

ABSTRACT

This chapter will examine the prison as a community. This enclosed community is a place for the incarceration of criminals tried in the courts. It is also a workplace for corrections officers, and a microcosm of wider society, with work related and prison related relationships developing within the institution's walls. The chapter examines these themes from the perspective of the corrections officer, a perspective not always discussed in penological literature, or understood in wider society. The focus of literature rarely involves discussion on prisons as places of work, or in terms of the individuals for which society invests the care of its incarcerated. The study of the history of imprisonment and prisons and its sociological implications is significant but outside the scope of this work.

INTRODUCTION:

Prison as an Institution

The existence and the use of prison is almost universal across cultures (Platek, 1991). Discussion in sociological and political texts, usually reflect the debate on, the integrity and nature of imprisonment on society, the state, and the individual (as a prisoner). The focus of literature rarely involves discussion on prisons as places

DOI: 10.4018/978-1-7998-6646-6.ch009

of work, or in terms of the individuals for which society invests the care of its incarcerated (Maguire, 2002). The study of the history of imprisonment and prisons and its' sociological implications is significant but, outside the scope of this work.

Prisons exist as physical entities which resemble their purpose of confinement as punishment. The modern prison as recognised today stems from Bentham's *Panopticon* or 'all seeing eye' (Carey, 2000), in which control of the body and soul of prisoners is invested in its' architecture. The discipline of the inmates is organised in terms of space and location. The *enclosure* surrounding this space was required to create the closed area required for discipline (Foucault, 1977). Further partitioning added to the control and discipline and this was modelled on the monastic cell. The cell as it is known collectively across jurisdictions, still retains the physicality of solitude and the ideal invested in soulful reflection.

The high walls of the prison provide a physical barrier to communication with wider society thus isolating the offender within. The importance of this is relevant today with the issue of prohibiting illegal mobile phones from inside Irish prisons. Goffman describes this barrier as a feature of the *Total Institution* where the staff monitor, not by observation alone but, by surveillance (Goffman, 1968). The barrier also extends to the wider community in which prison exist. Prison walls and security prohibit entry and inspection of prisons to a select few and censor all communications from within, thus protecting the prison regime from any scrutiny by the public (Gallo, 1995). This also had the effect of creating a social distance between the work of the prison officer and the perception in society of that work. In the absence of concrete reports, the imagination is fuelled by reference to media portrayals in film and television. Portrayed from mostly historical perspectives, the account of prison work is lacking a base in what is now known as the *Late Modern* prison environment (Liebling, 2004).

The legitimacy and necessity of prisons is a constant topic for debate between reformers and the idea that no realistic alternative exists. The most realistic reform is to limit the type and numbers incarcerated (O'Mahony, 1993. Rutherford, 1991). The recognition that reform from within by prison staff represents the best hope but, due to the vested interests involved, not a realistic one (Jenkins, 1987). In the UK and France and the US, the privatisation of prison services in competition to their traditional governmental organisations, has created a bunker mentality within the traditional organisations (Maguire, 2002).

Prison Organization

Historically, prison services have remained part of the governments security programme and managed by public servants. In Ireland this has been the case since 1878 and the setting up of the General Prisons Board. The Irish Prison Service has a continuous unbroken history as a service from the time of the General Prisons Board (Carey, 2000). This coincided with the formation of exactly the same institution in Britain. As an organisation the prison service remained as a minor function of the Dept of Justice until the setting up of the Irish Prison Service as an Agency in 1998. This was one of the key reccomendations of the Whitaker Report (Tomlinson, 1995).

The organisation of prison services in Ireland and Britain have evolved from the same basic structure. Based on the role of the prison and its' officers, and imbued with rules and regulations, it has defined structures and stability. Handy refers to this organisational structure as likened to a *Greek Temple,* whereby the pillars represent function and divisions of the organisation and the management is the *Pediment* at the top (Handy, 2000). Stability and predictability are features of this. However, from the 1960s onwards an explosion in the population numbers in prisons across Western Europe and the US, coupled with changes in the focus of imprisonment in terms of rehabilitation, destabilised the status quo (Rutherford, 1991, Ruggerio et al, 1995, Maguire, 2002). This trend followed at a later stage in Ireland (O'Mahony, 1993, Tomlinson, 1995, Carey, 2000). The organisational ability to deal with rapid changes was lacking due to its' structure (Handy, 2000), and to the financial constraints of those times (James et al, 1997).

Throughout Western Europe and the developed world, an ageing and decaying prison building structure belonging to victorian times, was inheritited (O'Mahony 1993, McCullagh, 1996, Ruggerio, 1995, James, 1997). Unsuited to modern forms of imprisonment and stretched to capacity, the prison services were operating crisis management. The brunt of this was felt by the prison officers working at the 'coalface' and led to more militant trade union activity (Liebling& Price, 2001, Coyle, 2005). The cost in monetary and management terms increased substantially, placing strains on prison budgets and leaving less capital for new building. The eighties brought about profound changes in the political landscape which was to have an immense effect on prison policies.

The eighties ushered in a period of Reagonomics and Thatcherism with the ideology of small government (James, 1997). A feature of this period was the practice of privatising prisons. In the US during the late seventies and early eighties, with declining faith in government coupled with the need to cut costs, the authorities embarked on a prison building spree financed by private companies. This shift in US policy occurred with the change in emphasis in imprisonment from one of rehabilitation and training to one of containment and deterence (King, 1994, James, 1997). Prison privatisation became the way forward in terms of cost, rising prison populations and the willingness of private corporations to invest in this 'Industry' (McDonald, 1994).

Imprisonment as an industry has gone through a rapid expansioist phase. In the US in 1986, there were 30 private prisons, this rose to 60 in 1991 (McDonald, 1994,

James, 1997). This trend occurred throughout the US, Britain, and Australia who after a late start became the biggest proponents by privatising 28% of its prisons (James, 1997). As part of the expansionist phase, a new term is being used, that of warehousing (Toch, 1985). This belief of an Anglo-American model of warehouse imprisonment being imposed on the Irish system has been made with regard to the proposed prison development at Thornton Hall in Co Dublin.

The prospect of privatisation has had an effect on the traditional public service prison officer unions. In most of the jurisdictions where prison privatisation has taken place, prison officer unions have negotiated changes to traditional work practices (Gallo, 1995,James, 1997, Maguire, 2002, Coyle, 2005, Arnold, 2007, Irish Times 2008).

Prison as a Workplace

The idea of prisons as workspaces are paid scant regard in literature. Mostly inhabited by men, both staff and prisoners, prisons can be seen as gendered workplace (Crawley, 2004, Coyle, 2005, Liebling, 2004, Arnold, 2007). In common with other prison services (UK and Australia), 10% of staff of the Irish prison Service are women (McGuckin, 2002) unlike that of Sweden where 46% of the workforce is made up of women (Kriminalvardan, 2009). The prison workplace can be frightening and dangerous (Kimmett, 2003), unhygeinic (O'Mahony, 1993, Carey, 2000), and stressful (Cheek, 1983, Dollard, 1998). The culture prevalent in prisons is one of 'machismo' (Crawley, 2004) or the 'John Wayne syndrome' as outlined by Cheek and Miller (1983).

Within the organisational make up of prison work, there are intrinsic factors which contribute toward stress. The literature tends to focus on the role problems of prison staff as particular contributors to stress (Shamir and Dory, 1982, Cheek, 1983, Poole and Regoli, 1983, Triplett, Mullings and Scarborough, 1996, Dollard, 1998). Poole and Regoli (1983) specifically cite the problem of shifting institutional policies and philosophies concerning the handling of prisoners as organisationally produced stress. They also found that this in turn created a cycle in which the officer intensified his/her commitment to their custodial role, leading to further conflict with both prisoners and management and exacerbating the stressful nature of the job.

The Custodial Role of the Officer

The minimum expectation of any prison service is that of the confinement of its charges. The removal from society of those deemed unfit for society is its primary function and the support functions are those deemed necessary by its jurisdiction. Traditionally this role of custody and security and the maintenance of order was the sole role of the prison officer. With the arrival of the late modern prison system, the role saw an expansion to fit the aspirations of society and its prison representation. The control element of the custodial role brings the officer into conflict with prisoners. Prisoners, nearly without exception, do not want to be there, there is no acquiescence on their part.

In order to control and hold them in their custody, staff have to censor, search, restrain and monitor all aspects of their interactions (Goffman, 1968). This imposition of control is unwarranted and unappreciated. The exercise of control is not done in any haphazard way. Prisons are highly regulated and rule orientated organisations with hierarchical management structures. The officer is managed by a set of rules and regulations and then in turn enforces another set of rules and regulations on the prisoner. This unique role is seen as unique among occupational groups (Cressy, 1961).

The maintenance of safe custody, routine and order in a prison, means searching and restraining and invasive surveillance (Thomas, 1972). This creates a source of tension where prisoners are to be found in a highly charged and emotional state and one wrong word by an officer can provoke a violent reaction. The constant readiness to react to potentially dangerous events is always lurking in the background (Williams, 1983). Some officers prefer this role. Williams (1983) found a correlation between officers' perception of being in conflict with prisoners, and their general beliefs regarding prisoners. These perceptions were linked with the officers' definition of their role and their concept of imprisonment. The more concerned the officer is with the custodial role, the more likely the officer is to see interactions with prisoners as one of conflict.

In the Irish context, research by McGowan (1982) found that officers inclined towards authoritarianism with rigid and '*inflexible views*' tended to favour tough treatment towards prisoners and have negative views of them. These officers tended to find the job difficult (McGowan, 1982). The traditional pure custodial role is one of less recent times and the officer of the late modern prison is expected to have input into the rehabiliative effects of imprisonment demanded by society.

The role of the prison officer has expanded across most prison regimes in the developed world, including Ireland. After the second world war a variety of specialist staff were introduced into prisons in Britain and later Ireland. These included, teachers, instructors, welfare officers and psychologists (McGowan, 1982, Coyle, 2005,). Their role was one of rehabilitation and reform. At first this tended to crystalise the custodial role of the officer by referencing this against the specialised care workers. Unionisation played a part in changing this. In order to get better work conditions for its members and prevent erosion of their status, prison officer unions recognised that prison officers had to specialise into areas previously reserved for care staff (Liebling, 2001,Coyle, 2005) . Yet, prison organisations are not ones that change very quickly and this was reported by McGowan in regard to the Irish prison officer. He found that prison officers saw professional groups within the prison as undermining their authority (McGowan, 1982).

The care nature of modern prison work is recognised in the mission statements of most western European, US and Australian prisons. The IPS mission statement reflects the twin roles of the prison officer. It references the custodial role as providing safe and secure and humane custody, while stressing ; '*The Service is committed to managing custodial sentences in a way which encourages and supports prisoners in their endeavouring to live law abiding and purposeful lives as valued members of society*' (IPS). The IPS is more explicit with regard to its' core values which states;

Core Values

The Prison Service:

- *Recognises its obligation to serve the community with full respect for the human dignity and rights of every person, both in custody and in the wider community*
- *Recognises that it is obliged to help every offender live as a law-abiding person and that the Service can contribute to their realising their potential*
- *Believes in making available to each person in custody conditions and services appropriate to their well-being and personal development*
- *Commits itself to minimising the detrimental effects of imprisonment*
- *Endeavours to help prisoners, where possible and appropriate, to maintain relationships with their families*
- *Values the resources available to it, especially all staff working in the prison system who are the most important asset in fulfilling the Service's mission*
- *Commits itself to being courteous and fair in all its dealings*
- *Accepts that it is accountable for its actions and endeavours to demonstrate this accountability in public* (Irish Prison Service mission statement).

The UK prison services statement of purpose is equally committed to its dual role:

Her Majesty's Prison Service serves the public by keeping in custody those committed by the courts. Our duty is to look after them with humanity and help them lead law-abiding and useful lives in custody and after release (HM Prison Service).

There seems to be remarkable similarity between the two jurisdictions in terms of their statements of intent. The Canadian Correctional Services makes similar statements of intent but has established an ethics board and a set of guidelines to proceed (CSC). The same sentiments are reflected in the oath taken by officers in other jurisdictions. The taking of an oath does not exist in the IPS. In Slovenia the officer pledges to respect human rights and basic freedoms. The US Federal Bureau of Prisons mission statement states that it is their duty

'to protect society by confining offenders in the controlled environments of prisons and community based facilities that are safe, humane, cost-efficient, and appropriately secure, and that provide work and other self-improvement opportunities to assist offenders becoming law-abiding citizens' (Liebling, 2001).

The US statement echoes different aspirations rather than stating any intent. Here the care role is relegated behind 'cost efficient' and 'appropriately secure'. The care nature of a prison officers role has become more definite in programmes that try to manage sentences. In the UK, the role of Personal Officer has been developed. This role is part of positive sentence management shemes whereby officers take on certain responsibilities regarding the development of prisoners. An officer is assigned a specific number of prisoner to communicate and interact with. Through this interaction the personal officer encourages and acts as a role-model to prisoners so that they may engage with the development regime. A similar scheme is being pilotted in the IPS at present. The Swedish prison service (Kriminalvardan) has gone one step further and seperated the role of their prison officers. They have developed two strands of prison officer where one is security orientated, and the other is a care officer or 'contact person' (Kriminalvardan).

The seperation of roles, and the recognition of enhanced and specialised working arrangements, highlights the conflict between the roles. *"It is difficult to define what prison officers do, let alone assess how well they have done it* (Gilbert, 1997: 50). In reference to the Irish case, McGowan (1982) stated that clarification of the role of the prison officer as one of the key issues in the prison service. The inability to define in concrete terms the role of a prison officer can lead to role conflict. Prison officers 'yearn' for a clearer definition of their work (Liebling, 2001). This has implications for their ability to carry out their duties, of which they have no clear definition, and cope with the resultant stresses involved.

Role conflict is the result of demands made of the officer to enforce prison routine and order, which relies on prisoner co-operation and on their personal privacy (Shamir and Dory, 1982). In order to maintain this role the officer has to utilise considerable interpersonal skill, which not all officers possess and are not adequately trained for. If an officer is under skilled in this area he/she would feel a sense of failure and helplessness and the resultant stress. Role overload might be a result of the inability of the officer to cope with the quality or the quantity of the work demanded. Role overload is directly related to burnout which is defined as emotional and or physical exhaustion, depersonalisation and lack of personal accomplishment, leading to cynicism and detachment (Whitehead and Lindquist, 1986). Pioneer work on burnout was carried out by Maslach (1976) and is seen as a result of frequent and intense interpersonal contact and occurs frequently among workers in human services. Worker alienation is a particular facet of this model and different studies of prison staff have found high levels of alienation. Shamir and Dory's (1982) study confirms this factor and relate it to organisational phenomena inherent in prison staff such as high absenteeism and sickness, a feature of the Irish prison system (IrishTimes, 2003).

Role conflict among senior officers is lessened with experience. They tend to exercise 'discretion' with regard to enforcement of rules and regulations and the handling of minor breaches (Crawley, 2004). This use of 'discretion' when viewed from a junior officers perspective, may be seen as being soft. The 'John Wayne Syndrome' as outlined by Cheek and Miller (1983) has been put forward as a peer pressure influence that junior officers are particularly affected by. This macho image is a feature of the role performance of officers who use 'masks' to hide their true feeling which may be of confusion and fear Goffman.E., 1969). The mask which is used to present the self in a prison setting can be confusing for the novice officer and contribute to feelings of cognitive dissonance (Howe, 2009). The inexperienced officer or RPOs have lesser feelings of control (McGuckin, 2002) and this can be frustrating. Their lack of autonomy/control over the work process, is in contrast with those of the more experienced officers. They are more willing to use their discretion and gain the benefit of this in their working relationships with prisoners. In studies, greater participation in decision making leads to more stisfaction among prison staff and in consequence to this, less absenteeism and less assaults by prisoners (Stohr, 1994).

Building Relationships in Prison

Officer-prisoner Dependency

The prison officer is in a power-relationship with the incarcerated. The nature of that power is based on the role provision of the officer. The officer may act as a role model, an enforcer, an enemy, a provider, a protector, a carer, a listener, a teacher, and yet, sometimes invisible or irrelevant. Prisons are like any closed or cloistered society. There is a self-sufficient/reliant society at work. All aspects of the prisoner's life is catered for and controlled by the prison officer (Crawley, 2004). This means a total reliance on the officer for their needs (Foucault, 1977, O'Mahony.P., 2000). These needs can be physical, mental, spiritual, educational, medical, recreational, familial, communicational, protectoral, and legal (Grant, 2005). The specialised nature of the prison officer's role is recognised as more than their base role (Liebling A., 2001).

The base-roles are those duties carried out that are at the minimum required to perform in a prison. They are the security duties that maintain the integrity of the security of the prison. Keeping prisoner numbers correct, observing prisoners, closing gates, keeping keys secure, controlling prisoner movement, and numerous other activities officers perform automatically on a daily basis (Foucault, 1977). The automaticity in these duties is apparent when established officers refer to being '*paid from the neck down*' when engaged in these routine duties which, some liken to '*watching paint dry*' (Fitzgerald, 1982)

Beyond base-line duties, it is more specialised and specific. An officer arrives at work and opens the school, another takes over the surgery, another stock-takes in the shop, another opens the visits area, another opens the kitchen, another gets his tools to fix the plumbing, another prepares the gym, another opens the library, another censors letters, another prepares the workshop, another opens the laundry, and the list goes on. For all these posts and many more, the prison officer is specialised and delivers this service to the prisoner. The prisoner depends on officers for all these services (Coyle, 2005, Crawley, 2004). This dependency defines part of the complex relationships between both sides (Liebling, 2008).

As the deliverer and controller of the services described above, the prison officer maintains the power to deny or delay their provision (Liebling, 2004). Simple requests take on dramatic significance for the prisoner when they are denied or obfuscated (Crawley, 2004). The provision of basic supplies such as; toilet roll, toothbrushes, soap, etc, can be of real significance to the prisoner who, is locked in his/her cell and has no other access (Sykes G., 2006) (Coyle, 2005). A delay in unlock at anytime can bring panic and rage. Some officers reduce the significance of the transactional nature of this relationship dismissing it as unimportant, in a form of cognitive dissonance. More cognitively aware officers realise its importance and either, use it as a lever for control, or acquiesce to demands as part of the nature of the role of the prison officer under regulations. Higher moral performance by some officers can be a factor of better training (HMIP, 2009) and a result of recruitment strategies (Crawley, 2004, Liebling A., 2004).

The strength of the cultural influence in individual prisons as a factor of staff behaviour should not be minimised. It has been recognised that each prison has an individual culture operating in regard to acceptable behaviour of staff regardless of the regulatory authority (Sparks, 1994; Liebling A., 2004). The kind of regime and behaviour that can be viewed as operating in moral vacuum is visible to prisoners, but may be invisible to staff operating it for different reasons. Highly regimented and rule-based institutions can operate a 'control model' in which little discretion is given to staff, and methods of control are secondary to the goal of management (McEvoy, 2006, Liebling, 2008). When prisons come under pressure due to issues such as; overcrowding, drugs, diseases and political strife, etc, the focus of prison management is on 'fire-fighting' (Liebling A., 2004) or 'crisis management' (O'Mahony.P., 2000; Carey, 2000).

The relationship between the officer and inmate in the prison can be described as one that takes place in an environment of constant tension. The tension can be alleviated based on the regime in place (Craig, 2004, Stohr M. H., 2000). Higher category security institutions are tenser, compared to the lower level security institutions such as open centres. Whatever the category though, some level of tension exists. The levels of tension in any individual prison can vary due to a variety of factors. Overcrowding, hot weather, and shortages of services can have significant effects on the tension levels (O'Mahony.P., 2000, Carey, 2000, Walmsley, 2001, Kimmett, 2003, Liebling A, 2004, Carrabine, 2004, Katherine Howard Foundation, 2007). Tension can be increased or alleviated to an extent by the actions of prison officers in the performance of their jobs (Carrabine, 2004, Crawley, 2004).

Tensions also exist in the nature of the interpersonal interactions between individual officers and prisoners within the wider considerations of the culture of the institutions involved (Liebling A., 2001, Crawley, 2004, Arnold, 2007). Prison officer work in confined spaces with their reluctant charges and have physical contact as part of their duties such as; searching, coralling, and in some cases, restraining (Liebling A, 2001, Crawley, 2004, Coyle, 2005)At this level of interaction, the tensions involved can be due to the actions and/or type of communications of either party. An officer can bring toxicity to the interaction (Grant, 2005). The reasons can be mutlitudinous and can be stable as in personality and/or beliefs system (Freeman, 2003, Tewkesbury, 2008).

The unstable conditions can include; officer alienation (Freeman, 2003, Lambert, 2004), burnout (Whitehead, 1986, Freeman, 2003), cynicism and job dissatisfaction (Lambert, 2004). External to the officers locus of control, other elements such as family problems, substance abuse etc, might intrude on their performance over their careers. These might be due to the stressful nature of the role (Maslach, 1976, Cheek, 1983, Whitehead, 1986, Carlson, 2003). The stable conditions described above can be eliminated by selection procedures at recruitment (Whitaker, 1985, Liebling A, 2001, Crawley, 2004). Unstable conditions within control of the officer can be changed by utilising interventions that reduce job-stress, heighten job-satisfaction, and allocate a certain amount of autonomy within organisational control (Lambert, 2004). Training in the early stages of an officers career can be of great benefit to them when dealing with prisoners (McGuckin, 2002, Coyle, 2005).

Problems with interpersonal communications between staff and prisoners, is normally less due to the characteristics of the officers intervention than with the prisoners, and their relationship with violence (Kimmett, 2003). It is universally understood that prisons are violent environments and that the prisoners, while in opposition to the prison officers are violent, the general violence is perpetrated against each other (Clemmer, 1940, Sykes, 2006). It is seen by prisoners as a matter of convention rather than a process of disruption (Bottoms, 1999).

Communications between staff and prisoners take place in confined spaces with aggression forming part of the interaction (Sykes G., 1958). Instrumental aggression is displayed quite often by prisoners in their dealings with staff and other prisoners (Kimmett, 2003), and generally in the presence of other prisoners. The hostility faced by staff in day to day dealings with prisoners has created a problematic working environment. This hostility can be reflective of the lack of trust and outright hostility by prisoners to the prison regime (Clemmer, 1940, Winfree, 2002, Arnold, 2007).

REFERENCES

Arnold, H. a. (2007). Prison Officers and prison culture. In Y. Jewkes (Ed.), *Handbook on Prisons* (pp. 471–495). Willan Publishing.

Canada, C. S. (n.d.). *Commisioner's Directive*. Retrieved February 13th, 2009, from Correctional Services of Canada: www.csc-scc.gc.ca/text/plcy/cdshtm/001-cde-eng.shtml#_5

Carey, T. (2000). *Mountjoy, The Story of a Prison*. The Collins Press.

Cheek, F. M., & Miller, M. D. S. (1983). The Experience of Stress in Prison Officers: A double-bind theory of correctional stress. *Journal of Criminal Justice*, *11*(2), 105–120. doi:10.1016/0047-2352(83)90046-6

Coyle, A. (2005). *Understandin Prisons; Key issues in policy and practice*. Open University Press.

Crawley, E. (2004). *Doing Prison Work*. Willan Publishing.

Cressy, D. E. (1961). The Prison: Studies in Institutional Organisations and Change. Reinhart & Winston.

Dollard, M., & Winefield, A. H. (1998). A test of the Demand-Control/Support Model of Work Stress in Correctional Officers. *Journal of Occupational Health Psychology*, *3*(3), 243–264. doi:10.1037/1076-8998.3.3.243

Foucault, M. (1977). *Discipline and Punish, the birth of the prison*. Allen Lane.

Gallo, E. (1995). The Penal System in France: from Correctionalism to Managerialism. In V. R. Ruggerio (Ed.), *Westen European Prison Systems. A Critical Anatomy* (pp. 71–92). Sage Publications.

Gilbert, M. (1997). The Illusion of Structure: A Critique of the Classical Model of Organisation and the Discretionary Power of Correctional Officers. *Criminal Justice Review*, *22*(1), 49–64. doi:10.1177/073401689702200105

Goffman, E. (1968). *Asylums, Essays on the Social Situation of Mental patients and other inmates*. Penguin Books.

Handy, C. (2000). *Gods of Management, The Changing work of Organisations*. Arrow Books.

HM Prison Service. (n.d.). *HM Prison Service, about the service*. Retrieved February 13th, 2009, from HM Prison Service: www.hmprisonservice.gov.uk/abouttheservice/statementofpurpose/

IPS. (n.d.). *About us*. Retrieved February 13th, 2009, from Irish Prison Service: / www.irishprisons.ie/about_us-home.htm

Irish Times. (2003). *Prison officers' sick leave costs over E18m more*. Retrieved January 10th, 2009, from Irish Times Archives: https://www.ireland.com/newspaper/ireland/2003/1001/1374848881HM10PRISON.html

James, A. B. (1997). *Privatising Prisons, Rhetoric and Reality*. Sage Publications.

Jenkins, M. (1987). Control Problems in Dispersals. In *A. &. Bottoms, Problems of long-term Imprisonment* (pp. 261–280). Gower.

Kimmett, E. M. (2003). *Prison violence, The dynamics of conflict, fear and power*. Willan Publishing.

King, R. M. (1994). Contexts of Imprisonment: An International Perspective. *British Journal of Criminology*, *34*, 1–13. doi:10.1093/oxfordjournals.bjc.34.S1.1

Kriminalvardan. (n.d.). *Organisation and employees*. Retrieved February 11th, 2009, from Kriminalvardan: www.kriminalvarden.se/templates/KVV_InfopageGeneral____3958.aspx

Liebling, A. (2001). *The Prison Officer.* Leyhill: Prison Service Journal.

Liebling, A. (2004). *Prisons and their Moral Performance, A study of Values, Quality, and Prison Life*. Oxford University Press.

Liebling, A. P. (1999). *An Exploration of Staff-Prisoner Relationships at HMP Whitmoor.* London: Prison Service Research Report No.6.

Maguire, M. M. (2002). *The Oxford Handbook of Criminology* (3rd ed.). Oxford University Press.

Maslach, C. (.-2. (1976). Burned-Out. *Human Behavior, 5*, 16–22.

McCullagh, C. (1996). *Crime in Ireland, a sociological Introduction*. Cork University Press.

McDonald, D. (1994). Public Imprisonment by Private Means, the re-emergence of private prisons and jails in the United States, the United Kingdom and Australia. *British Journal of Criminology, 34*, 29–48.

McGowan, J. (1984). The Role of the Irish prison Officer in the Irish prison Service. *Administration, 28*(3), 259–274.

McGuckin, J. (2002). *Characteristics and Attitudes of RPOs and Prison Officers in the Irish Prison Service*. Belfast: Unpublished Report for Dissertation in Criminology and Justice, Queens University.

O'Mahony, P. (1993). *Crime and Punishment in Ireland*. The Round Hall Press Ltd.

Organisation and Employees. (2009, Feb 12). Retrieved February 12th, 2009, from Kriminalvardan: https://www.kriminalvarden.se/templates/KVV_InfopageGeneral____3958.aspx

Platek, M. (1991). The Sluzewiec Prison in Warsaw, Poland. In D. E. Whitfield (Ed.), *The State of the Prisons- 200 years on* (pp. 56–69). Routledge.

Ruggerio, V. R. (1995). *Western European Penal Systems, A Critical Anatomy*. Sage Publications.

Rutherford, A. (1991). Penal Reform and Prison Realities. In D. Whitfield (Ed.), *The State of the Prisons - 200 years on* (pp. 1–13). Routledge.

Shamir, B. & Dory,A. (1982). Some Correlates of Prison Guards' Beliefs. *Criminal Justice and Behaviour, 8*, 223-249.

Sutherland, R. C. (1966). *Principles of Criminology* (7th ed.). Lippincott.

Thomas, J. (1972). *The English Prison Officer since 1850*. Routledge and Kegan Paul.

Toch, H. (1985). Warehouses for People. *The Annals of the American Academy of Political and Social Science, 478*(1), 58–72. doi:10.1177/0002716285478001006

Tomlinson, M. (1995). Imprisoned Ireland. In V. R. Ruggiero (Ed.), *Western European Penal System, A Critical Anatomy* (pp. 194–227). Sage Publications.

Whitehead, J., & Lindquist, C. A. (1986). Correctional Officer Burnout: A path model. *Journal of Research in Crime and Delinquency, 1*(1), 23–42. doi:10.1177/0022427886023001003

Chapter 10
Teaching Prisoners' Rights to Prison Officers to Improve Professional Performance

Liam J. Leonard
Northern Arizona University, USA

Paula Kenny
Dublin City University, Ireland

ABSTRACT

This chapter is based on the experiences of both authors as part of a multi-disciplinary team of academics who brought changes to the prison system in the Republic of Ireland by leading an academic training program for recruit corrections officers in that country's prison system. The goal was to improve the professional performance of the corrections officers and to increase their understandings of the significance of human rights and prisoner's rights as a key part of their daily work practices. The award-winning recruit prison officer training program was the first of its kind globally.

INTRODUCTION

This chapter will outline the planning, processes, challenges and successes of a unique and innovative teaching and training program for over 1000 recruits entering the Irish Prison Service (IPS), which took place in the Republic of Ireland between 2008 and 2013. The program was known as the Higher Certificate in Custodial Care (HCCC). Essentially, this program combined the expertise of academics from that

DOI: 10.4018/978-1-7998-6646-6.ch010

nation's Universities and the Irish Institutes of Technology sector and blended this with traditional prison training practices of Chief Officers of the IPS. By combining both academic and practical teaching, learning and mentoring, the program set out to extend the scope of knowledge, competence and professionalism of recruits to Ireland's national prison service. The chapter explores the planning and implementation of this innovative educational and training program, from development to delivery, through to the national recognition for the program from the National Academy for the Integration of Research, Teaching and Learning (NAIRTL) educational award to its educators in 2012.

The issue of prisoner's rights and access to justice has a long and contentious history in most jurisdictions. The Republic of Ireland has had a long tradition of problems within its prison system[1]. According to Leonard (2011, p.3.):

The issue of imprisonment in Ireland has traditionally been problematic for a number of reasons, including Ireland's colonial past and the struggle for Independence from British rule in both jurisdictions. This led, in turn, to the use (and abuse) of imprisonment by forces opposed to the independence project. Thus, a sentimental residue of tacit opposition to the prison system has remained a salient characteristic of contemporary Irish life. Essentially, the prevailing system of justice (and the prison system in particular) became a symbol of injustice and oppression throughout the history of British rule for Irish nationalists in either jurisdiction[2].

Therefore, we can see the conflict between the Irish authorities and the prisoner population as having political, historical and cultural aspects, in addition to the existence of complex issues within the criminal justice system for prisoners, particularly when it comes to rights and social justice. For many, the provision of rights and justice for prisoners was the duty and responsibility of the prison officers in the Irish system, many of whom had traditionally received a traditional basic training, focused on security issues rather than rights. Over a period of decades and in response to international covenants and obligations, the Irish Prison Service were required to reform their approach to training by collaborating with academics to implement a more comprehensive and rights based training and development program. The result was the introduction of the HCCC program for new recruits to the IPS[3].

The Higher Certificate in Custodial Care (HCCC) training and education program was an innovative approach to teaching corrections officers about rights and justice while they trained as recruits to a national prison service. It combined new departures in teaching recruit prison officers (RPOs) to recognize, appreciate and value the rights of those in their care in Ireland's prisons. The program has been recognized to be one of excellence and innovation in teaching, learning and research in higher education. The academics who devised and delivered the program were comprised of experts from across the spectrum of social sciences. While these disciplines each had their own emphasis, the presentation of different, though complementary, social science and health-related disciplines collectively provided a high quality, learner-centred blended educational experience informed by contemporary research[4].

The IPS programme was notable for its success in building correction officers' understanding of concepts of rights and justice through disciplines such as sociology, criminology and psychology. Many of the recruit officers had only experience of second level education, therefore program was devised with a focus on delivering rights-based competencies and knowledge. Furthermore, the IPS program was planned in a deliberate way, which would develop the officers' critical thinking, knowledge and skills. Ultimately, the goal was to create a sea of change in the thinking and approach of Ireland's correctional staff to the understanding of prisoners' rights, and to professionalize the prison service in a progressive manner for the benefit of both staff, prisoners and wider society.

The development of HCCC program would be characterized by the integration of the experts' pedagogy, andragogy, pedagogy, research, scholarship and planning skills. Essentially, the experts brought an array of salient research interests in subjects such as Human Rights, Social Justice, Criminology, Sociology, Psychology, Equality and Diversity, Restorative Justice and Penology/Prison Studies. The HCCC program was designed to be applied and had a reflective element, whereby the recruits journaled their experiences of prison work, chronicling the impact of the HCCC's modules on their performance and development as correction officers. While this innovative approach to correctional training would be met with some initial resistance from participants, it was ultimately one of the program's greatest successes, as the benefits of reflection on workplace performance led to improved treatment of prisoners under the RPO's care, it also provided a support network for RPO's to understand and deal with the challenges they faced in their initial years as correctional officers. One key area of focus for the program was the development of critical research skills, in addition to critical self-reflection competencies. The RPOs were asked to continuously assess and refine their work in the prison system, alongside their own perspectives on their academic development. Participants in the program participated in distance and online learning, work-based learning, problem based learning and widely used digital teaching technologies and learning programs.

In regards to curriculum design and subsequent revision, the academic team worked closely with the training staff of the Irish Prison Service Training and Development Centre, ensuring that the programme was informed by current best-practice in the provision of correctional care, prison operations and management. This combination of two very different professions was as unique, innovative and dynamic as the HCCC program itself. Both two groups worked diligently to merge the organizational cultures of the academic Institute and the national prison service and to knowledge transfer best practice and experiences from both. These two institutions had traditional differences in their objectives and methods of operation, but succeeded in achieving the goals and outcomes of the program. The foregrounding of social justice and human rights as key foci for the program was another area of innovative success, later recognized by their prestigious NAIRTL award.

Furthermore, the program was characterized by a focus on working in class and behind the prison walls to combine active learning with real world work experience. This presented challenges for the recruits as students and the educators alike. The experience of shadowing RPOs on their daily routines in prison was an innovative one, while interviews on learning outcomes, reflections and competency development also took place within the prison complex. Classes were given behind the walls of the Portlaoise Prison complex at the IPS Training and Development Centre. This complex also housed former Irish Republican Army (IRA), classified in the Irish system as political prisoners, as well as being the site of the new Midland Prison for other categories of prisoners. Work Place Visits (WPVs) and interviews occurred at Mountjoy Prison in Dublin, built in the 1840s, and the newer women's prison or "Dochas" Centre. WPVs also took place at the newer Wheatfield Prison and Cloverhill Remand Prison in County Dublin. The main goal of the program was to develop a professional competency framework which would enhance the development of the RPOs, protect the rights of the prison population in Ireland's penal system and raise the professional standard for the prison service as a whole.

We can examine the basis for this professionalization process which underpins the performance of prison officers in the execution of their daily workplace duties and responsibilities. At the heart of this is a desire to understand and explain how and why a prison officer will go beyond what is the basic requirement in their tasks, in order to deliver the 'safe, secure and humane' service required of them in the Irish Prison Service Mission Statement. As educators, it was central to our mission that the rights of both RPOs and prisoners in their care be protected as a result of this educational process. The degree of success in achieving this form of elevated integrity within the Irish prison system can be seen to impact upon the lives of the prisoners in the officer's care, and on wider prison system as a whole.

At the heart of this protection of rights was the development of a framework of professional development for the RPOs. Such qualities are invariably drawn upon when humans are faced with challenges to their character, and this can be borne out by the experiences of prison officers who are charged with maintaining the ethos of the Irish Prison Service (IPS) Mission Statement's call for 'safe secure and humane' approaches to custodial care. In particular, prison officers provide us with a good example of a group who must maintain a level of professionalism in the face of negative resistance (and on occasion, violence). The public perception of the prison officer is often surrounded in negativity, which adds to the difficulties in maintaining professionalism for individual officers and the IPS as an institution.

From the perspective of the academics delivering this program, our understanding of this moral dilemma and the manner in which it is challenged was built in part from our own experience working with IPS recruits as part of their Professional Development module on the IPS Custodial Care programme. Throughout this process, we were able to discuss these issues with recruits, and chart their progress over a number of years in prisons during our participation in workplace visits. One key issue which emerged from this process was an understanding of how difficult it was for recruit prison officers to come to terms with the dualistic demands they faced from internal as well as external concerns about professional behaviour. For the prison officer, this process incorporates what Goffman has described as a 'dramaturgical' process; the officer must develop a 'mask' for inside and outside of work in the prison. Crawley (2004) has developed this concept further to incorporate the 'front and back' stage performances which a prison officer must act out when they are involved in different aspects of their work. For instance, they may act and say things in the officer's canteen which they then will do differently during an incident on the prison landing.

Officers described different types of response to this ongoing challenge to their moral integrity when faced with this challenge. Mentoring, although an unofficial part of the IPS culture (Leonard, Kenny and McGuckin, 2009), also plays a role in the development of work-place integrity for prison officers. Recruit officers own moral understanding of their capacities at work are shaped by this unofficial mentoring process, which incorporates 'pro' and 'anti' social modelling (Cherry, 2004). Recruits must develop and maintain their own moral compass in the face of this overlapping process of negative and positive socialisation into workplace practices and dealings with the prison population. Crucially, the recruit must achieve this while both learning their trade in the prison while also dealing with sporadic episodes of violence on the landing or in the exercise yard (Edgar, O'Donnell and Martin 2004).

Externally, the recruit must also deal with misinformed public opinion shaped by a tabloid approach to prison stories by the media, as well as learning to leave the pressures of work behind when returning to their family in between shifts. Of course, such cultural connotations have also played a part in the development of the recruit's own perception of what is to be a prison officer before they joined the service. Therefore, the process of developing moral integrity can be seen to be a most difficult one as the recruit is faced with a series of challenges and dilemmas. These are both external and internal, and are manifest on their journey to becoming a professional correctional officer who can use their own moral integrity as a basis for performance at work alongside an ongoing process of personal and professional development. It is possible for the recruit to 'look within' themselves in order to find the capacity necessary to provide the prerequisite professional levels necessary to deal with their own development in congruence with a development in their humane and rights based response to those they are dealing with within the prison's walls. In addition, it is also possible for the personal integrity of one officer to shape the wider understandings of prisoner's rights in an institution like a prison. This would be the key question in the provision of rights and justice to the prisoners in their care.

The answer to this complex moral dilemma can be found in the statements provided in response to these questions by recruits, training officers and governors alike; 'if I can make the difference to just one person than it will all be worthwhile'. Taken in its totality this statement of intent from individuals in the prison service comes to underpin the overall ethos of the Irish Prison Service as a whole by way of their Mission Statement which calls for 'safe, secure and humane custody for people who are sent to prison'. In many ways, the moral integrity of any institution is bound up with the individual integrity of those who serve within it. Therefore, we can understand the significance of the development of personal levels of moral integrity for the individuals who are to be found on the landings of our prison system dealing with challenging situations such as overcrowding, drug related gang violence, addiction and prisoners with intellectual and learning disabilities. In such circumstances, each individual situation calls for a decision-making process by each officer which depends on a highly developed sense of personal integrity.

In that context, how can we come to understand the development of moral integrity amongst our prison officer population? How and why do they continue to maintain a highly developed sense of moral integrity within a system that has left them to deal with many of society's challenging issues such as asylum seekers, multicultural diversity, poverty and marginalisation, drug related gang violence and suicide? What are the virtues of a prison officer who develops their moral integrity in the face of state cutbacks and systemic overcrowding? In their chapter 'Prison officers and prison culture' in Yvonne Jewkes' (2007) *Handbook on Prisons*, Liebling, Arnold and Tait discuss the role of Prison Officers, who they see as an under researched group in Penology literature. They criticise the prevailing view of prison officers as being 'power-hungry enforcers of authority', claiming that 'prison work is complex and varied' and that POS actually 'under use their authority in the interests of their peacekeeping tasks far more often than they over use it' (ibid). They also acknowledge the varied nature of the prison officer's role as it changes from institution to institution. These were some of the issues that were addressed in the HCCC program.

Moreover, Prison Officers are rarely credited for their work as councillors, as institutional problem solvers, in suicide prevention and in engaging with prisoners by way of rehabilitation. Many surveys revealed that the camaraderie of their workmates and their role in helping others were significant factors in their motivations for work, despite the fact that many indicated that they had 'fallen into' the job due to financial reasons and had little knowledge of prisons before they signed up (ibid). This data reveals a professional group that has a much more public service-minded attitude than the 'power-hungry' misrepresentations would have many believe. The 'skills' of an effective prison officer include a set of values that require a Prison Officer to be 'loyal to decisions already made', but also 'flexible and able to change opinions when circumstances change', and to have these necessary characteristics:

- Physical characteristics: such as 'verbal skills...self-confidence, personal authority...strength for hard working conditions'
- Mental capacity: such as quick thought and retention of various forms of information at once
- Learning ability: such as watching, decision making, problem solving and undertaking administrative tasks
- Interactive ability: such as bearing difficult emotions, understanding other's thoughts and emotions, being interested in one's environment and self, to be sensitive, to have humour, to handle conflict situations...to be reliable, trustworthy and responsible and to acquire positive energy outside the institution (ibid).

Other studies have found that Prison Officers required a number of characteristics such as Moral Fibre; including 'confidence, integrity, honesty, good judgement and flexibility'. A Professional Orientation which underpins their engagements with staff and prisoners. An Optimistic Outlook, to maintain a pro-social approach to their work. An Understanding of the pain of imprisonment, to allow the officer to develop empathy with prisoners in their care. An Understanding of the effects of their own power, to keep power relations in check. Empathy and patience, to deal with the daily concerns of the prisoner. Consistency and resilience, to enhance the officer's reliability. Compassion and maturity, to improve officer-prisoner exchanges. Being Non-Confrontational and Non- Judgemental, to increase de-escalation and fairness. Observant and Communicative, for security and operative sucess (ibid p. 477).

Some negatives found in these studies included the outbreak of 'industrial disputes, challenges to management competence and public pronouncements on the favoured status of prisoners'. Other issues of concern which emerged in the studies included:

'Health and safety concerns, The quality of prison for prisoners, Low staff numbers, Resettlement, Productivity issues (ibid p. 480).

In the Irish case, prison officers are guided by their list of Officer Competencies, which were an integral part of the HCCC. These competencies include expected items such as 'Situational Awareness' and 'Team-Work'. However, there are more pastoral elements within these competencies; items such as 'People Orientation and Caring' and 'Developing Others' demonstrate the positive approach to professional development in the recruit's pathway towards the delivery of custodial care for prisoners and their families who visit them in difficult conditions (McGuckin 2008). This combination of internal and external motivations shape the 'elevation' that Haidt (2003) outlines in his description of the positivity which underpins the professional contribution of those requiring moral capacities in the face of challenging workplace environments. It is only through the combination of internal moral integrity and the reflection of the positive socialisation and mentoring of training officers and fellow professionals that a recruit can set out and maintain the elevation of their endeavour beyond the call of duty. This must be achieved while resisting the exhortations or conflicts with those negative mentors who may fall short of such a calling, or the prisoners who are caught up in a sea of personal negativity while in prison.

Once established however, any such negativity can be withstood and overcome by the onset of what Diessner calls 'Systemic Integrity'. This is built on through the extension of personal elevation and moral integrity throughout an institution, with the ultimate creation of systems and institutions that are built on a sense of shared integrity (Diessner, 2008). In many ways, the creation of systemic integrity is similar to a faith-based approach to life; one believer can come to influence the many to observe the codes and rituals of faith. In order for an institution such as a prison to work, there must be many believers, those who subsume their personal concerns for the good of their colleagues, and also for the prisoners in their care. In many ways this mobilisation of elevated or systemic forms of integrity defines the manner in which prisoners experience the primary forms of rehabilitation that occur during the duration of their sentence.

It is the officer with integrity that protects the incarcerated debt-defaulter from the worst aspects of the hardened criminals they may be surrounded by. The Irish justice system imprisons both minor and serious offenders within the walls of its medium security prisons, only paramilitary prisoners and white-collar criminals are afforded separate institutions for their periods of incarceration. Therefore, the prison officer must invest a good deal of time in protecting their prisoners; from the gang related violence they might inflict on each other, from an individual's suicidal tendencies and from the frustration or grief of news delivered by visitors from home. Prison officers also develop and support their colleagues through mentoring.

From the perspective of prison officers and mentoring, while the pragmatic aspect of helping to train a recruit's competencies are easily understood as underpinning the mentoring experience, many mentors are not sure of the bounds of their role in the unofficial context. What they are focussed on is the passing on of 'common-sense' approaches to issues that occur within the prison. This practical mentoring is demonstrated when the recruit is brought through the various procedures which occur in the cells, landings and during the transportation of prisoners. The process is three-fold. First, the mentor demonstrates a procedure to the mentee. Then, the mentee or protégé undertakes the procedure with the support of the mentor. Finally, the mentee begins to work without the mentor (while being observed from a distance). The success of this process is dependent on the pro-social modelling of the mentor, and from the wider team on their roster. This can vary from group to group and from institution to institution. Anecdotal evidence points to many institutions having a 'dark side' and a 'good side' to their rosters, where pro or anti-social modelling may be the prevalent ethos (Leonard, Kenny and McGuckin 2009).

The use of 'Dynamic Security' is another important part of developing the confidence of the mentee within the day to day handling of the inmate population. The use of dynamic security measures provides for increased competencies in dealing with issues, but allows the mentee to gain the confidence of his peers and of the inmates, who are also observing the new recruits. The procedures that appear to be out of the hands of the recruit during the initial mentoring process are 'handed over' by the mentor as professional competencies are developed. Again, communications and post incident de-briefings are used to underpin experiences gained through dynamic security processes. Nonetheless, some officers are more adept at de-briefing sessions than others, and may be better able to explain incidents in a relaxed manner.

Mentoring de-briefings occur in a variety of settings. These include the staff canteen, the exercise yard, during observations of prisoner recreation and even as we experienced during Work Place Visits (WPVs). Even here, the mentoring process continues. For example, if a fight breaks out in the yard, the recruit is often anxious to be seen to get involved. The mentor will hold the mentee back from this course of action, encouraging them to observe the techniques of experienced officers in handling the situation. This creates safety nets for both recruits and the other personnel, who can execute their duties without having to be concerned about protecting an inexperienced recruit from violence, injury or hostage taking. Alternatively, there may come a time when the mentor may need to push the mentor into action, or to encourage them to become more interactive with the prison population (ibid).

Mentoring is often about allowing the recruit to make a contribution. This can be seen in the development of the recruit's observational capacities. Observation is a major part of the prison officer's job. Good observation includes understanding the contexts and processes of prison, knowing when to let things go and knowing when to react. In many ways, it's about understanding human behaviour. Pro-social teaching encourages the mentee to develop their observational skills through learned processes, rather than every step being explained in detail. Here, mentors also appreciate the value of the mentoring process, as the team begins to benefit from the observations of the recruit. As the mentee is seen to contribute to the roster through their observations, confidence is developed amongst the team, enhancing the 'elevated' mentoring process (ibid).

CONCLUDING REMARKS

The full extent of supports that a prison officer provides to the prisoner is not fully understood or appreciated within our society. The professional competencies and humane ethos of the Irish Prison Service's mission statement provides us with the context for the elevation through service which is the bedrock of the prison officer's service to the prisoner in their care. Ultimately, it is this combination of personal integrity and professional elevation which provides us with the answer to the question 'why do we do it', and thereby indicated to wider society the nature of service provided by the custodians of our prisons in the face of ongoing challenges such as overcrowding, economic constraints and violence from the prison population. Achieving elevated integrity at work also begins the important process of primary rehabilitation (or in some cases) for prisoners, who are more likely to respond in a positive manner to this form of interaction.

FUTURE RECOMMENDATIONS

Ultimately, the extent to which the officer delivers on this elevated form of professional integrity is not always recognised or valued, sometimes even by the officers themselves who see themselves as simply 'just doing their job'. Their ability to attain levels of professionalism also inspires their colleagues to achieve the same. Similar police officers, prison officers deliver a form of professional care which requires a commitment to service to others. However, the extent to which they succeed in their attempts to maintain an elevated degree of professionalism within their careers needs be understood within a wider context of an evolving re-assessment of the issues of crime and punishment, and the protection of prisoner's rights in a wider system of justice. Prison Officer training programs should achieve a successful educational experienced which improved recruit officer's ability to deliver a safe and secure service for prisoners within the context of protecting the rights of those prisoners in their care.

REFERENCES

Cherry, S. (2004). *Transforming Behaviour*. William.

Crawley, E. (2004). *Doing Prison Work: The Public and Private Lives of Prison Officers*. Willan.

Edgar, K., O'Donnell, I., & Martin, C. (2004). *Prison Violence: The Dynamics of Conflict, Fear and Power*. Willan.

Goffman, E. (1962). *Asylums*. Penguin.

Haidt, J. (2003). Elevation and the positive psychology of morality. In C. L. M. Keyes & J. Haidt (Eds.), *Flourishing: Positive psychology and the life well-lived* (pp. 275–289). American Psychological Association. doi:10.1037/10594-012

Jewkes, Y. (2007). *Handbook on Prisons*. Wilian, Helen Arnold.

Kant, I. (1987). *Critique of Judgement*. Hackett.

Leonard, L. (Ed.). (2010). *The Prison Journal, Special issue. Irish Prisons, 91*(1).

Leonard, L. (2010). Introduction: The Significance of the Prison in Irish Nationalist Culture, *The Prison Journal, 91*(1), pp. 3-6.

Leonard, L., Kenny, P., & McGuckin, J. (2009, April). The Mentoring Processes of the Irish Prison Service: A Sociological Inquiry. *American Jails*.

Liebling, A., Arnold, H., & Tait, S. (2007). Prison staff culture. In Y. Jewkes (Ed.), *Handbook on Prisons*. Willan.

McGuckin, J. (2008) *Role Profile of Recruit Prison Officers In the Irish Prison Service*. Greenhouse Press.

ENDNOTES

1 See Leonard (2010).

2 See Leonard (2010).

3 The authors were part of the team of academics who devised and delivered the HCCC alongside IPS Chief Training Officers.

4 HCCC/NAIRTL Nomination Document (2012).

Section 3

Institutions: Policy and Practice

Chapter 11
Mob Justice in Contemporary Ghana

Daniel Tei
Mississippi State University, USA

ABSTRACT

Mob justice/instant justice/vigilantism in Ghana serves as an indictment on the 1992 Constitution of Ghana, creates a heightened sense of fear among citizens that they could become victims, and also undermines the legitimacy of the police and legal authorities. Several studies have shown that communities use mob justice as a tool to respond to crimes and an ineffective criminal justice system. The current study aims to describe the mob justice situation in Ghana through the lens of the procedural justice theory. Specifically, the study asks the following research question: How does the media in Ghana describe mob justice? Drawing data from two Ghanaian newspapers—the Daily Graphic and The Ghanaian Times—the study relies on the content analysis method to explore how media in Ghana describe mob justice. The study reveals that lynch mobs are more likely to subject males, especially between the ages of 20-29, to lethal punishment than their female counterparts. Men's overrepresentation and women's underrepresentation as victims are theorized to be based on gender stereotypes. Finally, the study does not find support for the procedural justice theory. Thus, the study finds that police effectiveness is not sufficient enough to elicit police legitimacy that will enhance widespread public compliance. The study recommends that the Ghana Police should embark on policing styles that respect the rights and dignity of citizens, in addition to being effective, to remedy the mob justice problem. Further research is needed to combine official homicide data from the Ghana Police and other sources of homicide to highlight the phenomenon in Ghana, given the data source of the current study.

DOI: 10.4018/978-1-7998-6646-6.ch011

INTRODUCTION

In Ghana, mob justice is a common practice that continues to grow as innocent people keep losing their lives. Despite the increase in police personnel over the last decade to contain crime, media houses in Ghana have been awash with reports of instant justice being meted out on alleged perpetrators of crime. Instant justice, also referred to as mob justice or vigilantism, occurs when a group of people imposes their own justice on a suspected offender or criminal. In most cases, instant justice is meted out on someone, in communities both large and small across Ghana, regardless of the victim's identity (Tankebe, 2009). For example, a mob does not care whether you are an upstanding citizen who contributes to society, the elderly, or even a military officer, one's status is irrelevant when it comes to justice.

One case that illustrates this occurred when a military officer was brutally attacked, despite making it known to the mob that he was in the military. In a horrific video that generated national outrage in Ghana, Major Maxwell Mahama, a member of the 5th Infantry Battalion of the Ghana Army, met his untimely death after he was murdered on the suspicion that he was an armed robber. Without verifying the identity of the soldier, the assemblyman and the townspeople accosted the military officer, chased and shot at him, and pounced on him using cement blocks and clubs, amongst other items. With blood oozing from his face, the mob continuously shoved the young soldier, dragging and pelting stones at him until he became motionless, later setting him ablaze. The young officer, a father of two, was callously murdered despite making his military identity known to his assailants.

In Ghana, there is seldom, if ever, a month that goes by without an alleged criminal being lynched by an angry mob. On the same day of the case mentioned above, a 67-year-old woman met a similar fate when she was accused of witchcraft and consequently stoned to death at a busy open-air market (Nyabor, 2017). This is a common response to suspicion of witchcraft as any form of witchery is seen as despicable, dangerous, and culturally unacceptable. Ghanaians have even gone so far as sending suspected witches to a "witch camp" where they are essentially exiled from the community.

Adinkrah (2005) suggests that public support for mob justice in Ghana is linked to people's judgments about the trustworthiness of the police. According to him, the public perceives the police to be corrupt and, therefore, not trustworthy to mete out justice to offenders. People who perceive the police to be trustworthy are less likely to support mob justice than people who perceive the police to be untrustworthy. In a series of interviews with law enforcement officers, in addition to news articles, Adinkrah (2005) provided support for the trustworthiness argument concluding that in Ghana, the public remains highly distrustful of the police. This is further supported by the widespread reports of mob justice in daily newspapers, where it can be inferred that there exists a lack of trust in the police to mete out justice. Adinkrah (2005) revealed that mob justice is a result of the strained relationship between the police and some members of the public. He found that this strained relationship stems from the widely held perception of police corruption that has led the public to lose faith in the criminal justice system. As such, this strained relationship motivates the public to resort to extralegal activities, such as mob justice.

Further, Tankebe (2009) employed quantitative methods to describe the mob justice situation in Ghana. In a survey data of 374 residents in Accra, Ghana, Tankebe (2009) concluded that the two most important predictors of mob justice are education and police trustworthiness. While Adinkrah (2005) concludes that the public resort to mob justice because of the diminished faith in the police that is brought about by perceived police corruption, Tankebe (2009) notes that police corruption does not necessarily incite the public to engage in mob actions in Ghana.

These two scholars, Adinkrah (2005) and Tankebe (2009), have explored issues of mob justice in Ghana. Adinkrah (2005) conducted a qualitative study on vigilante homicide using media reports. In a survey study on vigilante self-help, Tankebe (2009) examined the vigilante violence phenomenon through the lens of the procedural justice model. Whiles the two have already attempted a description of the problem, there is currently no qualitative study on how media reports describe mob justice through the lens of the procedural justice model. The current study seeks to do just this in an effort to contribute to the gap in the literature.

Specifically, the current study seeks to understand how the media, particularly newspapers in Ghana, describe mob justice as a phenomenon. The current study will explore how the media perceives and evaluates the actions of the police in terms of their responses to crime. Additionally, the current study will explore media descriptions surrounding the context of the offense to gain an understanding of possible factors that might influence mob reaction in the Ghanaian society. Newspaper depictions will provide insights into the modus operandi or mode of operation of lynch mobs, along with the role of bystanders and the consequences of mob actions. The media description of mob justice will enhance our understanding of the demographic characteristics of victims of mob justice and the regions or areas where mob justice is acute. Given that the current study focuses on how the media describe mob justice in Ghana, it will provide an opportunity to discern meaning about mob justice as a phenomenon in general.

Definition of Mob Justice

When discussing mob justice, it is important to address how scholars in the field define it. Johnston (1996) defined mob justice as “a social movement giving rise to premeditated acts of force—or threatened force—by autonomous citizens. It arises as a reaction to the transgression of institutionalized norms by people or groups—or to their potential or imputed transgression" (p. 232). These actions concentrate on crime control or social control and are intended to provide security guarantees to both participants and other members of a given established order (Johnston, 1996). By this, Johnston (1996) describes mob justice as a response to crime in which individuals who break the law are either leniently punished or not correctly held accountable by the state. As a result, the mob decides to enforce the law by dealing with matters themselves.

In his study on vigilante homicide in Ghana, Adinkrah (2005) resorted to Abrahams's (2003) definition of mob justice because of its comprehensiveness, as well as its general concordance with definitions elsewhere. According to Abrahams (2003), mob justice is the attempt by a group of citizens to enforce societal norms and maintain law and order through the use of violence to punish wrongdoings, often in the absence of an effective state justice system such as the police or the courts. An important aspect of this definition is how the people do not trust the police to maintain order competently. Other scholars have defined mob justice as a mechanism through which without recourse to the law, a crowd of people seeks justice by beating, inflicting injuries, or killing alleged criminals. Thus, people impose punishments on suspected criminals instead of handing them over to the law enforcement agency (Salihu & Gholami, 2018). This definition places more emphasis on the mode of operation of the mob. Also, it emphasizes the disregard for agents of the criminal justice system by lynch mobs.

All these definitions of mob justice indicate one notable feature; that is, it violates the law. The activities of a mob supplant the duties of the police and other agents of the criminal justice system to enforce the law, maintain law and order, and apprehend and punish suspected offenders (Adinkrah, 2005). When mob justice becomes pervasive, it is equated with rightness, and the public resort to it as a response to crime. It is usually initiated by individuals who allege that someone has committed an offense (Salihu & Gholami, 2018). In communities where mob justice occurs frequently, Salihu and Gholami (2018) stress that the mob typically increases in size when passersby join in to castigate the accused person.

During instances of mob justice, the mob takes the place of the criminal justice system and assumes the role of the police, prosecutor, judge, and at the same time, the executor (Salihu & Gholami, 2018). For example, when lynch mobs apprehend alleged criminals, they take on the role of a police officer. Then, by charging the person as a criminal, such as a thief, they assume the role of the prosecutor. In most cases, the victim ends up being seriously injured or beaten to death. This would not typically occur if the victim were to be handled by the police and other formal agents of social control.

It should be noted that the action of the mob is a reaction to crime or allegation of an offense (Cooper-Knock, 2014). The punishment that is meted out by the mob to the accused person does not follow any reasonable procedure for measuring the magnitude of the offense committed (Salihu & Gholami, 2018). In short, the punishment does not fit the crime. Further, the lack of reasonable procedures that lynch mobs follow suggests that innocent persons could be victims of mob justice and be subjected to assaults, maiming, or even killing in cases of mistaken identity or false accusations (Adinkrah, 2005).

Typically, the punishment the mob imposes on the accused person is the same for all kinds of crimes or types of perpetrators, regardless of their demographic characteristics, such as religion or education level (Salihu & Gholami, 2018). The mob subjects the accused offender to degrading and inhumane treatments, such as spanking, slashing, stripping, pounding, and burning (Salihu & Gholami, 2018). Usually, the severity of a punishment that is imposed on the accused offender is dependent on the mood of the mob. According to Salihu and Gholami (2018), the punishment that a mob imposes on an alleged criminal is rapid, baseless, unpredictable, and dangerous (Salihu & Gholami, 2018). Since mob justice is an affront to the laws that govern society and the dignity of victims in general, it is vital to explore the various reasons why people engage in such an act. The following section explores motivations and justifications for why persons engage in mob justice from the perspective of various countries.

Reasons People Resort to Mob Justice

Mob justice occurs in many parts of the world and the reasons for engaging in such behavior ranges. For example, in the United States, there is a history of mob justice in the form of lynching. From 1882 to 1951, evidence suggests that 4,730 people were killed from spontaneously formed lynch mobs in the United States (Adinkrah, 2005). Particularly, in Southern United States, studies show that Black males who were accused of sexually assaulting white women were subjected to "spectacle lynching" for hundreds of whites to witness the execution (Adinkrah, 2005; Hill, 2010). Hill (2010) stresses that as a result of emancipation, public discourse among white communities depicted Black males as people who were retrogressing to 'bestial' and 'sexually depraved' conditions. These Black males were described as "black beast rapist," and Whites were made to believe that such a retrogressive behavior by Black males was the reason why they were raping white women (Hill, 2010). To maintain power and subdue these black males, mob justice was viewed by Whites as a necessary and appropriate response (Hill, 2010).

In addition to the United States, mob justice is also a well-documented issue in Latin America due to its upsurge in the 1990s and the 2000s. For instance, Godoy

(2004) reports that 421 incidences of mob justice were recorded by the United Nations Missions to Guatemala from 1996 to 2000, representing an average of over 7 per month. Between October 2000 and September 2001, a human rights group in Venezuela documented 164 cases of mob justice in the country (Godoy, 2004). Additionally, lynching reports in Mexico indicated 103 cases of mob justice that occurred between 1987 and 1998, a figure that may be underestimated due to other lynching reports suggesting many more (Godoy, 2003). Other Latin American countries that have experienced mob justice over the years include Ecuador, Peru, and Brazil (Godoy, 2003).

Although seen as an insurgent mode of social control, mob justice in Latin America constitutes a form of political expression or democracy (Godoy, 2004; Goldstein, 2003). Both Godoy (2004) and Goldstein (2003) argue that through mob justice or lynching, people without access to formal legal venues address their grievances against a corrupt and an ineffective legal system. At the same time, lynch mobs use mob justice to deploy the rhetoric of justice and law to police their communities against crime (Goldstein, 2003). The practice takes place in both rural and urban places in Latin American countries (Godoy, 2004; Goldstein, 2003). It serves as a predominant tool for the poor and marginalized communities to respond to rising violent crime and a growing sense of insecurity. More importantly, communities use it to reassert their autonomy in legal and moral decision-making since the state has failed to govern effectively (Godoy, 2004). According to Godoy (2004) and Goldstein (2003), many Latin American countries, such as Bolivia and Guatemala, have experienced an increase in crime over the years, specifically, property crime.

Further, states have performed abysmally in dealing with the upsurge in crime through the formal justice system, which has consequently led to insecurity (Godoy, 2004; Goldstein, 2003). For many people in Latin American countries, the inability of their governments to combat crime indicates how their governments have failed to uphold the rule of law and govern effectively (Godoy, 2004; Goldstein, 2003). Due to widespread crime and woefully inefficient state justice systems that have thrown many citizens into a state of insecurity, citizens resort to mob justice as an alternative way of providing security for themselves (Godoy, 2004). Godoy (2004) refers to the logic mentioned above as the commonsense consensus in understanding mob justice in Latin America.

In his ethnographic studies on mob justice in Bolivia, Goldstein (2003) cited the commonsense consensus as the main explanation of the phenomenon. He contends that in Bolivia, citizens believe that the government has failed to honor its political promise of enhancing adequate security to its citizens and their properties. Bolivia's criminal justice system, imbued with corruption, is also unable to punish alleged malefactors (Goldstein, 2003). Driven by these happenings, most communities in Bolivia have been drawn into a state of anarchy (Goldstein, 2003). Thus, the absence of security for citizens and property has increased property crimes and violence as people steal, rob, and perpetrate violence on other people. (Goldstein, 2003). In particular, the absence of security for citizens has made it dangerous for individuals to roam the streets, especially at night, due to gangs of youths who are engaged in rampant murder, rapes, and other violent crimes (Goldstein, 2003). Citizens who work in the center city are affected the most because they usually have to leave their homes unattended during the day. This increases their vulnerability to thieves who often break in and steal household items (Goldstein, 2003). Faced with the immediacy of violence, property theft, and the state's failure to provide security, communities resort to extralegal activities, such as mob justice, to fend for themselves and their families. Thus, communities in Bolivia are forced to assume the role of arbiter of justice (Goldstein, 2003).

According to Goldstein (2003), lynch mobs do not only exist outside the law to punish suspected criminals, but they also function to achieve a political end by challenging the legitimacy of the state and the rule of law (Goldstein, 2003). He suggests that since modern democratic states have failed to provide security for persons and properties, lynch mobs turn to mob justice as a way of rejecting marginalization from the benefits promised them by the state (Goldstein, 2003). Thus, while communities seek to protect themselves and their properties by punishing criminals, they also "reassert themselves collectively as agents rather than victims" (Godoy, 2004, p. 36). Therefore, the actions of lynch mobs are supposed to compel the state to live up to its claims of legitimacy by providing security and order for its citizens (Goldstein, 2003).

Godoy (2004) also resorts to the commonsense consensus to explain mob justice in Guatemala. According to her, the state's apparent refusal to provide an effective criminal justice system has compelled citizens to resort to lynching as a way of protecting their communities and families from crime (Godoy, 2004). This is to notify the state that they can fend for themselves if the state is not ready to combat crime (Godoy, 2004). Such an action, Godoy (2004) argues, empowers communities in Guatemala to voice their frustration for an ineffective criminal justice system and reassert their autonomy to control crime since the state's justice system is not functioning (Godoy, 2004).

Interestingly, as a form of democracy, lynch mobs in Latin America usually mimic the procedures of the official justice system in punishing suspected criminals (Godoy, 2004). As a collective rite, lynch mobs initially detain suspected criminals, carry out investigations, obtain evidence, seek confessions under torture, and finally, pronounce sentences through lynching (Godoy, 2004). This indicates an alternative move by communities to control crime in a manner that resembles that of the state's justice system. This means that mob justice does represent not only an antagonism between communities and alleged offenders but also conflict between communities and the state. Here, the conflict between communities and the state can be tied to the authority that prevails in matters of life and death (Godoy, 2004). In this way, communities that resort to lynching to punish suspected criminals not only struggle to regain control over crime situations but also, decision-making authority in essential issues (Godoy, 2004). Therefore, in this context, lynching is a defiant manifestation of local autonomy (Godoy, 2004).

Even in certain communities, lynch mobs have affirmed their actions through the signing of documents indicating their unanimous intention to mete out instant justice to criminals (Godoy, 2004). In many instances, communities provide these signed documents to authorities to validate their actions and avoid potential prosecution by the state. For example, when the president of Guatemala paid a visit to a community where lynching is prevalent and made an attempt to ensure that the individuals who form lynch mobs are apprehended, he was presented with documents that affirm the actions of the communities to continue lynching suspected criminals (Godoy, 2004). This illustrates lynching as a collective rite that fosters cohesion among community members and also serves as a way of expressing popular will (Godoy, 2004).

As scholarly knowledge largely attributes mob justice to widespread crime and ineffective criminal justice systems, Godoy (2004) goes a step further and argues that lynching in Latin America deserves closer attention. For her, the reasons why mob justice occurs transcend the upsurge in crime and the failure of the state justice system to deal with the rising rate of crime. She argues that the commonsense consensus alone shades or impairs an understanding of mob justice in Latin America. Godoy's (2004) argument is that lynching is not about crime, or at least it is not only about crime. With this argument, Godoy (2004) notes that while crimes are considered most severe and pervasive in some urban areas in Guatemala, mob justice, on the other hand, is widespread in the non-urban areas. If indeed mob justice is a response to crime, why are people in urban areas not using to it to deal with suspected criminals? Although urban areas record high crime rates, mob justice is not used as a tool to combat crime.

Another reason why Godoy (2004) believes that lynching is not entirely about crime is because there is little known about the type of crime that elicits mob justice and the type of offense that actual victims of lynching were purported to have committed (Godoy, 2004). For instance, Godoy (2004) reveals that in communities where severe crimes, such as murder, are perpetrated with impunity, suspected criminals who suffer lynching are not necessarily accused of perpetrating those severe crimes. Rather, the victims of lynch mobs are typically accused of relatively minor property crimes (Godoy, 2004). Guatemala is not the only country in Latin America where there is disproportionality between the gravity of the offense and the often fatal outcome of lynching. In Ecuador, research suggests that 86% of people who were alleged to have committed theft were lynched as compared to 2.2% of people who were alleged to have committed murder, 3.2% of people who were accused of child rape, and 6.5% of people who were suspected of assault (Godoy, 2004). This disparity, therefore, underscores the need to disentangle explanations of mob justice to crime.

Furthermore, to say that mob justice is a product of a defective criminal justice system suggests that crime is better dealt with in areas where mob justice does not occur (Godoy, 2004). She points out that in some areas, crime has never been dealt with through the criminal justice system. Therefore, it will not be entirely accurate to explain the lynching in these areas with the state's failure to control crime (Godoy, 2004).

Transitioning to reasons for engaging in mob justice in Africa, in South Africa and Nigeria, lynch mobs serve as tool to respond to wrongdoings, committed or alleged to have been committed by the victim, including larceny/robbery, witchcraft, child abuse, and child murder (Adinkrah, 2005; Super, 2017). Usually, lynch mobs subject alleged offenders to necklacing—a style of killing where lynch mobs hang an old car tire that has been doused in gasoline around the neck of a suspected criminal and set him/her ablaze (Adinkrah, 2005). People engage in mob justice as a response to these crimes in Nigeria because they have become disenchanted and lost confidence in the justice system to deliver fair justice to suspected criminals (Salihu & Gholami, 2018).

Similar to South Africa and Nigeria, research findings in Ghana have revealed that mob justice usually surfaces in situations where lynch mobs accuse an individual of wrongdoings such as robbery, murder, and witchcraft (Adinkrah, 2005; Tankebe, 2009). In these situations of wrongdoings, African vigilante accounts stress police corruption as an instigating factor in why people resort to mob justice. The reasons for resorting to mob violence in these instances, versus relying on the police, stem from widespread dissatisfaction with law enforcement and other criminal justice agencies (Tankebe, 2009). Broadly held perceptions about police corruption and inefficiency in Ghana have resulted in a lack of faith in the police and other criminal justice agencies, such as the judiciary, and further encouraged citizens to resort to vigilantism (Adinkrah, 2005; Silke, 2001). Not only the police, but also prosecutors, judges, and other criminal justice officials routinely accept bribes in exchange for dropping criminal charges, discharging guilty offenders, giving favorable verdicts to defendants, and in some instances, facilitating the escape of convicted inmates from detention centers (Adinkrah, 2005). Additionally, most Ghanaians widely hold the belief that imprisonment is too lenient of a punishment and not only does it not dissuade criminal activity, dangerous and violent criminals deserve more punitive sanctions (Adinkra, 2005; Tankebe, 2009).

Mob justice in Ghana occurs as a result of police malfunctions and an ineffective criminal justice system (Adinkra, 2005; Tankebe, 2009). Studies show that policing activities, such as strategies used to enforce law and order and provide safety and security to the public, have come under public scrutiny due to the constant media spotlight on the work of the police (Adinkra, 2005; Tankebe, 2009). Public judgment about the work of the police tends to focus on the effectiveness of the police in combating crime and providing security and safety. Since policing involves daily and constant interactions with the public, these encounters leave an impression, not only on individuals at the receiving end of the interactions but also on the society as a whole as the public may judge or assess the behavior of the police. These assessments influence public attitude towards the police and the public's decision to cooperate and comply with the law in general. It is, therefore, essential to address the relationship between policing and citizen compliance. across people and communities, will lead to widespread cooperation of the public and compliance with the law in general (Tyler, 2003).

Studies show that instrumental compliance is minimally effective in promoting public compliance (Tyler, 2006; Tyler, 2003). Tyler (2003) argues that instrumental compliance strategies are costly since to achieve widespread public compliance, it is incumbent on the police or other legal authorities to create and maintain a credible threat of punishment for wrongdoing. For example, to ensure that such a strategy is effective, the authorities must credibly detect wrongdoing. To do this requires the police to deploy resources for surveillance and create credible sanctions (Tyler, 2003). This model of compliance is minimally effective because research shows that it is the probability of punishment that concerns people instead of the threat of punishment for wrongdoing (Tyler, 2003). Thus, a model that focuses on threats of severe punishment for wrongdoing is largely ineffective.

Normative Compliance

In normative compliance, citizens comply and cooperate with the police or legal authorities based on their feelings of obligation and responsibility (Tyler, 2004). In contrast to instrumental compliance, normative compliance operates on the premise that citizens hold the belief that their values will lead them to comply with the police or legal authorities (Tyler, 2006). The police or legal authorities draw on the internalized values of citizens to secure compliance and to gain cooperation (Tyler, 2004). In this model of compliance, an essential value that citizens hold is their widespread support for police legitimacy—the trust and confidence the police gain in their encounter with the public (Mazerolle, Antrobus, Bennett & Tyler, 2013). For instance, the public believes that they are entitled to be called upon by the police to help in combating crime. Once people realize that authority is legitimate, they allow the authority to determine what their actions will be in a given set of circumstances

(Tyler, 2004). This approval of authority compels the public to feel obligated to obeying and following the directives of legitimate authorities (Tyler, 2004).

One study by Tyler (2004) suggests that a normative-based strategy of policing increases cooperation with the law by drawing on people's feelings of responsibility and obligation. This strategy is effective in promoting widespread compliance since it can facilitate it voluntarily (Tyler, 2004). Unlike the instrumental compliance model, the normative compliance model is less costly since it draws on the personal values of members of the public to achieve widespread compliance as opposed to extra resources by the police to enforce public behavior (Tyler, 2004). Under this model, the maintenance of social order requires only minimal levels of societal resources which allows for resources to be channeled toward meeting other needs (Tyler, 2004).

Additionally, normative compliance is more reliable than instrumentally induced compliance because it is not dependent on the conditions or situations involved (Tyler, 2004). For instance, internal values motivate people to obey traffic rules on deserted roads at night, even when the probability of those people getting arrested and punished for breaking the law is minimal. Hence, legitimacy helps to shape peoples' feelings and willingness to obey the law (Tyler, 2003). Research has shown that peoples' willingness to obey and cooperate with the police or legal authorities is tied primarily to legitimacy (Mazerolle et al., 2013). For public support for mob justice, Tankebe (2009) argues that normative assessments of the police are essential. This is because, in instances where the public views the police or legal authorities as illegitimate, the public is likely to take the law into their own hands by administering justice to alleged offenders and withholding cooperation and compliance from the police. In his study, Tankebe (2009) found that when normative compliance is impaired, people are likely to engage in vigilantism. Tankebe (2009) reports that people who perceive the police to be trustworthy are less likely to support mob justice.

REFERENCES

Abrahams, R. (2003). What's in a name? Some thoughts on the vocabulary of vigilantism and related forms of 'informal criminal justice'. *Informal Criminal Justice*, 25-40.

Adinkrah, M. (2005). Vigilante homicides in contemporary Ghana. *Journal of Criminal Justice*, *33*(5), 413–427. doi:10.1016/j.jcrimjus.2005.06.008

Amamoo, J. G. (2011). Ghana: 50 Year of Independence. Xlibris Corporation.

Appiahene-Gyamfi, J. (2003). Urban crime trends and patterns in Ghana: The case of Accra. *Journal of Criminal Justice*, *31*(1), 13–23. doi:10.1016/S0047-2352(02)00196-4

Babbie, E. (2001). *The practice of social research. Belmont, CA: Wadsworth/ Thomson Learning*. Wiley.

Bayley, D. H. (1994). *Police for the future*. Oxford University Press.

Berg, B. L. (2004). *Methods for the social sciences. Qualitative Research Methods for the Social Sciences*. Pearson Education.

Bhattacherjee, A. (2012). *Social science research: Principles, methods, and practices*. Textbooks Collection.

Boateng, F. D. (2012). *Public Trust in the Police: Identifying factors that shape trust in the Ghanaian Police* (Doctoral dissertation). Washington State University.

Charmaz, K. (2006). *Constructing grounded theory: A practical guide through qualitative analysis*. Sage.

Chase, M. (2008). The Chivalry Hypothesis & Filicide: Are There Categorical Differences between Mothers and Fathers who kill their Children? *Undergraduate Review*, *4*(1), 41–50.

Constitution of Ghana, Art. 15, clause 2

Cooper-Knock, S. J. (2014). Policing in intimate crowds: Moving beyond 'the mob' in South Africa. *African Affairs*, *113*(453), 563–582. doi:10.1093/afraf/adu060

Creswell, J. W., & Poth, C. N. (2017). Qualitative inquiry and research design: choosing among five approaches (4th ed.). Academic Press.

Ekins, E. E. (2016). *Policing in America: Understanding public attitudes toward the police. Results from a national survey.* Results from a National Survey.

Erlingsson, C., & Brysiewicz, P. (2017). A hands-on guide to doing content analysis. *African Journal of Emergency Medicine*, *7*(3), 93–99. doi:10.1016/j.afjem.2017.08.001

Erlingsson, C., & Brysiewicz, P. (2017). A hands-on guide to doing content analysis. *African Journal of Emergency Medicine*, *7*(3), 93–99. doi:10.1016/j.afjem.2017.08.001

Ewuziem, I. K. (2019). *Moral and legal issues inherent in mob justice: A clarion call for a rethink*. Divinestone Publications.

Ghana Police Service. (2018). *Annual Report*. Retrieved from https://police.gov.gh/en/index.php/news-release-police-annual-crime-report-2015-2018/

Ghana. Statistical Service. (2014). *2010 population and housing census report*. Ghana Statistical Service.

Gibbs, G. R. (2007). *Thematic coding and categorizing. In Analyzing qualitative data*. Sage.

Godoy, A. S. (2002). Lynchings and the democratization of terror in postwar Guatemala: Implications for human rights. *Human Rights Quarterly*, *24*(3), 640–661. doi:10.1353/hrq.2002.0035

Hill, K. K. (2010). Black vigilantism: The rise and decline of African American lynch mob activity in the Mississippi and Arkansas deltas, 1883-1923. *Journal of African American History*, *95*(1), 26–43. doi:10.5323/jafriamerhist.95.1.0026

Hinds, L., & Murphy, K. (2007). Public Satisfaction with Police: Using Procedural Justice to Improve Police Legitimacy. *Australian and New Zealand Journal of Criminology*, *40*(1), 27–43. doi:10.1375/acri.40.1.27

Jernigan, D., & Dorfman, L. (1996). Visualizing America's drug problems: An ethnographic content analysis of illegal drug stories on the nightly news. *Contemporary Drug Problems*, *23*(2), 169–196. doi:10.1177/009145099602300203

Johnston, L. (1996). What is vigilantism? *British Journal of Criminology*, *36*(2), 220–236. doi:10.1093/oxfordjournals.bjc.a014083

Kneoma. (2019). *Ghana homicide rate*. Retrieved https://knoema.com/atlas/Ghana/Homicide-rate

Krippendorff, K. (2018). *Content analysis: An introduction to its methodology*. Sage publications.

Maunga, M., Mugari, I., & Tundu, M. (2015). Perspectives on vigilantism in the Republic of Zimbabwe. *Mediterranean Journal of Social Sciences*, *6*(5), 323. doi:10.5901/mjss.2015.v6n5s1p323

Mazerolle, L., Antrobus, E., Bennett, S., & Tyler, T. R. (2013). Shaping citizen perceptions of police legitimacy: A randomized field trial of procedural justice. *Criminology*, *51*(1), 33–63. doi:10.1111/j.1745-9125.2012.00289.x

Neuendorf, K. A. (2019). 18 Content analysis and thematic analysis. *Advanced Research Methods for Applied Psychology*, *211*(21).

Nyabor, J. (2017). *3 arrested over lynching of 'witch' at Nabdam*. Citifmonline. Retrieved from http://citifmonline.com/2017/06/06/3-arrested-over-lynching-of-witch-at-nabdam/

Nyavor, G. (2017). *Capt. Mahama lynching: Diaso turns ghost town as residents flee*. Retrieved from https://www.myjoyonline.com/news/2017/May-31st/photos-capt-mahama-lynching- diaso-turns-ghost-town-as-residents-flee-town.php

OSAC- Overseas Security Advisory Council. (2019). *Ghana 2019 Crime and Safety Report*. Available at: https://www.osac.gov/Country/Ghana/Content/Detail/Report/17cce973-2f6d-45de-bf74-15f4aec9e90a

Prasad, B. D. (2008). Content analysis. *Research Methods for Social Work, 5*, 1-20.

Salihu, H. A., & Gholami, H. (2018). Mob justice, corrupt and unproductive justice system in Nigeria: An empirical analysis. *International Journal of Law, Crime and Justice*, *55*, 40–51. doi:10.1016/j.ijlcj.2018.09.003

Silke, A. (2001). Dealing with vigilantism: Issues and lessons for the police. *The Police Journal*, *74*(2), 120–133. doi:10.1177/0032258X0107400204

Sunshine, J., & Tyler, T. R. (2003). The Role of Procedural Justice and Legitimacy in Shaping Public Support for Policing. *Law & Society Review*, *37*(3), 513–548. doi:10.1111/1540-5893.3703002

Super, G. (2017). What's in a name and why it matters: A historical analysis of the relationship between state authority, vigilantism and penal power in South Africa. *Theoretical Criminology*, *21*(4), 512–531. doi:10.1177/1362480617724830

Tankebe, J. (2009). Public cooperation with the police in Ghana: Does procedural fairness matter? *Criminology*, *47*(4), 1265–1293. doi:10.1111/j.1745-9125.2009.00175.x

Tankebe, J. (2009). Self-help, policing, and procedural justice: Ghanaian vigilantism and the rule of law. *Law & Society Review*, *43*(2), 245–270. doi:10.1111/j.1540-5893.2009.00372.x

Tankebe, J. (2009). Self-help, policing, and procedural justice: Ghanaian vigilantism and the rule of law. *Law & Society Review, 43*(2), 245-270.

Tyler, T. R. (2003). Procedural justice, legitimacy, and the effective rule of law. *Crime and Justice*, *30*, 283–357. doi:10.1086/652233

Tyler, T. R. (2004). Enhancing police legitimacy. *The Annals of the American Academy of Political and Social Science*, *593*(1), 84–99. doi:10.1177/0002716203262627

Tyler, T. R. (2006). *Why people obey the law*. Princeton University Press.

Tyler, T. R. (2011). Trust and legitimacy: Policing in the USA and Europe. *European Journal of Criminology*, *8*(4), 254–266. doi:10.1177/1477370811411462

Vaismoradi, M., Jones, J., Turunen, H., & Snelgrove, S. (2016). *Theme development in qualitative content analysis and thematic analysis*. Academic Press.

Wimmer, R. D., & Dominick, J. R. (2011). *Mass media research: An introduction* (International Edition). Wadsworth Cengage Learning.

World Bank. (2018). *World Bank open data*. Author.

Young, A. (1951). *A Report on the Gold Coast Police*. Government of Ghana.

Chapter 12
A Holistic Approach to Transitional Justice for Afghanistan

Parwez Besmel
Northern Arizona University, USA

ABSTRACT

This chapter will examine the transition from war to a form of peace that embraces justice for all participants in the long running civil war in Afghanistan. The chapter examines the initiatives for peace and justice established by the Afghan government and incorporates a review of the relevant literature on this approach to transitional justice. Finally, the chapter will examine the author's concept about the potential for the truth and recondition commission combined with amnesty as a pathway to a successful transitional justice framework.

INTRODUCTION

In February 2020, the United States signed a peace deal with the Taliban that facilitated direct talks between the Afghan government and the Taliban. After 19 years of bloody war against the Taliban and other militant groups, the United States and the Afghan government have come to the realization that a political solution is the only way to end the protracted war in Afghanistan. The announcement that the Afghan government is seeking unconditional peace talks shows that the main stakeholders are earnestly seeking a political solution. Thus, the prospects of a political settlement and a peace deal are highly likely. The question is, how will justice be meted out for those who are responsible for grave human rights violations, including

DOI: 10.4018/978-1-7998-6646-6.ch012

mass killings, torture, illegal imprisonments, and forced disappearances? Will it be retributive in the form of trial? Is lustration/vetting possible? Will the victims and their surviving families be compensated? Considering the current socio-political realities and the prominence of Islamic culture in Afghanistan, I argue that post-conflict justice takes a holistic approach in the form of a truth and reconciliation commission combined with amnesty. Amnesty will promote reconciliation while the truth commission will begin a recovery process by providing the victims a platform to express their fears and suffering and recommend reform to avoid future atrocities. Thus, truth commission combined with amnesty will ensure reconciliation, stability, and ultimately peace, which the Afghans need.

The organization of this chapter is as follows. First, I will provide an overview of the peace and justice initiatives of the Afghan government. Second, I will present an overview of the literature, highlighting the mechanisms of transitional justice. Next, I will present my argument for a holistic approach to transitional justice in Afghanistan. I will end the chapter with some concluding remarks..

Efforts Toward Reconciliation and Justice

The human cost of conflict is daunting, and Afghanistan is no exception to this rule. The estimated tally of deaths between 1979 and 2001 surpassed a million people (Rubin, 2003). 800,000 became disabled because of wounds and injuries[1], and another 100,000 disappeared under mysterious circumstances[2]. After the overthrow of the Taliban regime and the establishment of the Karzai administration, many believed that Afghanistan would slowly transition to a peaceful democratic society. The relative peace and the presence of the international community within the country was reassuring.

Starting 2002, the government embarked on some measures for peace and justice. These initiatives included perusal of transitional justice through the Afghanistan Independent Human Rights Commission and establishment of High Peace Council. Then President Hamid Karzai formally ordered the establishment of the Afghanistan Independent Human Rights Commission (AIHRC). Among others, the commission was specifically tasked with pursuing transitional justice. The Presidential decree directed the Afghanistan Independent Human Rights Commission to consult the nation on how to respond to violations of human rights and develop a national plan of action. Part of the decree issued by President Karzai stated that the commission:

Shall be charged with developing a national plan of action for human rights in Afghanistan, and with human rights monitoring, investigation of violations of human rights, development and implementation of a national program of human rights education, undertaking of national human rights consultations, and development of domestic human rights institutions.[3]

In compliance with the order, the Afghanistan Independent Human Rights Commission consulted Afghans in a national survey in 2005. Six thousand people from 32 provinces participated in this national consultation, and the findings of the survey were compiled in a report entitled "A call for Justice"[4] and submitted to the Afghan government for consideration. The findings of "Call for Justice" are interesting in the sense that both retributive and restorative justice captured the attention of respondents who asked for trial, lustration/vetting, and reparation, as well as a truth and reconciliation commission. According to the findings of the national survey, 76% of Afghans wanted trials, believing that only trials of the warlords and war criminals can ensure peace and stability in the country. The survey revealed that 90% of the Afghans wanted lustration/vetting, arguing that removal of those who committed severe human rights violations would enhance rule of law and peace. Additionally, 86% of the participants wanted compensation. Finally, a significant number—95%—of the respondents believed that establishing a truth and reconciliation commission is critical to the country's stability and peace. This survey is of great importance because it was the only survey conducted at the national level concerning the question of transitional justice in Afghanistan.

Nonetheless, the Afghan government could not take action at that time following the receipt of the report "A call for Justice" for fear of further destabilization, as the Taliban had regrouped and engaged in intense fighting across Afghanistan. Several theories can explain the re-emergence and regrouping of the Taliban and an increase in violence in Afghanistan. According to Jones (2008), ideology is their main motivation, as the Taliban and other militant groups fight to establish a government based on their narrow interpretation of Islam. Jones likens the group to former Mujahidin who rose against Soviet Union occupation of Afghanistan, claiming the fight as a religious obligation against invaders. The failure of the government and the international community in delivering essential services, curbing corruption, and providing job opportunities are other factors that led to discontent and led some segments of the population to support the Taliban. As a result, the Afghan government lost control of around 45% of the territory (SIGAR, 2018).[5] Weir and Azamy (2015), who interviewed the Taliban insurgents in Herat and Helmand provinces, present a different theory. They found that money is the main motivation among the rank and file. They placed local grievances and ideology as the second and third motivating factors. Self-interest as the main motivation was also supported by Peters (2009), who asserted that the Taliban had increased criminal activities such as kidnapping, smuggling and running heroin factories.

Regardless of their motivations, the Taliban managed to take control of the main cities of the Kundoz province in 2015 and later the Ghazni province in 2018. They also managed to take partial control of Farah City for a day in 2018. The Taliban, who lost control of Afghanistan in 2001, solidified their reach over 45% of the land and began to practice and implement laws and render justice in their own exclusive court system.

On the topic of reconciliation, President Karzai established the Peace and Reconciliation Commission in 2005. The goal of the peace commission was to reach out to the Taliban and other militant groups and invite them to lay down their arms and join the legitimate Afghan government. While the commission did reach out to the Taliban, it was not successful in starting peace talks. To further the cause of reconciliation, the Afghan government established a new commission entitled High Peace Council in 2010, which was more representative and included members of the former Mujahidin, religious figures, women, and Taliban members who had joined the government. To encourage the Taliban and other militant groups, the High Peace Council announced that they are ready to make concessions and offer positions, housing, and salaries. This was a change in the tone of the government position, as the government had previously stated that they would welcome the Taliban if they accepted the constitution of Afghanistan. In May 2019, the government summoned a traditional consultative peace Loya Jirga[6], in which 3,200 people from different walks of life participated, including tribal leaders, academics, artists, influential figures, religious leaders, and athletes, as well as representatives from the private sectors, civil society, and political parties. The goal of the Jirga was to consult the nation on the framework and limits of peace talks and negotiation between the Afghan government and the Taliban. In the final communique, among others, the members of consultative peace Loya Jirga urged the Afghan government to accelerate facilitation of peace talks and respond to the legitimate demands of the Taliban. They also demanded that the international community, regional powers, and relevant parties take sincere and practical steps for a lasting peace in Afghanistan. In his remarks in the closing of the peace Jirga, President Ashraf Ghani said that the government would use the recommendations made by the members of the Jirga as a roadmap to the peace process[7]. These new developments are indications that the peace talks, while lengthy and complex, may lead to a political settlement.

The peace council received more political weight and attention in May 2020 when two presidential contenders Ashraf Ghani and Abdullah Abdullah reached political settlement and power sharing deals. Based on the political agreement, Abdullah will lead the Afghanistan High Council of National Reconciliation, and his team will have 50% of the cabinet seats.

While the Afghan government has been pushing for reconciliation, some human rights activists and political figures criticized the government and expressed concerns. For example, Sima Samar, former head of Afghanistan Independent Human Rights Commission, stated that peace without justice is a deal that will not solve the problem[8]. Former Director of Afghan Intelligence Agency and current Vice President Amrullah Salih had voiced a similar concern in the past and stated that a rushed peace deal would sacrifice justice.[9]

Recognizing the dire need for a reconciliation, the United States government started direct talks with the Taliban. After 18 months of negotiations, the U.S. Peace Envoy for Afghanistan, Zalmay Khalilzad, signed a peace deal with the Taliban in February 2020. The peace deal between the Taliban and the US stipulates that the Afghan government releases 5,000 Taliban prisoners and the Taliban 1,000 prisoners as a gesture of goodwill prior to the peace talks between the Afghan government and the Taliban. From the get-go, this became a point of contention, as the Afghan government wanted gradual release and a ceasefire prior to the direct peace talks. The Taliban, on the other hand, demanded the release of all 5,000 prisoners immediately prior to any direct talks with the Afghan government. The Taliban also rejected ceasefire as they see violence as a leverage in peace talks. While the Afghan government released more than 5,000 Taliban prisoners and the direct peace talks between the Afghan government and the Taliban began in September 2020, the level of violence and killings did not decrease. This indicates that the road to peace will be complex and difficult. Nonetheless, considering the high number of casualties and the stalemate at war, reconciliation through a peace settlement is necessary to stop the bloodshed. Based on a tally by the Watson Institute of Brown University, from 2001–2019, more than 157,000 individuals from different sides lost their lives in war in Afghanistan (Crawford and Lutz, 2019)[10]. Here is the breakdown of the causalities.

Table 1.

No	Category	Death	Grand Total
1	**US Military and Contractors**	6,118	157,052
2	**Other Allied Troops**	1,145	
3	**Afghan National Forces**	64,124	
4	**Opposition Fighters**	42,100	
5	**Afghan Civilians**	43,074	
6	**Aid Workers and Journalist**	491	

The war not only caused human casualties and suffering, but also destroyed the social fabric and physical infrastructure of the country. The Afghan people still suffer from a variety of problems, including psychological, emotional, and social trauma.

Overview of Transitional Justice Literature

Transitional justice refers to judicial and non-judicial measures adopted by post-authoritarian and post-conflict societies to address past atrocities (Hayner, 2009; Sandoval, 2011). The aim of transitional justice is to bring justice, reconciliation, stability and peace (David and Choi, 2009; Kerr and Mobeck, 2007; Hayner 2009). Proponents of transitional justice contend that there are political, moral, and legal obligations to uphold transitional justice. Kerr and Mobekk (2007:4) astutely summarize this obligation by asserting that transitional justice brings about:

Individual accountability, deterring future violations, establishing an historical record, promoting reconciliation and healing, providing victims a means of redress, removing perpetrators, and supporting capacity-building and rule of law.

Today, several mechanisms fall within the sphere of transitional justice, including trial, lustration, truth and reconciliation commissions, and reparation (Hayner, 2009; Forsythe, 2011). To elaborate on each mechanism of transitional justice, I will use Olsen et al.'s (2010) categorization of transitional justice. Olsen et al. categorized transitional justice into four categories: maximalist, moderate, minimalist, and holistic approaches.

Maximalist Approach

To address past atrocities, the maximalist approach stresses retributive justice in the form of trials and tribunals. This approach does not favor amnesties as it sees them going against international law, which rejects amnesties for crimes such genocide, war crimes, and crimes against humanity. Proponents of this approach argue that it is the victims' right that their perpetrators be punished as stipulated by international law. The proponents of this approach argue that trials are necessary for deterrence, and if the government and international community do not hold perpetrators of human rights violations accountable, impunity will perpetuate, which will result in further atrocities (Schabas, 2011; Kritz, 1996).

For example, Rwanda opted for international tribunal and domestic trials after the genocide of 1994, which killed "900,000 Tutsis" and some Hutus (Corey and Joireman 2004; Akhavan, 2001). Following the 10-year genocide, Rwandan courts prosecuted and tried a significant number of genocide perpetrators, as shown in the table below:

Table 2. Number of Suspected Genocide Perpetrators Imprisoned and Tried

Incarcerated	Tried	Received Death Penalty	Total
85,000	6500	700	92,200

Adopted from Graybill, 2004, p.1120

Similarly, the International Criminal Tribunal for Rwanda (ICTR) indicted 93 individuals in the span of 10 years following the genocide in Rwanda.[11]

Table 3. Individuals Indicted by the ICTR

Sentenced	Acquitted	Referred to National Jurisdiction for Trail	Fugitive Referred to MICT	Deceased Prior to Judgment	Indictment Withdrawn Before Trial	Total
62	14	10	3	2	2	93

Adopted from the United Nations ICTR website

Although there was not a full-blown genocide in Peru, during the conflict and state repression around 69,000 were killed and between 6,000 and 15,000 individuals were disappeared, mostly by the government forces (Burt, 2009). During the Presidency of Alberto Fujimori, while the state was at war with the Shining Path, an insurgent group, the state resorted to atrocities such as torture, massacres, forced disappearances, and arbitrary detention. Additionally, President Fujimori suspended the constitution, annulled the parliament, and took full control of the judiciary (Burt, 2009; Cueva, 2006). Following some political scandals, President Fujimori stepped down from power in 2001. In 2009, in an unprecedent move, the Peruvian court convicted Fujimori and "sentenced him to 25 years in prison" (Burt, 2009, p. 384). This is a historic moment in transitional justice because a president was held accountable in a domestic court for the atrocities committed under his presidency. In compliance with domestic and international law and honoring victims' rights, several countries such as Germany, Rwanda, Greece, Argentina, Sierra Leon, former Yugoslavia, and Peru have implemented retributive justice in the form of trials and tribunals.

Although there are valid reasons for punishment and legal approaches to addressing mass atrocities, it is also true that punishment negatively affects reconciliation and integration of the party engaged in the conflict. As Besmel and Alvarez (2017: 187) put it:

If reconciliation and enduring peace are true goals of international mechanisms of justice, great care must be taken with legal proceedings. Trials do not transcend politics; they are inherently political, and if the purpose of justice is to promote post-conflict peace and stability, then legalistic mechanisms for punishing offenders may not always be the best solution.

Thus, to integrate an opposition group/warring party through reconciliation, several countries have taken on a moderate approach, as explained below.

Moderate Approach

This approach stresses the truth commission because it promotes reconciliation, peace, and the protection of human rights. The moderate approach asserts that post-conflict and post-authoritarian nations suffer from various challenges, including weak judicial institutions, corruption, poor infrastructure, and financial constraints, which are obstacles to a fair trial. A truth commission is attractive for the government and for the opposition because both parties will try not to derail peace settlements to get impunity from domestic or international trials. The first truth commission ever was established in Argentina in 1983 (Sikkink and Walling, 2006). Argentina's truth commission, which became a model for subsequent truth commissions, investigated violations under the military government from 1976 to 1983. The commission recommended reparation to the victims, which was approved by the government.

The literature widely discusses South Africa's truth and reconciliation commission as a success story that helped the country in national reconciliation. During almost half a century of apartheid, more than 18,000 people were killed and 80,000 were imprisoned (Graybill, 2004). The truth and reconciliation commission established by Nelson Mandala was authorized to look into human rights violations that occurred from 1960-1994 and give individuals amnesty in return for disclosure about their past atrocities. (Graybill, 2004, p. 1117; Gibson, 2004; Owens et al., 1996). The Truth and Reconciliation Commission proved useful in South Africa because it resulted in national reconciliation and led the country to a peaceful transition from apartheid to democracy (Gibson 2006). The truth commission is a non-judicial, temporary, autonomous, and state-appointed entity whose job is to investigate past atrocities committed by the warring parties (Dancy et al., 2010). Truth commissions are attractive to post-conflict societies when their priority is peace and there is a fear that retributive justice would destabilize a country. Many countries, including Peru, Sri Lanka, Nepal, Chad, El Salvador, Liberia, Guatemala Sierra Leone, Chile, East Timor, Uganda, and Nigeria, have implemented truth commissions. Not all countries that implement truth commissions get favorable outcomes, however. For example, the outcome of truth commissions in Sri Lanka, Chad, Uganda, and Nigeria was not favorable as it did not result in reconciliation and peace. (Besmel, 2020) The political leaders in these nations established commissions to boost internal legitimacy and international image to gain donor attraction.

Minimalist Approach

A minimalist approach promotes amnesties. Proponents of amnesties argue that amnesties help deter and neutralize spoilers (Olsen et al., 2010). Like the truth commission, amnesty helps bring reconciliation to post-conflict societies. Amnesty is a useful tool used as a bargaining chip in seeking immunity following a peace deal. Additionally, there are cultures and religions that emphasize amnesties, including South Africa and Mozambique (Laplante, 2008; Millender, 2009). Several countries, such as Mozambique, Chile, Uruguay, Guatemala, El Salvador, and Haiti, used amnesties to promote "political change, peace, and reconciliation" (Tietle, 2000, p. 53). Two prominent cases of countries using amnesties are Spain and Mozambique. In Mozambique, after 17 years of civil war that claimed the lives of "one million civilians," the government reached a peace deal with the rebel group Mozambique National Resistance (Renamo) in 1992 that resulted in blanket amnesty. Amnesty proved effective as the country did not return to civil war and never sought trial or lustration (Ricci, 2013; Graybill, 2004). Spain passed an amnesty law in 1977 that covered the civil war of 1936–1939 and the subsequent 36 years of Franco dictatorship (Paredes, 2010). Based on an estimated tally, "the Franco regime executed approximately 50,000 people" and imprisoned "300,000" in concentration camps, with "hundreds of thousands more forced into exile" (Aguilar, Balcells and Cebolla-Boada, 2011, p. 1399). The amnesty helped the country strengthen its democracy (Teitle, 2000). While some researchers and activities reject the notion of amnesty altogether, arguing that it is not permitted under international law, McEvoy and Mallender present a counter argument and state that "no international convention has explicitly prohibited amnesty law". In fact, on average, 12 amnesty laws were approved annually from 1997 to 2010 (McEvoy and Mallinder, 2012, p. 415). Gibson (2002) asserts that globally, countries managed to develop processes in which amnesties were given in return for "truth, reconciliation and acquiescence to the new political order" (p. 540).

Holistic Approach

The holistic approach promotes a combination of different transitional justice mechanisms. The belief behind this approach is that a single measure does not address the complex conditions of post-conflict countries. Thus, joining several mechanisms would prove more useful in post-conflict justice. David and Choi (2009) argue that each of the transitional justice measures in one way or the other re-establish equality between the victims and the perpetrators. While retributive justice measures such as trial and lustration bring accountability and strengthen rule of law, restorative justice such as truth and reconciliation commissions and reparation contribute to peace and reconciliation. Several counties, such as Peru, Sierra Leone, Argentina, and South Africa, used a combination of transitional justice mechanisms to move their country forward.

Looking at 421 cases of transitional justice since 1970, Olsen et al. (2010) argued, "trials provide accountability and amnesties provide stability, advancing democracy and respect for human rights". These scholars contend, "if all else being equal, truth commissions alone have a negative impact on the two political objectives but contribute positively when combined with trials and amnesty" (Olsen et al., 2010, p. 980). Similarly, Ricci (2013) found a positive relationship between using two transitional justice mechanisms and long-standing peace. El Salvador endorsed amnesty laws from 1979 to 1993, yet in 1993 the country established a truth commission and trials in between. Argentina used trials, truth commission, amnesty, and reparation. Similarly, Germany implemented trials and reparation; Peru used trials, truth commissions and lustration, and South Africa implemented amnesty, truth commission and reparation.

A Holistic Approach to Transitional Justice for Afghanistan

Transitional justice has been viewed as a worthwhile policy measure by the Afghan government since 2002, when the former Afghan President, Hamid Karzai, established the Afghanistan independent Human Rights Commission. It has also been an important issue to the Afghan public, as exemplified in a national survey conducted in 2005 by the Human Rights Commission. While this survey is outdated, it is significant because it is the only national survey conducted in Afghanistan on transitional justice. Nevertheless, things have changed dramatically in Afghanistan since 2005. Therefore, some demands are incompatible with the current socio-political realities, meaning that both retributive and restorative justice cannot be implemented simultaneously, as was suggested by the Afghans in the national survey.

I argue that a holistic approach in the form of restorative justice only is more congruent with the current situation considering the looming reconciliation between the Taliban and the Afghan government. Below, I will first explain why trial, lustration, and reparation are not viable transitional justice measures for Afghanistan and then present my argument for a restorative holistic approach, i.e., truth and reconciliation commission combined with amnesty.

First, history shows that countries that have ended the war are more likely to resort to either national or international trials or tribunals. The Nuremberg trials, the International Criminal Tribunal for former Yugoslavia and Rwanda, the Tokyo and Yokohama trials, and Greece are some examples indicating that trials are possible when one side of the conflict ends the war. In Afghanistan, however, both the Afghan government and NATO failed to end the war. On the other hand, the Taliban appeared stronger and gained more momentum and territory on the battlefield. By 2018, the Taliban managed to regain control of almost half of the Afghan territory as the government control shrank to "55.5%".[12] Considering the military stalemate, NATO involvement, and the willingness of both sides for reconciliation, domestic and international trials are out of the question in immediate post-conflict Afghanistan.

Two important factors will hinder the International Criminal Court (ICC) should it decide to initiate criminal investigation of mass atrocities in Afghanistan. These are the absence of political will by the Afghan government and the United States' involvement in war in Afghanistan. As a court of last resort, the ICC admits cases only when referred to it by the United Nations Security Council, a state party, and when a prosecutor from the ICC opens a case. The United States is still a global superpower and will not permit the ICC to prosecute any US troops for alleged war crimes and torture in Afghanistan. Realpolitik and the United States soft power were shown to have worked in April 2019 when the ICC reversed its decision on an investigation initiated in 2017 by Fatou Bensouda, ICC Prosecutor. In a unanimous decision, the judges in ICC ruled that the possible investigation cannot go ahead because "the prospects for a successful investigation and prosecution [is] extremely limited" in Afghanistan[13]. The United States welcomed the ruling of the ICC, and President Trump warned that any action by the ICC that would implicate the U.S troops will meet with a tough and quick response[14]. In an interesting development, the ICC's appeal chamber invalidated the April 2019 ruling and re-authorized the prosecutor to initiate investigation of war crimes in Afghanistan. Regardless of the new ruling, the US had made its position clear as Mike Pompeo, former US Secretary of State, asserted that hauling US troops to the ICC will never happen[15]. The 2020 peace deal between the US and the Taliban and the looming peace settlement between the Afghan government and the Taliban cancel the likelihood of any involved party in the conflict appearing before any national or international court in the foreseeable future. Thus, trial as a post-conflict measure is not likely in the Afghanistan post-conflict scenario. So far, there is no indication that the Afghan government is willing to reach out to the ICC, as the government is desperate for a peace settlement to avoid undue bloodshed in the country.

Second, I argue that lustration/vetting also does not work in the current socio-political climate because it can further exacerbate the partial political stability in Afghanistan. After 9/11, the new government under the leadership of Hamid Karzai was formed from various heterogeneous groups—loyalist of former King Zahir Shah, former Mujahidin, pro-communist elements, defected Taliban—some of whom are known for their roles in armed conflict and violations of human rights. In Karzai's administration, the political process was grounded on impunity, as many who were suspected of war crimes were given a higher position in the Afghan cabinet and other government institutions. Political structure and institutions were assembled with a quota mindset based on ethnicity. Ethnic alignments and affiliations had provided a shield for many of the alleged war criminals and warlords to grab government posts. Ethnic divisions were clearly exemplified in both the 2014 and 2019 presidential elections. In the 2014 election, the majority of Pashtuns and Uzbeks stood behind Ashraf Ghani, while the majority of Hazaras and Tajiks supported Abdullah Abdullah. When both contenders disputed the result, many feared that Afghanistan would witness another ethnic conflict, but thanks to John Kerry, former United States Secretary of State, they were able to agree on a unified government. As a result, Ghani became President and Abdullah became Chief Executive Officer. The story of the 2019 election was similar, as ethnic alignments and disputes erupted over the result of the election. While the Afghanistan Election Commission announced Ghani as President by winning 50.64% of the votes, Abdullah disputed these results and claimed victory. When Ghani was sworn in as President of Afghanistan, Abdullah held a parallel inauguration and was also sworn in as President. Later, both contenders reached a deal, creating a shared cabinet with a 50–50 split and appointing Abdullah Abdullah as head of the Afghanistan High Council of National Reconciliation. The ethnic quota in the post-Taliban regime in 2001 was intended to increase the legitimacy of the interim administration, but instead it has increased the ethnic power struggle. Considering the frail political structure and prospects of an imminent peace settlement with the Taliban, I argue that lustration/vetting is not an option, and removing any influential figure or party further destabilizes the country.

Third, I argue that reparation to the victims and their surviving families is another unviable post-conflict justice measure because the Afghan government is not even near a position to compensate. The Afghan government heavily relies on international aid not only for developing budgets, but also to remain operational. For example, in the fiscal year of 2017–2018, the Afghan government managed to fund only 33 percent of its national budget; the remaining amount was funded through foreign aid[16]. Therefore, given the fragile economy, compensation to the victims or surviving victims is not likely to happen in immediate post-reconciliation Afghanistan.

Considering the current socio-political realities, I have disqualified the options for trials/tribunals, reparation and lustration- the three important mechanisms of transitional justice—and suggest that a holistic approach in the form of a truth and reconciliation commission combined with amnesty are the most viable options for transitional justice in Afghanistan.

To that end, a strong foundation is already in place on which this restorative holistic approach can be built. For example, there exists an amnesty law passed by the Afghan parliament in 2007 and later endorsed by the then President, Hamid Karzai. *The National Stability and Reconciliation Law*—or the amnesty law—stipulates that individuals involved in the conflict, prior to the establishment of the interim government in late 2001, are protected, and will "enjoy all their legal rights and shall not be prosecuted"[17]. The Afghan parliament in close collaboration with the executive branch can amend the law to cover the later years.

Additionally, the spirit of Islamic teaching is more oriented toward reconciliation, truth telling and preference for "non-violence over violence, and for forgiveness (afu) over retribution" (Said et al., 2001, p.8; Bassiouni, 2014). According to Rye et al., in the Quran, forgiveness is expressed in three different terminologies, including *ghafara* (forgive or remit), *afu* (to pardon), and *safhu* (ignore or turn away), each repeated 243 times, 35 times, and 8 times respectively (Rye et al., 2000). Afghanistan is an Islamic country where Islamic teachings are highly valued and ingrained in tradition and law. Therefore, Islamic teachings and amnesty law can go hand in hand as foundations for the truth and reconciliation commission.

Moreover, the traditional or communal conflict resolution method known as *Jirga* or *Shura* (assembly, council or gathering) can be another cornerstone for the truth and reconciliation commission. Jirga is deeply rooted in Afghan culture and practiced mainly by the Pashtun ethnic group (Ahmadi, 2012; Wardak, 2003). Jirga is used by the Afghans for resolving a wide variety of conflicts, including family disputes, violent crimes like murder, and important national political issues such as changes in the country's constitution. Different governments imposed formal legal systems, but ordinary people, especially those residing in villages and rural areas, have used Jirga to resolve their disputes. A preference for quick and internal dispute resolutions, concerns about corruption, long delays in the state court system, and the failure of the government to extend its authority to rural areas and villages are the three prominent reasons why people avoid the formal state court system and turn to Jirgas (Wardak, 2003; Mukhopadhyay, 2009).

Thus, amnesty law, Islamic teachings, and traditional conflict resolution *Jirga* provide strong foundations for creating a truth and reconciliation commission. For the truth commission to work and secure cooperation of the Taliban, the Afghan government can establish a conditional amnesty or extend the current law to cover the last 19 years of the conflict.

Concerning the timeline from when truth about past atrocities be uncovered, the former Head of Afghanistan Independent Human Rights Commission already suggested a starting date of April 27, 1978, which is a reasonable proposal. It is the day when the pro-Communists overthrew President Daud's government via a bloody coup. It is known that pro-Communist regimes, Mujahidin factions, and the Taliban all committed heinous atrocities, including killings, illegal imprisonments, torture, and disappearances. For example, the Parcham faction of the pro-communist regime "published a list of about 12,000 people said to have disappeared in Pul-i Charkhi prison" (Rubin, 2003, p. 568). Mujahidin factions during the civil war in 1992 killed and injured "tens of thousands of civilians" (Human Rights Watch, 2005). During the same year, they forced more than 500,000 people to flee Kabul (Human Rights Watch, 2005, p. 1 & 35). Based on the United Nations Assistance Mission in Afghanistan (UNAMA), from 2009–2020 there were 110,893 civilian casualties[18.] UNAMA attributed anti-government forces to most civilian casualties. Therefore, it is important for the truth commission to cover atrocities committed from 1978 to the present.

Regarding the mandate of the truth commission, it should investigate massive human rights violations that were committed by the pro-communist governments, Mujahidin, the Taliban, and the Afghan governments established post 9/11. The mandate should include an investigation of crimes, including illegal imprisonments, killings, torture, and disappearances. The commission should provide a forum for the victims and their surviving families to express their fear, anger, and demands. It should also have the subpoena power to summon individuals at a higher level to provide testimony to the commission. The truth commission should dig deep into the root causes of the atrocities to recommend corrective measures. To ensure impartiality and funding, UN involvement in the process is crucial.

CONCLUSION

With the imminent peace settlement between the Taliban and the Afghan government, the prospect of reconciliation is highly likely. Transitional justice will remain an essential task in Afghanistan's post-peace settlement, but it will not be retributive. I argued that a holistic approach, i.e., truth and reconciliation commission combined with amnesty, is the appropriate transitional justice approach for Afghanistan's post-peace settlement. This restorative justice approach will promote reconciliation, peace, and stability, which is the priority in Afghanistan to end the bloodshed. While truth commission is a non-judicial mechanism, it does serve as a form of accountability, moral accountability, which entails "shame, opprobrium and disgrace" that perpetrators would feel and live with (Daly, 2001, p.135). I have also contended that trial, reparation, and lustration/vetting are not possible in the immediate post-peace settlement due to NATO's involvement, lack of political will, civilians' predicament, and fragile economy. It is essential to highlight that truth and reconciliation commissions are the first steps toward accountability. Depending on the situation, countries may further pursue retributive justice once stability, strong judicial institutions, and the rule of law have been established.

REFERENCES

Afghanistan, H. R. W. (2005, June 7). Blood-Stained Hands: Past Atrocities in Kabul and Afghanistan's Legacy of Impunity. *Human Rights Watch.*

Aguilar, P., Balcells, L., & Cebolla-Boado, H. (2011). Determinants of attitudes toward transitional justice: An empirical analysis of the Spanish case. *Comparative Political Studies*, *44*(10), 1397–1430. doi:10.1177/0010414011407468

Ahmadi, H. (2012). *The overview of traditional Jirga in Afghanistan*. Xlibris Corporation.

Akhavan, P. (2001). Beyond impunity: Can international criminal justice prevent future atrocities? *The American Journal of International Law*, *95*(1), 7–31. doi:10.2307/2642034

Barnett, R. R. (2003). Transitional Justice and Human Rights in Afghanistan. *International Affairs*, *79*(3), 567–581.

Bassiouni, M. C. (2014). *The shari'a and Islamic criminal justice in time of war and peace*. Cambridge University Press.

Bauer, P. (2000). *From Subsistence to Exchange: And other Essays*. Princeton University Press. doi:10.1515/9781400824649

Besmel, P. (2020). The Pathway to Transitional Justice in Afghanistan. *Journal of Global South Studies*, *37*(2), 240–269.

Besmel, P., & Alvarez, A. (2017). Transitional Justice and the Legacy of Nuremberg: The Promise and Problems of Confronting Atrocity in Post-Conflict Societies. *Genocide Studies International*, *11*(2), 182–196. doi:10.3138/gsi.11.2.03

Burt, J. M. (2009). Guilty as charged: The trial of former Peruvian president Alberto Fujimori for human rights violations. *The International Journal of Transitional Justice*, *3*(3), 384–405. doi:10.1093/ijtj/ijp017

Comprehensive National Disability Policy in Afghanistan (2003): 7.

Corey, A., & Joireman, S. F. (2004). Retributive justice: The Gacaca courts in Rwanda. *African Affairs, 103*(410), 73–89. doi:10.1093/afraf/adh007

Cueva, E. G. (2006). The Peruvian Truth and Reconciliation Commission and the challenge of impunity. *Transitional Justice in the Twenty-First Century: Beyond Truth versus Justice*, 70.

Daly, E. (2001). Transformative justice: Charting a path to reconciliation. *Int'l Legal Persp., 12*(73), 73–183.

Dancy, G., Hunjoon, K., & Wiebelhaus-Brahm, E. (2010). The turn to truth: Trends in truth commission experimentation. *Journal of Human Rights, 9*(1), 45–64. doi:10.1080/14754830903530326

David, R., & Choi, S. Y. (2009). Getting even or getting equal? Retributive desires and transitional justice. *Political Psychology, 30*(2), 161–192.

Forsythe, D. P. (2011). Forum: Transitional Justice: The Quest for Theory to Inform Policy. *International Studies Review, 13*(3), 554–578. doi:10.1111/j.1468-2486.2011.01016.x

Gibson, J. L. (2004). Truth, reconciliation, and the creation of a human rights culture in South Africa. *Law & Society Review, 38*(1), 5–40. doi:10.1111/j.0023-9216.2004.03801001.x

Gibson, J. L. (2006). The Contributions of Truth to Reconciliation Lessons from South Africa. *The Journal of Conflict Resolution, 50*(3), 409–432. doi:10.1177/0022002706287115

Graybill, L. S. (2004). Pardon, punishment, and amnesia: Three African post-conflict methods. *Third World Quarterly, 25*(6), 1117–1130. doi:10.1080/0143659042000256922

Hayner, P. B., & Centre for Humanitarian Dialogue. (2009). *Negotiating justice: Guidance for mediators*. HD Centre for Humanitarian Dialogue.

Jones, S. G. (2008). The Rise of Afghanistan's Insurgency: Sate Failure and Jihad. *International Security, 33*(4), 7–40. doi:10.1162/isec.2008.32.4.7

Kerr, R., & Mobekk, E. (2007). Peace and justice. *Polity*.

Kritz, N. J. (1996). Coming to terms with atrocities: A review of accountability mechanisms for mass violations of human rights. *Law and Contemporary Problems, 59*(4), 127–152. doi:10.2307/1192195

Laplante, L. J. (2008). Transitional justice and peace building: Diagnosing and addressing the socioeconomic roots of violence through a human rights framework. *The International Journal of Transitional Justice*, *2*(3), 331–355. doi:10.1093/ijtj/ijn031

Mallinder, L. (2009). *Exploring the practice of States in introducing amnesties.* Springer Berlin Heidelberg. doi:10.1007/978-3-540-85754-9_6

McEvoy, K., & Mallinder, L. (2012). Amnesties in transition: Punishment, restoration, and the governance of mercy. *Journal of Law and Society*, *39*(3), 410–440. doi:10.1111/j.1467-6478.2012.00591.x

Mukhopadhyay, D. (2009). *Warlords as bureaucrats: The Afghan experience.* Carnegie Endowment for International Peace.

Olsen, T., Payne, L., & Reiter, A. (2010). The justice balance: When transitional justice improves human rights and democracy. *Human Rights Quarterly*, *32*(4), 980–1007. doi:10.1353/hrq.2010.0021

Owens, I., Wildschut, G., Orr, W., & Goboda-Madikezela, P. (1996). Stories of silence: Women, truth and reconciliation. *Agenda (Durban, South Africa)*, *12*(30), 66–72. doi:10.2307/4065784

Paredes, T. C. F. (2010). Transitional Justice in Democratization Processes: The Case of Spain from an International Point of View. *International Journal on Rule of Law. Transitional Justice and Human Rights*, *1*(1), 120–135.

Peters, G. (2009). How opium profits the Taliban (Vol. 31, No. 19-62). Washington DC: United States Institute of Peace.

Ricci, N. (2013). *Eroding the Barrier between 'Peace 'and 'Justice': Effects of Transitional Justice Mechanisms on Post-Conflict Stability*. Academic Press.

Rye, M. S., Pargament, K. I., Ali, M. A., Beck, G. L., Dorff, E. N., Hallisey, C., ... Williams, J. G. (2000). Religious perspectives on forgiveness. *Forgiveness: Theory, Research, and Practice*, 17-40.

Said, A. A., Funk, N. C., & Kadayifci, A. S. (2001). *Peace and conflict resolution in Islam: precept and practice*. University Press of Amer.

Sandoval, C. (2011). *Transitional Justice: Key Concepts*. Processes and Challenges.

Schabas, W. (2011). *Transitional justice and the norms of international law.* Academic Press.

Sikkink, K., & Walling, C. B. (2006). Argentina's contribution to global trends in transitional justice. *Transitional justice in the twenty-first century: beyond truth versus justice*, 301-324.

Wardak, A. (2003). *Jirga–A Traditional Mechanism of Conflict Resolution in Afghanistan*. Institute of Afghan Study Center.

Wardak, A. (2010). State and non-state justice systems in Afghanistan: The need for synergy. *U. Pa. J. Int'l L.*, *32*, 1305.

Weir, J., & Azamy, H. (2015). Afghanistan's "Transformation Decade" Depends on the Taliban's Foot Soldiers. *Foreign Policy*.

ENDNOTES

1 Afghanistan National Disability Action Plan 2008-2011. Full report can be accessed at: Microsoft Word - SCVA-Afghanistan-ANDAP.doc (un.org)

2 This is a piece by Patricia Gossman of The Human Rights Watch. For more information check: Agony of Afghanistan's Enforced Disappearances | Human Rights Watch (hrw.org)

3 Decree on establishment of Afghanistan Independent Human Rights Commission can be accessed at: http://www.aihrc.org.af/2010_eng/Eng_pages/about/decree.pdf

4 Full report can be accessed at: https://www.refworld.org/pdfid/47fdfad50.pdf

5 For more information see "Quarterly Report of Special Inspector General for Afghanistan Reconstruction," which can be accessed at https://www.sigar.mil/pdf/quarterlyreports/2018-10-30qr.pdf

6 Full communique of the consultative peace jirga can be accessed at: https://www.canberra.mfa.af/news/communique-the-consultative-peace-loya-jirga-2019.html

7 Ghani comments and the main highlights of the peace jirga can be accessed at: https://ariananews.af/grand-consultative-peace-jirga-ends-in-kabul/

8 Interview in Dari language, Daud Sultanzoy Show, June 2011, Tolo TV. The interview can be watched at: http://www.tolonews.com/en/daoud-sultanzoy?start=5

9 Interview in Dari Language with BBC Persian, 2011.Interview with can be watched at http://www.bbc.co.uk/persian/tvandradio/2011/05/110505_hardtalk_amrullah_saleh_final.shtml

10 For more information you can look at: Direct War Deaths COW Estimate November 13 2019 FINAL.pdf (brown.edu)

11 Adopted from United Nations ICTR website: https://unictr.irmct.org/en/tribunal

12 . Quarterly report of Special Inspector General for Afghanistan Reconstruction (October 30, 2018), page 69. Accessed from: https://www.sigar.mil/pdf/quarterlyreports/2018-10-30qr.pdf

13 Merrit, Kennedy (2019).World Criminal Court Rejects Probe into U.S. Actions in Afghanistan. National Public Radio. Retrieved April 8 2020 from **Error! Hyperlink reference not valid.**

[14] Jennifer, Hansler, (2019).International Criminal Court rejects call to investigate war crimes in Afghanistan. *CCN*. Retrived April, from https://www.cnn.com/2019/04/12/politics/icc-rejects-afghanistan-investigation/index.html

[15] Full Story of the US Secretary of State can be accessed at:, https://www.yahoo.com/news/pompeo-signals-impending-action-against-160041290.html

[16] Aid Effectiveness in Afghanistan (2018) a joint report commissioned by Swedish Committee for Afghanistan and Oxfam with support from CAFOD. According to this report in 2008 the Afghan revenue was roughly 750 million so there is a huge increase if compared to several years back, https://swedishcommittee.org/sites/default/files/media/aid_effectivenessin_afhganistan_march_2018_0.pdf (accessed in November 2018)

17 For details of Human Rights Watch Reaction go to:http://www.hrw.org/news/2010/03/10/afghanistan-repeal-amnesty-law

18 For more on the civilian casualties check: https://unama.unmissions.org/surge-civilian-casualties-following-afghanistan-peace-negotiations-start-un-report

Chapter 13
Foster Children and Deviance Risks After Emancipation

Gianna M. Strube
Independent Researcher, USA

ABSTRACT

The subject of this chapter is how foster children may become at risk of displaying deviant behavior after emancipation from care. The chapter argues that there is a special need to provide for young people's legal protection and care after emancipation. The chapter then highlights the issues surrounding of foster children being abused and neglected, aging out of the system, and the programs offered as they overcome certain measures during their adolescent years. This research advocates for foster children in this category and outlines how their deviant behavior is perceived and defined and asks if this perception is just a stereotype. The research methodologies included interviews from those involved in the foster care system, in addition to literature and research from professional foster agencies.

INTRODUCTION

Foster care is a system in which a minor has been placed into a ward, group home, or private home of a state-certified caregiver, referred to as a "foster parent" or a family member approved by the state. The placement of the child is normally arranged through the government or a social service agency. The institution, group home, or foster parent is then compensated for the expenses unless the child is with a family member. Children who grow up within the foster care system are more likely to partake in deviant behavior, and with certain programs, it will limit the deviance of those being released. The researcher involved mixed methods as my methodology,

DOI: 10.4018/978-1-7998-6646-6.ch013

consisting of fieldwork, interviews, and a review of relevant agencies and literature about foster children.

Furthermore, across the United States, we can find up to half a million children placed in foster care services (U.S Department of Health and Human Services, 2010). Young people who have become legal adults are 'aged out' of foster care and stop receiving assistance from child protective services, and they reach eighteen to twenty-five years of age and the juvenile or family court terminates its jurisdiction. In many states, childhood is seen to end legally at age eighteen. On top of that, children who have suffered abuse or neglect cannot safely remain with their families and child welfare officials are obligated to provide them safe and appropriate homes to ensure their wellbeing and recover from the trauma. Many children are further maltreated at the hands of the people entrusted with their protection.

Foster children experience a wide variety of different forms of abuse and neglect that no child should face alone or be exposed to at all. Many programs are offered to help these adolescents but not in time for something to be done or fixed. Later stated in my interviews I will discuss commonalities of treatment, programs provided, and age groups of the interviews and their unique experiences.

Abuse and Neglect

From 1993 through 2002 there were 107 recorded deaths within foster homes; there are approximately 400,000 children in out-of-home care in the United States. Almost 10% of children in foster care have stayed in foster care for five or more years. Nearly half of all children in the foster care system have chronic medical problems:

About 8% of all children in foster care have serious emotional problems, 11% of children exiting foster care aged out of the system in 2011 (Wexler, 2017).

Children in foster care experience high rates of child abuse, emotional deprivation, and physical neglect. A recent study of foster children found that nearly one third reported being abused by a foster parent, another adult in a foster home, social workers, religious advisors, teachers, or anyone else in the child's life. It becomes common for sexual predators to use their position in the child's life to take advantage of the child. Many of these abusers don't usually have a criminal record of abuse This further leads to PTSD (Post Traumatic Stress Disorder), resulting in many children within foster care:

Studies show that 60% of children in foster care who had experienced sexual abuse had PTSD, and 42% of those who had been physically abused met the PTSD criteria (Child Trauma Academy, 2002).

PTSD was also found in 18% of the children who were not abused, although many experienced trauma simply by witnessing violence within the home. Many children from ages 14-18 were found to experience the highest levels of PTSD. In addition, when foster children experience physical or mental abuse within the first 5 years of their lives they are at a greater risk for being arrested as juveniles, nonviolent and status offenses. Starting at such a young age high levels of abuse and neglect can continue those levels of PTSD into adulthood. In continuum, physically and mentally abused adolescents were less likely to have graduated from high school, been a teen parent, these being more prevalent for females than males. Much of the delinquency is led by aggression, malnutrition, and sexual abuse and neglect starting at a very young age and only progressing as time goes by and they age within the system.

Aging out of the System

Young people who have become legal adults are 'aged out' of foster care and stop receiving assistance from child protective services. Ranging from 18-25 years of age the juvenile or family court terminates its jurisdiction. In much of the United States, you 'age out' of childhood at 18. This means that nearly 30,000 youth age out of the foster care system according to the 2009 statistics.

This then leads to many issues and problems when released such as; finding a house, getting a job, research and enrolling in post-secondary or vocational educational opportunities, taking care of their basic needs, and function independently as an adult (HHS, 2010).

Many face this fear and tasks alone without much, if any support from other adults, family members, or friends that look out for their success. On top of aging out, there are many important life skills that later help them overcome these problems as well as developing better self-esteem and competencies. Living within the foster care system can be very traumatic, both physically and emotionally, thus leading to many psychological issues such as depression and isolation for many young individuals. Without the relationships with others, many of those can be strained or lost. On top of that as stated before many children do and will experience different levels of abuse and neglect within the system. This further leads to a loss of confidence and alienation caused by neglect and abuse, therefore, leading to the increased risks of drug and alcohol abuse as well as antisocial behavior.

"Research on developing brains of adolescents and young adults points to the importance of understanding the "vulnerability of teens, and the significance of

this stage" and highlights the importance of positive, supportive relationships in the context of the continuing development of the adolescent brain (HHS, 2010).

However, when young people experience the positive support of families and mentors, they are to have improved life courses and a significant improvement to their physical and mental health and wellbeing. Negative outcomes such as delinquency, drug, and alcohol abuse, and depression are also reduced by positive engagement with family and mentors. Unfortunately, when young people 'age out' of the care systems and networks provided by fostering, this may lead to multiple negative outcomes, some including; instability and homelessness, lack of education, lack of employment, issues with health and wellbeing, poor health care, problems with the justice system, and few social connections.

Aging out of the foster care system can increase the likelihood of being homeless for many young individuals. More than one fifth of youth within this aging out category experience some level of homelessness during their first year of emancipation from the system. The rate of homelessness increases drastically for those in the LGBTQ community as youths, as well as comprising between 5-10% of this overall group. Although with positive mentoring those certain individuals' percentage was significantly reduced. Furthermore, the LGBTQ community may already be disproportionally represented in the homeless population by being a youth and being a youth of color (National Alliance to End Homelessness, 2007).

Because these adolescents age out of the system and later become homeless, they are left to become deviant and participate in deviant behavior. This results in drug and alcohol abuse and sometimes even stealing and looting from other individuals and stores. Many that age out steal to get by and survive on the streets because only they can support and help themselves when so many others pushed them away.

Next, is their lack of education, the young experience after being emancipated, facing many difficulties when trying to complete educational studies. Due to being stuck in the system, they missed out on a valuable education system and life lessons learned while participating. Furthermore, because the young were slowly aging out and moving from foster home to foster home their school and social bonds were continuously changing.

Research has shown that students in foster care score 16-20% points below their peers in state standardized testing and fewer than 60% graduate from High School (National Working Group on Foster Care, 2008).

Only a few, around 3% go on to secondary education to better their educational and social skills. This further led to their lack of employment or training. When many are forced to leave foster care at 18 they have very few job skills or experience. With few skills and training many find the process to move up career-wise or lifestyle-wise they can't due to their current education level.

Youth who do obtain employment may find jobs with lower-paying wages, which makes them vulnerable to poverty, and the inability to establish independence (Lenz-Rashid, 2004).

Issues with foster children's health and wellbeing are diminished and around 25% of the youth from foster homes experience higher than average health problems in their lives. Many of these individuals suffer from health problems such as;

"depression, dysthymia, post-traumatic stress disorder (PTSD), alcohol dependence, substance abuse, or substance dependency (Courtney et al., 2005).

On top of that healthcare is very poor and only some states will offer Medicaid for youth until they become 21 years of age but can be denied or taken away as well as any other forms of assistance. This forces the youth's mental and physical state to diminish after emancipation and can no longer support the child welfare system or themselves. Consequently, these all later tie into the Justice System and delinquency. When adolescents face abuse and neglect before or during foster care services they are more likely to partake in delinquent behavior as well as become involved with criminals. This is due to the 'lack of support networks, low-income skills, and unstable living arrangements. Arizona's statistics state that;

"45% had been in trouble with law enforcement, 41% spent time in jail, 26% were involved in the court system(with formal charges filed), and 7% were incarcerated (Reilly, 2003).

Lastly, those who age out have few social connections and are in need of permanent mentors who provide a positive relationship and well as mentor role. Although it is found that the youth within the foster system have these good adult relationships with child welfare professionals, and those may be lost once emancipated. Aging out of the system diminishes many social bonds, communication skills, and a fight to provide for yourself. Without these social bonds, many of these teens age out and commit delinquent behavior to survive off the streets if living isn't accommodated.

Programs and Institutions Offered

It is said that there are many programs and institutions offered for children in foster care, but it seems to only be offered to those who have been adopted and taken into their forever families. The terms and guidelines differ in each state as to where the child is being sent next and if any precautions are taken beforehand. The following requirements are reviewed and taken into account before adopting, those include; 18 years of age, married or single, financially stable, emotionally ready for parenting, in good physical health, free of serious DCS or criminal background, flexible schedule to meet needs of children in care, able to provide transportation for children, willing to consider sibling groups, available to take in children on emergency notice, and are committed to reunification with the child's biological family if need be (Arizona Children Association).

Although in many cases the foster kids may be moved from house to house, they never provided any programs or support, just being pushed and pulled through the system until they age out. Furthermore, the Children's Bureau states that many of the programs and funding go to assisting the youth from aging out of the system and achieving self-sufficiency (Children's Bureau).

Statistics previously showing that many age-out without receiving any of that assistance. For those children that do get adopted, they are offered far more programs and assistance in improving their physical and mental emotions as well as creating a kinship with their new adopted parent or parents. Some of these programs include;

behavioral health and trauma response, family preservation and reunification, kinship services, family education, and support, young adult services, and lastly neurosequential model of therapeutics.

With the lack of these programs, support, and research it may lead to further delinquency and a life without self-sufficiency and struggles. Foster care systems and group homes need to show and give these children the mentors and support they need all the way through the time they are adopted or even aged out of the system. These relationships create social bonds and the information needed to survive and thrive while being brought from home to home or watching out for yourself on the streets.

Discussion

Many foster kids that aren't provided with the mentoring or support they require and this may lead to delinquency. According to Cusick et al (2010) there is a strong correlation between maltreatment, (such as physical abuse and neglect) and crime. This is also dependent on the length and quality of placements, as well as the number of transfers undertaken by the foster child:

For example, the length of stay in out-of-home care across all children who exited care in 2001 varied from less than 1 month (19 percent) to greater than 5 years

(9 percent), with a median duration of 12 months (U.S. Department of Health and Human Services, 2003).

There are large variables when it comes to the age of the young people in foster care. For instance, children up to 8 years of age tend to stay with one foster family far longer than teenagers, and those at the end of the teenage years tend to stay the least amount of time with one family. The type of placement also proved to be of considerable significance to the foster child, according to the US Department of Health and Human Services:

Of the 542,000 children in out-of-home care in 2001, 48 percent were in non-relative foster family homes, 24 percent were in relative family homes, 18 percent were in group homes or institutions, 4 percent were in pre-adoptive homes, and 6 percent were in other placement types (U.S. Department of Health and Human Services, 2003).

Studies have demonstrated a correlation between higher amounts of foster home placements and post foster home criminal behavior. This would seem to indicate a link between stability and duration of early foster care and subsequent positive outcomes for the foster child as they grow into adulthood and out -row the foster care system. Multiple placements in the foster child's early years can therefore be linked with increased criminal behavior in adolescence.

By observing the 'life-course' of the foster child in this manner, we can come to understand the significance of various points within the wider life-course and the subsequent impact on behavior and potential criminal activities as the foster child ages:

For youth leaving out-of-home care, behavior during the transition may be partially explained by earlier experiences of abuse or neglect as well as unstable or negative experiences within the child welfare system. It may be that these negative experiences decrease child well-being and result in greater behavior problems among youth. It may also be that instability or placement in a group home setting is an indicator of a difficult case; a youth already showing significant problem behavior, a parent, caregiver, or household environment with problems, or both (Cusik et al, 2010).

Race is another factor which impacts on post foster care outcomes. As in so many aspects of American life, the foster system is shown to fail minorities at higher levels than white youth. African-American youth have higher rates of offending than Caucasians, and also higher rates of serious offending when studies are examined in that category:

Although African-American children comprised 15 percent of the U.S. child population in 1999, they constituted 45 percent of the children in out-of-home care. Conversely, white children, who comprised 60 percent of the child population, accounted for only 36 percent of children in out-of-home care (Cusik 2010).

The lack of family engagement with minority children who are housed within the foster-care system is seen as a further issue which may also affect post childhood and post foster care behaviors, possibly leading to increased criminal activities and further to that, arrest and imprisonment. With families providing emotional support during the life-course, a child in foster care may transition into adolescence (and later adulthood) with a better pathway for success. Certainly, research demonstrates that when this family engagement is lacking (as is too often the case with minority youth in care), the odds of the young person ending up in criminal activity increases exponentially. It would seem obvious that more significance needs to be placed on supports for minority youth within the foster-care system as it exists, with more resources and a system of safety nets for relevant minority youth in this category.

Conclusion/Outcomes & Preliminary Findings

The primary goal of this study was to test and research whether children who grow up within the foster care system are more likely to partake in deviant behavior and if certain programs, it will limit the deviance of those children being released. The results of this study suggest that mentors and support groups influence foster children to make good decisions. When it came to abuse and neglect it was found that high numbers of foster children are abused and neglected, that being emotional, physical, or sexual abuse. This further leads to many psychological issues such as depression, PTSD, and so many others. These numbers were a lot higher in teens aging from 14-18. If these teens and adolescents do take part in deviant behavior is usually led by aggression, malnutrition, and sexual abuse and neglect starting at a very young age and progressing as they age within the system. Furthermore, the high rates on individuals aging out of the system and losing all assistance from child protective services, leaving many to end up on the street and commit these deviant acts.

Many of the homeless foster children that age out have limited resources to provide for themselves which further leads them to steal, abuse drugs and alcohol, as well as become highly depressed. The connection between having a good education and becoming a delinquent is tied in many ways, meaning if you grew up with a poor education than you are more likely to become deviant. Having an education while in the foster system kept many children on the right track, social bonds were created, and they became very self-sufficient. Lastly, while many of these individuals were placed in one home after another many of them didn't know where they were going, if there were any programs or groups to help them physically and mentally, and social groups and bonds are lost when you keep getting moved around.

This data provided evidence that although there are a high number of foster children that lead to delinquency, it seems to be more so those who age out of the system that partakes in it. A lack of resources and support can really affect a person, especially one that has dealt with it their whole life. The provided hypothesis was institutional support and many foster children do end up living a delinquent lifestyle. In order to help these individuals 'falling through the cracks', the provision of more social work and education needs to be a priority at this crucial juncture of a foster child's transition out of care and into wider society.

This would require a greater number of professional and volunteer mentors and support groups to help these young people as they age, go through puberty, and their mental and physical issues they have been through. This support may lead to more self-sufficient children and teens as well as the ability to socialize and create positive relationships, thus later helping them in the real world when in need of a job. In relation to education, connections are needed between children or youth as they move and educational institutions. In addition to enhanced learning outcomes, this connection creates and maintains important social bonds with others, teaches young people life skills, which ideally will lead them to success in their later life. There are significant ways to improve the foster child's odds of not partaking in delinquency and crime, and more needs to be done to support these children as they face these life challenges. More institutional support should result in more successful life outcomes for children after foster care.

Foster Care and Criminal Justice

Child welfare is one of the most overlooked and underrepresented systems, from the child entering foster care, the child's emotional, mental, and physical state. The three most prevalent concept where this occurs is courts, police, and corrections. Within these sectors, foster children are lost in the criminal justice system risk being lost in the system. With the lack of support or a stable environment these foster children have higher rates of becoming a delinquent or being involved with law enforcement. The court is very significant when determining a child's best interest, that meaning the safest and loving home as well as whether the foster parents present information that is both good and detailed or it may fall through.

The foster child must attend multiple court hearings and the foster parents have a right to attend these hearings. If notices of the hearings do not arrive, you must contact the clerk of juvenile matters or your social worker. Although these foster parents have the legal right to this information, these hearings usually occur every 6 months until the foster child receives permanency or the case is closed. These permanency hearings must be held before the child reaches one year in foster care, and again every six months thereafter. There are also two other types of hearings in which parents are informed but legally obligated to be notified or participate in. These two hearings include termination of parental rights hearings and adoption finalization or permanent guardianship hearings. Although the most important part is always making sure your child will still and always have a voice. Furthermore, in many cases, they are dragged on from court to court and on top of that they must attend court for weeks as a time. When cases run for strenuous amounts of time the child's mental and physical state must be taken into account. This further leading to many foster children turning to delinquency, whether they plan it or not. This increasing the number of arrests and consultations with law enforcement. Juvenile Law Center states that:

"Youth placed in group homes are more than 2.5 times more likely to get involved with the criminal justice system (Juvenile Law Center, 2020)."

And "90% of youth with 5 or more foster placements will enter the justice system within the first two years of being a foster care alumni, one quarter will become involved in the criminal justice system (Juvenile Law Center, 2020).

Many foster children, especially those of color, LGBTQ community, and those with mental illness are the ones being targeted by law enforcement.

"Only 13 states have laws protecting youth from discrimination based on sexual orientation and gender identity (JLC, 2018)."

Furthermore, another study found that

"By age 17, over half of youth in foster care experienced an arrest, conviction, or overnight stay in a correctional facility (JLC, 2018).

It becomes very common for the police to be called on by their caregiver and face incarceration for small infractions, this becoming more frequent in government-run group homes. Many foster children who are taken home believe they are safe and no longer can be harmed, yet so many leave with bruises, scars, and mental challenges.

Children in the foster care system are a very vulnerable population with a wide variety of complex history. Moving from different placements, schools, educational difficulties, and mental symptoms, and lastly just living multiple years with no permanent family. More research needs to be done in order to correlate foster care involvement with adult crime and to determine if those factors lead to criminal involvement. Further research should focus not so much on those who age out of the system, but those who have spent any time within the system. Although many efforts have been made in improving these practices, policies, and previous research it shows that many individuals, especially those that age out are still struggling into adulthood.

Many policymakers should address more fully the safety and care of children, especially in terms of abuse and neglect. The criminal justice system plays a big role in whether or not these children are treated correctly and are sent to good homes, as well as little improvements that need to be made in order to give foster children what they deserve. While as for law enforcement, precautions and new laws need to be set in place to ensure safety and proper training when dealing with anyone who is or was a foster child, part of the LGBTQ community, or just have mental challenges, Ensuring this will provide a long and positive future for the children that have been or aged out of the system.

REFERENCES

Adoption.com is the world's most-visited adoption site to help adopt or foster a child, baby or orphan. (n.d.). Retrieved May 26, 2020, from https://adoption.com/

American Psychological Association. (n.d.). psycnet.apa.org/record/2006-01693-001

Child Abuse and Neglect. (n.d.). *Children's Rights*. www.childrensrights.org/newsroom/fact-sheets/child-abuse-and-neglect/

Cusick, Courtney, Havlicek, & Hess. (2010). *Crime during the Transition to Adulthood: How Youth Fare as They Leave Out-of-Home Care*. Academic Press.

Foster Care. (n.d.). *ACF*. www.acf.hhs.gov/cb/focus-areas/foster-care

PTSD and Children in the Child Welfare System. (n.d.). www.practicenotes.org/vol10_n3/basics.htm

Reilly, T. (1970). Transition from Care: Status and Outcomes of Youth Who Age out of Foster Care.: Semantic Scholar. *Undefined*. www.semanticscholar.org/paper/Transition-from-care:-status-and-outcomes-of-youth-Reilly/1f29ee69eb603aba46cd97327ed0ca9e0fa1c6e6

Report submitted to the U.S. Department of Justice. (n.d.). NCJRS. https://www.ncjrs.gov/pdffiles1/nij/grants/229666.pdf

Services. (n.d.). *Arizona's Children Association*. www.arizonaschildren.org/services/

The National Working Group on Foster Care and Education. (n.d.). *NCJFCJ*. www.ncjfcj.org/publications/the-national-working-group-on-foster-care-and-education/

Wexler, R. (2018). Abuse in Foster Care: Research vs. the Child Welfare System's Alternative Facts. *Youth Today*. youthtoday.org/2017/09/abuse-in-foster-care-research-vs-the-child-welfare-systems-alternative-facts/.

What Is the Foster Care-to-Prison Pipeline? (n.d.). Retrieved May 26, 2020, from https://jlc.org/news/what-foster-care-prison-pipeline

Working With the Courts for Permanency. (n.d.). Retrieved May 26, 2020, from https://www.childwelfare.gov/topics/permanency/legal-court/courts/

Chapter 14
Restorative Justice as an "Informal" Alternative to "Formal" Court Processes

Paula Kenny
Dublin City University, Ireland

Liam J. Leonard
Northern Arizona University, USA

ABSTRACT

This chapter will examine the manner in which restorative justice provides an informal alternative to the formal processes of the adversarial court within the criminal justice system overall. In so doing, the chapter highlights the significance of restorative justice as a facet of a 'Sustainable Justice' within the community. While members of the public may be intimidated by the formal processes of the court system, the informal nature of the restorative justice conference may provide the community with a better exchange, and thereby see true justice served more fully.

INTRODUCTION:

The notorious rape case involving Brock Turner highlighted the need to establish a more victim-centered approach to our system of justice. Rather than have both the accused and the victim be on the sidelines throughout the legal process, a system that focuses on restoring the victims, their friends and family and even the offender should be pursued. This chapter will develop a comparative study examining the formal criminal justice court system and the informal restorative justice process

DOI: 10.4018/978-1-7998-6646-6.ch014

using a social psychological framework. The authors will examine the structure of power within the two systems and how both perceived and actualized forms of power impact the various invested parties.

In so doing, the authors aim to identify problems associated with power that have emerged in the formal court system while subsequently highlighting potential possibilities associated with power equity within the restorative approach. Questions of offenders' guilt, remorse, potential rehabilitation and desistance through restorative practices will be contrasted with the relative dismissal and re-victimization of victims in the formal court system. The chapter will also examine key issues surrounding formal and informal processes in contemporary society, as new challenges involving politics, race and gender draw attention to the need for victim-centered approaches and outcomes from the legal sector.

The chapter will also examine the emergence and influence of the restorative justice movement as a bridge between communities, civil society and the state. The analysis will be divided into a number of sections, each reflecting the emergence of a movement dedicated to the promotion of restorative justice as a vehicle for a holistic form of community-based justice. The chapter covers the history, scope, and philosophical-political background of the restorative justice movement, providing specific examples of the interchange between this restorative justice movement and civil society. Through this discussion the wider potential of the restorative justice movement will be highlighted.

This potential is demonstrated in the restorative movement's challenge to understandings of failed punitive approaches, and through its socially redemptive alternative which emphasises collective responsibility for crime amongst all of the community. The chapter will also explore the international background to restorative justice, and its theoretical understandings, with a focus on key theorists such as Strang and Braithwaite, amongst others. It will examine salient issues that underpin social justice and social control, including the potential impacts of restorative justice policy and practice for the wider community and the state.

Existing literature on the alienating nature of the legal process has produced little analysis of the links between communities and possible alternatives in the area of law and justice. Moreover, the pursuit of forms 'informal' alternatives as restorative justice, once at the heart of traditional societies, remains central to a victim-centred, rights-based approach to justice.

One of the key issues at the heart of this debate is the acceptance of 'justice' as a salient issue within the rubric of 'community', whether it is in the context of development or cultural expression. Furthermore, any debate about justice in the community must first acknowledge the impact of social inequality on all levels of society in recent years. All too often networks of power which underpin levels of privilege and inequality in society pervade all levels of the formal legal system and create a justice dichotomy for many excluded by the elitist nature of the legal process as it exists. This body of criticism has tended to incorporate a critique of such inequalities as a contributory element to societal inequity and injustice. Nonetheless, this section will highlight both the benefits and difficulties which emerge from an 'informal' approach to restorative justice policy and practice.

Civil Society and Restorative Justice

In the main, the relationship between civil society and justice can be seen as one which has been embedded in a community-oriented move towards restoration, as opposed to the legal system's overriding concern for retribution. We can locate this process of community healing within the bounds of civil society by establishing which networks are working in the field and by identifying the outcomes of the interactions between civil society groups and the agencies of the state. Further understandings of the social, cultural and legal outcomes of the mobilization of the various elements of the restorative justice movement can then be established. As stated earlier, the conceptualisation of 'civil society' is itself contested. Therefore, the four contemporary understandings of 'civil society' set out by Scholte (2007, p. 16) will be applied to the wider restorative justice movement here. These understandings, which are congruent with the key principles of restorative practices, include:

i). the 'quality of human collectivity', based on tolerance, trust and non-violence
ii). a 'political space, an arena where citizens congregate to deliberate'
iii). the 'sum total of associational life within a given human collectivity'
iv). 'third sector non-governmental organisations (NGOs)' (Scholte, 2007: p. 16).

'Informal Justice' in the Community:

The restorative element in traditional understandings of the relationship between justice and civil society can be traced back through history. Early Native, Indigenous and Celtic laws contained elements of social restoration.

Justice based movements have mobilised in pursuit of social change throughout the recent past, including the trade union movement, the civil rights movement, the women's movement, the environmental movement and the alter-globalisation movement (Allen, 2007, Leonard, 2006, 2008). In recent decades, paramilitaries and vigilante groups have presented a darker form of community justice. In many of these cases, a form of community restoration has been undertaken in the aftermath of periods of intolerance or inequality (Tomlinson, Varley and McCullagh, 1988). The following section will examine the theoretical concepts which underpin the formation of restorative justice movements in society.

Restorative Justice Theory:

Restorative Justice is a separate concept of justice, which focuses on making reparations for harm or damages (Wright, 1999; Edgar & Newell, 2006). Essentially, restorative justice can achieve the fundamental requirements of the 'social contract' which according the concepts of Hobbes and Rousseau form the framework of civil society. The fundamental principle of restorative philosophy holds that when a citizen has harmed another, the best overall response is to try to repair that damage (Consedine, 1995; Johnstone and Van Ness, 2007). Restorative justice moves far beyond mainstream concepts criminal justice to encompass 'civil renewal, individual responsibility, conflict resolution, empowerment, shaming and forgiveness' (Braithwaite, 1998; Hudson, 2003). While contemporary understandings of 'restorative justice' are relatively recent, when reviewed in a more historic context it becomes understood that key phrases such as 'restitution, reparation, compensation, reconciliation, atonement, redress, community service, mediation', are all used interchangeably in the literature (Weitekamp. 2002). These key terms have collectively been absorbed into the approach to resolution which is now known as restorative justice.

Restorative justice operates within and outside of the criminal justice process, through policy initiatives and civil society responses (Morris and Maxwell, 2002; McCold, 2004). Whilst it may have only come to prominence in Western societies in the 1980s, the concept is far from new and can be linked to traditions of the Celts, Maori, Samoans, other indigenous peoples, as well as having roots in various religious communities (Consedine, 1995; Gelsthorpe and Morris, 2002). For some commentators it is not a new form of justice but rather dates back and returns society to pre-modern forms of justice (Zehr, 1990).

In this context restorative justice is seen as ageless approach, with the modern criminal justice system as something of an aberration (Crawford and Newburn, 2002; Daly, 2002). The modern state and legal system can be seen to have *'stolen the conflict'* from the communities, victims and offenders who require justice be served, and in the process buried longstanding traditions of a more natural restorative justice (Christie, 1977). Some go as far to suggest that restorative justice has been 'the dominant model of criminal justice throughout most of human history for indigenous peoples globally' (Braithwaite, 1998). Furthermore, restorative justice's contemporary re-emergence in can be linked to a number of social, political and cultural changes, for example the 're-articulation of rights and responsibilities between the state and civil society particularly inspired by neo-liberal assaults on the welfare state, and the increasing salience given to victims of crime' (Crawford and Newburn, 2003).

The practice of restorative justice in its many forms in in different countries led to be coined as an 'umbrella concept (Shapland, Robinson, Sorsby, 2011). They all however, share common values a reflection of international instruments such as the UN Basic Principles on the use of restorative justice in criminal matters (E/2002/INF/2/Add.2). These include free consent of parties invited e.g. victim and offender, adequate information about the process, inclusivity by including all affected by the offence, the use of trained, impartial facilitator and the facilitation of communication between parties in a safe and secure manner.

"Informal Justice" in Practice

The goal of restorative justice is to undertake an evaluation of overall impacts on victims and community members, including family, friends, peers or neighbours (Sharpe, 1998). It also endeavours to explore this impact upon the community and essentially looks to reduce the role of legal professionals. Advocating Christie's call 'let's have as few experts as we dare' (1977:12), restorative justice instead looks to empower victims, offenders, relatives and practitioners as partners in the justice process. According to Crawford and Newburn (2003: p. 22):

'these are the new stakeholders of a revised vision of justice, which seeks to recognise and bring into play, through their active involvement, a broader conceptualisation of the appropriate key actors in dispute processing and resolution'.

Therefore, restorative justice re-directs authority in response to crime away from the state to community stakeholders who are provided with the greatest amount of control over deliberation and decision-making (Hudson, 2003). In the case of 'bottom-up' practices such as restorative justice, the relocation of authority from the formal criminal justice system to the informal justice within a community context is key to restructuring systems of justice to foreground the needs of the victim, families and communities which have been harmed by criminal activity.

Furthermore, the significance of participatory and deliberative processes highlights the importance of participation, empowerment, communication, dialogue and negotiated agreements. Informal environments in which stakeholders are comfortable are conducive to good communication and exchange between parties. An integral part of restorative justice is a concern with a particular mode of participatory conflict resolution that focuses on 'consensus building through a problem-solving approach to crime that is grounded in local knowledge and local capacity' (Johnstone and Van Ness, 2007). Restorative processes highlights the importance of offender and victim participation- choice and control in the process of face-to-face encounters and decision-making. Restoring a sense of control to the central parties is an important part of the restorative process (Wright, 1999). One positive outcome of community-centred control and participation is the restoration of accountability to participants, with the belief that this will encourage offenders to be more responsible for their actions while encouraging others to take responsibility for ensuring the successful implementation of any agreement reached (Morris and Maxwell, 2002).

Sharing concerns about the consequences of crime is seen to be a more powerful way of highlighting the wider impacts of their crime to offenders. This can be achieved by focusing on the impact felt by victims (Morris, 2002). By treating participants with respect, this approach encourages empowerment. Ultimately this can be more impactful for those participating. Furthermore, it encourages a greater understanding and respect for the law and 'understandings of the consequences of individual crimes on others' (McCold, 2001). Informal community based restorative justice programmes encourage participation, empowerment, communication, dialogue and negotiated agreements between parties. Furthermore, this promotes particular restorative outcomes or resolutions such as desistance (Claes & Shapland, 2017). Repairing the harm caused by the criminal activity to all of the community, including those directly and indirectly affected can be seen as the ultimate goal of restorative conferences.

Reparations may be symbolic as well as material, with the intention that outcomes should 'seek to heal relationships' (Braithwaite, 1998). Often, this may include 'verbal or written apologies, compensation or direct reparation to the victim for the harm and indirect reparation to the community', which may take a variety of forms (Hudson, 2002). It is suggested that restorative outcomes should be flexible and party centred as well as problem-oriented (Johnstone, 2002). The actions and influence of those around the offender and in some cases the influence of the victim themselves (Kenny, 2010) can be vital in decisions to desist from further criminal behaviour/activity and in maintaining desistance (Claes & Shapland, 2017).

Restorative practices in the community have increased over the past forty years, and as a result a range of approaches have been applied to different problems, including domestic relationships, bullying, work related training, industrial relations as well as complaints against law enforcement. In addition, it has been applied to address different types of crime. Nonetheless the variety of restorative justice programmes are too widespread for there to be an overall definition (Daly, 2002). While some jurisdictions focus on core values and principles, others emphasis outcomes or highlight specific programmes or practices (Hoyle & Young, 2002; Hudson, 2003). Despite this difficulty it's come to be accepted that restorative justice is a person to person process that involves 'offenders, victims, their representatives and representatives of the community coming together to agree a response to a crime' (Zehr, 1990; Bazemore & Walgrave, 1999; Braithwaite, 1999).

Civil Society

The 'informal' version of the restorative justice movement has its roots in the international movements which have shaped understandings of restorative justice for over thirty years. The inception of the modern restorative justice movement can be found within the civil rights and women's movements of the 1960s. The U.S. civil rights movement was, in their view, partially rooted in critiques of institutional racism in the American justice system. This racial critique also framed their arguments around the disproportionate imprisonment of African-Americans and other minority groups, such as Native Americans. Campaigns for prisoners' rights and alternatives to imprisonment can also be traced back to the 'new left' era.

In addition to the United States, challenges to unfair formal justice systems occurred in other jurisdictions, including Australia, Canada, New Zealand, and South Africa. The women's movement also provided an important focus on the increase in crimes of violence against women and argued for better alternatives in justice practices for women. According to Daly and Immarigeon (ibid) 'feminist organising, and feminist groups were among the first to call attention to the mistreatment of victims in the criminal justice process' and prisoners' rights campaigns. These early advocates in the informal restorative justice movement mobilized around issues for society which stemmed from an over-use of incarceration in addition to the lack of stronger advocacy for victims in the formal justice process.

Daly and Immarigeon (ibid) also outline the various kinds of initiatives which gave rise to the wider mobilization of the restorative justice movement. These included the following initiatives which empowered victims and communities including: 'Prisoner Rights and Alternatives to Prisons; Conflict Resolution; Victim-Offender Reconciliation Programs (VORPs); Victim-Offender Mediation (VOMs); Victim Advocacy; Family Group Conferences/the 'Wagga' Model (FGCs); Sentencing Circles; Victim Impact Panels (originally established by Mothers against Drunk Driving or MADD)' (ibid). Varona (1996) links improving prisoner rights with the rise of restorative justice initiatives. Many of the social movement that emerged from the end of the 20th century gave rise to research and academic inquiry into informal justice alternatives, and this ran in parallel with such social movement activism in the pursuit of alternatives to formal justice system practices.

Civil Society and Informal Justice

In order to better understand the potential of civil society as an informal element of the criminal justice system through the activities of the restorative justice movement, we must first outline the basis of civil society as it operates in the United States. Civil society as a sector in society includes a diverse range of actors ranging from trade unions, local development agencies, business interests, advocates and academics, media interests, and the various strata of local and national government who create improved conditions for most informal justice agencies active across society. In addition, the civil society sector incorporates a range of rights-based non-governmental organisations (NGOs) and social movements, including social justice groups, women's rights groups and ethnic and equality advocates. All of these work within the context of an engaged civil society sector that had been given some access to the structures of justice in recent years (Leonard and Kenny 2010).

It must be recognised that those advocating for restorative justice had to operate within this dichotomous socio-political culture. Nonetheless, as players within the realm of civil society, those advocating for restorative justice have had some degree of success through the introduction of the concept as an aspect of informal justice practices in the United States which overlap at both the institutional and community levels.

Essentially, a wider restorative justice movement can be said to exist internationally, based on civil society groups which are connected through various networks, both nationally and globally. This justice movement has been mobilized through the four elements of civil society outlined above. Although lacking the counter-hegemonic basis of other civil society movements[1], the restorative justice movement is in many ways representative of a radical approach to grassroots governance based on a conceptualisation of justice which is embedded in the community. Within this public space, existing notions of punitiveness are challenged in a manner which promotes collective responsibility and inclusive deliberation. The mediation processes of restorative practice can be applied to individual, group or community issues, and can be extended out to provide a wider extent of engagement by concerned parties. By providing this extensive and collective range of community-based mediation, the restorative justice movement can address the provision of justice within the parameters of local discourse and situational habitus.

The most significant aspects of the informal restorative justice sector in are often embedded within the structures of civil society. This can incorporate multiple local and national non-governmental organisations (NGOs), relevant agencies and community-based groups who are advocating for justice reforms. The overlapping elements within these aspects of community and state sector help to build a smoothly operating civil society which has the potential to enact reforms in the area of justice across the informal sector, making the restorative justice a more effective element of contemporary civil society activism. Across the United States, religious and pastoral groups have extended the remit of the informal justice sector in restorative justice and community mediation.

According to Gormally (2006): 'The idea of restorative justice is sweeping through communities. The ideas of restorative justice have formed the core of what has become a real social movement'. The framing processes of the restorative justice movement have lacked sufficient research. In addition, this has led to limited understandings about the most significant issues, influences and direction of the system.

What the Informal Justice Process Provides

The benefits for victims and offenders who engage in restorative justice processes may out weight those offered by more formal approaches, by providing a shared or community-based platform for dealing with crime. This also includes dealing with criminal activities' private and public impacts such as pain, remorse and guilt. Initially, victims are provided the opportunity to meet the offender and relate to him or her of their perspective on events and how the offence has affected them. Meeting with the offender also gives the victim the opportunity to understand the reason behind the offence and perhaps realise that they were not singled out. The conference may also empower them to overcome worries about possible re-victimisation. Research demonstrates that victims can be empowered through restorative justice. In addition, they can be satisfied by receiving an apology, reparation for the harm caused along with an assurance that there will not be a reoccurrence. The community, who can be said to have failed the offender as much as the victim from a Durkheimian or 'anomic' perspective, can also partake in a community-based restoration process.

Restorative conferences provide the offender with the opportunity to take responsibility and account for their actions. The restorative approach empowers them to express genuine remorse, to apologise directly to the victim and make some form of reparation financial or otherwise. It further empowers offenders to address underlying problems, which they may be having, and provides them with the opportunity to work with their parents and authorities to fully integrate themselves back into society. Restorative Justice may provide the Criminal Justice System with an informal alternative means of dealing with crime control across society, and even within a wider political context, such as post-conflict mediation. The benefit of restorative justice for society and the criminal justice system is that is has implications for social control in the form of reducing future rates of crime. The juvenile offenders of today are the major criminals of tomorrow. For offenders, restoring a sense of security and empowerment can rebuild their confidence in finding employment, achieving educational success, sporting success and of feeling confident and secure in the future. Restorative justice practices that involve victims and (ex-) offenders can help to maintain and strengthen those ex-offenders' desires to desist (Claes & Shapland, 2011).

Community Empowerment

The restorative justice philosophy involves all of those affected by the criminal behaviour be they victims, offenders, the families involved, or the wider community all play their part in resolving the issues that flow from the offending. As Braithwaite contends, the restorative justice process 'empowers all parties to restore the deliberative control of justice by its citizens' (Braithwaite, citied in Johnstone et al, 2003, p.87). The remaining terms of the agreement came about as a result of dialogue, interaction and agreement between all parties. The community may acknowledge its own failings and address the best outcome through mediation. However, the process can empower the community, who can present their shared grievance in a public forum to key actors from the state or multinationals. With such processes embedded in civil society, the third sector could provide a vital bridge between concerned communities and the de-legitimised state.

Wheeldon (2009) has outlined concerns about the co-optation of restorative justice movement within the wider socio-political system of justice due to the bridging role restorative justice can play through the links created between civil society and agencies of the state. However, the pitfalls of co-optation can be avoided through the development of a framework which allows the 'third sector' groups of civil society to work with the community orientated projects of state justice agencies within the formal criminal justice system. Once established, this creates a viable role for civil society groups within the criminal justice system, while also providing a forum for the presentation of community grievances. Essentially, the establishment of informal frameworks provides community members and victims with a degree of access to the 'political opportunity structures' of both the justice system and the wider political frameworks surrounding any dispute. The community conferencing outlined can subsequently be seen to represent a 'political mediation model' based on 'transformative mediation' (Bush and Folger, 1994).

Theoretical Framework

In this section, we construct our theoretical framework around Zajonc's "Drive Theory": We can also apply "Affect Theory" to these processes and highlight some outcomes in both categories.

There may be evidence that formal and informal approaches provide two competing outcomes in non-professional participants:

- Social Facilitation (informal)
- Social Inhibition (formal)

We will further contextualize the impact of participation in formal and informal processes by extending our framework to incorporate the use of Steiner's "Task taxonomy" in relation to behavior and roles adopted in proceedings. For instance, does the formal criminal justice court process allow for a division of labor that facilitates input from non-professionals? Those who comprise the non-professional section (Juries, victims and the accused) are all corralled into a formal process, whereas the tasks and division of labor within the informal restorative justice setting actually require some social innovation to work.

Formal versus informal processes of justice

Zajonc's (1965) drive theory of social facilitation demonstrates that formal processes lead to the 'social inhibition' of non-professionals such as juries, family members, even victims; whereas informal restorative events provide a platform for the 'social facilitation' of participants, including victims, families and even the accused. This is based on the settings which provide a contextual concern for being perceived to be 'legally correct' (formal context) in comparison to the ability of informal processes to deliver 'socially correct' outcomes which are beneficial to both participants and the wider community. In addition, the informal and non-adversarial structures of restorative justice allow for a greater expression of genuine emotions such as grief and remorse, delivering what the authors have termed a 'functionalist exchange' (Kenny and Leonard, 2014). This leads to an uninhibited social facilitation. We will apply these concepts to understandings of restorative justice as an informal alternative to formal courts in this chapter.

We can then go on to adapt Steiner's (1972, 1976) "Three Questions" to ask whether the formal or informal process develops a multifaceted division of labor within the "Task taxonomy":

1. Is the task divisible or unitary?
    - A divisible task is one that benefits from a division of labor, where different people perform different subtasks. ie. *Informal Restorative Justice Conferences*
    - A unitary task cannot sensibly be broken into subtasks. ie *Formal Criminal Justice courts*
2. Is it a maximising or an optimising task?
    - A maximising task is an open-ended task that stresses quantity: the objective is to do as much as possible.ie. *Formal Courts*
    - An optimising task is one that has a set standard: the objective is to meet the standard, neither to exceed nor fall short of it.ie. *Informal RJ Conferencing*
3. How are individual inputs related to the group's product?

- An additive task is one where the group's product is the sum of all the individual inputs.ie. *Informal RJ Conferencing*
- A compensatory task is one where the group's product is the average of the individuals' inputs ie.. *Informal RJ Conferencing*
- A disjunctive task is one where the group selects as its adopted product one individual's input.ie. *Formal Courts*
- A conjunctive task is one where the group's product is determined by the rate or level of performance of the slowest or least able member. ie *Informal (Victim)*
    - A discretionary task is one where the relationship between individual inputs and the group's product is not directly dictated by task features or social conventions; instead, the group is free to decide on its preferred course of action. ie *Informal RJ Conferencing* (Adapted from Steiner 1972 & 1976).

Restorative Models of Community Policing:

The restorative justice movement provides an opportunity to achieve a fairer and more satisfactory criminal justice system for all members of society. In this way, the 'gaps' which exist in the provision of justice through civil society participation in alternative forms of policing through conferencing is established. Restorative Justice Principles are slowly being accepted as alternatives to sentencing and as a community or individual mediation process in the community in several cases. There is a growing acknowledgement among professionals and academics that society needs to develop other responses to crime. The Restorative Justice process has much to offer, by way of community policing initiatives as it centres on the greater use of non-custodial sentences will bring about changes not only in the community's relationship with the law but will have significant implications for improved and deeper methods of providing social justice.

These restorative measures improve the context of policing and crime prevention in the community and enhance the processes of justice across society. Through rehabilitation and reintegration rather than traditional punitive measures offenders come to realise that there is nothing to be gained from leading a life or crime. Ultimately, as an alternative system of policing the community, restorative justice provides a significant alternative based on concepts of sustainable justice rather than short-term punitiveness:

History is teaching us every day that if we continue to operate a criminal justice system oriented principally towards punishment based on vengeance and continue to reap its bitter harvest of high crime rates, fear and insecurity. The time for change is now if we are to bequeath the 21st century a criminal justice system worthy of its name (Consedine, 1999, p.196).

CONCLUSION:

The informal restorative justice movement has been demonstrated to have an impact in the areas of community development, civil society, governmentality and policy delivery. These impacts have been demonstrated to occur on at least two levels; the first is at the level of extending the remit of the state through civil society's engagement with community policing in the form of the various conferencing initiatives outlined in this chapter. The second impact reflects a more contentious outcome. Such contention is demonstrated through the capacity of restorative justice to serve as a facilitator of 'informal' community empowerment which strengthens civil society and third sector engagement, creating a form of social capital which has true implications for the establishment of a broader and more inclusive justice base across society.

The mobilization of any social movement has limited potential to secure complete social or cultural change in the area of contention chosen by its advocates as the social issue requiring attention. And so it is with the informal restorative justice movement. No movement can completely restore the losses incurred as a result of any injustice which occurs. Nonetheless, this chapter demonstrates that the restorative justice movement can contribute to an active civil society by creating the conditions whereby certain outcomes which are compatible with the movement's aims are achieved. These outcomes include the following:

- The amelioration of grief and suffering in the community.
- The creation of networks which facilitate dialogue between opposing parties.
- The strengthening of civil society through the facilitation of processes of engagement with the various elements of the justice system such as the police, courts and welfare services.
- The extension of the concept of justice beyond that of punishment, creating a deeper form of sustainable justice throughout society.
- The creation of 'sustainable justice' in society.

Moreover, the chapter demonstrates that the basic philosophies and aims of the restorative justice movement are congruent with the essential basis of civil society set out by Scholte's (2007: p. 16) civil society orientated criteria of creating public space for discussion, tolerance, associational living, and the engagement of the third sector in civic affairs. Furthermore, the restorative justice movement can provide a bridge between civil society and the justice system through the provision of restorative conferencing in community-based disputes[2].

Future Recommendations

According to Wheeler (2009), 'The restorative justice project is challenged today by a desire both from within and outside the movement to more fully engage with the criminal justice system'. This chapter demonstrates that while the risks of co-option are real for the restorative justice movement, the processes of restorative justice hold out a much deeper promise of providing a real alternative to narrow punitive or the cycles of negativity that characterise many social or criminal disputes. In many ways, the restorative conferencing established by the police in this section of the chapter provide the type of access to political opportunity structures required by both communities and the state in the pursuit of full mediation and the resolution of publicly held grievances.

This chapter also establishes the degree to which restorative conferencing can provide an alternative to disputes about the provision of social justice, whether in areas such as community participation in policing and judication processes, through to the creation of a positive and neutral space for social expression and dialogue on different levels (including protests) through public conferencing. This creation of a 'political mediation model' based on 'transformative mediation' (Bush and Folger, 1994) addresses many of the points raised by McAdam, Tarrow and Tilly (2001: pp. 139-143) about the 'possible interactions and outcomes' that emerge at the end of an episode of contention.

This 'transformation' (or 'innovation' for movement theorists) addresses what Bush and Folger (1994) refer to as the 'destabilizing' of relationships through conflict, transforming relations through processes of mediation and the development of mutual understandings by all parties. The processes of transformative mediation discussed here uses the creation of dialogue (or 'the communication of claims as opposed to direct confrontation' according to McAdam, Tarrow and Tilly 2001: pp. 139-143) as a measure of success, rather than successful attainment of preconceived outcomes which may jeopardize the attainment of full restoration within the community.

Findings:

The Motivated Performance in our Formal and Informal cases can be dived into two outcomes:

- **Formal:** Motivation to fulfill the desired outcomes of the Criminal Justice system (as represented by the judge and legal professionals; and

- **Informal**: Motivation to fulfill the desired outcomes of the community (as represented by the restorative justice participants).

Therefore, the presence of others automatically produces arousal, which 'drives' dominant responses.

In addition, performance is improved by a 'correct' dominant response but is impaired by an 'incorrect' dominant response.

REFERENCES

Allen, K. (2000). *The Celtic Tiger: The Myth of Social Partnership in Ireland.* Manchester University Press.

Allen, K. (2007). *The Corporate Takeover of Ireland.* Irish Academic Press.

Bazemore, G., & Walgrave, L. (Eds.). (1999). Restorative Juvenile Justice. Monsey, NY: Criminal Justice Press.

Bernstein, E., & Zajonc, R. B. (1965). Individual Task Performance in the Changing Social Structure. *Sociometry, 28*(1), 16–29. doi:10.2307/2786082

Braithwaite, J. (1996). *Restorative Justice and A Better Future. Dorothy J. Killam Memorial Lecture.* Dalhousie University.

Braithwaite, J. (1998). Restorative Justice. In M. Tonry (Ed.), *Handbook of Crime and Punishment.* Oxford University Press.

Bush, R. A. B., & Folger, J. P. (1994). *The Promise of Mediation.* Jossey-Bass.

Christie, N. (1977). *'Conflicts as property'. British Journal of Criminology, 17*(1), 1–15. doi:10.1093/oxfordjournals.bjc.a046783

Christie, N. (1992). *Crime Control as Industry: Towards Gulags, Western Style?* Blackwell.

Claes, B., & Shapland, J. (2016). Desistance from crime and restorative justice. *Restorative Justice, 4*(3), 302–322. doi:10.1080/20504721.2016.1245912

Connolly, L. (2002). *The Irish Women's Movement: From Revolution to Devolution.* Lilliput Press. doi:10.1057/9780230509122

Connolly, L. (2003). *The Irish Women's Movement: From Revolution to Devolution.* Macmillan/Palgrave.

Connolly, L., & Hourigan, N. (Eds.). (2006). *Social Movements and Ireland.* Manchester University Press.

Consedine, J. (1995). *Restorative Justice: Healing the Effects of Crime.* Ploughshares Publications.

Crawford, A., & Newburn, T. (2002). Recent Developments in Restorative Justice for Young People in England and Wales: Community Participation and Representation. *British Journal of Criminology, 42*(3), 476–495. doi:10.1093/bjc/42.3.476

Daly, K. (2002). Restorative Justice: The Real Story. *Punishment & Society, 4*(1), 55–79. doi:10.1177/14624740222228464

Daly, K., & Immarigeon, R. (1998). The past, present, and future of restorative justice: Some critical reflections. *Contemporary Justice Review, 1*(1), 21–45.

Doran, P. (2008). Absent Friends of the Earth: Minding the environmental gap in Ireland's Social Partnership. In *Governance and Public Policy in Ireland.* Irish Academic Press.

Edgar, T., & Newell, T. (2006). *Restorative Justice in Prisons: A guide to making it happen.* Waterside Press.

Gelsthorpe, L., & Morris, A. (2002). Restorative youth justice the last vestiges of welfare? In J. Muncie, G. Hughes, & E. McLaughlin (Eds.), *Youth Justice Critical Readings.* Sage.

Geoghegan, M., & Powell, F. (2009). *Community development, the Irish state and the contested meaning of civil society. In Power, Dissent and Democracy: Civil Society and the State in Ireland.* A & A Farmar.

Gormally, B. (2006). Community Restorative Justice in Northern Ireland: An Overview. *Restorative Justice Online.* http://www.restorativejustice.org/editions/2006/april06/gormallyarticle

Hobbes, T. (1985) Leviathan (C.B. MacPherson, Ed.). London: Penguin. (Originally published 1651)

Hoyle, C., & Young, R. (2002). Restorative Justice: Assessing the prospects and pitfalls. In M. McConville & G. Wilson (Eds.), *The handbook of the criminal justice process.* Oxford University Press.

Hudson, B. (2003). Understanding Justice (2nd ed.). McGraw-Hill Education Open University Press.

Johnstone, G. (2002). *Restorative Justice: Ideas, Values, Debates.* Willan Publishing.

Johnstone, G., & Van Ness, D. W. (Eds.). (2007). *Handbook of Restorative Justice*. Willan Publishing.

Keenan, M., Zinsstag, E., & Aertsen, I. (2017). Towards a better understanding of justice: concluding thoughts on restorative processes to sexual violence. In *Restorative Responses to Sexual Violence: Legal, Social & Therapeutic Dimensions*. London: Routledge.

Kenny, P. (2010). *Restorative Justice in Ireland.* Galway: Greenhouse Press. www.greenhousepress.webs.com

Kenny, P., & Leonard, L. (2014). The Sustainability of Restorative Justice. Emerald.

Leonard, L. (2008). *The Environmental Movement in Ireland.* Springer.

Leonard, L., & Barry, J. (Eds.). (n.d.). *The Transition to Sustainable Living*. Emerald Publishing.

Leonard, L., & Kenny, P. (2009). *Submission to the White Paper on Crime*. Dublin: Department of Justice.

Leonard, L., & Kenny, P. (2010). *Sustainable Justice*. Emerald.

MacNeill, E. (1935). *Early Irish Law and Institutions*. Burns, Oates and Washbourne.

McCold, P. (2001). Primary Restorative Justice Practices. In Restorative Justice for Juveniles: Conferencing, Mediation and Circles. Oxford: Hart Publishing.

McCold, P. (2004). What is the role of community in Restorative Justice Theory and Practice? In Critical Issues in Restorative Justice. Monsey, NY: Criminal Justice Press and Devon: Willan Publishing.

McEvoy, K., & Eriksson, A. (2008). Who owns justice? Community, state and the Northern Ireland transition. In J. Shapland (Ed.), *Justice, Community and Civil Society*. Willan Publishing.

Morris, A. (2002). Critiquing the critics: A brief response to critics of restorative justice. *British Journal of Criminology*, *42*(3), 596–615. doi:10.1093/bjc/42.3.596

Morris, A., & Maxwell, G. (Eds.). (2002). Restorative Justice for Juveniles: Conferencing, Mediation and Circles. Oxford: Hart Publishing.

Ó Broin, D., & Kirby, P. (2009). *Power, Dissent and Democracy: Civil Society and the State in Ireland*. A & A Farmar.

Rousseau, J. J. (1762). *The Social Contract or Principles of Political Right (Du contrat social ou Principes du droit politique)*. Chez Marc/Michel Rev.

Scholte, J.A. (2007). Global civil society-Opportunity or obstacle for democracy. In *Global Civil Society: More or Less Democracy*. Academic Press.

Shapland, J. (Ed.). (2008). Justice, Community and Civil Society. London: Willan.

Shapland, J., Robinson, G., & Sorsby, A. (2011). *Restorative justice in practice*. Routledge. doi:10.4324/9780203806104

Sharpe, S. (1998). *Restorative Justice: A Vision for Healing and Change*. Edmonton Victim Offender Mediation Society.

Sherman, L. W., & Strang, H. (2007). *Restorative Justice: the Evidence*. Smith Institute.

Stenson, K., & Lea, J. (2007). Canadian Journal of Law and Society / Revue Canadienne. *Droit Social*, *22*(2), 9–27.

Strang, H., & Braithwaite, J. (2001). *Restorative Justice and Civil Society*. Cambridge University Press.

Tomlinson, M., Varley, T., & McCullagh, C. (1988). *Whose Law and Order? Aspects of Crime and Social Control in Irish Society*. Studies in Irish Society Series. Sociology Association of Ireland.

Varona, G. (1996). *Restorative justice: new social rites within the penal system. Onati*. International Institute for the Sociology of Law.

Weitekamp, E. G. M., & Kerner, H. J. (Eds.). (2002). Restorative Justice Theoretical Foundations. Devon: Willan Publishing.

Wheeldon, J. (2009). Finding common ground: Restorative justice and its theoretical construction(s). *Contemporary Justice Review*, *12*(1), 91–100. doi:10.1080/10282580802681774

Wright, M. (1999). *Restoring Respect for Justice*. Waterside Press.

Zajonc, R. B. (1965). Social facilitation. *Science*, *149*(3681), 269–274. doi:10.1126cience.149.3681.269

Zajonc, R. B. (1968). Attitudinal effects of mere exposure. *Journal of Personality and Social Psychology*, *9*(2, Pt.2), 1–27. doi:10.1037/h0025848

Zehr, H. (1990). Changing Lenses: A new focus for crime and justice. Herald Press.

ENDNOTE

1 Stenson and Lea examine the manner in which movements representing non-state governance from below work *with* and then *against* the State through different relationships in civil society:
Civil society 'with the state' is presented as follows: 'Private welfare, private security, neighbourhood activism, voluntary associations, restorative justice, the courts, NGOs and private commercial regulation' (Stenson and Lea, 2007: pp 9-27)

Compilation of References

Constitution of Ghana, Art. 15, clause 2

Abrahams, R. (2003). What's in a name? Some thoughts on the vocabulary of vigilantism and related forms of 'informal criminal justice'. *Informal Criminal Justice*, 25-40.

Abrego, L. (2011). Legal Consciousness of Undocumented Latinos: Fear and Stigma as Barriers to Claims-Making for First- and 1.5-Generation Immigrants. *Law & Society Review*, *45*(2), 337–370. doi:10.1111/j.1540-5893.2011.00435.x

Abrego, L. J. (2014). *Sacrificing Families: Navigating Laws, Labor, and Love Across Borders*. Stanford University Press. doi:10.1515/9780804790574

Adinkrah, M. (2005). Vigilante homicides in contemporary Ghana. *Journal of Criminal Justice*, *33*(5), 413–427. doi:10.1016/j.jcrimjus.2005.06.008

Adoption.com is the world's most-visited adoption site to help adopt or foster a child, baby or orphan. (n.d.). Retrieved May 26, 2020, from https://adoption.com/

Afghanistan, H. R. W. (2005, June 7). Blood-Stained Hands: Past Atrocities in Kabul and Afghanistan's Legacy of Impunity. *Human Rights Watch*.

Aguilar, P., Balcells, L., & Cebolla-Boado, H. (2011). Determinants of attitudes toward transitional justice: An empirical analysis of the Spanish case. *Comparative Political Studies*, *44*(10), 1397–1430. doi:10.1177/0010414011407468

Ahmadi, H. (2012). *The overview of traditional Jirga in Afghanistan*. Xlibris Corporation.

Akhavan, P. (2001). Beyond impunity: Can international criminal justice prevent future atrocities? *The American Journal of International Law*, *95*(1), 7–31. doi:10.2307/2642034

Allen, K. (2000). *The Celtic Tiger: The Myth of Social Partnership in Ireland*. Manchester University Press.

Allen, K. (2007). *The Corporate Takeover of Ireland*. Irish Academic Press.

Alper, M., Durose, M. R., & Markman, J. (2018). *2018 Update on Prisoner Recidivism: A 9-Year Follow-Up Period (2005-2014)*. Available at https://www.bjs.gov/index.cfm?ty=pbdetail&iid=6266

Alper, M., Durose, M. R., & Markman, J. (2018). *2018 update on prisoner recidivism: A 9-year follow-up period (2005-2014)*. Bureau of Justice Statistics.

Altman, R. J. (2007). *The health of incarcerated women: An analysis of existing conditions and recommendations for future programs*. Retrieved from http://d-scholarship.pitt.edu/10135

Amamoo, J. G. (2011). Ghana: 50 Year of Independence. Xlibris Corporation.

American Psychological Association. (n.d.). psycnet.apa.org/record/2006-01693-001

Amuedo-Dorantes, C., Pozo, S., & Puttitanun, T. (2015). Immigration Enforcement, Parent–Child Separations, and Intent to Remigrate by Central American Deportees. *Demography*, *52*(6), 1825–1851. doi:10.100713524-015-0431-0

Andreas, P. (2000). *Border Games: Policing the U.S.-Mexico Divide*. Cornell University Press.

Andrews, K. (2017). *The Dark History of Forced Sterilization of Latina Women*. Retrieved on April 3rd, 2020, https://www.panoramas.pitt.edu/health-and-society/dark-history-forced-sterilization-latina-women

Andrews, D. A., Zinger, I., Hoge, R. D., Bonta, J., Gendreau, P., & Cullen, F. T. (1990). Does correctional treatment work? A clinically relevant and psychologically informed meta- analysis. *Criminology*, *28*(3), 369–404. doi:10.1111/j.1745-9125.1990.tb01330.x

Appiahene-Gyamfi, J. (2003). Urban crime trends and patterns in Ghana: The case of Accra. *Journal of Criminal Justice*, *31*(1), 13–23. doi:10.1016/S0047-2352(02)00196-4

Arkles, G. (2008). Safety and solidarity across gender lines: Rethinking segregation of transgender people in detention. *Temp. Pol. & Civ. Rts. L. Rev.*, *18*, 515.

Armstrong, B. (2012). Notes on Recidivism. *Alaska Justice Forum, 28*(4), 4-5.

Arnold, H. a. (2007). Prison Officers and prison culture. In Y. Jewkes (Ed.), *Handbook on Prisons* (pp. 471–495). Willan Publishing.

Arowolo, O. O. (2000). Return Migration and the Problem of Reintegration. *International Migration (Geneva, Switzerland)*, *38*(5), 59–82. doi:10.1111/1468-2435.00128

Aslam, M. (2009). *Education Gender Gaps in Pakistan: Is the Labor Market to Blame?* The University of Chicago Press.

Ayón, C., Messing, J. T., Gurrola, M., & Valencia-Garcia, D. (2018). The oppression of Latina mothers: Experiences of exploitation, violence, marginalization, cultural imperialism, and powerlessness in their everyday lives. *Violence Against Women*, *24*(8), 879–900. doi:10.1177/1077801217724451

Babbie, E. (2001). *The practice of social research. Belmont, CA: Wadsworth/Thomson Learning*. Wiley.

Baker, B. F., & Marchevsky, A. (2019). Gendering deportation, policy violence, and Latino/a family precarity. *Latino Studies*, *17*(2), 207–224. Advance online publication. doi:10.105741276-019-00176-0

Balderrama, F. E., & Rodriguez, R. (2006). *Decade of Betrayal: Mexican Repatriation in the 1930s*. University of New Mexico Press.

Baldursson, E. (2000). Prisoners, Prisons and Punishment in Small Societies. *Journal of Scandinavian Studies in Criminology and Crime Prevention*, *1*(1), 6–15. doi:10.1080/14043850050116228

Baldwin, J. (1963). *The Fire Next Time*. Dial Press.

Barnett, R. R. (2003). Transitional Justice and Human Rights in Afghanistan. *International Affairs*, *79*(3), 567–581.

Barthel, M. (2019). Employers are Still Avoiding Former Inmates. *Atlantic (Boston, Mass.)*.

Bassiouni, M. C. (2014). *The shari'a and Islamic criminal justice in time of war and peace*. Cambridge University Press.

Bauer, P. (2000). *From Subsistence to Exchange: And other Essays*. Princeton University Press. doi:10.1515/9781400824649

Bayley, D. H. (1994). *Police for the future*. Oxford University Press.

Bazemore, G., & Walgrave, L. (Eds.). (1999). Restorative Juvenile Justice. Monsey, NY: Criminal Justice Press.

Benedict, W. R., Huff-Corzine, L., & Corzine, J. (1998). Clean up and go straight: Effects of drug treatment on recidivism among felony probationers. *American Journal of Criminal Justice*, *22*(2), 169–187. doi:10.1007/BF02887256

Berg, B. L. (2004). *Methods for the social sciences. Qualitative Research Methods for the Social Sciences*. Pearson Education.

Bernstein, E., & Zajonc, R. B. (1965). Individual Task Performance in the Changing Social Structure. *Sociometry*, *28*(1), 16–29. doi:10.2307/2786082

Besmel, P. (2020). The Pathway to Transitional Justice in Afghanistan. *Journal of Global South Studies*, *37*(2), 240–269.

Besmel, P., & Alvarez, A. (2017). Transitional Justice and the Legacy of Nuremberg: The Promise and Problems of Confronting Atrocity in Post-Conflict Societies. *Genocide Studies International*, *11*(2), 182–196. doi:10.3138/gsi.11.2.03

Bhattacherjee, A. (2012). *Social science research: Principles, methods, and practices*. Textbooks Collection.

Bissonnette, A. (2020). "Caged Women": Migration, Mobility and Access to Health Services in Texas and Arizona. Journal of Borderlands Studies, 1-22.

Blust, K. (2020). Migrant Aid Group Opens New Shelter in Nogales, Sonora. *Fronteras Desk.* Accessed May 12, 2020. https://fronterasdesk.org/content/1441501/migrant-aid-group-opens-new-shelter-nogales-sonora

Boateng, F. D. (2012). *Public Trust in the Police: Identifying factors that shape trust in the Ghanaian Police* (Doctoral dissertation). Washington State University.

Bolivar, A. (2017). For Chicago's Trans Latina Sex Workers, A Cycle of Fear, Violence, and Brutality: From employment discrimination to incarceration to deportation, trans Latina sex workers face a triple threat of sexism, racism, and classism through policing. *NACLA Report on the Americas, 49*(3), 323–327. doi:10.1080/10714839.2017.1373959

Bonta, J., & Andrews, D. A. (2017). *The psychology of criminal conduct* (6th ed.). Routledge.

Borjas, G. J. (1990). *Friends or Strangers: The Impact of Immigrants on the U.S. Economy.* Basic Books.

Braithwaite, J. (1996). *Restorative Justice and A Better Future. Dorothy J. Killam Memorial Lecture*. Dalhousie University.

Braithwaite, J. (1998). Restorative Justice. In M. Tonry (Ed.), *Handbook of Crime and Punishment*. Oxford University Press.

Brangan, L. (2019). Pastoral penality in 1970s Ireland: Addressing the pains of imprisonment. Theoretical Criminology, 1-22.

Briggs, L. (2002). La Vida, Moynihan, and other libels: Migration, social science, and the making of the Puerto Rican welfare queen. *Centro Journal, 14*(1), 75–101.

Brotherton, D. C., & Barrios, L. (2011). *Banished to the Homeland: Dominican Deportees and their Stories of Exile*. Columbia University Press.

Bureau of Justice Statistics. (2018). *2018 Update on Prisoner Recidivism: A Nine-Year Follow-Up Period.* Bureau of Justice Statistics.

Burt, J. M. (2009). Guilty as charged: The trial of former Peruvian president Alberto Fujimori for human rights violations. *The International Journal of Transitional Justice, 3*(3), 384–405. doi:10.1093/ijtj/ijp017

Bush, R. A. B., & Folger, J. P. (1994). *The Promise of Mediation*. Jossey-Bass.

Cacho, L. M. (2012). *Social death: Racialized rightlessness and the criminalization of the unprotected.* NYU Press.

Calavita, K. (1999). Mexican Immigration to the USA: The Contradictions of Border Control. In R. Cohen (Ed.), *The Cambridge Survey of World Migration*. Cambridge University Press.

California Department of Corrections and Rehabilitation. (2015). *Transition Program Curriculum, "Another Chance A Better Choice" Part 1: Participant Guide.* Division of Rehabilitative Programs, Office of Offender Services.

Cammett, A. (2016). Welfare Queens Redux: Criminalizing Black Mothers in the Age of Neoliberalism. *S. Cal. Interdisc. LJ*, *25*, 363.

Canada, C. S. (n.d.). *Commisioner's Directive*. Retrieved February 13th, 2009, from Correctional Services of Canada: www.csc-scc.gc.ca/text/plcy/cdshtm/001-cde-eng.shtml#_5

Cardoso, J. B., Hamilton, E. R., Rodriguez, N., Eschbach, K., & Hagan, J. (2016). Deporting Fathers: Involuntary Transnational Families and Intent to Remigrate among Salvadoran Deportees. *The International Migration Review*, *50*(1), 197–230. doi:10.1111/imre.12106

Carey, T. (2000). *Mountjoy, The Story of a Prison*. The Collins Press.

Carroll, E., & Warner, K. (Eds.). (2014). *Re-Imagining Imprisonment in Europe: Effects, Failures and the Future*. Liffey Press.

Carson, E. A. (2016). *Prisoners in 2018*. U.S. Department of Justice.

Castillo, J. (2014). Tolerance in schools for Latino students: Dismantling the school-to-prison pipeline. *Harvard Journal of Hispanic Policy*, *26*, 43–58.

Charmaz, K. (2006). *Constructing grounded theory: A practical guide through qualitative analysis*. Sage.

Chase, M. (2008). The Chivalry Hypothesis & Filicide: Are There Categorical Differences between Mothers and Fathers who kill their Children? *Undergraduate Review*, *4*(1), 41–50.

Chaudry, A., & Wimer, C. (2016). Poverty is not just an indicator: The relationship between income, poverty, and child well-being. *Academic Pediatrics*, *16*(3), S23–S29.

Cheek, F. M., & Miller, M. D. S. (1983). The Experience of Stress in Prison Officers: A double-bind theory of correctional stress. *Journal of Criminal Justice*, *11*(2), 105–120. doi:10.1016/0047-2352(83)90046-6

Cherry, S. (2004). *Transforming Behaviour*. William.

Child Abuse and Neglect. (n.d.). *Children's Rights*. www.childrensrights.org/newsroom/fact-sheets/child-abuse-and-neglect/

Christian, S. (2009). Children of Incarcerated Parents. *National Conference of State Legislatures*.

Christie, N. (1977). *'Conflicts as property'*. *British Journal of Criminology*, *17*(1), 1–15. doi:10.1093/oxfordjournals.bjc.a046783

Christie, N. (1992). *Crime Control as Industry: Towards Gulags, Western Style?* Blackwell.

Christie, N. (2000). *Crime Control as Industry: Towards Gulags Western Style* (3rd ed.). Routledge.

Claes, B., & Shapland, J. (2016). Desistance from crime and restorative justice. *Restorative Justice*, *4*(3), 302–322. doi:10.1080/20504721.2016.1245912

Clemmer, D. (1950). Observations on Imprisonment as a Source of Criminality. *The Journal of Criminal Law and Criminology*, *41*(3), 311–319. doi:10.2307/1138066

Coalition on Urban Girls Chicago (CUG). (2018) Girls in the City: A Status Report on Teen Girls Residing in Chicago. Retrieved May 8, 2020, from http://cugchicago.org/wp-content/uploads/2018/12/CUG-2018-REPORT-UPLOAD-1.pdf

Comprehensive National Disability Policy in Afghanistan (2003): 7.

Connolly, L. (2002). *The Irish Women's Movement: From Revolution to Devolution*. Lilliput Press. doi:10.1057/9780230509122

Connolly, L., & Hourigan, N. (Eds.). (2006). *Social Movements and Ireland*. Manchester University Press.

Consedine, J. (1995). *Restorative Justice: Healing the Effects of Crime*. Ploughshares Publications.

Cooper-Knock, S. J. (2014). Policing in intimate crowds: Moving beyond 'the mob' in South Africa. *African Affairs*, *113*(453), 563–582. doi:10.1093/afraf/adu060

Corey, A., & Joireman, S. F. (2004). Retributive justice: The Gacaca courts in Rwanda. *African Affairs*, *103*(410), 73–89. doi:10.1093/afraf/adh007

Cornelius, W. (2018). Constructing Deterrence in the Age of Trump: Restricting Asylum, Separating Families, and Criminalizing Migration. *LASA Forum, 49*(4), 37-41.

Cornelius, W. A., & Salehyan, I. (2007). Does Border Enforcement Deter Unauthorized Immigration? The Case of Mexican Migration to the United States of America. *Regulation & Governance*, *1*(2), 139–153. doi:10.1111/j.1748-5991.2007.00007.x

Costelloe, A., & Warner, K. (2014). Prison education cross Europe: Policy, practice, politics. *London Review of Education*, *12*(2).

Council of Europe CPT. (2008). *Report to the Government of Denmark on the visit to Denmark carried out by the European Committee for the Prevention of Torture and Inhuman or Degrading Treatment or Punishment (CPT) from 11 to 20 February 2008*. Strasbourg. Download from www.cpt.coe.int

Council of Europe CPT. (2011a). *Report to the Government of Ireland on the visit to Ireland carried out by the European Committee for the Prevention of Torture and Inhuman or Degrading Treatment or Punishment (CPT) from 25 January to 5 February 2010*. Strasbourg. Download from www.cpt.coe.int

Council of Europe CPT. (2011b). *Response of the Government of Ireland to the report of the European Committee for the Prevention of Torture and Inhuman or Degrading Treatment or Punishment (CPT) on its visit to Ireland from 25 January to 5 February 2010*. Strasbourg. Download from www.cpt.coe.int

Council of Europe. (1990). *Education in Prison*. Author.

Council of Europe. (2006). *European Prison Rules*. Author.

Coutin, S. B. (2010). Confined Within: National Territories as Zones of Confinement. *Political Geography*, *29*(4), 200–208. doi:10.1016/j.polgeo.2010.03.005

Coutin, S. B. (2013). In the Breach: Citizenship and its Approximations. *Indiana Journal of Global Legal Studies*, *20*(1), 109–140. doi:10.2979/indjglolegstu.20.1.109

Covington, S. S., & Bloom, B. E. (2003). *Gendered Justice: Women in the Criminal Justice System*. Carolina Academic Press.

Cox, R. (2012). The Impact of Mass Incarceration on the Lives of African American Women. *The Review of Black Political Economy*, *39*(2), 203–212. doi:10.100712114-011-9114-2

Coyle, A. (2005). *Understandin Prisons; Key issues in policy and practice*. Open University Press.

Coyle, A. (2005). *Understanding prisons: key issues in policy and practice*. Open University Press.

Crank, B. R., & Brezina, T. (2013). 'Prison Will Either Make Ya or Break Ya': Punishment, Deterrence,and the Criminal Lifestyle. *Deviant Behavior*, *34*(10), 782–802. doi:10.1080/01639625.2013.781439

Crawford, A., & Newburn, T. (2002). Recent Developments in Restorative Justice for Young People in England and Wales: Community Participation and Representation. *British Journal of Criminology*, *42*(3), 476–495. doi:10.1093/bjc/42.3.476

Crawley, E. (2004). *Doing Prison Work*. Willan Publishing.

Crawley, E. (2004). *Doing Prison Work: The Public and Private Lives of Prison Officers*. Willan.

Cressy, D. E. (1961). The Prison: Studies in Institutional Organisations and Change. Reinhart & Winston.

Creswell, J. W., & Poth, C. N. (2017). Qualitative inquiry and research design: choosing among five approaches (4th ed.). Academic Press.

Crewe, B. (2009). *The Prisoner Society: Power, Adaptation, and Social Life in an English Prison*. University Press. doi:10.1093/acprof:oso/9780199577965.001.0001

Criminal Sanctions Agency. (2004). Assessment and Allocation Unit Handbook, Version 1.0. Helsinki: Author.

Cueva, E. G. (2006). The Peruvian Truth and Reconciliation Commission and the challenge of impunity. *Transitional Justice in the Twenty-First Century: Beyond Truth versus Justice*, 70.

Cusick, Courtney, Havlicek, & Hess. (2010). *Crime during the Transition to Adulthood: How Youth Fare as They Leave Out-of-Home Care*. Academic Press.

Customs and Border Patrol (CBP). (2020). *Border Wall System*. Customs and Border Patrol, Department of Homeland Security. Retrieved June 10, 2020. https://www.cbp.gov/border-security/along-us-borders/border-wall-system

Daly, E. (2001). Transformative justice: Charting a path to reconciliation. *Int'l Legal Persp.*, *12*(73), 73–183.

Daly, K. (2002). Restorative Justice: The Real Story. *Punishment & Society*, *4*(1), 55–79. doi:10.1177/14624740222228464

Daly, K., & Immarigeon, R. (1998). The past, present, and future of restorative justice: Some critical reflections. *Contemporary Justice Review*, *1*(1), 21–45.

Dancy, G., Hunjoon, K., & Wiebelhaus-Brahm, E. (2010). The turn to truth: Trends in truth commission experimentation. *Journal of Human Rights*, *9*(1), 45–64. doi:10.1080/14754830903530326

David, R., & Choi, S. Y. (2009). Getting even or getting equal? Retributive desires and transitional justice. *Political Psychology*, *30*(2), 161–192.

Davidson, R. D., Morrissey, M. W., & Beck, C. J. (2019). The Hispanic Experience of the Child Welfare System. *Family Court Review*, *57*(2), 201–216.

Davis, A. (2003). *Are prisons obsolete*. Seven Stories Press.

Davis, A., & Shaylor, C. (2001). Race, Gender, and the Prison Industrial Complex California and Beyond. *Meridians (Middletown, Conn.)*, *2*(1), 1–25. doi:10.1215/15366936-2.1.1

De-Bug, S. V. (2015). *East Palo ALto and Crack Epidemic That Tried to Kill the Black Family*.

DeGenova, N. (2002). Migrant "Illegality" and Deportability in Everyday Life. *Annual Review of Anthropology*, *31*(1), 419–447. doi:10.1146/annurev.anthro.31.040402.085432

Dilts, A. (2014). *Punishment and Inclusion: Race, Membership, and the Limits of American Liberalism*. Fordham University Press.

Dingeman-Cerda, K. (2017). Segmented Re/integration: Divergent Post-Deportation Trajectories in El Salvador. *Social Problems*, (0), 1–19.

Dollard, M., & Winefield, A. H. (1998). A test of the Demand-Control/Support Model of Work Stress in Correctional Officers. *Journal of Occupational Health Psychology*, *3*(3), 243–264. doi:10.1037/1076-8998.3.3.243

Doran, P. (2008). Absent Friends of the Earth: Minding the environmental gap in Ireland's Social Partnership. In *Governance and Public Policy in Ireland*. Irish Academic Press.

Dreby, J. (2015). *Everyday Illegal: When Immigration Policies Undermine Immigrant Families*. University of California Press. doi:10.1525/9780520959279

Drotbohm, H., & Hasselberg, I. (2015). Deportation, Anxiety, Justice: New Ethnographic Perspectives. *Journal of Ethnic and Migration Studies*, *41*(4), 551–562. doi:10.1080/1369183X.2014.957171

Drug Policy Alliance. (2018). *Women, Prison, and the Drug War*. https://www.drugpolicy.org/sites/default/files/women-and-the-drug-war_0.pdf

Dunbar, I. (1985). *A Sense of Direction*. Home Office.

Dunning-Lozano, J. L. (2018). Secondary discipline: The unintended consequences of zero tolerance school discipline for low-income Black and Latina mothers. *Urban Education*. doi:10.1177/0042085918817343

Durose, M. R., Cooper, A. D., & Snyder, H. N. (2014). *Recidivism of prisoners released in 30 states in 2005: Patterns from 2005 to 2010*. Bureau of Justice Statistics.

Edgar, K., O'Donnell, I., & Martin, C. (2004). *Prison Violence: The Dynamics of Conflict, Fear and Power*. Willan.

Edgar, T., & Newell, T. (2006). *Restorative Justice in Prisons: A guide to making it happen*. Waterside Press.

Edwards, A. (2019). Hispanic Poverty Rate. *United States Census*. Retrieved May 8, 2020, from https://www.census.gov/library/stories/2019/02/hispanic-poverty-rate-hit-an-all-time-low-in-2017.html

Ekins, E. E. (2016). *Policing in America: Understanding public attitudes toward the police. Results from a national survey*. Results from a National Survey.

Ellison, M., Szifris, K., Horan, R., & Fox, C. (2017). A Rapid Evidence Assessment of the effectiveness of prison education in reducing recidivism and increasing employment. *Probation Journal*, *64*(2), 108–128. doi:10.1177/0264550517699290

Erlingsson, C., & Brysiewicz, P. (2017). A hands-on guide to doing content analysis. *African Journal of Emergency Medicine*, *7*(3), 93–99. doi:10.1016/j.afjem.2017.08.001

Escobar, M. (2009). Understanding the Roots of Latina Migrants' Captivity. *Social Justice (San Francisco, Calif.)*, *36*(2), 7.

Escobar, M. D. (2016). *Captivity beyond prisons: Criminalization experiences of Latina (im) migrants*. University of Texas Press.

Evans, M., & Morgan, R. (1998). *Preventing Torture: A Study of the European Convention for the Prevention of Torture and Inhuman or Degrading Treatment or Punishment*. Oxford: Clarendon Press.

Ewick, P., & Silbey, S. S. (1992). Conformity, Contestation, and Resistance: An Account of Legal Consciousness. *New England Law Review*, (26), 731–749.

Ewuziem, I. K. (2019). *Moral and legal issues inherent in mob justice: A clarion call for a rethink*. Divinestone Publications.

Falcon, S. (2001). Rape as a weapon of war: Advancing human rights for women at the US-Mexico border. *Social Justice*, *28*(2 (84), 31-50.

Ferdaush, Jannantul, & Rahman. (2011). *Gender Inequality in Bangladesh, Unnayan Onneshan-The Innovators*. Christian Aid Trust.

Flores, J. (2016). *Caught up: Girls, surveillance, and wraparound incarceration*. Univ of California Press. doi:10.1525/california/9780520284876.001.0001

Flores, J., Camacho, A. O., & Santos, X. (2017). Gender on the run: Wanted Latinas in a southern California barrio. *Feminist Criminology*, *12*(3), 248–268.

Florida International. (2011, June 10). *Slavery and the Prison Industrial Complex-Angela Davis*. Retrieved from Youtube: https://www.youtube.com/watch?v=yQ2cC7LHMxA

Forsythe, D. P. (2011). Forum: Transitional Justice: The Quest for Theory to Inform Policy. *International Studies Review*, *13*(3), 554–578. doi:10.1111/j.1468-2486.2011.01016.x

Foster Care. (n.d.). *ACF*. www.acf.hhs.gov/cb/focus-areas/foster-care

Foucault, M. (1977). *Discipline and Punish, the birth of the prison*. Allen Lane.

Gainey, R. R., Payne, B. K., & O'Toole, M. (2000). The relationships between time in jail, time on electronic monitoring, and recidivism: An event history analysis of a jail-based program. *Justice Quarterly*, *17*(4), 733–752. doi:10.1080/07418820000094741

Gallo, E. (1995). The Penal System in France: from Correctionalism to Managerialism. In V. R. Ruggerio (Ed.), *Westen European Prison Systems. A Critical Anatomy* (pp. 71–92). Sage Publications.

García Hernández, C. C. (2014). Immigration detention as punishment. *Immigr. & Nat'lity L. Rev.*, *35*, 385–453.

García, A. M. (1982). *La Operación* [Film]. Latin American Film Project.

García, L. (2009). "Now Why Do You Want To Know About That?": Heteronormativity, Sexism, and Racism in the Sexual (Mis)education of Latina Youth. *Gender & Society*, *23*(4), 520–541. doi:10.1177/0891243209339498

Garland, D. (2001). *The Culture of Control: Crime and Social Order in Contemporary Society*. University Press. doi:10.7208/chicago/9780226190174.001.0001

Gelb, A., & Velázquez, T. (2018). *The Changing State of Recidivism: Few People Going Back to Prison*. Available at https://www.pewtrusts.org/en/research-and-analysis/articles/2018/08/01/the-changing-state-of-recidivism-fewer-people-going-back-to-prison

Gelsthorpe, L., & Morris, A. (2002). Restorative youth justice the last vestiges of welfare? In J. Muncie, G. Hughes, & E. McLaughlin (Eds.), *Youth Justice Critical Readings*. Sage.

Gendreau, P., Little, T., & Goggin, C. (1996). A meta-analysis of the predictors of adult offender recidivism: What works! *Criminology*, *34*(4), 575–607. doi:10.1111/j.1745-9125.1996.tb01220.x

Geoghegan, M., & Powell, F. (2009). *Community development, the Irish state and the contested meaning of civil society. In Power, Dissent and Democracy: Civil Society and the State in Ireland*. A & A Farmar.

Ghana Police Service. (2018). *Annual Report*. Retrieved from https://police.gov.gh/en/index.php/news-release-police-annual-crime-report-2015-2018/

Ghana. Statistical Service. (2014). *2010 population and housing census report*. Ghana Statistical Service.

Gibbs, G. R. (2007). *Thematic coding and categorizing. In Analyzing qualitative data*. Sage.

Gibson, J. L. (2004). Truth, reconciliation, and the creation of a human rights culture in South Africa. *Law & Society Review, 38*(1), 5–40. doi:10.1111/j.0023-9216.2004.03801001.x

Gibson, J. L. (2006). The Contributions of Truth to Reconciliation Lessons from South Africa. *The Journal of Conflict Resolution, 50*(3), 409–432. doi:10.1177/0022002706287115

Gilbert, M. (1997). The Illusion of Structure: A Critique of the Classical Model of Organisation and the Discretionary Power of Correctional Officers. *Criminal Justice Review, 22*(1), 49–64. doi:10.1177/073401689702200105

Godoy, A. S. (2002). Lynchings and the democratization of terror in postwar Guatemala: Implications for human rights. *Human Rights Quarterly, 24*(3), 640–661. doi:10.1353/hrq.2002.0035

Goffman, E. (1962). *Asylums*. Penguin.

Goffman, E. (1968). *Asylums, Essays on the Social Situation of Mental patients and other inmates*. Penguin Books.

Golash-Boza, T. (2015). *Deported: Immigrant Policing, Disposable Labor, and Global Capitalism*. New York University Press. doi:10.18574/nyu/9781479894666.001.0001

Golash-Boza, T., & Hondagneu-Sotelo, P. (2013). Latino immigrant men and the deportation crisis: A gendered racial removal program. *Latino Studies, 11*(3), 271–292. doi:10.1057/lst.2013.14

Golden, D. (2013). The Federal Bureau of Prisons: Willfully Ignorant or Maliciously Unlawful? *Michigan Journal of Race & Law, 18*(2), 275–294.

Gonzales, R. G. (2015). *Lives in Limbo: Undocumented and Coming of Age in America*. University of California Press. doi:10.1525/9780520962415

Gonzalez, F. R., Benuto, L. T., & Casas, J. B. (2018). Prevalence of interpersonal violence among Latinas: A systematic review. *Trauma, Violence & Abuse*. doi:10.1177/1524838018806507

González, G. (2006). *Guest Workers or Colonized Labor: Mexican Labor Migration to the United States*. Paradigm Publishers.

González, G., & Fernández, R. (2003). *A Century of Chicano History: Empire, Nations and Migration*. Routledge.

Goodman, R. D., Vesely, C. K., Letiecq, B., & Cleaveland, C. L. (2017). Trauma and resilience among refugee and undocumented immigrant women. *Journal of Counseling and Development, 95*(3), 309–321. doi:10.1002/jcad.12145

Goodmark, L. (2018). *Decriminalizing domestic violence: A balanced policy approach to intimate partner violence*. Univ of California Press. doi:10.1525/9780520968295

Goodwin, M. (2015). Invisible Women: Mass Incarceration's Forgotten Casualties. *Texas Law Review, 94*(2), 353.

Görg, N., Priebe, K., Böhnke, J. R., Steil, R., Dyer, A., & Kleindienst, N. (2017). *Trauma-related emotions and radical acceptance in dialectical behavior therapy for posttraumatic stress disorder after childhood sexual abuse*. Retrieved from https://ncbi.nlm.nih.gov/pmc/articles/pmc5508787

Gormally, B. (2006). Community Restorative Justice in Northern Ireland: An Overview. *Restorative Justice Online*. http://www.restorativejustice.org/editions/2006/april06/gormallyarticle

Gramlich, J. (2020). panic dropout rate hits new low, college enrollment at new high. *Pew Research Center.* Retrieved on April 3rd, 2020, from https://www.pewresearch.org/fact-tank/2017/09/29/hispanic-dropout-rate-hits-new-low-college-enrollment-at-new-high/

Graybill, L. S. (2004). Pardon, punishment, and amnesia: Three African post-conflict methods. *Third World Quarterly, 25*(6), 1117–1130. doi:10.1080/0143659042000256922

Gutíerrez, J., & Portillo, S. (2018). Trans (formation) of a Movement: Roxsana Hernández, an immigrant transgender woman from Honduras, died in ICE detention earlier this year. LGBTI activists refuse to let her death be in vain. *NACLA Report on the Americas, 50*(4), 392–394. doi:10.1080/10714839.2018.1550983

Hagan, J., Eschbach, K., & Rodriguez, N. (2008). U.S. Deportation Policy, Family Separation, and Circular Migration. *The International Migration Review, 42*(1), 64–88. doi:10.1111/j.1747-7379.2007.00114.x

Hagan, J., & Wassink, J. H. (2020, July 30). Return Migration Around the World: An Integrated Agenda for Future Research. *Annual Review of Sociology, 46*(1), 533–552. Advance online publication. doi:10.1146/annurev-soc-120319-015855

Haidt, J. (2003). Elevation and the positive psychology of morality. In C. L. M. Keyes & J. Haidt (Eds.), *Flourishing: Positive psychology and the life well-lived* (pp. 275–289). American Psychological Association. doi:10.1037/10594-012

Hairston, C. F., & Oliver, W. (2005). *Domestic Violence and Prisoner Reentry*. Vera Institute of Justice.

Hamilton, C. (2014). *Reconceptualising Penality: A Comparative Perspective in Ireland, Scotland and New Zealand*. Ashgate.

Handy, C. (2000). *Gods of Management, The Changing work of Organisations*. Arrow Books.

Harding, D. J., Morenoff, J. D., & Herbert, C. W. (2013). Home Is Hard to Find: Neighborhoods, Institutions, and the Residential Trajectories of Returning Prisoners. *The Annals of the American Academy of Political and Social Science, 647*(1), 214–236. doi:10.1177/0002716213477070

Harper, S. B. (2017). No way out: Severely abused Latina women, patriarchal terrorism, and self-help homicide. *Feminist Criminology*, *12*(3), 224–247. doi:10.1177/1557085116680743

Harris, J. R., & Todaro, M. P. (1970). Migration, unemployment and development: A two-sector analysis. *The American Economic Review*, *60*(1), 126–142.

Haverkate, D. L., Meyers, T. J., Telep, C. W., & Wright, K. A. (2020). On PAR with the yard: Participatory action research to advance knowledge in corrections. *Corrections: Policy, Practice and Research*, *5*(1), 28–43. doi:10.1080/23774657.2019.1576149

Hay, C., & Meldrum, R. (2016). *Self-Control and Crime Over the Life Course*. Sage Publications. doi:10.4135/9781483397726

Hayner, P. B., & Centre for Humanitarian Dialogue. (2009). *Negotiating justice: Guidance for mediators*. HD Centre for Humanitarian Dialogue.

Heidbrink, L. (2019). The Coercive Power of Debt: Migration and Deportation of Guatemalan Indigenous Youth. *Journal of Latin American and Caribbean Anthropology*, *24*(1), 263–281. doi:10.1111/jlca.12385

Hepburn, J. R., & Albonetti, C. A. (1994). Recidivism among drug offenders: A survival analysis of the effects of offender characteristics, type of offense, and two types of intervention. *Journal of Quantitative Criminology*, *10*(2), 159–179. doi:10.1007/BF02221157

Hernández, G., & Cuauhtémoc, C. (2013). Creating Crimmigration. *Brigham Young University Law Review*, 1457–1516.

Hernández-Leon, R. & Zuniga, V. (2016). Introduction to the Special Issue: Contemporary Return Migration from the United States to Mexico-Focus on Children, Youth, Schools and Families. *Mexican Studies/Estudios Mexicanos*, *32*(2), 171–198.

HHS. (2018). *Medicaid Fraud Control Units*. HHS.

Hill (2016). Nobody: Casualties of America's War on the Vulnerable, from Ferguson to Flint and Beyond. Atria Publishing Group: Miami, FL.

Hill, K. K. (2010). Black vigilantism: The rise and decline of African American lynch mob activity in the Mississippi and Arkansas deltas, 1883-1923. *Journal of African American History*, *95*(1), 26–43. doi:10.5323/jafriamerhist.95.1.0026

Hinds, L., & Murphy, K. (2007). Public Satisfaction with Police: Using Procedural Justice to Improve Police Legitimacy. *Australian and New Zealand Journal of Criminology*, *40*(1), 27–43. doi:10.1375/acri.40.1.27

HM Prison Service. (n.d.). *HM Prison Service, about the service*. Retrieved February 13th, 2009, from HM Prison Service: www.hmprisonservice.gov.uk/abouttheservice/statementofpurpose/

Hobbes, T. (1985) Leviathan (C.B. MacPherson, Ed.). London: Penguin. (Originally published 1651)

Horn, M. (2001). Rethinking Sentencing. *Corrections Management Quarterly*, *5*(3), 34–40.

Hossain, A. (2012). *Beyond Emasculation:Pleasure, Power and masculinity in the making of Hijrahood in Bangladesh* (PhD Thesis). University of Hull.

Hossain, A. (2010). Bangladesh. In C. Stewart (Ed.), *The Greenwood encyclopedia of LGBT Issues Worldwide* (Vol. 1, pp. 333–346). Greenwood press.

Houses of the Oireachtas, Joint Committee on Justice, Defence and Equality. (2013). *Report on Penal Reform*. Author.

Hoyle, C., & Young, R. (2002). Restorative Justice: Assessing the prospects and pitfalls. In M. McConville & G. Wilson (Eds.), *The handbook of the criminal justice process*. Oxford University Press.

Hudson, B. (2003). Understanding Justice (2nd ed.). McGraw-Hill Education Open University Press.

Hughes & Wilson. (n.d.). *Reentry Trends in the United States*. Washington, DC: Bureau of Justice Statistics.

Human Rights Watch (HRW). (2015). *Forced Apart: Families Separated and Immigrants Harmed by U.S. Deportation Policies*. HRW.

INCITE! (2000). *Mission Statement*. Retrieved on April 3rd, 2020, from https://incite-national.org/history/

IPS. (n.d.). *About us*. Retrieved February 13th, 2009, from Irish Prison Service: /www.irishprisons.ie/about_us-home.htm

Iriondo, J. (2018). Income, Poverty and Health Insurance Coverage in the United States: 2017. *U.S. Census*. Retrieved on April 3rd, 2020, from https://www.census.gov/newsroom/press-releases/2018/income-poverty.html

Irish Penal Reform Trust. (2019). *Progress in the Penal System (PIPS): a framework for penal reform*. Dublin: IPRT. Download from www.iprt.ie

Irish Times. (2003). *Prison officers' sick leave costs over E18m more*. Retrieved January 10th, 2009, from Irish Times Archives: https://www.ireland.com/newspaper/ireland/2003/1001/1374848881HM10PRISON.html

James, A. (2019). *Ending the Incarceration of Women and Girls*. The Yale Law Journal Review.

James, A. B. (1997). *Privatising Prisons, Rhetoric and Reality*. Sage Publications.

Jenkins, M. (1987). Control Problems in Dispersals. In *A. &. Bottoms, Problems of long-term Imprisonment* (pp. 261–280). Gower.

Jernigan, D., & Dorfman, L. (1996). Visualizing America's drug problems: An ethnographic content analysis of illegal drug stories on the nightly news. *Contemporary Drug Problems*, *23*(2), 169–196. doi:10.1177/009145099602300203

Jesuit Centre for Faith and Justice. (2012). *The Irish Prison System: Vision, Values, Reality.* Dublin: JCFJ. Download from www.jcfj.ie

Jesuit Centre for Faith and Justice. (2016). *Developing Inside: Transforming Prison for Young Adults.* Dublin: JCFJ. Download from www.jcfj.ie

Jewkes, Y. (2007). *Handbook on Prisons*. Wilian, Helen Arnold.

Jimenez, A. (2020). El Milagro Temporarily Closes Plant. *Chicago Tribune.* Retrieved May 8, 2020, from https://www.chicagotribune.com/coronavirus/ct-coronavirus-chicago-el-milagro-closing-factories-20200427-v5onmmvgvfhs5bwl64z4j2x4eq-story.html

Johnstone, G. (2002). *Restorative Justice: Ideas, Values, Debates*. Willan Publishing.

Johnstone, G., & Van Ness, D. W. (Eds.). (2007). *Handbook of Restorative Justice*. Willan Publishing.

Johnston, L. (1996). What is vigilantism? *British Journal of Criminology, 36*(2), 220–236. doi:10.1093/oxfordjournals.bjc.a014083

Jones, N. (2009). *Between good and ghetto: African American girls and inner-city violence*. Rutgers University Press. doi:10.36019/9780813548258

Jones, S. G. (2008). The Rise of Afghanistan's Insurgency: Sate Failure and Jihad. *International Security, 33*(4), 7–40. doi:10.1162/isec.2008.32.4.7

Kajsturua, A. (2019). Women's Mass Incarceration: The Whole Pie 2019. *Prison Policy Initiative.* Retrieved on April 3rd, 2020, from https://www.prisonpolicy.org/reports/pie2019women.html

Kanstroom, D. (2007). *Deportation nation: Outsiders in American history*. Harvard University Press.

Kant, I. (1987). *Critique of Judgement*. Hackett.

Karliner, L., Marks, A., & Mutha, S. (2016). Reducing health care disparities for minority women in the era of the affordable care act: Opportunities within primary care. *Journal of Health Care for the Poor and Underserved*, *2*(27), 392–415. doi:10.1353/hpu.2016.0098

Keenan, M., Zinsstag, E., & Aertsen, I. (2017). Towards a better understanding of justice: concluding thoughts on restorative processes to sexual violence. In Restorative Responses to Sexual Violence: Legal, Social & Therapeutic Dimensions. London: Routledge.

Kenny, P. (2010). *Restorative Justice in Ireland.* Galway: Greenhouse Press. www.greenhousepress.webs.com

Kenny, P., & Leonard, L. (2014). The Sustainability of Restorative Justice. Emerald.

Kerr, R., & Mobekk, E. (2007). Peace and justice. *Polity.*

Kerwin, D., Alulema, D. & Nicholson, M. (2018). *Communities in Crisis: Interior Removals and Their Human Consequences*. Kino Border Initiative (KBI), Center for Migration Studies (CMS), and Office of Justice and Ecology (OJE).

Khan, Hussain, M. I., Parveen, S., Bhuiyan, M. I., Gourab, G., Sarker, G. F., Arafat, S. M., & Sikder, J. (2009). Living on the Extreme Margin: Social Exclusion of the Transgender Population *(hijra)* in Bangladesh. *Health. Population and Nutrition*, *27*(4), 441–451. doi:10.3329/jhpn.v27i4.3388

Khan, S. I., Hudson-Rodd, N., Saggers, S., & Bhuiya, A. (2005). Men who have sex with men's sexual relations with women in Bangladesh. *Culture, Health & Sexuality*, *7*(2), 159–169. doi:10.1080/13691050412331321258

Kilcommins, S., O'Donnell, I., O'Sullivan, E., & Vaughan, B. (2004). *Crime, Punishment and the Search for Order in Ireland*. Institute of Public Administration.

Kilpatrick, C. (1973). *Nixon Tells Editors, 'I'm Not a Crook'*. Washington, DC: The Washington Post.

Kimmett, E. M. (2003). *Prison violence, The dynamics of conflict, fear and power*. Willan Publishing.

King, R. M. (1994). Contexts of Imprisonment: An International Perspective. *British Journal of Criminology*, *34*, 1–13. doi:10.1093/oxfordjournals.bjc.34.S1.1

Kneoma. (2019). *Ghana homicide rate*. Retrieved https://knoema.com/atlas/Ghana/Homicide-rate

Kriminalomsorgen (Norwegian Correctional Service). (n.d.). *Halden Prison: Punishment that Works – Change that Lasts!* Halden: Halden fengsel.

Kriminalvardan. (n.d.). *Organisation and employees*. Retrieved February 11th, 2009, from Kriminalvardan: www.kriminalvarden.se/templates/KVV_InfopageGeneral____3958.aspx

Krippendorff, K. (2018). *Content analysis: An introduction to its methodology*. Sage publications.

Krissman, F. (2005). Sin Coyote Ni Patron: Why the "Migrant Network" Fails to Explain International Migration. *The International Migration Review*, *39*(1), 4–44. doi:10.1111/j.1747-7379.2005.tb00254.x

Kristoffersen, R. (Ed.). (2019). *Correctional Statistics of Denmark, Finland, Iceland, Norway and Sweden 2013-2017*. Lillestrom: University College of Norwegian Correctional Service. Download from www.krus.no

Kritz, N. J. (1996). Coming to terms with atrocities: A review of accountability mechanisms for mass violations of human rights. *Law and Contemporary Problems*, *59*(4), 127–152. doi:10.2307/1192195

Kubal, A. (2015). Legal consciousness as a form of social remittance? Studying return migrants' everyday practices of legality in Ukraine. *Migration Studies*, *3*(1), 68–88. doi:10.1093/migration/mnu032

Lakhani, S. M. (2013). Producing Immigrant Victims' 'Right' to Legal Status and the Management of Legal Uncertainty. *Law & Social Inquiry*, *38*(2), 442–473. doi:10.1111/lsi.12022

Lang, K. (1993). What kind of prisoners do we meet in the 1990s? In Report from 'Beyond the Walls', conference of European Prison Education Association, Sigtuna, Sweden.

Laplante, L. J. (2008). Transitional justice and peace building: Diagnosing and addressing the socioeconomic roots of violence through a human rights framework. *The International Journal of Transitional Justice*, *2*(3), 331–355. doi:10.1093/ijtj/ijn031

Lappi-Seppala, T. (2007). Penal Policy in Scandinavia. In Crime, Punishment and Politics in Comparative Perspective. Crime and Justice: A Review of Research, Vol. 36. Chicago: University Press. doi:10.1086/592812

Law, V. (2015). Pregnant and behind bars:How the US Prison System Abuses Mothers-to-be. *The Guardian*, 15.

Leonard, L. (Ed.). (2010). Special issue. Irish Prisons, 91(1).

Leonard, L., & Barry, J. (Eds.). (n.d.). The Transition to Sustainable Living. Emerald Publishing.

Leonard, L., & Kenny, P. (2009). *Submission to the White Paper on Crime*. Dublin: Department of Justice.

Leonard, L., & Kenny, P. (2010). Sustainable Justice. Emerald.

Leonard, L., Kenny, P., & McGuckin, J. (2009, April). The Mentoring Processes of the Irish Prison Service: A Sociological Inquiry. *American Jails*.

Leonard, L. (2008). *The Environmental Movement in Ireland*. Springer.

Liebling, A. (2001). *The Prison Officer.* Leyhill: Prison Service Journal.

Liebling, A. P. (1999). *An Exploration of Staff-Prisoner Relationships at HMP Whitmoor.* London: Prison Service Research Report No.6.

Liebling, A. (2004). *Prisons and their Moral Performance, A study of Values, Quality, and Prison Life*. Oxford University Press.

Liebling, A., Arnold, H., & Tait, S. (2007). Prison staff culture. In Y. Jewkes (Ed.), *Handbook on Prisons*. Willan.

Lira, N., & Stern, A. M. (2014). Mexican Americans and eugenic sterilization: Resisting reproductive injustice in California, 1920–1950. *Aztlán*, *39*(2), 9–34.

Listwan, S. J., Sundt, J. L., Holsinger, A. M., & Latessa, E. J. (2003). The effect of drug court programming on recidivism: The Cincinnati experience. *Crime and Delinquency*, *49*(3), 389–411. doi:10.1177/0011128703049003003

Loader, I., & Sparks, R. (2014). Beyond mass incarceration. *The Good Society - PEGS*, *23*(1), 114–120. doi:10.5325/goodsociety.23.1.0114

Lonergan, J. (2010). *The Governor: the life and times of the man who ran Mountjoy*. Penguin Ireland.

Lopez, C., & Cohn, D. (2011). Hispanic Poverty Rate Highest In New Supplemental Census Measure. *Pew Research Center-Hispanic Trends*. Retrieved on April 3rd, 2020, from https://www.pewresearch.org/hispanic/2011/11/08/hispanic-poverty-rate-highest-in-new-supplemental-census-measure/

Lopez-Aguado, P. (2018). *Stick Together and Come Back Home: Racial Sorting and the Spillover of Carceral Identity*. University of California Press. doi:10.1525/california/9780520288584.001.0001

Lopez, V. (2017). *Complicated lives: Girls, parents, drugs, and juvenile justice*. Rutgers University Press. doi:10.36019/9780813586571

Lorde, A. (1984). *Sister Outsider:Essays and Speeches*. Crossing Press.

Love, M. C., & Shay, G. (2012). *Incarceration in the United States: Issues in America's Jails and Prisons: Gender & Sexuality in the ABA Standards on the Treatment of Prisoners*. Retrieved from https://papers.ssrn.com/sol3/papers.cfm?abstract_id=2063916

Lytle Hernandez, K. (2010). *Migra! A History of the U.S. Border Patrol*. University of California Press. doi:10.1525/9780520945715

MacDonald, M. (2013). Women prisoners, mental health, violence and abuse. *International Journal of Law and Psychiatry*, *36*(3), 293–303. doi:10.1016/j.ijlp.2013.04.014

Macias, J. K. (2020). *Rompiendo Alambres: Immigrant Youth Navigating School and Life in St. Louis* (Doctoral dissertation). Washington University in St. Louis.

MacNeill, E. (1935). *Early Irish Law and Institutions*. Burns, Oates and Washbourne.

Maguire, M. M. (2002). *The Oxford Handbook of Criminology* (3rd ed.). Oxford University Press.

Mallinder, L. (2009). *Exploring the practice of States in introducing amnesties*. Springer Berlin Heidelberg. doi:10.1007/978-3-540-85754-9_6

Maltz, M. D. (1984). *Recidivism*. Academic Press.

Maruna, S. (2012). Elements of Successful Desistance Signaling. *Criminology & Public Policy*, *11*(1), 73–86. doi:10.1111/j.1745-9133.2012.00789.x

Maslach, C. (.-2. (1976). Burned-Out. *Human Behavior*, *5*, 16–22.

Massey, D. S., & Espinosa, K. E. (1997). What's Driving Mexico-U.S. Migration? Theoretical, Empirical, and Policy Analysis. *American Journal of Sociology*, *102*(4), 939–999. doi:10.1086/231037

Massey, D., Durand, J., & Malone, N. J. (2002). *Beyond Smoke and Mirrors: Mexican Immigration in an Era of Economic Integration*. Russell Sage Foundation.

Maunga, M., Mugari, I., & Tundu, M. (2015). Perspectives on vigilantism in the Republic of Zimbabwe. *Mediterranean Journal of Social Sciences*, *6*(5), 323. doi:10.5901/mjss.2015.v6n5s1p323

Mazerolle, L., Antrobus, E., Bennett, S., & Tyler, T. R. (2013). Shaping citizen perceptions of police legitimacy: A randomized field trial of procedural justice. *Criminology*, *51*(1), 33–63. doi:10.1111/j.1745-9125.2012.00289.x

McBeth, M. K., & Lybecker, D. L. (2018). The narrative policy framework, agendas, and Sanctuary cities: The construction of a public problem. *Policy Studies Journal: the Journal of the Policy Studies Organization*, *46*(4), 868–893. doi:10.1111/psj.12274

McCold, P. (2001). Primary Restorative Justice Practices. In Restorative Justice for Juveniles: Conferencing, Mediation and Circles. Oxford: Hart Publishing.

McCold, P. (2004). What is the role of community in Restorative Justice Theory and Practice? In Critical Issues in Restorative Justice. Monsey, NY: Criminal Justice Press and Devon: Willan Publishing.

McCullagh, C. (1996). *Crime in Ireland, a sociological Introduction.* Cork University Press.

McDonald, D. (1994). Public Imprisonment by Private Means, the re-emergence of private prisons and jails in the United States, the United Kingdom and Australia. *British Journal of Criminology*, *34*, 29–48.

McEvoy, K., & Eriksson, A. (2008). Who owns justice? Community, state and the Northern Ireland transition. In J. Shapland (Ed.), *Justice, Community and Civil Society*. Willan Publishing.

McEvoy, K., & Mallinder, L. (2012). Amnesties in transition: Punishment, restoration, and the governance of mercy. *Journal of Law and Society*, *39*(3), 410–440. doi:10.1111/j.1467-6478.2012.00591.x

McGowan, J. (1984). The Role of the Irish prison Officer in the Irish prison Service. *Administration*, *28*(3), 259–274.

McGuckin, J. (2002). *Characteristics and Attitudes of RPOs and Prison Officers in the Irish Prison Service.* Belfast: Unpublished Report for Dissertation in Criminology and Justice, Queens University.

McGuckin, J. (2008) *Role Profile of Recruit Prison Officers In the Irish Prison Service.* Greenhouse Press.

McNair-Williams, S. S. (2019). *The Impact of a Felon's Overall Well-Being on Education, Employment, and Recidivism.* Retrieved from https://digitalcommons.liberty.edu/doctoral/2197

McWhirter, E. H., Garcia, E. A., & Bines, D. (2018). Discrimination and other education barriers, school connectedness, and thoughts of dropping out among Latina/o students. *Journal of Career Development*, *45*(4), 330–344. doi:10.1177/0894845317696807

Mears, D. P., Cochran, J. C., Bales, W. D., & Bhati, A. S. (2016). Recidivism and Times Served in Prison. *Criminology*, *106*(1), 81–122.

Mears, D., & Cochran, J. C. (2016). *Prisoner Reentry in the Era of Mass Incarceration*. Sage Publications.

Meiners, E. R. (2015). Trouble with the Child in the Carceral State. *Social Justice (San Francisco, Calif.)*, *41*(3), 120–144.

Menjívar, C. (2011). The Power of the Law: Central Americans' Legality and Everyday Life in Phoenix, Arizona. *Latino Studies*, *9*(4), 377–395. doi:10.1057/lst.2011.43

Merry, S. E. (1990). *Getting Justice and Getting Even: Legal Consciousness Among Working-Class Americans*. University of Chicago Press.

Messing, J. T., Vega, S., & Durfee, A. (2017). Protection Order Use Among Latina Survivors of Intimate Partner Violence. *Feminist Criminology*, *12*(3), 199–223. doi:10.1177/1557085116678924

Ministry of Justice (Denmark). (1994). *A Programme of Principles for Prison and Probation Work in Denmark.*

Ministry of Justice (Finland). (1994). *Survey of the Enforcement of Imprisonment Sentences in Finland.*

Ministry of Justice (Finland). (1999). *Mission and Short-term Policies of the Prison Administration and the Probation Association of Finland*. University Press.

Morenoff, J. D., & Harding, D. J. (2014). Incarceration, Prisoner Reentry, and Communities. *Annual Review of Sociology*, *40*(1), 411–429. doi:10.1146/annurev-soc-071811-145511

Morris, A., & Maxwell, G. (Eds.). (2002). Restorative Justice for Juveniles: Conferencing, Mediation and Circles. Oxford: Hart Publishing.

Morris, A. (2002). Critiquing the critics: A brief response to critics of restorative justice. *British Journal of Criminology*, *42*(3), 596–615. doi:10.1093/bjc/42.3.596

Mujeres Latinas en Accion. (2020). *A Letter from our President and CEO*. Sent to Listserv.

Mukhopadhyay, D. (2009). *Warlords as bureaucrats: The Afghan experience*. Carnegie Endowment for International Peace.

Nanda, S. (1984). The Hijras of India: Preliminary Report. *Medicine and Law*, *3*, 59–65.

Nanda, S. (1986). The Hijras of India. *Journal of Homosexuality*, *11*(3-4), 3–4, 35–54. doi:10.1300/J082v11n03_03

National Institute of Justice. (2008). *Measuring Recidivism*. Available at https://nij.ojp.gov/topics/articles/measuring-recidivism

Neuendorf, K. A. (2019). 18 Content analysis and thematic analysis. *Advanced Research Methods for Applied Psychology*, *211*(21).

Nevins, J. (2002). *Operation Gatekeeper: The Rise of the "Illegal Alien" and the Remaking of the US-Mexico Boundary*. Routledge.

Newbold, G., Ross, J. I., Jones, R. S., Richards, S. C., & Lenza, M. (2014). Prison Research From the Inside: The Role of Convict Autoethnography. *Qualitative Inquiry*, *20*(4), 439–448. doi:10.1177/1077800413516269

Ngai, M. (2004). *Impossible Subjects: Illegal Aliens and the Making of Modern America*. Princeton University Press.

Nillson, A. (2003). Living Conditions, Social Exclusion and Recidivism Among Prison Inmates. *Journal of Scandinavian Studies in Criminology and Crime Prevention*, *4*(1), 57–83. doi:10.1080/14043850310005321

Norwegian Ministry of Justice and the Police. (2008). *Punishment that works – less crime – a safer society. Report to the Storting on the Norwegian Correctional Services*. English Summary.

Nyabor, J. (2017). *3 arrested over lynching of 'witch' at Nabdam*. Citifmonline. Retrieved from http://citifmonline.com/2017/06/06/3-arrested-over-lynching-of-witch-at-nabdam/

Nyavor, G. (2017). *Capt. Mahama lynching: Diaso turns ghost town as residents flee*. Retrieved from https://www.myjoyonline.com/news/2017/May-31st/photos-capt-mahama-lynching-diaso-turns-ghost-town-as-residents-flee-town.php

Ó Broin, D., & Kirby, P. (2009). *Power, Dissent and Democracy: Civil Society and the State in Ireland*. A & A Farmar.

O'Donnell, I. (2013, Autumn). Penal Policy in Ireland: The Malign Effect of Sustained Neglect. In *Studies: An Irish. The Quarterly Review*, *102*(407), 315–323.

O'Mahony, P. (1993). *Crime and Punishment in Ireland*. The Round Hall Press Ltd.

O'Mahony, P. (Ed.). (2002). *Criminal Justice in Ireland*. Institute of Public Administration.

Olsen, T., Payne, L., & Reiter, A. (2010). The justice balance: When transitional justice improves human rights and democracy. *Human Rights Quarterly*, *32*(4), 980–1007. doi:10.1353/hrq.2010.0021

Organisation and Employees. (2009, Feb 12). Retrieved February 12th, 2009, from Kriminalvardan: https://www.kriminalvarden.se/templates/KVV_InfopageGeneral____3958.aspx

OSAC- Overseas Security Advisory Council. (2019). *Ghana 2019 Crime and Safety Report*. Available at: https://www.osac.gov/Country/Ghana/Content/Detail/Report/17cce973-2f6d-45de-bf74-15f4aec9e90a

Owens, I., Wildschut, G., Orr, W., & Goboda-Madikezela, P. (1996). Stories of silence: Women, truth and reconciliation. *Agenda (Durban, South Africa)*, *12*(30), 66–72. doi:10.2307/4065784

Pager, D. (2007). *Marked: Race, Crime, and Finding work in an Era of Mass Incarceration*. The University of Chicago Press. doi:10.7208/chicago/9780226644851.001.0001

Palloni, A., Massey, D. S., Ceballos, M. K., & Spittel, M. (2001). Social Capital and International Migration: A Test Using Information on Family Networks. *American Journal of Sociology, 106*(5), 1262–1298. doi:10.1086/320817

Paredes, T. C. F. (2010). Transitional Justice in Democratization Processes: The Case of Spain from an International Point of View. *International Journal on Rule of Law. Transitional Justice and Human Rights*, *1*(1), 120–135.

Parish. (2017). Gender-Based Violence against Women: Both Cause for Migration and Risk along the Journey. *Migration Policy Institute.* Retrieved on April 3rd, 2020, from https://www.migrationpolicy.org/article/gender-based-violence-against-women-both-cause-migration-and-risk-along-journey

Pasko, L., & Lopez, V. (2018). The Latina penalty: Juvenile correctional attitudes toward the Latina juvenile offender. *Journal of Ethnicity in Criminal Justice*, *16*(4), 272–291. doi:10.1080/15377938.2015.1015196

Passel, J. S., & Cohn, D. (2019). *Mexicans Decline to Less than Half the U.S. Unauthorized Immigrant Population for the First Time*. Pew Research Center.

Paz, K., & Massey, K. (2016). Health Disparity among Latina Women: Comparison with Non-Latina Wome. *U.S. Library of Medicine National Institutes of Health.* Retrieved on April 3rd, 2020, from https://www.ncbi.nlm.nih.gov/pmc/articles/PMC4955974/

Peguero, A. A., & Shekarkhar, Z. (2011). Latino/a student misbehavior and school punishment. *Hispanic Journal of Behavioral Sciences*, *33*(1), 54–70. doi:10.1177/0739986310388021

Peters, G. (2009). How opium profits the Taliban (Vol. 31, No. 19-62). Washington DC: United States Institute of Peace.

Peutz, N. (2007). Out-laws: Deportees, Desire, and "The Law.". *International Migration (Geneva, Switzerland), 45*(3), 182–191. doi:10.1111/j.1468-2435.2007.00415.x

Pew Center on the States. (2011). *State of recidivism: The revolving door of America's prisons.* The Pew Charitable Trusts.

Phillips, A. (2017). 'They're rapists.' President Trump's campaign launch speech two years later, annotated. *Washington Post.* Retrieved June 10, 2020. https://www.washingtonpost.com/news/the-fix/wp/2017/06/16/theyre-rapists-presidents-trump-campaign-launch-speech-two-years-later-annotated/

Pickering, S. (2011). Women, borders, and violence. In *Women, Borders, and Violence* (pp. 109–119). Springer. doi:10.1007/978-1-4419-0271-9_6

Platek, M. (1991). The Sluzewiec Prison in Warsaw, Poland. In D. E. Whitfield (Ed.), *The State of the Prisons- 200 years on* (pp. 56–69). Routledge.

Pope, B. (2020). Little Village residents rip Chicago officials during virtual town hall on botched smokestack demolition. *Chicago Sun Times.* Retrieved May 25th, 2020, from https://chicago.suntimes.com/2020/5/23/21268518/little-village-chicago-residents-hilco-smokestack-power-plant-demolitions-frydland-arwady

Prasad, B. D. (2008). Content analysis. *Research Methods for Social Work, 5*, 1-20.

Pratt, J. (2008). Scandinavian Exceptionalism in a Time of Penal Excess. British Journal of Criminology, 48, 119-137, 275-292.

Pratt, J., Brown, D., Brown, M., Hallsworth, S., & Morrison, W. (Eds.). (2005). *The New Punitiveness: Trends, theories, perspectives.* Willan Publishing.

Prison Policy Initiative. (2019). *Policing Women: Race and gender disparities in police stops, searches, and use of force.* Retrieved on April 3rd, 2020, from https://www.prisonpolicy.org/blog/2019/05/14/policingwomen/

PTSD and Children in the Child Welfare System. (n.d.). www.practicenotes.org/vol10_n3/basics.htm

Rabin, N. (2008). Unseen prisoners: Women in immigration detention facilities in Arizona. *Geo. Immigr. LJ*, *23*, 695–717.

Rascon-Canales. (2020). "If they come for her child in the morning…": Detained/Incarcerated Children in the time of COVID-19, retrieved on April 3rd, 2020, https://abolitionjournal.org/if-they-come-for-her-child-in-the-morning-detained-incarcerated-children-in-the-time-of-covid-19/

Reilly, T. (1970). Transition from Care: Status and Outcomes of Youth Who Age out of Foster Care.: Semantic Scholar. *Undefined.* www.semanticscholar.org/paper/Transition-from-care:-status-and-outcomes-of-youth-Reilly/1f29ee69eb603aba46cd97327ed0ca9e0fa1c6e6

Rentzmann, W. (1992). Cornerstones in a modern treatment philosophy: normalisation, openness and responsibility. Prison Information Bulletin, 16, 19-23.

Report of Expert Group (McAuley Report). (1997). *Towards an Independent Prison Agency.* Dublin: Department of Justice.

Report submitted to the U.S. Department of Justice. (n.d.). NCJRS. https://www.ncjrs.gov/pdffiles1/nij/grants/229666.pdf

Restrepo, I. C. (2019). Pathologizing Latinas: Racialized Girlhood, Behavioral Diagnosis, and California's Foster Care System. *Girlhood Studies*, *12*(3), 1–17.

Ricci, N. (2013). *Eroding the Barrier between 'Peace 'and 'Justice': Effects of Transitional Justice Mechanisms on Post-Conflict Stability.* Academic Press.

Richard, K. (2014). The wealth gap for women of color. *Center for Global Policy Solutions.* Retrieved on April 3rd, 2020, from http://www.globalpolicysolutions.org/wp-content/uploads/2014/10/Wealth-and-women-of-color.pdf

Rios, V. M., Carney, N., & Kelekay, J. (2017). Ethnographies of Race, Crime, and Justice: Toward a Sociological Double-Consciousness. *Annual Review of Sociology*, *43*(1), 492–513. doi:10.1146/annurev-soc-081715-074404

Ritchie, A. J. (2017). *Invisible no more: Police violence against Black women and women of color*. Beacon Press.

Rogan, M. (2011). *Prison Policy in Ireland: Politics, penal-welfarism and political imprisonment*. Routledge. doi:10.4324/9780203828885

Rosales, W. E. (2017). *Effects of Neighborhood Diversity on Civic Engagement and Social Trust* (Doctoral Dissertation). Retrieved from ProQuest Dissertations & Theses Global database. (UMI ID: 0031D_16507)

Rousseau, J. J. (1762). *The Social Contract or Principles of Political Right (Du contrat social ou Principes du droit politique)*. Chez Marc/Michel Rev.

Rubino, E. P. (n.d.). *White Collar Crime - An Overview*. Retrieved 5 3, 2020, from https://www.frankrubino.com/CM/FSDP/PracticeCenter/Criminal-Law/White-Collar-Crime.asp?focus=overview

Ruggerio, V. R. (1995). *Western European Penal Systems, A Critical Anatomy*. Sage Publications.

Runell, L. L. (2017). Identifying Desistance Pathways in a Higher Education Program for Formerly Incarcerated Individuals. *International Journal of Offender Therapy and Comparative Criminology*, *61*(8), 894–918. doi:10.1177/0306624X15608374

Rutherford, A. (1991). Penal Reform and Prison Realities. In D. Whitfield (Ed.), *The State of the Prisons - 200 years on* (pp. 1–13). Routledge.

Rye, M. S., Pargament, K. I., Ali, M. A., Beck, G. L., Dorff, E. N., Hallisey, C., ... Williams, J. G. (2000). Religious perspectives on forgiveness. *Forgiveness: Theory, Research, and Practice*, 17-40.

Said, A. A., Funk, N. C., & Kadayifci, A. S. (2001). *Peace and conflict resolution in Islam: precept and practice*. University Press of Amer.

Salihu, H. A., & Gholami, H. (2018). Mob justice, corrupt and unproductive justice system in Nigeria: An empirical analysis. *International Journal of Law, Crime and Justice*, *55*, 40–51. doi:10.1016/j.ijlcj.2018.09.003

Sánchez, G. J. (1993). *Becoming Mexican American: Ethnicity, Culture, and Identity in Chicano Los Angeles, 1900-1945*. Oxford University Press.

Sandoval, C. (2011). *Transitional Justice: Key Concepts*. Processes and Challenges.

Schabas, W. (2011). *Transitional justice and the norms of international law*. Academic Press.

Schnittker, J. (2014). The Psychological Dimension and Social Consequences of Incarceration. *The Annals of the American Academy of Political and Social Science*, *651*(1), 112–138. doi:10.1177/0002716213502922

Scholte, J.A. (2007). Global civil society-Opportunity or obstacle for democracy. In *Global Civil Society: More or Less Democracy*. Academic Press.

Schram, S. F., Soss, J., Fording, R. C., & Houser, L. (2009). Deciding to discipline: Race, choice, and punishment at the frontlines of welfare reform. *American Sociological Review*, *74*(3), 398–422. doi:10.1177/000312240907400304

Schultheis, R., & Ruiz Soto, A. G. (2017). *A Revolving Door No More? A Statistical Profile of Mexican Adults Repatriated from the United States*. Migration Policy Institute.

Schuster, L., & Majidi, N. (2015). Deportation Stigma and Re-migration. *Journal of Ethnic and Migration Studies*, *41*(4), 635–652. doi:10.1080/1369183X.2014.957174

Scott, J., Faulkner, M., Cardoso, J. B., & Burstain, J. (2014). Kinship Care and Undocumented Latino Children in the Texas Foster Care System: Navigating the Child Welfare-Immigration Crossroads. *Child Welfare*, *93*(4).

Sentencing Project. (n.d.). *Incarcerated Women and Girls*. Retrieved on April 3rd, 2020, from: https://www.sentencingproject.org/publications/incarcerated-women-and-girls/https://www.sentencingproject.org/publications/incarcerated-women-and-girls/

Services. (n.d.). *Arizona's Children Association*. www.arizonaschildren.org/services/

Sevelius, J., & Jenness, V. (2017). Challenges and opportunities for gender-affirming healthcare for transgender women in prison. *International Journal of Prisoner Health*, *13*(1), 32–40. doi:10.1108/IJPH-08-2016-0046

Shamir, B. & Dory,A. (1982). Some Correlates of Prison Guards' Beliefs. *Criminal Justice and Behaviour, 8,* 223-249.

Shapland, J. (Ed.). (2008). Justice, Community and Civil Society. London: Willan.

Shapland, J., Robinson, G., & Sorsby, A. (2011). *Restorative justice in practice*. Routledge. doi:10.4324/9780203806104

Sharpe, S. (1998). *Restorative Justice: A Vision for Healing and Change*. Edmonton Victim Offender Mediation Society.

Sherman, R. (2019). *Understanding Mass Incarceration of African American Women*. Retrieved from https://wisc.pb.unizin.org/english100coursereader/chapter/understanding-mass-incarceration-of-african-american-women

Sherman, L. W., & Strang, H. (2007). *Restorative Justice: the Evidence*. Smith Institute.

Shinn, D. (2020). *Corrections at a glance, August 2020*. Available at https://corrections.az.gov/reports-documents/reports/corrections-glance

Sikkink, K., & Walling, C. B. (2006). Argentina's contribution to global trends in transitional justice. *Transitional justice in the twenty-first century: beyond truth versus justice*, 301-324.

Silke, A. (2001). Dealing with vigilantism: Issues and lessons for the police. *The Police Journal*, *74*(2), 120–133. doi:10.1177/0032258X0107400204

Skardhamar, T. (2003). Inmates' Social Background and Living Conditions. *Journal of Scandinavian Studies in Criminology and Crime Prevention*, *4*(1), 39–56. doi:10.1080/14043850310012314

Slack, J., Martinez, D., & Whiteford, S. (2018). *In the Shadow of the Wall: Violence and Migration on the US-Mexico Border*. University of Arizona press. doi:10.2307/j.ctt20krzfr

Smith, R. C. (2005). *Mexican New York: Transnational Lives of New Immigrants*. University of California Press. doi:10.1525/9780520938601

Smyth, J. (2012). *Dual Punishment: Incarcerated Mothers and Their Children*. Retrieved from https://cswr.columbia.edu/article/dual-punishment-incarcerated-mothers-and-their-children

Snacken, S., & Dumortier, E. (Eds.). (2012). Resisting Punitiveness in Europe? Welfare, human rights and democracy. Abingdon: Routledge.

Stecklov, G., Winters, P., Stamini, M., & Davis, B. (2005). Do Conditional Cash Transfers Influence Migration? A Study Using Experimental Data From the Mexican PROGRESA Program. *Demography*, *42*(4), 769–790. doi:10.1353/dem.2005.0037

Stenson, K., & Lea, J. (2007). Canadian Journal of Law and Society / Revue Canadienne. *Droit Social*, *22*(2), 9–27.

Stern, K. (2014). *Voices from American Prisons: Faith, education and healing*. Routledge. doi:10.4324/9780203374573

Strang, H., & Braithwaite, J. (2001). *Restorative Justice and Civil Society*. Cambridge University Press.

Sugie, N. F. (2012). Punishment and welfare: Paternal incarceration and families' receipt of public assistance. *Social Forces*, *90*(4), 1403–1427. doi:10.1093fos055

Sunshine, J., & Tyler, T. R. (2003). The Role of Procedural Justice and Legitimacy in Shaping Public Support for Policing. *Law & Society Review*, *37*(3), 513–548. doi:10.1111/1540-5893.3703002

Super, G. (2017). What's in a name and why it matters: A historical analysis of the relationship between state authority, vigilantism and penal power in South Africa. *Theoretical Criminology*, *21*(4), 512–531. doi:10.1177/1362480617724830

Sutherland, R. C. (1966). *Principles of Criminology* (7th ed.). Lippincott.

Sykes, G. (1971). *The Society of Captives: A Study of a Maximum Security Prison*. Princeton University Press. (Original work published 1958)

Tankebe, J. (2009). Self-help, policing, and procedural justice: Ghanaian vigilantism and the rule of law. *Law & Society Review, 43*(2), 245-270.

Tankebe, J. (2009). Public cooperation with the police in Ghana: Does procedural fairness matter? *Criminology*, *47*(4), 1265–1293. doi:10.1111/j.1745-9125.2009.00175.x

Tankebe, J. (2009). Self-help, policing, and procedural justice: Ghanaian vigilantism and the rule of law. *Law & Society Review*, *43*(2), 245–270. doi:10.1111/j.1540-5893.2009.00372.x

Terriquez, V. (2011). Schools for Democracy: Labor Union Participation and Latino Immigrant Parents' School-Based Civic Engagement. *American Sociological Review*, *76*(4), 581–601. doi:10.1177/0003122411414815

Terriquez, V., & Kwon, H. (2015). Intergenerational Family Relations, Civic Organisations, and the Political Socialisation of Second-Generation Immigrant Youth. *Journal of Ethnic and Migration Studies*, *41*(3), 425–447. doi:10.1080/1369183X.2014.921567

The National Working Group on Foster Care and Education. (n.d.). *NCJFCJ*. www.ncjfcj.org/publications/the-national-working-group-on-foster-care-and-education/

Thomas, J. (1972). *The English Prison Officer since 1850*. Routledge and Kegan Paul.

Thrasher, J., Maloney, E., Mills, S., House, J., Wroe, T., & White, V. (2019). Reimagining prison research from the inside-out. *Journal of Prisoners on Prisons*, *28*, 12–28.

Toch, H. (1985). Warehouses for People. *The Annals of the American Academy of Political and Social Science*, *478*(1), 58–72. doi:10.1177/0002716285478001006

Tomlinson, M. (1995). Imprisoned Ireland. In V. R. Ruggiero (Ed.), *Western European Penal System, A Critical Anatomy* (pp. 194–227). Sage Publications.

Tomlinson, M., Varley, T., & McCullagh, C. (1988). *Whose Law and Order? Aspects of Crime and Social Control in Irish Society*. Studies in Irish Society Series. Sociology Association of Ireland.

Tonry, M. (2004). *Thinking About Crime: Sense and Sensibility in American Penal Culture*. Oxford University Press.

Trask, H. K. (2006). The Color of Violence. In *INCITE! Women of Color Against Violence (Ed.), Color of Violence the incite! Anthology* (pp. 81–87). South End Press.

Travis, J. (2005). *But They All Come Back: Facing the Challenges of Prison Reentry*. The Urban Institute.

Triplett, N. P., Allen, A., & Lewis, C. W. (2014). Zero tolerance, school shootings, and the post-Brown quest for equity in discipline policy: An examination of how urban minorities are punished for white suburban violence. *The Journal of Negro Education*, *83*(3), 352–370. doi:10.7709/jnegroeducation.83.3.0352

Turanovic, J. J., Rodriguez, N., & Pratt, T. C. (2012). The collateral consequences of incarceration revisited: A qualitative analysis of the effects on caregivers of children of incarcerated parents. *Criminology*, *50*(4), 913–959. doi:10.1111/j.1745-9125.2012.00283.x

Twillie, J. (2019). November 20, 2019, is Latina Equal Pay Day. It's not a celebration, it's a day of awareness. Retrieved on April 3rd, 2020, from: https://publicmediawomeninleadership.org/announcements/2019/11/20/november-20-2019-is-latina-equal-pay-day-its-not-a-celebration-its-a-day-of-awareness

Tyler, T. R. (2003). Procedural justice, legitimacy, and the effective rule of law. *Crime and Justice*, *30*, 283–357. doi:10.1086/652233

Tyler, T. R. (2004). Enhancing police legitimacy. *The Annals of the American Academy of Political and Social Science*, *593*(1), 84–99. doi:10.1177/0002716203262627

Tyler, T. R. (2006). *Why people obey the law*. Princeton University Press.

Tyler, T. R. (2011). Trust and legitimacy: Policing in the USA and Europe. *European Journal of Criminology*, *8*(4), 254–266. doi:10.1177/1477370811411462

Ugelvik, T., & Dullum, J. (2012). *Penal Exceptionalism? Nordic Prison Policy and Practice*. Routledge.

United States Commission on Civil Rights. (2020). *Women in Prisons: Seeking Justice Behind Bars*. Retrieved on April 3rd, 2020, from: https://www.usccr.gov/pubs/2020/02-26-Women-in-Prison.pdf

United States Sentencing Commission. (2004). *Measuring Recidivism: The Criminal History Computation of the Federal Sentencing Guidelines*. Available at https://www.ussc.gov/sites/default/files/pdf/research-and-publications/research-publications/2004/200405_Recidivism_Criminal_History.pdf

United States Sentencing Commission. (2016). *Recidivism among federal offenders: A comprehensive overview*. Available at https://www.ussc.gov/sites/default/files/pdf/research-and-publications/research-publications/2016/recidivism_overview.pdf

United States Sentencing Commission. (2020). *Length of Incarceration and Recidivism*. Available at https://www.ussc.gov/sites/default/files/pdf/research-and-publications/research-publications/2020/20200429_Recidivism-SentLength.pdf

USDHS. (2019). *Yearbook of Immigration Statistics*. Office of Immigration Statistics. Department of Homeland Security.

Vaismoradi, M., Jones, J., Turunen, H., & Snelgrove, S. (2016). *Theme development in qualitative content analysis and thematic analysis*. Academic Press.

Varona, G. (1996). *Restorative justice: new social rites within the penal system. Onati*. International Institute for the Sociology of Law.

Vázquez, Y. (2015). Constructing crimmigration: Latino subordination in a "post-racial" world. *Ohio State Law Journal*, *76*(3), 599–657.

Velasco-Mondragon, E., Jimenez, A., & Palladino-Davis, A. G. (n.d.). *Hispanic health in the USA: A scoping review of the literature*. Retrieved on April 3rd, 2020, from: https://www.latinaequalpay.org/about

Vidales, G. T. (2010). Arrested justice: The multifaceted plight of immigrant Latinas who faced domestic violence. *Journal of Family Violence, 25*(6), 533–544. doi:10.100710896-010-9309-5

Visher, C. A., Debus-Sherrill, S. A., & Yahner, J. (2011). Employment After Prison: A Longitudinal Study of Former Prisoners. *Justice Quarterly, 28*(5), 698–718. doi:10.1080/07418825.2010.535553

Wacquant, L. (2010). Prison reentry as myth and ceremony. *Dialectical Anthropology, 34*(4), 605–620. doi:10.100710624-010-9215-5

Wardak, A. (2003). *Jirga–A Traditional Mechanism of Conflict Resolution in Afghanistan*. Institute of Afghan Study Center.

Wardak, A. (2010). State and non-state justice systems in Afghanistan: The need for synergy. *U. Pa. J. Int'l L., 32*, 1305.

Warner, K. (2009). *Resisting the New Punitiveness? Penal Policy in Denmark, Finland and Norway* (Unpublished PhD thesis). University College Dublin. Download from www.pepre.ie

Warner, K. (2011). 'Valued members of society?' Social Inclusiveness in the Characterisation of Prisoners in Ireland, Denmark, Finland and Norway. *Administration, 59*(1), 87-109. Download from www.pepre.ie

Warner, K. (2012a). Redefining Standards Downwards: The Deterioration in Basic Living Conditions in Irish Prisons and the Failure of Policy. *Working Notes, 70*, 3-10. Download from www.pepre.ie

Warner, K. (2012b, July 31). Negative, miserly, punitive. *Irish Examiner*. Download from www.pepre.ie

Warner, K. (2018). Every possible learning opportunity: the capacity of education in prison to challenge dehumanisation and liberate 'the whole person'. *Advancing Corrections Journal, 6*, 30-43. Download from www.icpa.org

Warner, K. (2014). Regimes in Irish Prisons: 'Inhumane' and 'degrading': An analysis and the outline of a solution. *Irish Journal of Applied Social Studies, 14*(1), 3–17.

Warner, K. (2016). What's the Difference between Ireland and Iceland? One Letter and a Decent Prison System…. *Irish Probation Journal, 13*(October), 234–248.

Weir, J., & Azamy, H. (2015). Afghanistan's "Transformation Decade" Depends on the Taliban's Foot Soldiers. *Foreign Policy*.

Weitekamp, E. G. M., & Kerner, H. J. (Eds.). (2002). Restorative Justice Theoretical Foundations. Devon: Willan Publishing.

Western, B. (2018). *Homeward: Life in the Year After Prison*. Russell Sage Foundation. doi:10.7758/9781610448710

Wexler, R. (2018). Abuse in Foster Care: Research vs. the Child Welfare System's Alternative Facts. *Youth Today*. youthtoday.org/2017/09/abuse-in-foster-care-research-vs-the-child-welfare-systems-alternative-facts/.

What Is the Foster Care-to-Prison Pipeline? (n.d.). Retrieved May 26, 2020, from https://jlc.org/news/what-foster-care-prison-pipeline

Wheeldon, J. (2009). Finding common ground: Restorative justice and its theoretical construction(s). *Contemporary Justice Review*, *12*(1), 91–100. doi:10.1080/10282580802681774

Whitaker Report. (1985). *Report of the Committee of Inquiry into the Penal System*. Dublin: Stationery Office.

Whitehead, J., & Lindquist, C. A. (1986). Correctional Officer Burnout: A path model. *Journal of Research in Crime and Delinquency*, *1*(1), 23–42. doi:10.1177/0022427886023001003

Wilson, J. A. (2005). Bad behavior or bad policy? An examination of Tennessee release cohorts, 1993-2001. *Criminology & Public Policy*, *4*(3), 485–518. doi:10.1111/j.1745-9133.2005.00304.x

Wimmer, R. D., & Dominick, J. R. (2011). *Mass media research: An introduction* (International Edition). Wadsworth Cengage Learning.

Winnick, T. A., & Bodkin, M. (2008). Anticipated Stigma and Stigma Management Among Those to be Labeled 'Ex-Con'. *Deviant Behavior*, *29*(4), 295–333. doi:10.1080/01639620701588081

Wong, T. K. (2018). *Do Family Separation and Detention Deter Immigration?* https://www.americanprogress.org/issues/immigration/reports/2018/07/24/453660/family-separation-detention-deterimmigration/

Working With the Courts for Permanency. (n.d.). Retrieved May 26, 2020, from https://www.childwelfare.gov/topics/permanency/legal-court/courts/

World Bank. (2018). *World Bank open data*. Author.

Wright, K.A., Haverkate, D.L., Meyers, T.J., Matekel, C.G., Telep, C.W., Maloney, E., … Wroe, T. (2017). *Recidivism reduction in Arizona*. Report submitted to the Governor's Office Recidivism Reduction Project Team.

Wright, K. A., & Khade, N. (2018). Offender recidivism. In O. H. Griffin & V. H. Woodward (Eds.), *Routledge handbook of corrections in the United States* (pp. 494–502). Routledge.

Wright, K. A., Morse, S. J., & Sutton, M. M. (in press). The limits of recidivism reduction: Advancing a more comprehensive understanding of correctional success. In J. Gould & P. Metzger (Eds.), *Big ideas in criminal justice reform*. NYU Press.

Wright, M. (1999). *Restoring Respect for Justice*. Waterside Press.

Young, A. (1951). *A Report on the Gold Coast Police*. Government of Ghana.

Zajonc, R. B. (1965). Social facilitation. *Science*, *149*(3681), 269–274. doi:10.1126cience.149.3681.269

Zajonc, R. B. (1968). Attitudinal effects of mere exposure. *Journal of Personality and Social Psychology*, *9*(2, Pt.2), 1–27. doi:10.1037/h0025848

Zayas, L. H. (2015). *Forgotten Citizens: Deportation, Children, and the Making of American Exiles and Orphans*. Oxford University Press.

Zehr, H. (1990). Changing Lenses: A new focus for crime and justice. Herald Press.

About the Contributors

Liam J. Leonard (BA; M. Phil; PhD) is a researcher and international academic. Employment history: Department of Criminology & Criminal Justice, Northern Arizona University, California State University, Los Angeles and National University of Ireland. Previously, Liam has been Chair of the Criminology Association of Ireland and former Member Secretary and President of the Sociological Association of Ireland. The author/editor of over 20 books and numerous journal articles, Liam is Editor of IGI Global's Advances in Criminology series, and formerly Senior Editor of the Advances in Sustainability and Environmental Justice Book Series and Founding Editor of the CRIMSOC: Journal of Social Criminology. Dr. Leonard was awarded the Sage Publishing Research Excellence Award in New York as well as the NAIRTL Research & Teaching Award in 2012, and a California State University Author's Award in 2015.

* * *

Parwez Besmel earned his Ph.D. in Politics and International Affairs from Northern Arizona University. He has taught at Kabul University and his research interests are Transitional Justice, Peace Building, Ethnic Conflict, Political Crimes and Afghanistan. He is currently a Lecturer in the Department of Criminology and Criminal Justice at Northern Arizona University.

Katie Dingeman, Ph.D. Sociology (UC Irvine, 2014). Research Interests: Undocumented Migration, Detention & Deportation, Qualitative Methods.

Adiba Fannana has been a Graduate Teacher's Assistant at California State University, Los Angeles, where she graduated with an MA in Sociology. She is currently working towards a second MA at Ontario Tech University, Canada.

Jim Howe is a retired Assistant Chief Officer with the Irish Prison Service. He completed his MA with Limerick University in Ireland.

Paula Kenny was a Board Member and leading criminologist working with the Irish Prison Service (IPS) on their award-winning Recruit Prison Officer Training Programme, devised and delivered with IPS Training Officers within the Irish Prison complex. She is the co-author of two books; The Sustainability of Restorative Justice and Sustainable Justice, and is currently working on a study of her work in the Irish prison system.

Cassandra Little is a 56-year-old woman and mother. Upon graduating from high school she studied Criminal Justice at California State Fullerton and California Baptist University. She later earned her Masters in Social Work and her Doctorate in Counseling from University Nevada Reno. Dr. Little is a native of California but resided in Reno, Nevada for over 25 years prior to returning home to California in 2018. For over 28 years she had worked professionally in Child Welfare. She is currently an Adjunct Professor at California State University of Fresno and Fresno Pacific University. She is committed to speaking truth to power and combating systemic racism. Her current writing interests are focused on how the Criminal Justice System impacts communities of color.

Rebecca Hubbard Maniglia is an Associate Professor in the Department of Criminology and Criminal Justice at Northern Arizona University. She is also the Faculty Advisor for the Hood Initiative. Her areas of research include mass incarceration and its impact on families as well as race and pedagogy.

Kayla Marie Martensen is a doctoral candidate at the University of Illinois Chicago in the Criminology, Law and Justice department and an Instructor at Northeastern Illinois University in the Justice Studies department. Broadly, her area of focus is issues related to social justice and the criminal legal system, particularly around issues of race, ethnicity, nationality, gender, and class. Her specific areas of research include carceral state studies, prison abolition, women of color feminisms, and juvenile justice. Her dissertation research is concerned with Latinx girls that are caught in what she calls a 'web of detainment' between juvenile detention centers and other court-ordered (or suggested) residential placements that act as social service agencies, but as she will argue, actually replicate the ideologies and practices of juvenile detention, and the larger agendas of the carceral state in general.

Luis Nuño is Assistant Professor, Department of Sociology. Dr Luis Nuno has worked at CSULA since 2014. Courses Taught include Criminology, Deviant Behavior, Violence in American Society, Policing America. Dr. Nuno gained his PhD at the New School.

William Rosales is an assistant professor in the Department of Sociology at California State University, Los Angeles. Primarily invested in researching migration processes, Dr. Rosales has extended interest in the role that legal institutions have in affecting social and legal processes that affects marginalized populations.

Gianna Strube is an Independent Researcher and University Teaching Assistant in Arizona, United States.

Daniel Tei is a Ph.D. Candidate at Mississippi State University. He earned his MA in Northern Arizona University and his BA at the University of Cape Coast, Ghana. He has worked as a researcher and Graduate Assistant.

Kevin Warner has been National Co-ordinator of Education in the Irish Prison Service, main author of the Council of Europe report 'Education in Prison', a Fulbright Scholar at California State University San Bernardino and a researcher into penal policy in Nordic and other countries. He now teaches at two Irish universities, University College Cork and NUI Maynooth. His writing can be found on www.pepre.ie.

Kevin Wright is an associate professor in the School of Criminology and Criminal Justice and director of the Center for Correctional Solutions at Arizona State University. His work focuses on enhancing the lives of people living and working in the correctional system through research, education and community engagement. His published research on these topics has appeared in Justice Quarterly, Criminology & Public Policy, and Journal of Offender Rehabilitation. He developed and taught the first Inside-Out Prison Exchange Program class in the state of Arizona and is a co-founder of the Arizona Transformation Project. Wright earned his PhD in Criminal Justice from Washington State University in 2010.

Index

A

adolescents 215-218, 221
alternative 42, 128, 156, 185-186, 225-227, 234, 236-237, 239
Arizona 13, 27-28, 31, 43, 47, 50-51, 58, 144, 147, 149-150, 152-154, 168, 195, 218-219, 224, 226

B

behavior 9, 36-37, 39, 57, 61-62, 69, 84, 86, 88-89, 92, 102, 105, 107, 109, 144-148, 150-151, 154, 167, 184, 189-190, 214, 216-218, 220-221, 236

C

Carceral State 30, 40, 46, 73, 75, 77-78, 82
children 2, 7-10, 15-16, 21, 26, 29, 33, 39, 41, 47-48, 55-56, 60, 62, 65-67, 71, 76, 79, 85, 92, 118, 152, 191, 214-216, 218-224
class 3, 11, 38, 72, 90, 171
colonialism 42, 86
community 5, 13-16, 21-22, 39-40, 43, 58, 74, 76-77, 83, 87-88, 90, 94, 102, 104, 106, 114, 118, 122-123, 125, 129, 142, 144, 150-153, 155-156, 160-161, 181, 187, 196-198, 200, 217, 223-224, 226-231, 233-243
competencies 168, 170, 175-177, 216
corrections 50-51, 71, 103, 107, 140, 150-151, 153-155, 168-169, 222
courts 35, 155, 160, 183, 200, 210, 222, 225, 236-238, 244
criminal 2-3, 30, 34, 36-42, 47, 50-51, 69, 72, 74-76, 80-84, 99-103, 105-108, 119, 122, 124, 128, 131, 137, 139, 144-147, 149, 151, 153-154, 165-167, 169, 180-188, 190-191, 197, 201, 205, 209, 213, 215, 219-224, 226, 229-232, 234-242
Criminology 45, 47, 85, 102, 107-108, 121, 137, 139, 143, 146, 152-154, 166-167, 170, 192-194, 240-242

D

Denmark 110, 113-114, 116-118, 120, 123-124, 127, 129, 137-140, 142
deportation 1-7, 9-19, 21-24, 26-29, 33, 39, 42-43
deviance 86-88, 91, 93-94, 214, 221

E

emancipation 184, 214, 217-218
exclusion 3, 86-87, 90-92, 96, 123, 139

F

facility 79, 99, 102, 104, 223
fear 24, 42-43, 53, 55, 70, 118, 162, 166, 178, 180, 197, 202, 208, 216, 237
Finland 110, 113-114, 116, 118-119, 122, 124-125, 127, 129, 138-142
formal 16, 29, 50, 145, 183, 185, 207, 218, 226-227, 230, 232, 234-237, 239

foster care 10, 39, 48, 75-77, 82, 214-225

G

gender 32-34, 38, 41, 43, 45, 47, 72, 77, 82, 84-85, 87-95, 180, 223, 227
Ghana 180-183, 188, 190-194
girls 30-44, 46, 48, 74, 80, 85

H

human rights 3, 27, 44, 86, 94, 122, 127, 132, 139, 161, 168, 170-171, 185, 192, 195-200, 202, 204, 206, 208-213

I

immigration 1-6, 9, 15, 17-18, 22-25, 27, 29, 31, 33, 37, 40-42, 45, 47
incarceration 2, 33, 39-41, 43-44, 46, 48, 50-51, 54-60, 63, 67, 69-70, 72-74, 76, 78-85, 99-100, 102, 104-106, 108-109, 111-113, 115, 128-129, 146-147, 149, 151-153, 155, 175, 223, 232
informal 3, 59, 103, 145, 190, 226-228, 230-240
institution 91, 99-100, 116, 119, 141, 152, 155-157, 172-176, 214
Intersections 72
Ireland 110-111, 113, 116, 127-130, 132-133, 136-142, 155-157, 159, 166-171, 226, 240-243

J

justice 3, 13, 26-27, 31, 39, 44, 46-51, 63, 71-72, 75, 80-84, 99-102, 107-109, 111, 115, 118-119, 121-123, 125-126, 128, 130-134, 138-139, 141-145, 149, 153-154, 157, 165-167, 169-171, 173, 175, 177, 180-188, 190-193, 195-212, 217-218, 222-224, 226-244

K

knowledge 8, 12, 87, 97, 153, 168-171, 174, 187, 230

L

labeling 86-87, 146
Latinx 30-43, 49
legal 1, 3-4, 9, 11-12, 14-16, 18, 20-27, 31, 34, 37-39, 41, 69, 75, 81-82, 88, 146-147, 151, 162, 180, 185, 189-191, 200, 202, 207, 210, 214-216, 222, 226-230, 239, 242

M

Mexico 1-14, 16, 21, 24, 32-33, 185
migratory decision-making 22, 24
mob 180-188, 190-193

N

neglect 88, 139, 215-216, 218-221, 224
Norway 110, 113, 115-116, 119-122, 126-127, 129, 138, 140, 142

P

penal 108, 110-115, 121, 123-128, 130-133, 135-136, 138-142, 165, 167, 171, 193, 243
police 18, 35, 38, 40-42, 47-48, 63, 74, 77, 115, 119, 126, 139, 142, 177, 180-183, 185, 188-194, 222-223, 238-239
policy 3, 7, 24, 26-28, 31, 38-40, 44-48, 73, 75, 79, 82, 94, 100, 102, 107, 110-114, 119, 122-124, 126-128, 130-134, 137-141, 145-146, 152-154, 157, 165, 204, 209-210, 212, 227-229, 238, 241
prison 6, 23, 30, 40, 42-44, 46-48, 50-57, 59-61, 63-64, 66-67, 69-76, 78-85, 99-178, 201, 208
prison officer 155-156, 158-164, 166-168, 171-177
prisoner 48, 50-51, 55-60, 63, 71, 80, 99-101, 105-108, 111, 116, 118, 120, 122, 125-126, 134, 137, 153, 155, 159, 161-163, 168-169, 173-174, 176-177, 232

prisoners 47, 51, 57-60, 85, 102, 107, 109, 115-129, 132, 134-138, 140-141, 151-154, 156, 158-165, 168-171, 173-177, 199, 232
prisons 6, 40, 43-44, 48, 55, 59, 66, 72, 75, 78-79, 81, 84-85, 101-102, 106, 110, 112-123, 129-137, 140-143, 145, 149-150, 154-167, 169, 172-175, 177-178, 232, 241
process 4, 6, 8-9, 12-14, 18, 23-24, 50-51, 56, 59-60, 64, 67, 70, 78, 80, 92, 94, 100, 119, 126, 134, 146, 162, 165, 171-173, 176-177, 196, 198, 206, 208, 218, 226-232, 234-237, 241
punitiveness 110-112, 115, 121-122, 127-128, 130, 132, 139-140, 233, 237

R

Race 32, 37-38, 47-48, 72, 82, 84, 106-108, 120, 145, 220, 227
rearrest 101-103
recruits 168-173, 176
reentry 16, 50-51, 55, 57, 59-60, 63, 69-71, 82, 99-106, 108-109, 148-150, 152
re-entry 29, 50, 83, 99, 144, 149, 151-152
rehabilitation 51, 69-70, 107, 111, 115, 121, 124, 126, 132, 134-135, 142, 150, 157, 159, 173, 175, 177, 227, 237
reimprisonment 144-145
reintegration 10-11, 23-24, 57, 116, 119, 134, 237
relationships 8-9, 39, 67, 69-70, 74-75, 84, 100, 116, 135, 142, 147, 153, 155, 160, 162-163, 166, 216-219, 222, 231, 239, 244
remigration 1, 4, 7, 9-11, 14, 18, 21-23
restorative 170, 197, 204-205, 207-208, 226-244
rights 2-4, 23, 27, 33, 40-42, 44, 48, 57-58, 86, 94, 112, 122, 124, 127, 132-133, 139, 160-161, 168-171, 173, 177, 180, 185, 192, 195-202, 204, 206-213, 223-224, 228-229, 232-233

S

sanctuary 30-31, 34-37, 40-43, 46
social 1-2, 4, 6, 8-11, 13, 16, 18, 22-23, 25, 27-31, 36-37, 39-40, 42-44, 46, 48, 57, 59, 75-76, 86-88, 90-97, 100, 103, 107-108, 111-112, 119-120, 122-128, 134, 137-140, 146, 153, 156, 166-167, 169-172, 182-183, 185, 190-193, 200, 214-215, 217-219, 221-222, 227-229, 232-243
society 3, 12-13, 24, 30, 32, 36, 38-39, 41-42, 45, 50-51, 57-58, 60, 63, 85, 87-93, 100, 103-106, 108, 111-113, 119, 121-122, 124-127, 130, 134, 137-140, 148, 151-152, 155-156, 158-162, 170, 173, 177, 181-182, 184, 189, 193, 196, 198, 210-211, 222, 227-229, 232-235, 237-239, 241-244
state violence 30-32, 36-38, 42
stigma 10, 24, 28, 87, 104-105, 109, 148
system 1-3, 7, 10-11, 23, 25, 30-31, 34-35, 37-41, 43-44, 48, 50, 57, 70, 72, 75-77, 81-85, 93, 99-100, 111-112, 114, 118-123, 125, 127, 129-133, 135-136, 138, 140-141, 144-145, 148, 150-151, 158-160, 162, 164-165, 167-171, 173, 175, 177, 180, 182-183, 185-188, 193, 198, 207, 214-230, 232, 234-235, 237-239, 243

T

teaching 120, 168-170, 176, 207, 237
transgender 43, 45, 48, 86-97
trends 6, 46, 71, 110-111, 113, 130, 139, 191, 210, 212

U

US-Mexico Border 1, 28, 44

V

victims 27, 125, 152, 180, 182, 184, 186-187, 196, 200-202, 204, 206, 208, 226-227, 229-232, 234-236 vigilantism 180-181, 188, 190, 192-193

W

well-being 34, 41, 44, 85, 160, 220
women 30-49, 55, 66-67, 70, 72-73, 79-85, 89, 91, 96, 99-106, 116, 118, 122, 127, 129, 131, 150, 152-153, 158, 171, 180, 184, 198, 211, 228, 232-233, 240
work 13, 16, 24, 30-31, 34, 36-37, 39, 42, 49, 52-54, 56, 58-59, 64, 67, 69, 75-76, 80-81, 89, 102-106, 108, 112, 117-125, 127, 133, 136, 139, 142, 151-153, 155-156, 158-166, 168, 170-178, 186, 189, 193, 206-207, 222, 231, 233-236, 244

www.ingramcontent.com/pod-product-compliance
Lightning Source LLC
LaVergne TN
LVHW061540290926
849162LV00004B/857